I0797765

Mining Language

Mining Language

RACIAL THINKING, INDIGENOUS KNOWLEDGE, AND COLONIAL METALLURGY IN THE EARLY MODERN IBERIAN WORLD

Allison Margaret Bigelow

Published by the
OMOHUNDRO INSTITUTE OF
EARLY AMERICAN HISTORY AND CULTURE,
Williamsburg, Virginia,
and the
UNIVERSITY OF NORTH CAROLINA PRESS,
Chapel Hill

The Omohundro Institute of Early American History and Culture is sponsored by the College of William and Mary. On November 15, 1996, the Institute adopted the present name in honor of a bequest from Malvern H. Omohundro, Jr.

Manufactured in the United States of America

Cover images: Watercolor painting of Cocorote, Venezuela, by Rebecca Graham (2017); contact-era ear flare depicting a *cacique* (The Metropolitan Museum of Art, New York)

Library of Congress Cataloging-in-Publication Data
Names: Bigelow, Allison Margaret, author.
Title: Mining language : racial thinking, indigenous knowledge, and colonial metallurgy in the early modern Iberian world / Allison Margaret Bigelow.
Description: Chapel Hill : Omohundro Institute of Early American History and Culture : University of North Carolina Press, 2020. | Includes bibliographical references and index.
Identifiers: LCCN 2019052077 | ISBN 9781469654386 (cloth) | ISBN 9781469654393 (ebook)
Subjects: LCSH: Mineral industries—Latin America—Language—History. | Mines and mineral resources—Latin America—History. | Language and culture—Latin America—History. | Indians—Language—Influence on Spanish. | Indians—Language—Influence on Portuguese. | African languages—Latin America—Influence on Spanish. | African languages—Latin America—Influence on Portuguese.
Classification: LCC HD9506.L29 B54 2020 | DDC 622.01/4—dc23
LC record available at https://lccn.loc.gov/2019052077

The University of North Carolina Press has been a member of the Green Press Initiative since 2003.

For Lily

PREFACE

RECREATING THE ARCHIVE

Allison Bigelow and Rebecca Graham

Allison:

Between the spring of 2010, when I first read don Manuel Gaytán de Torres's *Relación, y vista de ojos* (1621) as a graduate student working in the John Carter Brown Library, and the fall of 2016, when I finished writing the chapter on colonial copper projecting, I searched high and low for the painting that don Manuel described in his report. I looked in a variety of libraries and archives that held materials by Gaytán de Torres, including the Newberry Library (Chicago), British Library (London), Biblioteca Nacional de España (Madrid), and Archivo General de Indias (Seville). At the AGI, I found manuscript drafts of don Manuel's plan for Cocorote and two years' responses to his colonial designs. At the Biblioteca Nacional, I uncovered legal cases of disputed inheritances that were important enough to have been printed as books. The British Library and Newberry collections hold multiple editions of the *Relación* and other published works that bear don Manuel's signature. But I never found the painting. The subject librarian for Iberian studies at UVa, Miguel Valladares-Llata, even stopped by the Biblioteca Real del Palacio Real in Madrid to download an eighteenth-century *recopilación* of another proposal that don Manuel had authored; the handwritten edition included a family tree but no painting or navigational chart.

I thus was faced with a pressing methodological challenge: seventeenth-century manuscript sources provided testimony of the painting's existence, but the work itself was lost. Historians often speak of following our sources, but there are few guidelines on how to treat sources that testify to their own fragmentation. Don Manuel's vision for a kind of autonomous slavery in Cocorote offers a very different model of community life and artisan labor than the dominant models of plantation monocultures that later took root in Venezuela and those that were practiced throughout the Americas. Nor does it resemble the forms of royal slavery that characterized the mines of El Cobre in eastern Cuba. The mines of Cocorote went on to become part of Simón Bolívar's family estate, gesturing toward the intimate relationship between enslaved labor, commercial gain, and independence movements. The painting is an evidentiary form and means of persuasion that don Manuel specifically included in his proposal. By making visible don Manuel's vision of Cocorote, the painting promises to capture a key moment in imperial imagining of possibility, and an important—if almost entirely overlooked—part of the story of Afro-Venezuelans and Afro-Latin communities in the early Americas. Archival evidence could only take me so far in my effort to tell this story, and I was stuck.

In the summer of 2016, while writing Chapter 7 of this book, it struck me that a skilled painter who had studied colonial Latin America could use the *Relación, y vista de ojos* to recreate the missing painting of Cocorote. Most important, I knew a Spanish-speaking artist who might be willing to give it a try. Rebecca Graham, an undergraduate student majoring in Spanish and Media Studies with an extensive background in studio art, and I then designed a three-credit independent study that we called "Recreating the Archive" (SPAN 4993). I had taught Rebecca in a survey of colonial Latin American literature and a research-intensive seminar in colonial translation. There, she formed part of a team of students who translated the testimonies of a colonial Spanish official and an Arawak woman regarding Walter Ralegh's attack on Venezuela in 1617. The class project from Fall 2014, now published on the Early Americas Digital Archive, proved that Rebecca was a dedicated researcher and an excellent collaborator. I also served as her adviser for the major. Over the years, as we mapped out her schedule during advising office hours, I learned about her diverse background and deep interest in visual communications, from silkscreening and printmaking to film studies and American Sign Language. I had a sense of her intellectual curiosities and creative interests, and I suspected that this kind of experimental approach to archival remediation might be right up her alley.

We spent the fall semester of 2016 in Charlottesville, meeting every other week to talk about the text and sketch the mine site. We worked through print and manuscript editions of Gaytán de Torres's plan, consulted military historians to determine how far "two shots of an arquebus" ought to be (our sincere thanks to Wayne Lee at the University of North Carolina–Chapel Hill), and pored over early modern paintings of copper mines and colonial settlements in Venezuela.

In January 2017, we traveled to Spain with support from UVa's Center for Global Inquiry and Innovation. We pulled sources at the Biblioteca Nacional in Madrid, studied seventeenth-century masterpieces in the Prado, and analyzed modern experiments that resembled our own efforts. At the Museo Reina Sofía, we were most inspired by Czech filmmaker Harun Farocki's "La plata y la cruz," which maps onto the present-day landscape of the Andean city elements of eighteenth-century Bolivian artist Gaspar Miguel de Berrío's painting of Potosí, "Descripción del zerro rico e ymperial villa de Potosí" (1758). With this iconographic base, we traveled to Seville to consult archival documents, maps, and images.

Rebecca:

At the Archivo General de Indias, I found an image that is probably the closest model of what the missing painting would have looked like. On May 15, 1623, two years after Gaytán de Torres sent his report, the governor of Venezuela, Capitán don Andrés Rodríguez de Villegas, asked the crown to reconfigure the main fort of the province into a triangular form that would be easier to defend from Dutch, French, and English pirates. He commissioned Cristóbal de Roda Antonelli to paint his vision. That painting, "Planta irregular para el sitio sobre el surgidero de Ancón de refriegas en la salina de Araya, hecha por el capitán don Andrés Rodríguez de Villegas, governador de esta isla Margarita por el Rey, nuestro señor," accompanied Rodríguez de Villegas's letter. Below the painting, someone wrote a four-column description of the site, which specified the scale and dimensions of the fort. These two elements gave us a sense of how prose and pictures conveyed information from Venezuela to imperial officials.[1]

Upon finding the work by Antonelli, I experienced a sense of relief. The most difficult aspect of this project was trying to emulate the Gaytán de Torres's description without knowledge of scale or how elements were expressed visually in colonial Venezuela. After seeing it, I had a better idea of how our painting

1. Archivo General de Indias (hereafter cited as AGI), Santo Domingo, 622; "Planta del castillo de Araya, en Sucre," ca. May 15, 1623, AGI, Mapas y Planos, 14 (Irregular design for the site above *Ancón de Refriegas* ["Cove of Skirmishes"] in the Araya Salt Marsh, made by Capitán don Andrés Rodríguez de Villegas, governor of this island of Margarita for the King our Lord). At the AGI, I found manuscript drafts of don Manuel's plan for Cocorote and two years' responses to his colonial designs ("Minas de cobre del valle de Cocorote: Expediente sobre las minas de cobre del valle de Cocorote, provincia de Caracas," 1621–1663, AGI, Santo Domingo, 740). At the Biblioteca Nacional de España, I uncovered legal cases of disputed inheritances that were important enough to have been printed as books. See Andrés de Ávila y Ciguenza et al., *Por don Andres de Avila y Ciguenza vezino de la ciudad de Xerez de la Frontera, contra don Manuel Gaytan de Torres ventiquatro de la dicha ciudad de Xerez de la Frontera, y contra, don Pedro Riquelme Valera Ponce de Leon, Cavallero de la Orden de Alcantara, vezino de la dicha ciudad, y contra don Pedro de Guzman Cavallero del Orden de Calatrava, vezino de la ciudad de Senilla por Antonio René de Lacazno* (1632), Porcones 121(35).

For the British Library edition, see Manuel Gaytán de Torres, *Relacion, y vista de ojos...* ([Havana], 1621), C.62.i.19, no. 49. At the Newberry Library, Chicago: *Que se de diferente modo al govierno de las Indias, q̃ se van perdiendo muy apriessa con el que oi tienen, y modo para su pratica* (n.p., n.d.), Ayer 652 .G28 A. The handwritten edition included a family tree but no painting or navigational chart; see "Discursos que disponen medios para la restauracion de España con mayor Cantidad de Renta en la rl hacienda y menos Gabelas en estos Reynos, y aumento de su Poblacion y en las fuerzas de la Mar . . . ," Madrid, ca. 1747, MS, Biblioteca del Palacio Real, DIG/II/1452_B.

FIGURE 1. "Cocorote, ca. 1621." Painting by Rebecca Graham (2017), following Manuel Gaytán de Torres, *Relación, y vista de ojos* (1621)

might have looked. I used the 1623 image as a reference for both scale and style of our "recreated" image from 1621.

I also had a better understanding of how realistic the recreation should be, keeping in mind the importance of a maplike layout and taking note of which objects were emphasized by size and detail. More specifically, I had a much greater reference for coloring and shading. Allison and I had a good sense of what colors were used at the time, but after visiting the archive and comparing colonial images with those in the Prado, I could see how they were used and how they differentiated between different areas.

Allison:

After looking at images of Cocorote on Google Maps, we bought gouache paints, brushes, and sketchbooks of different sizes from the Winsor & Newton line at The Art Box in Charlottesville. Rebecca selected colors that allowed her to convey contrasting pasture lands, marshes, mountains, and the open pit mine, as well as elements of the built environment, like family homes, refining houses, and a defensive fortress ("el castillo"). To paint miners and herders in Cocorote, she had to unlearn all of her training as a modern artist and instead emulate the works that she studied in Seville—the people had to be the size of giants.

Rebecca and Allison:
We are proud of our painting and the journey that led to its completion. It represents exciting opportunities for faculty-student collaborations that combine creative work, archival research, and multiple forms of media, from colonial reports, paintings, and maps to modern-day films and Google Maps data. We learned a lot along the way, and we hope that our project will encourage others to experiment with new methods of reading around colonial archival silences.

ACKNOWLEDGMENTS

This book has benefited from the thoughtful responses and insightful suggestions of many colleagues in colonial studies. For generously sharing their ideas and encouraging me in this project, I thank deeply James Amelang, Rossana Barragán, Ralph Bauer, Alexandre Belmonte, Orlando Bentancor, Daniela Bleichmar, Ben Breen, Larissa Brewer-García, Kendall Brown, Kathryn Burns, Hugh Cagle, Alejandro Cañeque, David Chang, Matthew Crawford, Teresa Cribelli, Pablo Cruz, Surekha Davies, Davide Domenici, Lydia Fossa, Mariana Françozo, Barbara Fuchs, Juliana Gandini, Guadalupe García, Pablo Gómez, Ximena Gómez, Miles Grier, Sandra Gustafson, Amanda Herbert, LuAnn Homza, Alejandra Irigoin, Jane Landers, Carina Johnson, Sara E. Johnson, Ryan Kashanipour, Heather Miyano Kopelson, Kris Lane, Hal Langfur, Clara López Beltran, Diana Magaloni, Peter Mancall, Stuart McMannus, Iris Montero Sobrevilla, Barbara Mundy, David Navarrette, Marcy Norton, Karl Offen, Eduardo Paiva, Pepe Pardo, Joshua Piker, Fabrício Prado, Nick Popper, Matthew Restall, Lorena Rodríguez, Neil Safier, Elena Schneider, Casey Schmitt, Heidi Scott, Cassander Smith, Carmen Solís, Dana Velasco Murillo, Lisa Voigt, Molly Warsh, Nicolas Wey-Gómez, Mark Wright, Mary van Buren, Carmina Vargas, Miguel Valerio, Chi-ming Yang, Paula Zagalsky, and Zac Zimmer.

For their help with translations from German and French, I thank Claudia Engelmann, Patrick Erben, and Soufyane Meftah. For teaching me about the material processes of copper mining, I thank my students at the Compañía Minera Cerro Colorado, especially Mario Vallejos, Jorge Hidalgo, and Luis Benvenuto. I also thank my fellow teachers at CMCC, especially Lenka Vitaglich and Mónica Zelada, for encouraging me to apply to graduate school and for supporting me along the way.

At the University of North Carolina, I thank my dissertation committee members, Tim Marr, Jessica Wolfe, Rosa Perelmuter, and Philip Gura. I also thank Beatriz Riefkhol Muñiz at the Institute for the Study of the Americas for coordinating the fellowships and cultivating partnerships that allowed students like me to work at La Universidad de la Habana, study in Yukatek-speaking communities, and complete our dissertations. To the Durham crew, Lee James and Pablo Robles, I am grateful for your friendship, love, and support over the years. You have kept me sane, grounded, and inspired to work for good. For generously sharing ideas and encouraging each other, I thank my fellow graduate students, Raghu Halvader, Deepali Jeere, Flora Luk, Kelly Bezio, Angie Calcaterra, Evan Gurney, Zach Hutchins, Ashley Reed, and Pamela Hamilton (†), who is deeply missed by family and friends.

At the University of Virginia, all of my colleagues in the Department of Spanish, Italian, and Portuguese have supported my work, especially Eli Carter, who answered questions about Portuguese phrases from Goa to Brazil; Michael Gerli, Omar Velázquez-Mendoza, and Alison Weber, who took questions about medieval paleography; and, most notably, Ricardo Padrón, my mentor and friend. Ricardo embodies the kind of rigorous, well-caffeinated, intellectual curiosity that is shared generously and communicated with pure, nerdy joy. No question is too small or too silly to ponder.

Outside of the department, I am grateful for conversations and feedback from colleagues in anthropology, art history, history, and literature, especially Rafael Alvarado, Alison Booth, Anna Brickhouse, Eve Danziger, Marlene Daut Zaka, Douglas Fordham, Thomas Klubock, Carmen Lamas, Brian Owensby, Jennifer Tsien, and Amanda Wagstaff. For support in finding materials and generating projects, I thank Miguel Valladares-Llata, Jeremy Boggs, John Unsworth, and David Whitesell at the UVa Library. I also thank the library staff for coordinating hundreds of Interlibrary Loan requests. For coordinating the Maya K'iche' program while I was on leave, my sincere thanks to my colleague and friend, Esther Poveda Moreno.

Without year-long fellowships from the American Council of Learned Societies (2017–2018) and the Huntington Library (2017–2018), short-term fellowships at the John Carter Brown Library (2010, 2018), and a postdoctoral fellowship from the National Endowment for the Humanities (2012–2014), the research and writing of this book would not have been possible. I thank the anonymous reviewers of those selection committees. For creating the conditions that enable scholars like me to develop and complete ambitious, cross-disciplinary, multilingual projects like this book, I thank the teams of professionals at all of the archives and libraries where I have conducted research for this book, especially archivists who helped me during weeks- and months-long stays at the Archivo y Biblioteca Nacional de Bolivia in Sucre, Chuquiscaca; Archivo General de Indias in Seville; Archivo General de la Nación in Lima; Archivo Nacional de la República de Cuba in Havana; Biblioteca Nacional de España in Madrid; British Library in London; Center for Southwest Research in Albuquerque, N.M.; JCB in Providence, R.I.; Newberry Library in Chicago; National Archives in Kew; and—especially—the Huntington. For coordinating grants within the College of Arts & Sciences at UVa, including fellowships in 2015, 2016, and 2019, and a subvention in 2020, I thank Ian Baucom, Francesca

Fiorani, Neal Grandy, Joel Rini, Tally Sanford, Octavia Wells, the Buckner W. Clay Dean of Arts & Sciences, and the Vice President for Research.

At UVa, conversations with graduate students in colonial and early modern studies have reminded me of the joys of research and encouraged me to consider new avenues of inquiry. I am grateful to Catherine Addington, Karina Baptista, Melissa Frost, Kimberly Hursh, Matthew Richey, Loreto Romero Martínez Eiroa, and Eric Romig for sharing their expertise—and especially to Nasser Meerkhan and Andrea Pauw, who did so while guiding me through transcriptions and translations of Arabic-language materials. I have been fortunate to collaborate with whip-smart, highly motivated undergraduates who inspired me to look into old archives in new ways—especially Angel Estremera, my research assistant; Aldo Barriente, a keen reader, critical thinker, and tireless fact checker; Rachel Gardella and Will Norton, digital collaborators in Mesoamerican studies; Rebecca Graham, whose artwork graces the cover of this book and is described in the preface; and Taneen Maghsoudi, who answered my questions about Avicenna while balancing her own experiments in the lab and a demanding medical career. Collaborating with student leaders like Claudia Bonilla, Kate Eagan, Paola Sánchez Valdez, Carina Rodríguez, Lisa Trinh, and Andrea Villena, inside and outside of the classroom, inspires me to be a better teacher and scholar.

At the Huntington Library, where I finished the manuscript among a supportive group of colonial historians, including Andrew Lipman, Dan Richter, and Jim Sidbury, I am grateful to colleagues who workshopped ideas, methods, and sources across the disciplines, especially Leah Astbury, Janet Brown, Josh Chafetz, Alejandra Dubcovsky, Michelle Navakas, Mary E. Mendoza, David O'Shaughnessey, Catherine Roach, and Amanda Vickery. Their timely intellectual interventions, encouragement to keep putting finger to keyboard, and sincere friendship are felt throughout the book, and their book deadline care packages sustained me with beer and gummy bears (not taken together). Leah, Kate, and Mary deserve my extra thanks for helping me with the cover design. For their help in coordinating the fellowship program and making possible this intellectual community, I thank Juan Gómez, Catherine Wehrey-Miller, and Steve Hindle. For help navigating the collections in 2012, 2016, and 2017–2018, I thank Sara Couch, Manuel Flores, Sue Hodson, Leslie Jobsky, Dan Lewis, Frank Osen, Mary Robertson, Clay Stalls, Jaeda Snow, Olga Tsapina, Vanessa Wilkie, and Emmy Zhang.

For giving me the opportunity to be a postdoctoral fellow at the Omohundro Institute of Early American History and Culture and to learn from historians at William & Mary (2012–2014), I thank the Institute directors, Ron Hoffman and Karin Wulf, acquisitions editors Fredrika Teute and Nadine Zimmerli, and copy-editor Kathy Burdette. I am especially grateful to Nadine for reading chapters as I wrote them, responding enthusiastically to outlines sketched on the fine stationery that is an American Airlines napkin, and challenging me to define the theoretical and methodological stakes of my project in ways that would resonate with scholars across the disciplines. Every page of this book reflects her scholarly insight; for her knowledge, expertise, and friendship, I am very much indebted to Nadine. I am also grateful to the Swem Library staff who coordinated my many Interlibrary Loan requests during my appointment.

When I had back surgery in Williamsburg, an amazing group of people stepped up to help before, during, and after the operation. Anne Condon, Paul Polgar, Fabrício Prado, and Beverly Smith kept me well supplied with the scholarly trifecta of coffee, sugar, and books. Nadine artfully learned how to fold the backseat of her car and fit me into the trunk, diagonally, and drove me to and from the hospital more times than I can count. Chris Bancells and Yuen Lau came down from Maryland, and Patricia Bigelow came up from Carolina, to change lightbulbs, mow the lawn, shuttle me around, and keep me company. In Los Angeles, John Bianchi's excellent care ensured that I avoided a second surgery. Although the chairs were probably not great for my back, I was grateful for thought-provoking engagement with artists, activists, and scholars at the Women's Center for Creative Work in downtown L.A., especially Harpreet Kaur and the co-organizers of the Feminist Book Club, Dawn Finley and Eileen Ybarra.

For their help balancing chemical equations and deciphering metallic transformations described in colonial treatises, I thank Yuen Lau and Fernando Uribe Romo. Thank you, Bigs and Owen, for always answering questions about raw changes, percent changes, and all things mathematical with [teasing ≤ deserved]. For encouraging hard work, I thank Patricia, Thomas, and Alane Bigelow. And for supporting me as a partner through the thick and thin of writing, I thank Isaac Mbiti, who since 2014 has left no pun behind, coined some of the most memorable punch lines to describe this project, and always found a way to impart love and laughter into these pages. Above all else, this book is dedicated to my daughter, Lily Kendi Mbiti, who kept me company during the final stages of manuscript revisions and waited until I submitted copy-edits for all of the chapters in my inbox before starting contractions. Lily was born the next day, changing our world for the better.

CONTENTS

ILLUSTRATIONS

FIGURES

MAPS

Mining Language

INTRODUCTION

THE MEANING OF METALS

Before metals were converted, stamped, and coined into money, early American miners and refiners throughout the hemisphere created a technical lexicon for what they observed under- and aboveground. This was no small feat, as imperial Iberian officials and colonial agents were generally unfamiliar with the technical vocabularies, instruments, and practices of mining and metallurgy in Europe. They were even less familiar with the nuanced, varying, and local understandings of organic matter that circulated within diverse metalworking communities in the lands colonized by Spain and Portugal after 1492. These regions—known as the geographic imaginary of "the Indies," a term that linked Asia and the Americas into a shared "Indian" territory—were knitted together in real terms. They formed part of a shared knowledge economy, system of global trade, and community of artisans, scientists, and medical practitioners whose ways of knowing circulated within the lettered networks of early modern Iberian empires.

Language was central to these scientific communications, often sparking confusion as much as it offered clarification of technical concepts. Royal gold refiner Gonzalo Fernández de Oviedo y Valdés, writing in the extended Caribbean (present-day Panama, Colombia, and the Greater Antilles), and physician Juan de Cárdenas, working in Mexico, remarked in similar ways about the difficulties of translating specialized mining vocabularies into everyday Spanish. Oviedo defined the techniques that Indigenous and African women used to wash gold in La Española with a specific register: "en lengua o estilo delos que son mineros platicos" (in the language or style of people fluent in mining). In his detailed study of minerals, plants, and herbs, published as the *Historia general y natural delas Indias* (1535), Oviedo treated mining terminologies as yet another tongue that required translation into Spanish—much as he rendered expressions from Indigenous languages like Taíno and Arawak into Castilian nouns, verbs, and adjectives. Cárdenas, in his *Problemas y secretos maravillosos de las Indias* (1591), prefaced his explanation of the new method of amalgamating silver with mercury, which had been developed by Indigenous, Spanish, and Fugger refiners in central Mexico in the 1550s, with a promise that he would be "macipecificada" (more particular) as he described technical concepts in a language that was intelligible to his readers, "aquellos aquiē Dios ha hecho tā señaladas mercedes, de no hazer los mineros" (those to whom God has shown such good mercy in not making them miners). For physicians like Cárdenas and overseers like Oviedo, to know mining vocabularies was to understand the logic of specialized techniques and complex refining technologies. *Mining Language* integrates linguistic, literary, and visual analysis of colonial sources authored by writers like Oviedo and Cárdenas (all men, unlike the miners) to show where and how diverse ideas of metals and metalwork influenced the colonial Iberian mining industry, a critical scientific domain and engine of imperial expansion.[1]

This preoccupation with the language of mining and refining was not limited to the Spanish and Portuguese colonies but was instead shared by other global imperial powers. In 1696, William III of England ordered a nationwide melting down and recasting of silver currency. The great recoinage was supervised by Sir Isaac Newton at the Royal Mint, located in the Tower of London. By 1675, Newton had tabulated all of the gold and silver coined in England and for export from October 1599 through November 1657, revealing the monetary effects of the East India trade. Newton's calculations, broken into twenty-year intervals, showed "how the coyn of this Kingdom did Encrease in the three first parts proportionable to the Exercise of Trade and Navigation, and how much it hath decreased in the fourth part, being since this present East India Company was erected in the year 1657." Imperial agents mined, refined, and exported gold and silver from India in such enormous quantities that the price of "standard silver"—clearly, no longer standard—was "so much in value above his Maj[es]t[y]s coyne that it doth not only hinder the Bullion of Gold and silver imported from being coyned but hath occasioned all the weighty coyn to be culled out and melted into Bullion." In other words, merchants directed silver and gold from India toward commodity markets, where precious metals fetched higher prices than they did at royal refineries. Newton understood the cause of the disparate prices of English and Indian silver: the shortage of coin in England "brought down the prices of Land, Lead, Tinn, Woolen and other Manufactures."[2]

Twenty years later, Newton's assessment became a matter of national policy. As part of the recoinage, Newton's deputies provided regional mint officers with rubrics whose sample grids and vocabularies were designed to help

1. [Gonzalo Fernández de Oviedo y Valdés], *La historia general delas Indias* (Seville, 1535), lxvi; Juan de Cárdenas, *Problemas y secretos maravillosos de las Indias . . .* (1591) (Valladolid, 2003), 90.

2. Isaac Newton, "Account of All the Gold and Silver Coined in the Mint within the Tower of London from 1599 Oct. to 1675 Nov., Divided into Four Parts," 2 fols., 9/26, Records of the Royal Mint, National Archives, Kew, U.K. (hereafter cited as Mint).

county clerks report the amount of silver brought to their offices, who brought it, and what it amounted to after it was melted down and recoined. For example, instead of reporting that silver was "delivered," they were instructed to say that it had been "cleared" and "solved." However, local officials, such as Israel Hayes, an operator of the Exeter Mint, ignored these lexical prescriptions and continued to report data on coinage and casting using the customary verbs. He announced that he found the entire matter hard to follow, drawing a harsh reproach from Hopton Haynes, weigher and teller in the London Mint. Israel Hayes responded that it was "a little surprising to see You threaten me"; the local minter concluded that "such little surds sure are not worth a censure." Hopton Haynes replied with a sharp reminder of the preferred terms "according to the practice of Yr Mint, and the express words of the Act of Parliament." Haynes's supervisor, Newton, approved of his command of language enough to have him translate *Historical Account of Two Notable Corruptions of Scripture* into Latin. Newton later praised Haynes's "steady hand" and disposition "skilled in all the business of the Mint and in the Recoynage instructed the Officers and Clerks of the five Country Mints and did other great service."[3]

Histories of science and technology readily place figures like Newton within the trajectories of early modern scientific thought—more so for his study of physics, mathematics, and natural science than for his work on language, coins, and biblical history. However, in the early modern era, the distinctions between grammar, science, and the spirit would not have been so easily made. This book, by attending to the key terms of mining and metallurgy in the sixteenth and seventeenth centuries, illustrates how technical languages indexed broader cultural patterns of life, thought, meaning, and value. Although I focus on lands colonized by early modern Iberian empires—Spanish- and Portuguese-speaking communities in Latin America, the Caribbean, Goa, and La Florida (an expansive stretch of what is now the Southeast region of the United States)—the testy exchanges between Newton, officials in the Tower of London, and officers in the English countryside reveal that the language of mining and money animated global debates about standardization, political power,

3. Letter of H. Hayes, London, Sept. 26, 1696, letter of Israel Hayes, Exeter, Sept. 29, 1696, both in "Letters Directed to and Received from the Dep. Comptrolers of the Country Mints, 1696," Mint 10/3; "To the Right Honourable the Lords Commissioners of His Majesties Treasury," Sept. 5, 1701, Mint 19/1.121, available on the Newton Project: http://www.newtonproject.ox.ac.uk/view/texts/normalized/MINT00044; Isaac Newton, *Corruptelae duorum celebrium in sacris literis locorum historica narratio . . .* ([London?], 1609), Yahuda MS 20, National Library of Israel, Jerusalem. See also Richard S. Westfall, *The Life of Isaac Newton* (New York, 2015).

and local expressions throughout the pre-1800 world. This book examines the interconnected spaces of Iberian colonization to show how technical and scientific lexicons can help us to better understand the diverse ways of knowing that shaped vernacular scientific industries—even, and especially, when such subaltern knowledge systems were not recognized as "scientific." *Mining Language* thus builds on histories of metallurgy and alchemy in the early modern Atlantic world by providing new evidence of Indigenous knowledge production, African refining agencies, and South Asian mineralogical beliefs as collected and conveyed within Iberian imperial letters.[4]

Histories of mining in colonial Latin America have made important contributions to our knowledge of the early Americas, the early modern Spanish empire, and global capitalism. Rich and informative studies have focused variously on economic history, environmental history, labor history, legal history, historical geography, and social history.[5] Joining historians in these efforts are

4. See, for instance, Ralph Bauer, *The Alchemy of Conquest: Science, Religion, and the Secrets of the New World* (Charlottesville, Va., 2019); Karin A. Amundsen, "Thinking Metallurgically: Metals and Empire in the Projects of Edward Hayes," *Huntington Library Quarterly,* LXXIX (2016), 561–590; Walter W. Woodward, *Prospero's America: John Winthrop, Jr., Alchemy, and the Creation of New England Culture, 1606–1676* (Williamsburg, Va., and Chapel Hill, N.C., 2010); Eric H. Ash, "Introduction: Expertise and the Early Modern State," *Osiris,* XXV (2010), 1–24, and the essays in the special issue.

5. For comprehensive histories, see Kendall W. Brown, *A History of Mining in Latin America: From the Colonial Era to the Present* (Albuquerque, N.M., 2012); Kris Lane, *Potosí: The Silver City That Changed the World* (Oakland, Calif., 2019). For economic histories, see Earl J. Hamilton, "Spanish Banking Schemes before 1700," *Journal of Political Economy,* LVII (1949), 134–156; Pierre Villar, *A History of Gold and Money, 1450–1920,* trans. Judith White (London, 1976); Dennis O. Flynn and Arturo Giráldez, eds., *Metals and Monies in an Emerging Global Economy* (Aldershot, U.K., 1997); Flynn and Giráldez, "Born with a 'Silver Spoon': The Origin of World Trade in 1571," *Journal of World History,* VI (1995), 201–221; John J. TePaske, *A New World of Gold and Silver,* ed. Kendall W. Brown (Boston, 2010); Elvira Vilches, *New World Gold: Cultural Anxiety and Monetary Disorder in Early Modern Spain* (Chicago, 2010); Jason Moore, "'This Lofty Mountain of Silver Could Conquer the Whole World': Potosí and the Political Ecology of Underdevelopment, 1545–1800," *Journal of Philosophical Economics,* IV (2010), 58–103; Regina Grafe and Alejandra Irigoin, "A Stakeholder Empire: The Political Economy of Spanish Imperial Rule in America," *Economic History Review,* LXV (2012), 609–651; Leticia Arroyo Abad and Jan Luiten van Zanden, "Growth under Extractive Institutions? Latin American per Capita GDP in Colonial Times," *Journal of Economic History,* LXXVI (2016), 1182–1215. For environmental histories, see Elizabeth Dore, "Environment and Society: Long-Term Trends in Latin American Mining," *Environment and History,* VI (2000), 1–29; Daviken Studnicki-Gizbert and David Schecter, "The Environmental Dynamics of a Colonial Fuel-Rush: Silver Mining and Deforestation in New Spain, 1522 to 1810," *Environmental History,* XV (2010), 94–119; Nicholas A. Robbins, *Santa Bár-*

multidisciplinary approaches that integrate insights from fields like art history, philosophy, linguistics, and literary studies.[6] One of the most robust multidisciplinary research areas is archaeometallurgy, a field whose grounding in material cultures, archaeology, and anthropology uncovers local perspectives on the history of metals in pre-Columbian and colonial communities.[7]

---

bara's Legacy: An Environmental History of Huancavelica, Peru (Boston, 2017); Studnicki-Gizbert, "Exhausting the Sierra Madre: Mining Ecologies in Mexico over the Longue Durée," in J. R. McNeill and George Vrtis, eds., *Mining North America: An Environmental History since 1522* (Oakland, Calif., 2017), 19–46. For labor histories, see Peter Bakewell, *Miners of the Red Mountain: Indian Labor in Potosí, 1545–1650* (Albuquerque, N.M., 1984); Enrique Tandeter, *Coacción y mercado: La minería de la plata en el Potosí colonial, 1692–1826* (Buenos Aires, 1992); Rossana Barragán, "Working Silver for the World: Mining Labor and Popular Economy in Colonial Potosí," *Hispanic American Historical Review,* XCVII (2017), 193–222. For legal histories, see Alejandro Vergara Blanco, *Principios y sistema del derecho minero: Estudio histórico-dogmático* (Santiago, 1992); Francisco José Tejada Hernández, *El derecho minero romano ante la ilustración hispanoamericana* (Madrid, 2017). For historical geography, see Heidi V. Scott, "Taking the Enlightenment Underground: Mining Spaces and Cartographic Representation in the Late Colonial Andes," *Journal of Latin American Geography,* XIV (2015), 7–34; Scott, "The Contested Spaces of the Subterranean: Colonial Governmentality, Mining, and the Mita in Early Spanish Peru," ibid., XI (2012), 7–33. For social histories, see P. J. Bakewell, *Silver Mining and Society in Colonial Mexico: Zacatecas, 1546–1700* (Cambridge, 1971); Bakewell, *Silver and Entrepreneurship in Seventeenth-Century Potosí: The Life and Times of Anthony López de Quiroga* (Albuquerque, N.M., 1988); Jane E. Mangan, *Trading Roles: Gender, Ethnicity, and the Urban Economy in Colonial Potosí* (Durham, N.C., 2005); Dana Velasco Murillo, *Urban Indians in a Silver City: Zacatecas, Mexico, 1546–1810* (Stanford, Calif., 2016).

6. For art history, see Mario Chacón Torres, *Arte virreinal en Potosí: Fuentes para su historia* (Seville, 1973); Gerardo Estrada, P. Gregory Warden, and Alfredo Ruy Sánchez Lacey, *Escultura en plata,* no. 52 of *Artes de México* (2000); Thomas DaCosta Kaufmann, *Toward a Geography of Art* (Chicago, 2004); Luisa María Vetter Parodi, *Plateros indígenas en el virreinato del Perú: Siglos XVI y XVII* (Buenaventura, 2008). For philosophy, see Orlando Bentancor, *The Matter of Empire: Metaphysics and Mining in Colonial Peru* (Pittsburgh, 2017). For linguistics, see Mary Money, *Oro y plata en los Andes: Significado en los diccionarios de Aymara y Quechua, siglo XVI–XVII* (La Paz, 2004); Frédérique Langue and Carmen Salazar-Soler, *Dictionnaire des termes miniers en usage en Amérique espagnole, XVIe–XIXe siècle* (Paris, 1993). For literature, see Stephanie Merrim, *The Spectacular City, Mexico, and Colonial Hispanic Literary Culture* (Austin, Tex., 2010); Lisa Voigt, *Spectacular Wealth: The Festivals of Colonial South American Mining Towns* (Austin, Tex., 2016).

7. For the Caribbean, see Marcos Martinón-Torres et al., "Metallic Encounters in Cuba: The Technology, Exchange and Meaning of Metals before and after Columbus," *Journal of Anthropological Archaeology,* XXXI (2012), 439–454. For Mexico and Central America, see Aaron N. Shugar and Scott E. Simmons, eds., *Archaeometallurgy in Mesoamerica: Current Approaches and New Perspectives* (Boulder, Colo., 2013); Dorothy Hosler, *The Sounds and*

By focusing on the language of mining communities, this book provides scholars in multiple fields with new analysis of moments when miners throughout the early modern Iberian world collaborated and competed against each other to promote and sometimes prevent the production of colonial wealth. Without denying the weighty forces of imperial power and the consistently asymmetrical deployment of colonial violence, I show how diverse women and men made their lives and provided for their families within extractive imperial systems. Attention to mining communities' language, tools, and metallurgical technologies suggests that the Spanish empire was less of a monolithic imposition from above and more like the protean, contingent human, plant, and metallic matter that composed it—dynamic, locally defined, and contextual. By 1535, colonial writers found themselves forced to redefine terms like "gold," recognizing, as did Oviedo, that Amerindian ideas about matter and value had been thoroughly incorporated into Spanish metalworking discourse. During the colonial period, a range of scientific practitioners and technical agents came to learn what literary scholar James Potter argues in his study of aesthetics: "Matter never leaves meaning untouched."[8]

My approach owes much to the work of art historians and historians of science, especially Daniela Bleichmar, Hugh Cagle, Lorraine Daston, Pablo F. Gómez, Ursula Klein and Emma C. Sparry, Iris Montero Sobrevilla, Marcy Norton, Brian Ogilvie, and Pamela H. Smith. Their studies of the raw materials of scientific inquiry, from glass flowers and medicinal plants to metals and the making of liquid ethers, reveal how "obdurate objecthood" asserted itself in the workshops, laboratories, and intellectual debates of early modern scientific communities. Centering scientific objects and raw materials does not remove human actors from these stories, because human beings organize matter through alphabetic and visual language and then communicate their ideas to specific audiences. Because sixteenth- and seventeenth-century sources, and the archives that house them, are so deeply invested in denying the humanity

---

Colors of Power: The Sacred Metallurgical Technology of Ancient West Mexico (Cambridge, Mass., 1994). For the Andes, see Mary Van Buren and Barbara H. Mills, "*Huayrachinas* and *Tocochimbos:* Traditional Smelting Technology of the Southern Andes," *Latin American Antiquity,* XVI (2005), 3–25; Van Buren and Brendan J. M. Weaver, "Contours of Labor and History: A Diachronic Perspective on Andean Mineral Production and the Making of Landscapes in Porco, Bolivia," *Historical Archaeology,* XLVI (2012), 79–101; and the excellent essays included in Pablo José Cruz and Jean-Joinville Vacher, eds., *Mina y metalurgia en los Andes del Sur: Desde la época prehispánica hasta el siglo XVII* (Sucre, 2008).

8. James I. Porter, *The Origins of Aesthetic Thought in Ancient Greece: Matter, Sensation, and Experience* (New York, 2010), 11.

of the women and men whose labor transformed colonial metals into imperial wealth, we need to approach texts about metals in new ways. My focus on metallic matter reframes the study of the colonial mining industry and opens up new avenues of inquiry and modes of analysis, indicating, with lexical data and iconographic evidence, where and how Indigenous, African, and South Asian ideas influenced critical infrastructure, technologies, and ideas about metals and minerals—from mining calendars that aligned the cycles of gold refining in La Española with Taíno cosmologies (Part 1) to silver amalgamation technology transfers between Mexico and the Andes, both enabled by Indigenous expertise in metalworking (Part 4).[9]

Instead of beginning with a philosophical question, as do works of the new materialism that push us into urgent debates about ecological, economic, and social sustainability, this book centers the materials themselves—as they were made and understood by diverse actors and artisans in the colonial period. A careful attention to materiality has informed literary, philosophical, and art historical studies of silver, labor, race, and empire in the early modern era. In his study of silver mining and money in colonial Peru, Orlando Bentancor insists that to understand the paradoxes of the Spanish empire—the coeval impulse to produce silver through Indigenous labor and evangelize among Indigenous communities who died in the mines—we must conceive of mining in terms of the commodity fetishism wherein silver metals were converted into currency that acquired value in circulation, generated capital from itself, and could be stored as surplus. Chi-ming Yang also applies Marxist theory to her study of silver, but instead of the history of ideas that Bentancor charts, Yang analyzes the materiality of silver metals in transpacific artistic and commercial

9. The phrase "obdurate objecthood" is from Lorraine Daston, ed., *Things That Talk: Object Lessons from Art and Science* (New York, 2004), 11. I refer to Daniela Bleichmar, *El imperio visible: Espediciones botánicas y cultural visual en la ilustración hispánica*, trans. Horacio Pons (Mexico City, 2016); Hugh Cagle, *Assembling the Tropics: Science and Medicine in Portugal's Empire, 1450–1700* (Cambridge, 2018); Pablo F. Gómez, *The Experiential Caribbean: Creating Knowledge and Healing in the Early Modern Atlantic* (Chapel Hill, N.C., 2017); Ursula Klein and E. C. Sparry, eds., *Materials and Expertise in Early Modern Europe: Between Market and Laboratory* (Chicago, 2010), esp. Pamela H. Smith, "Vermilion, Mercury, Blood, and Lizards: Matter and Meaning in Metalworking," 29–49; Iris Montero Sobrevilla, "The Slow Science of Swift Nature: Hummingbirds and Humans in New Spain," in Patrick Manning and Daniel Rood, eds., *Global Scientific Practice in an Age of Revolutions, 1750–1850* (Pittsburgh, 2016), 127–146; Marcy Norton, *Sacred Gifts, Profane Pleasures: A History of Tobacco and Chocolate in the Atlantic World* (Ithaca, N.Y., 2008); Brian W. Ogilvie, *The Science of Describing: Natural History in Renaissance Europe* (Chicago, 2008).

exchanges. In these moments of exchange, "the sensory experiences of silver's touch, sight, weight, and sound" were converted into "aesthetic and affective value," such as racial classifications, tangible media, and the haptic materiality of jet-black objects that "embed layers of colonial history in a collage of color-coded intersections." *Mining Language* builds on the work of scholars like Bentancor and Yang by studying the moments before metals became money—moments when miners classified, sorted, and processed ores that were then sent out for minting. As we saw with the examples of Oviedo, Cárdenas, and Newton, early modern scientific actors were preoccupied with the language and form of metals before and after coinage. This book thus traces through spoken, written, and visual languages the "old material" ways in which miners throughout the Iberian world understood the animacy of matter and the ability of metallic objects to shape human experiences.[10]

Histories of science and technology have not often considered coercive labor systems and the coloniality of power as mining technologies. They instead take "technology" literally, focusing, as do historians Modesto Bargalló, Manuel Castillo Marcos, and Saul Guerrero, on the development of large-scale methods of amalgamation, the sophisticated natural knowledges that informed these metallurgical techniques, and the skilled practices that allowed miners, refiners, and engineers to build new kinds of instruments to process precious metals. These are foundational concepts in the history of mining, and they have been central to my own work.[11]

Yet, as Marcy Norton argues, it is time for a new scholarly understanding of technology. Or, rather, it is time for an older understanding—one that reflects the term's meaning in the sixteenth and seventeenth centuries. Included in colonial definitions of "technology" were diverse human interventions into the order of nature and the ensuing ways in which such efforts transformed organic matter. Colonial technologies referred to all manners of preparing

10. Jane Bennett, *Vibrant Matter: A Political Ecology of Things* (Durham, N.C., 2010); Bentancor, *Matter of Empire*, 24–25, 28; Chi-ming Yang, "Silver, Blackness, and Fugitive Value, 'from China to Peru,'" *Eighteenth Century*, LIX (2018), 141–166. See also Cyra Levenson, Yang, and Ken Gonzales-Day, "Haptic Blackness: The Double Life of an 18th-Century Bust," *British Art Studies*, I (2015), https://doi.org/10.17658/issn.2058-5462/issue-01/harwood.

11. Modesto Bargalló, *La minería y la metalurgía en la América española durante la época colonial: Con un apéndice sobre la industria del hierro en México desde la iniciación de la Independencia hasta el presente* (Mexico City, 1955); Bargalló, *La amalgamación de los minerales de plata en Hispanoamérica colonial* (Mexico City, 1969); Manuel Castillo Martos, *Bartolomé de Medina y el siglo XVI* (Santander, 2006); Saul Guerrero, *Silver by Fire, Silver by Mercury: A Chemical History of Silver Refining in New Spain and Mexico, 16th to 19th Centuries* (Boston, 2017).

foodstuffs and medical recipes, designing new forms of communication, and fashioning materials to construct things—whether such a thing was a house, a hammock, or a human life that was understood as convertible matter. By understanding technology as a "process and product" or "a set of practices and processes designed to transform matter . . . as well as the transformed matter itself," we can situate diverse colonial technologies in local contexts and analyze them according to such particulars. Instead of a linear march toward scientific modernity in which European imperialism is imposed from above, this expansive approach reveals entangled histories of globalization and colonization. It throws into sharp relief the subaltern miners whose humanity was denied even as colonial forces appropriated and adapted their scientific, technical, and medical ideas.[12]

This understanding of technology is beginning to appear in certain areas of the history of science, such as cartography, and in studies of the colonial mining industry. Historian Sherwin K. Bryant argues, in his study of gold mining in Ecuador and Colombia, that the institution of slavery "was not merely a labor system" but rather a central juridical framework and series of legal practices that authorized imperial claims to land, labor, and resources under- and aboveground. It was, Bryant writes, "one of the chief European technologies used to exercise dominion over the Indies." Viewing the institution of slavery, and its daily practices, as a European technology allows scholars to consider the entangled operations of mining, knowledge production, and coerced labor in a new light.[13]

By following metallic matter as it was shaped into culturally specific objects, symbols, technologies, and lexicons, *Mining Language* sheds light on aspects of the colonial mining industry that have gone largely overlooked in the historiography of colonial science and technology. Parts 1, 3, and 4 of the book analyze Indigenous and African miners' contributions to the tools, technologies, and cultures of metalworking as they unfolded in colonial designs for gold, copper, and silver in the Americas. Part 2 examines how Spanish and Portuguese writers positioned iron metals, minerals, and medical rituals in the East and West Indies as part of a larger dialogue on the nature of empire. In this way, this book explores the grammar of empire as it helped to shape—and was ultimately shaped by—the colonial mining industry and its technologies.

12. Marcy Norton, "Subaltern Technologies and Early Modernity in the Atlantic World," *Colonial Latin American Review,* XXVI (2017), 18–38, esp. 26.

13. Sherwin K. Bryant, *Rivers of Gold, Lives of Bondage: Governing through Slavery in Colonial Quito* (Chapel Hill, N.C., 2014), 3; see also Stuart Elden, *The Birth of Territory* (Chicago, 2013).

It is, I believe, the first monograph-length study of mining lexicons in the early modern Iberian world.

The book is organized according to the loose chronological order in which miners, refiners, and writers encountered metallic materials in Iberian colonies: gold (1492–1530s), iron (1492–1570s), copper (1540s–1620s), and silver (1550s–1790s). I say "loose chronological order" because I move back and forth between the pre-Columbian and colonial periods, juxtaposing evidence from pre-Columbian material cultures and narrative traditions with colonial-era assessments of Indigenous technologies. This necessary series of contrapuntal readings of objects and words allows me to investigate where colonial authors understood and misunderstood Indigenous mining communities' beliefs about metals, metalworking, and the nature of life itself. The conclusion briefly reflects on archives, comparison, and future directions in colonial studies and the history of science and technology. In this way, the structure of this book riffs on the notion, often articulated or assumed within science studies, that human society progresses in a linear manner through distinct stages of social development and that such stages can be classified archaeologically by materials like stone, bronze, and iron.

This kind of materials-based periodization is as old as the poetry of Roman imperial writer Ovid. In his *Metamorphoses* (8 CE) Ovid defined the march of human civilization as a progression (or, more properly, a declension) of Gold, Silver, Bronze, and Iron Ages. In Ovid's telling, the chaos of creation gave birth to a hierarchical model of human existence, one whose greed and loss of innocence was marked by declining metallic purity. All was held in common in the Golden Age, an era of perfect harmony with an eternally fertile Nature. From untilled lands flowed "Streams of milk and streams of sweet nectar," and "yellow honey was distilled from the verdant oak." With the advent of seasons and shelter, "the silver race came in, lower in the scale than gold, but of greater worth than yellow brass." The Bronze Age, or "brazen race" *(aenea proles),* presaged the end of human happiness, marked by the Iron Age, in which "all evil burst forth into this age of baser vein," and human beings divided the land into units of property from which they demanded always-increasing outputs. They explored the world below the surface and across oceanic horizons, using new technologies to delve "into the very bowels of the earth" and "spread sails to the winds ... insolently over unknown waves." Metallic epochs were rewritten with advances in agriculture, navigation, and mining: "And now baneful iron had appeared, and gold more baneful still; war came, which fights with both, and brandished in its bloody hands the clashing arms. Men lived on plunder." In this world of scientific knowledge turned upside down, family structures fell apart: "Guest was not safe from host, nor father-in-law from son-in-law; even among brothers 'twas rare to find affection. The husband longed for the death of his wife, she of her husband; murderous stepmothers brewed deadly poisons, and sons inquired into their fathers' years before the time."[14]

Ovid's idea that human civilization can be measured in units of metallic matter has shaped colonial scientific writing and contemporary classifications. In the early modern era, writers who recuperated ideas and ideologies from antiquity began to interpret non-European peoples through metallic chronologies and the material facts of their everyday lives. Spanish and Portuguese writers, those based in colonial communities and those writing from the Iberian Peninsula, classified human development through visible data like clothing, food, houses, medicines, metals, and weapons (see Part 2). Even today, scholars periodize human history by metallic materials. From the Stone Age to the Ages of Bronze and Iron, such classifications imply a steady march toward modernity—one that collapses the diverse chronologies of periods like "The Bronze Age," which unfolded at different times in the Middle East (ca. 3300–1230 BCE), India (ca. 3000–1000 BCE), China (ca. 2000–700 BCE), and Europe (ca. 2300–600 BCE), and instead gives pride of place to a single historical epoch that is based on European precedent. These classifications and categories of development are not only restricting in their homogenization; they are also bound up in traditional Western ideas about progress. As archaeologist Dorothy Hosler notes in her study of the sensory values of copperwork in pre-Columbian and early colonial Michoacán, chronologies that move from Stone to Iron suggest a teleology that flattens the dynamic cultural complexities of ancient societies who negotiated issues of change and continuity over time; this teleology also restricts our analysis of the sociocultural domains of scientific cultures and our understandings of technologies. The linguistic focus of *Mining Language* offers one way to center material and view critically these received frames of historical analysis.[15]

14. Ovid, *Metamorphoses,* trans. Frank Justus Miller, 3d ed., I (Cambridge, Mass., 1977), 9–13.

15. Jack Goody, *Metals, Culture and Capitalism: An Essay on the Origins of the Modern World* (New York, 2012), xviii; Hosler, *Sounds and Colors of Power,* 4–5. On stone, see Carolyn Dean, *A Culture of Stone: Inca Perspectives on Rock* (Durham, N.C., 2010). Despite such critiques, these periodizations continue to circulate. A Boolean search in JSTOR for the terms "Bronze Age" + "Stone Age" + "Iron Age" returned 152 results published between 2010 and 2019. For examples of how these ideas circulate in diverse undergraduate classrooms, from classes on world history to programs in materials engineering, see John P. McKay et al., *Understanding World Societies,* II, *since 1450* (Boston, 2015); xxxix; William D.

Although language has always been fundamental to mining communications, it has not often played a key role in histories of mining and metallurgy. The preeminent historian of mining in colonial Latin America, Modesto Bargalló, famously dismissed colonial mining vocabularies as nonsensical, maintaining that writers in the colonial Iberian world were unfamiliar with the learned theories of minerogenesis and mercury-sulfur doctrine that authors articulated, as *sevillano* physician Nicolás Monardes did in his *Diálogo del hierro, y de sus grandezas* (1574). But these technical lexicons are central to our understanding of the history of mineral extraction, processing, and circulation in the early modern Iberian world. In particular, a careful attention to the language of mining and refining allows us to document the intellectual contributions of people whose ways of knowing have gone underacknowledged in the colonial scientific historiography, such as mining women, Afro-Latin artisans, and Indigenous experts.[16]

Iberian writers' preoccupation with language was not just about the difficulty of reducing dynamic, organic matter into stable, standardized terms or translating eyewitness testimony into textual passages that were intelligible to readers in Europe. The care with which writers like Oviedo, Cárdenas, and authors throughout the Americas crafted a technical lexicon indicates their serious concern about the nature of colonial society and the ways in which new cultural and demographic mixtures violently yoked together diverse ways of knowing, believing, and being in the so-called *Siglo de Oro* (Golden Age). The story of Spain's golden empire—traditionally construed as a hegemonic imposition of language and religion, extraction of knowledge and resources, and denial of humanity and sovereignty—looks quite different when we highlight the metals that were classified by miners from different cultural, linguistic, and scientific traditions. Such an emphasis does not deny the unbalanced doctrinal, epistemological, political, and socioeconomic powers of imperial Spanish agents versus artisan miners in colonized spaces, but it does reveal a

---

Callister, Jr., and David G. Rethwisch, *Materials Science and Engineering: An Introduction,* 10th ed. (New York, 2018), 2.

16. Bargalló, *La amalgamación,* 221. The full passage reads, "Los mineros cronistas del Perú apenas conocieron la doctrina azogue-azufre para los metales: a lo sumo jugaban con palabras de sentido poco preciso como 'frialdad' o 'calidez' de los metales, o su 'sequedad' o 'humedad'; las de 'calentamiento' o 'enfriamiento' del azogue durante el beneficio, que era un modo de expresar la actividad de dicho metal; o las de la 'amistad' o 'simpatía' y los de 'enemistad' o 'antipatía' entre los metales, para indicar su capacidad de combinación mutua; o con las frases de que 'el azogue abraza a la plata,' o 'la sal limpia las maletías de la plata' para que mejor le abrace el azogue, o la de que 'el azogue se calienta con la sal' o 'con los repasos.'"

more nuanced exchange of ideas than is suggested by the traditional historiography on metals and empire.[17]

Before African, Amerindian, Asian, and European people were brought into economic, social, and linguistic community, variously and asymmetrically by force and by choice, there was nothing new about the New World. It was a quite-old place whose communities had domesticated maize and crops around 5000–3000 BCE and were well established when Colón disembarked with African and European sailors in 1492. After that first, formative act of colonization in the Caribbean, the mining industry was made new each day. Miners uncovered new veins, refiners developed new methods to treat diverse mineralogical compositions, and writers conveyed these ways of knowing by coining new vocabularies, repurposing existing expressions, and fashioning new forms of communication.[18]

Throughout the territories colonized by Spain and Portugal, the gold and silver industries—later joined by explorations of copper and discussions of iron—indexed broader social, cultural, and economic developments within colonial mining communities, imperial councils, and the transoceanic world of print. The expressions that writers invoked to voice these changes underscore early modern perceptions of mining and metallurgy. For example, some of the foundational terms shifted dramatically or came into being as a result of Spanish imperial extractions in the Americas. Consider the case of the word *minero* (male miner / a mine). By tracing how the meaning of the word changed over time, from a medieval concept of underground deposits to that of a colonial laborer whose body and knowledge generated imperial riches, we can better understand broader developments in Spanish imperial law, language, and writing about the sources of extractive wealth.

Between 1286 and 1399, the mercury mines of Almadén, in Andalusia, were bought, sold, and leased in negotiations involving artisans, unskilled laborers, religious officials, landed Spanish elites, Knights of Calatrava, and Genovese merchants. Notaries named all of these actors. There were merchants ("mercaderes que compran et lievan azogue," "aquellos que fallaredes trayendo azogue, o conprando o vendiendo o en otra manera qualquier"); mine owners *(vecinos, moradores),* some of whom bought on contract ("arrendadores de los pozos del Almaden") and some of whom acquired titles through military

17. See, for instance, Stanley J. Stein and Barbara H. Stein, *Silver, Trade, and War: Spain and America in the Making of Early Modern Europe* (Baltimore, 2000).

18. Janine Gasco et al., "Origins and Development of Mesoamerican Civilization," in Robert M. Carmack, Gasco, and Gary H. Gossen, eds., *The Legacy of Mesoamerica: History and Culture of a Native American Civilization,* 2d ed. (1996; rpt. New York, 2007), 39.

networks ("maestre de la orden de la cavallería de Calatrva"); and administrative officials who regulated and recorded mine operations, including officers *(alamines, alguaciles, alcaldes),* lawyers *(procuradores),* and notaries *(escribanos).* There were also workers ("omes que labraran," "omes que tovieredes en la lavor"), squadron members *(quadrilleros),* operators *(cozedores),* peons *(peones),* and an unclassified group of "others" ("los otros," "aquellos"), including skilled craftsmen in related industries, such as *maestros* who made refining devices. In this impressive range of vocabularies and mining professions, including mining women ("los cuerpos de los tales omes o mugeres que sean presos e estén a la nuestra merçed"), there was no word for "miner." Although the mining industry had developed sophisticated legal protocols to authorize international transfers of deeds and titles and to coerce people from southern Spain into enriching merchants from Italy, by 1399 it had not yet coined a word to name the women and men who labored underground.[19]

Throughout the medieval era, *minero* was understood symbolically as "a source," a metaphorical extension of its primary, spatial definition. These definitions circulated in works like the anonymous thirteenth-century treatise *Bocados de oro* (Mouthfuls of Gold), which argues, "La verdadera sapiencia es minero de toda ventura e demostrador de todos enseñamientos e amatador de todo mal" (True wisdom is the source of all fortune, revealer of all learning, and vanquisher of all evil). They also appear in fifteenth-century poet Juan de Mena's philosophical verses, which tell how "Amarillo faze el oro al que sigue su minero, y tenblador el tesoro del azogue" (Yellow becomes gold for he who follows the vein / And from the treasure of mercury, a trembler is made).[20]

19. See the following in A. Matilla Tascón, *Historia de las minas de Almadén* (Madrid, 1958), I: "Sancho IV concede a la orden de Calatrava autorización para fabricar bermellón y poder explotarlo," Mar. 22, 1286, 273; "Privilegio de Alfonso XI, confirmación de otro de 1308 en que se concedió a la orden de Calatrava monopolio de venta del azogue," Aug. 18, 1316, 279; "Relación de los delitos cometidos por los arrendadores de la mina," Sept. 4, 1316, 281–284; "Traslado de la escritura de arrendamiento de los pozos de azogue de Almadén, otorgada por el maestre de Calatrava a favor del rey Alfonso XI," Mar. 13, 1348, 287; "Escritura de arrendamiento de los pozos de azogue del Almadén, otorgada por el maestre de Calatrava a favor de unos mercaderes genoveses," Aug. 10, 1387, 299; "Escritura de arrendamiento de los pozos de azogue del Almadén, otorgada por el maestre de Calatrava a favor de unos mercaderes genoveses," Mar. 26, 1399, 307. I thank Reneé Raphael for pointing me toward these sources.

20. *Bocados de oro* (ca. 1250), and Mena, *Debate razón* (ca. 1445–1456), in Gómez Manrique, *Cancionero,* ed. Francisco Vidal González (Madrid, 2003), cited in the Real Academia Española's Banco de datos, *Corpus diacrónico del español* (CORDE), s.v. "minero," http://www.rae.es.

Only after the collision of African, Indigenous, and Spanish knowledge, labor, and belief systems in the Americas would the meaning of *minero* shift from a physical or metaphorical source of wealth to a human body whose labor generated revenue for an overseas empire. According to the Real Academia Española's historical database of the Spanish language, *Corpus diacrónico del español* (CORDE), *minero* was first used to mean "miner" rather than "mineral" in ordinances concerning the treatment of Indigenous people in Puerto Rico. In 1513, the crown ordered all masters whose estates were located far from the mines to form partnerships ("conpañya") with owners of agriculturally productive lands in mining districts. As one provided labor ("los dhos yndios") and the other provided food ("los dhos mantenimios"), the crown, equating human beings and foodstuffs, reasoned that Indigenous miners would be guaranteed the basic sustenance they needed to do their work. For good measure, the ordinances insisted "q̄ el dueño de los dhos yndios ponga el mynero q̄ a de andar conllos poq̄ste no consenyra que le fala cossa nynga" (that the owner of the aforesaid Indians appoint a miner to accompany them because he will not allow them to want for anything). For the first time in the recorded history of the Spanish language, *minero* was now a technical expert who was appointed to oversee acts of colonial extraction, not a place where metals were found in alluvial deposits or generated below the surface of the earth. This shifting meaning indexes larger historical tensions about the relationship between imperial wealth, colonial society, and human, nonhuman, and less-than-human bodies. A series of legal institutions, economic practices, and intellectual frameworks enabled the transmutation of American gold into imperial money and the transformation of human beings into sources of wealth—even, and most important, when their humanity was not acknowledged.[21]

However, this new understanding of human and mineral bodies did not displace older definitions of the term *minero.* Rather, writers layered their texts with both meanings, creating a palimpsest of signifiers that resounded in transatlantic letters and literary markets. Throughout the sixteenth century, *minero* appeared in multilingual dictionaries as the English "myne," or "vaine of mettal," and the Latin *vena* or *metallum.* The noun *mina* was translated as "a myne" in English and *cuniculus* in Latin, following the distinction of Spanish lexicographer Elio Antonio de Nebrija between *vena,* "minero de algun

21. "Orden sobre tratamiento de indios," Valladolid, Jan. 23, 1513, Archivo General de Indias (hereafter cited as AGI), Indiferente, 419, legajo 4, fols. 83–96v, 94. The ordenanzas are transcribed in Paulo Suess, *La conquista espiritual de la América española: 200 documentos–siglo XVI* (Quito, 2002), 320–327, esp. 325, law 26.

metal" (vein of some metal) and *metallum,* "minero de metal en griego" (vein of metal in Greek). Nicolás Monardes described "mineros distintos" (different minerals) and noted, "Ay mineros do[nde] es el Hierro mas fuerte que otro" (There are mines in which the iron is stronger than in other places). Translators in England and Germany easily understood the two meanings of *minero*-as-mineral and *minero*-as-mine, expressing the lines as "mynes, how deep so ever they bee" ("den tieffesten Gängen") and "there are mynes where some Iron is more strong then other some" ("Es werden zwar Gänge gefunden / da einer weicher und schmeidiger Eisen gibt / als der ander welcher sprödes und hartbrüchiges Eisen gibt"). Only by the seventeenth century would dictionary authorities define *minero* primarily as a human being with skilled knowledge of mineral extraction.[22]

The presence or absence of a word in a language does not tell us much about the worldview or lived realities of the speakers of that language. But as one measure of the way in which human beings make meaning in the world, language—when read alongside historical sources as an index of change, continuity, accommodation, and adaptation—is an important avenue through which we can access the past. In the study of New World mining and metallurgy, we have not often approached language in this way. By treating mining lexicons as archives that record the contributions of women and men who

22. [Nicolás] Monardes, *Diálogo del hierro, y de sus grandezas, y como es el más excelente metal de todos, y la cosa más necesaria para servicio del hombre, y de las grandes virtudes medicinales que tiene* . . . (Seville, 1574), 161v, 163; Monardes, *Dialogue of Iron* . . . , in John Frampton, trans., *Joyfull Newes out of the Newfound World* . . . (London, 1580), 144, 145v; Jeremiam Gesner, ed. and trans., *Ein nützlich und lustig Gespräche, Von Stahl und Eisen: Darinnen dieser Metallen Würdigkeit und Artzney Tugenden angezeiget werden* . . . (Leipzig, 1615), 10, 14, orig. in Bayerische Staatsbibliothek, Münchener Digitalisierungs Zentrum Digitale Bibliothek, http://reader.digitale-sammlungen.de/resolve/display/bsb10904545.htmlsammlungen.de/de/fs1/object/display/bsb10904545_00001.html; Richard Percyvall, *Bibliothecae Hispanicae pars Altera: Containing a Dictionarie in Spanish, English, and Latine* . . . (London, 1591), 125; Elio Antonio de Nebrija, *Vocabulario español-latino* (Salamanca, [1495?]), 133; Hierosme [Girolamo] Vittori, *Tesoro de las tres lenguas francesa, italiana y española / Thresor des trois langues françoise, italienne, et espagnolle* (Geneva, 1609), 423; John Minsheu, *Hēgemōn Eis Tas Glōssas Id Est, Ductor in Linguas: The Guide into Tongues . . . with Their Agreement and Consent One with Another, as Also Their Etymologies, That Is, the Reasons and Derivations of All or the Most Part of Wordes, in These Eleven Languages* . . . (London, 1617), 128. In early modern texts, "mineral" and "metal" are used interchangeably. Today, "metal" refers to a hard, solid material, whereas "mineral" refers to a chemical compound with a specific elemental signature. In sixteenth- and seventeenth-century records, silver and argentine are variously called "metal" and "mineral," but today we say that silver is a metal and argentine is a mineral.

worked under- and aboveground, we gain a deeper understanding of what metallic matter meant—both in physical and ideological terms—and how various technical experts gave shape, form, and texture to those meanings.[23]

Rather than departing from a theoretical paradigm about matter, materialism, or cultural contact, this book is organized around the raw materials of Iberian colonial spaces as they were refined into sources of imperial wealth and read as markers of human civilization. The chapters contained within the four parts of the book—"Gold," "Iron," "Copper," and "Silver"—use different methods and theoretical approaches, including historical linguistics, visual analysis, and comparative literary interpretation, to reveal different stories about the place of metals in colonial history. Because the sections focus on different metals, they also analyze different geographic areas. "Gold" focuses on the extended Caribbean (Panama, Colombia, and the Antilles), whereas "Iron" extends to the literary space of "the Indies," a geographic imaginary along which early moderns analogized Amerindians to Southeast Asians. "Copper" takes us to Cuba, the Southeast United States, and the Venezuelan Andes, whereas the story of "Silver" unfolds in technology transfers between Mexico and Peru, where imperial agents negotiated contracts with mercury suppliers in Europe and Asia and refiners sent silver to the markets of China and Japan.

This range of metallic materials and geographic sites requires a variety of literary and historical methods. By combining language data, folklore, iconographic analysis, and print histories—that is, considering books and manuscripts as physical objects and analyzing variant translations—"Gold" (Chapters 1–3) and "Silver" (Chapters 8–10) show how Indigenous knowledges shaped Spanish colonial technologies of metallic extraction and processing. Part 1 focuses on mining tools and geographies that were developed with Taíno and

23. Whorfian conclusions have been replaced with new research, in no small part because of the small sample size of informants (n = 1) in Benjamin Lee Whorf, "The Hopi Language, Toreva Dialect," in Harry Hoijer et al., *Linguistic Structures of Native America,* ed. Cornelius Osgood (New York, 1946), 158–183; Whorf, *The Hopi Language* (1935; rpt. Chicago, 1956), but the idea that human beings cannot think of something without a word for it persists in numerous studies of language. Bill Bryson's encomium to the English language and the mind that melded it, *The Mother Tongue: English and How It Got That Way* (New York, 2001) was first published in 1990. When I first wrote these lines in October 2012, Bryson's book was number 11 on Amazon's list of top-selling English-language dictionaries and thesauruses. When I looked for it in December 2017, it was number 8 in Linguistics. On Whorf's legacy, see Ekkehart Malotki, *Hopi Time: A Linguistic Analysis of the Temporal Concepts in the Hopi Language* (New York, 1983); John B. Carroll, Stephen C. Levinson, and Penny Lee, eds., *Language, Thought, and Reality: The Selected Writings of Benjamin Lee Whorf,* 2d ed. (1956; rpt. Cambridge, Mass., 2012).

Afro-Taíno knowledges, gold refineries that were designed after Taíno-style *bohíos* (huts), and the ways in which early modern visual culture erased critical details about Taíno mining practices and Indigenous and black women miners from the extended Caribbean region. Because there is more robust lexical data for Mexico and the Andes, Part 4 uses historical linguistics and translation analysis to reveal Indigenous contributions to New World methods of silver metallurgy. After central Mexican miners redefined the borders of "like" and "unlike" and developed industrial-scale amalgamation methods, these technologies were transferred to South America. There, Quechua-speaking miners accommodated the Mexican *patio* technique to the different silver mineralogies and colder ambient temperatures of the Andes. By comparing moments when Mexican and Andean vocabularies overlap and diverge, and by tracing how Andean etymologies are systematically translated out of scientific writing in Western Europe, these chapters create a documentary record of Indigenous knowledge production in the colonial Andean silver industry.

"Iron" (Chapters 4–5) and "Copper" (Chapters 6–7) focus on base metals to address questions of genre and form. Part 2 uses genre, print history, and translation to compare how Portuguese physician García d'Orta and Spanish medic Monardes engage with writers from classical antiquity, medieval Christendom and the Middle East, and their own Iberian empires, and how they reconcile these authorities with information from Hindu and Islamic informants in Asia (d'Orta) or Indigenous experts in the Americas (Monardes). Both authors use the genre of the dialogue to engage in larger issues of imperial knowledge production and scientific communication, but Monardes's *Diálogo del hierro* was translated as a dialogue, whereas d'Orta's *Colóquios dos simples* was converted into a natural history. Part 3 attends to form, rather than genre, in a game of colonial telephone in which Portuguese footsoldier o Fidalgo de Elvas retold tales of Spanish explorer Álvar Núñez Cabeza de Vaca, and English polymath Richard Hakluyt fashioned Elvas's *Relaçam verdadeira* (1552) into promotional material for different audiences (1609, 1611). In these tellings and retellings of copper mining, refining, and trading in what is now the Southeast of the United States, copper—even when absent—became evidence that supported various colonization schemes. By the seventeenth century, when copper currencies were in crisis throughout western Europe and the metal played a critical role in granting European access to West African markets, writers began to imagine new kinds of futures for the colonial copper industry. Projectors like Manuel Gaytán de Torres, a politician from Andalusia, inspired by the Cuban case of El Cobre, surveyed the copper mines of Cocorote, Venezuela, and created a blueprint for a new type of colonial society—one in which enslaved African copper miners and Indigenous farmers and ranchers would operate largely outside of Spanish control. The complex was organized, as don Manuel explained in his *Relación y vista de ojos* (1621) and its accompanying painting, around the three stages of copper metallurgy: crushing, purifying, and casting. These were also foundational practices of empire, insofar as imperial policy makers and colonial agents treated subaltern communities violently: crushing human spirits, reducing Native communities to colonial governance, and converting non-Catholics into bearers of the faith. In this way, Gaytán de Torres, like Hakluyt and o Fidalgo de Elvas, transformed the material potential of copper metals into a malleable discursive medium through which to articulate visions of colonization and imperial wealth.

By analyzing diverse historical sources (archival manuscripts and papers, printed books, and visual representations) through the frames of linguistic, literary, and iconographic interpretation, *Mining Language* situates human responses to metals, both real and imagined, within particular cultural, epistemological, and geographic contexts. It reveals how a mélange of people, including Indigenous miners, African refiners, South Asian healers, Spanish colonial officials, and Iberian imperial agents, interpreted the physical and symbolic registers of metallic materials as part of a broader signifying tradition—one that laid bare questions of knowledge, empire, and power. Colonial scientific texts have not often been subject to this kind of discursive analysis. We have, instead, considered the forms of Spanish and Portuguese that circulated in natural histories, medical dialogues, proposals, and technical treatises as languages imposed upon colonized communities by dominant imperial forces and thus as unproductive sites for documenting subaltern knowledge production. This book takes a different approach. It treats colonial Iberian scientific languages as an archive that offers a variety of methods to document the things that have gone undocumented—namely, the intellectual contributions of women and men from Indigenous, African, and South Asian metalworking communities. Like other recent scholarship in colonial studies and the history of science and technology, *Mining Language* enables us to approach fragmented colonial scientific archives and reframe their historical silences.

Gold

1 : GATHERING INDIGENOUS KNOWLEDGES

As soon as Cristóbal Colón made landfall on the island of present-day Haiti and the Dominican Republic, he began searching for the metal whose promise had underwritten his voyage. The very next day, October 13, 1492, the admiral set about "de saber si avía oro" (to know if there was gold). Following the directions of Indigenous captives, Colón resolved to sail south, southeast, and northeast "a buscar el oro, y piedras preçiosas" (in search of gold and precious stones). From October 15 until the twenty-third, Colón expressed his single-minded pursuit of gold in a variety of terms: finding gold ("fallar oro"), following gold ("adonde es el oro"), locating underground mines ("ay mina de oro," "no ay mina de oro"), trading for gold ("aguardando si el rey de aquí o otras personas traerían oro"), and seeing whether there was gold ("si puedo aver del oro," "avia en ella oro").[1]

Colón's diary continues in a similar tenor until, one month after arriving in the Antilles, he sailed toward an island that his Lucayan informants called "Baveque," which he quickly amended to "Baneque" (present-day Inagua Island, Bahamas). There, Native men told him through signs, "La gente d'ella coge el oro con candelas de noche en la playa y después con martillo diz que hazían vergas d'ello" (The people there gather gold by candlelight at night along the beach, and afterward it is said that they hammer it into sheets). Language, signs, and extractive economies become conjoined in the diary: that same day, Colón determined to capture Indigenous women and children, following a practice that he learned from Portuguese traders in West Africa, so that male prisoners would stay with their families and women would teach their language to "los nuestros" (our men). One month later, on December 18, when Colón learned the word *cacique* (chief), he gained more insight into mining methods on islands where "nasçe mucho oro, hasta dezirle que avía isla que

1. Cristóbal Colón, *Los cuatro viajes: Testamento,* ed. Consuelo Varela (1986; rpt. Madrid, 2011), 61 (Oct. 13, 1492), 66 (finding), 67, 68–69 (following), 67, 76 (locating), 75 (trading), 75, 77 (seeing). Although he later grafted the goal of religious conversion onto his letters, the passenger list from the first voyage, like Colón's reluctance to investigate botanical sources of wealth, reveals a truer story. Colón departed with a diverse crew of Spanish, Italian, and African men. There were plenty of newly released prisoners, practiced apothecaries, and interpreters fluent in Arabic, Aramaic *(caldeo),* Hebrew, Portuguese, and Spanish, but not a single priest traveled with them (85). See 7–38, esp. 9–10.

era toda oro, y en las otras que ay tanta cantidad que lo cogen y ciernen como con çedaço y lo funden y hazen vergas y mill labores" (a lot of gold springs forth, so much that they say there is one made of pure gold, and in the others there is so much that they gather it and sift it as you would with a sifter and they smelt it and make sheets and a thousand works). His informant demonstrated these techniques through signs ("figurava por señas la hechura").[2]

Unlike earlier expressions of seeking *(buscar)* or finding *(hallar)* what there was *(haber)*, Colón's new, more precise vocabulary included gathering *(coger)*, sorting *(cernar)*, smelting *(fundir)*, and hammering into shape *(hacer vergas)*. These terms provide a critical linguistic index of knowledge transfers from Indigenous informants. By tracing moments when new terms were coined and when they began to appear in early-sixteenth-century books, this chapter combines linguistic data and historical sources to show how Indigenous ideas about mining and metals influenced the grammar of the colonial gold industry. This approach allows me to situate metallic cosmologies of the Taínos, Indigenous people of La Española, within a web of human, plant, and mineral relationships. As the sources analyzed here—written, published, and circulated between 1492 and the 1530s—will show, such relationships were both material and symbolic (Map 1).[3]

First, a note about the definition of Taíno and how it shifts in the years covered in this chapter. There is a vibrant debate in the archaeological literature regarding the definition of Taíno peoples and cultures; some scholars, such as Irving Rouse, divide Taínos into Taíno and sub-Taíno groups (and, later, Western Taínos), whereas others, including Marcio Veloz Maggiolo, argue that Taínos are only "associated with Boca Chica, a highly developed style of ceramics named after the site in the Dominican Republic." Others still, surveying the state of extant Taíno material cultures, insist that these categories "have limited archaeological support." This chapter, and the subsequent two chapters on goldwork in the extended Caribbean, follows Roberto Valcárcel Rojas, Marcos Martinón-Torres, Jago Cooper, and Thilo Rehren, who acknowledge the limitations of the term Taíno yet conclude that it is the best word we have to describe the particular cultural contexts of an Antillean commu-

2. Ibid., 90–92 (Nov. 12, 1492), 133 (Dec. 18, 1492). Baveque enters Colón's records on November 12, when he first mentions the Río del Sol; the last mention of the island occurs on January 6, 1493, two days after he wrote of the Río del Oro, solidifying the connection between Baveque and gold. See Evelina Gužauskytė, *Christopher Columbus's Naming in the "Diarios" of the Four Voyages (1492–1504): A Discourse of Negotiation* (Toronto, Ont., 2014), 95.

3. Julian Granberry and Gary S. Vescelius, *Languages of the Pre-Columbian Antilles* (Tuscaloosa, Ala., 2004), 35.

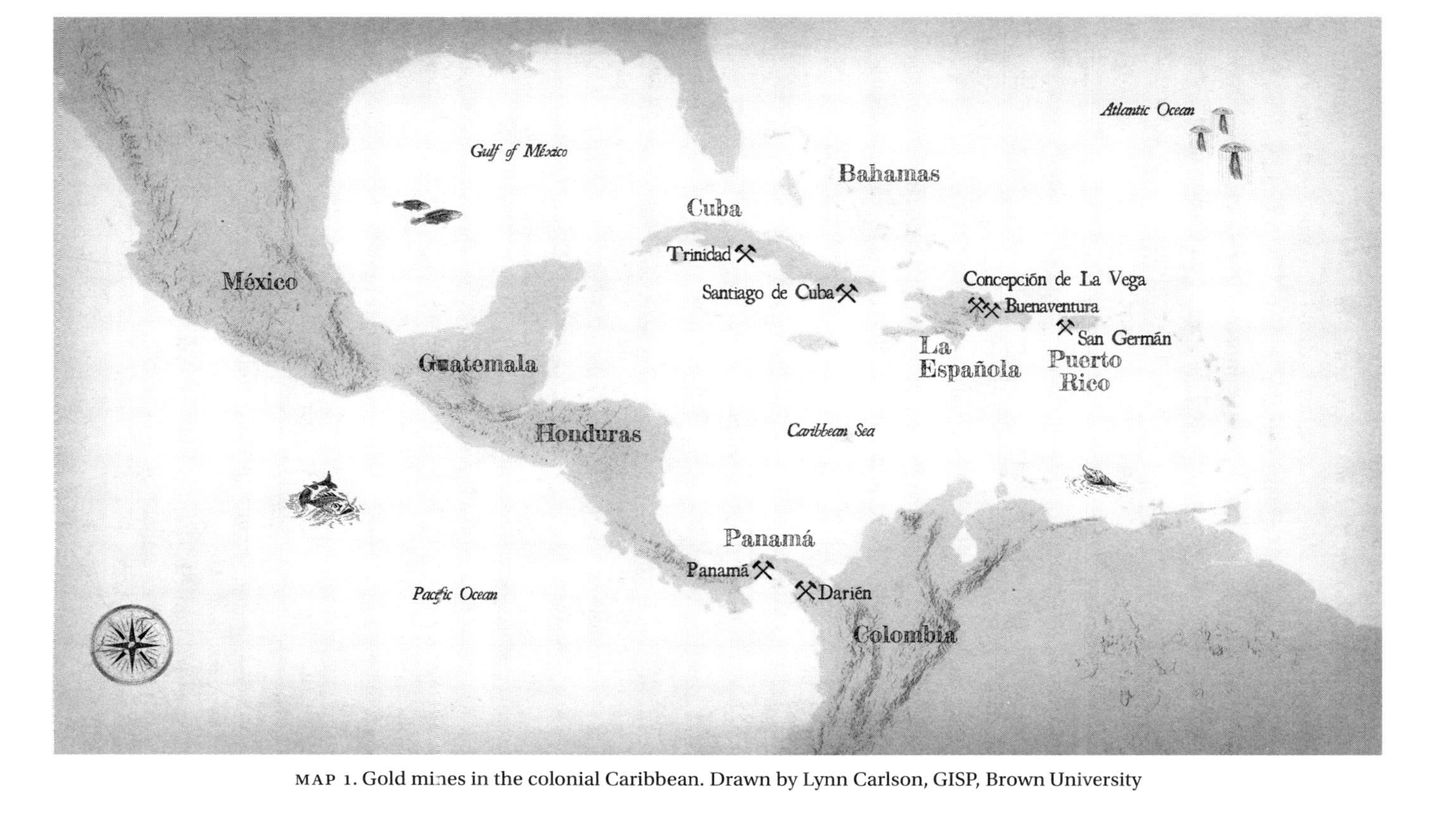

MAP 1. Gold mines in the colonial Caribbean. Drawn by Lynn Carlson, GISP, Brown University

nity whose history was shaped by contact with Indigenous communities from Mesoamerica, South America, and the Caribbean. Here, the term Taíno refers, not to a self-contained Indigenous population, but to a broader community of Taínos from various Antillean islands and Afro-Taíno miners in the sixteenth-century Caribbean. This usage reflects the imprecise ethnic identities listed in colonial documents and the Afro-Indigenous metallurgical cultures that came to define metalwork in La Española and the extended Caribbean.[4]

Long before the arrival of Africans and Europeans, Taíno societies were shaped by cultural, linguistic, and economic contact with diverse communities throughout the Americas. The earliest material artifacts from the Antilles suggest that the region was first populated by speakers of Tolan languages from Mesoamerica, around 4000 BCE. In La Española, known in the pre-Columbian era as Haiti or Quisqueya, a second wave of Waraoid speakers arrived from what is now Venezuela. By 1000 BCE, Waraoid seems to have replaced Tolan as the language of daily life everywhere but in Ciguayo communities (a northeastern sliver of Haiti / Quisqueya). In Puerto Rico and eastern Haiti / Quisqueya, Taíno replaced Waraoid, whereas in Cuba and western Haiti / Quisqueya, they blended into a hybrid language that is known as Ciboney Taíno (Map 2). By 1200 CE, Taíno cultures consolidated their power and became a dominant force in the Greater Antilles.[5]

4. Irving Rouse, *The Tainos: Rise and Decline of the People Who Greeted Columbus* (New Haven, Conn., 1992), 7; Marcio Veloz Maggiolo, "The Daily Life of the Taíno People," trans. Ana Maria Simo, in Fatima Bercht et al., eds., *Taíno: Pre-Columbian Art and Culture from the Caribbean* (New York, 1997), 34–45, esp. 37; L. Antonio Curet, "Colonialism and the History of Archaeology in the Spanish Caribbean," in Ludomir R. Lozny, ed., *Comparative Archaeologies: A Sociological View of the Science of the Past* (New York, 2011), 641–672, esp. 647; Roberto Valcárcel Rojas et al., "Oro, *guanines* y latón: Metales en contextos aborígenes de Cuba," *El caribe arqueológico,* X (2007), 116–131. See also Reniel Rodríguez Ramos, "What Is the Caribbean? An Archaeological Perspective," *Journal of Caribbean Archaeology,* Special Publication no. 3 (2010), 19–51; and Curet, "The Taíno: Phenomena, Concepts, and Terms," *Ethnohistory,* LXI (2014), 467–495. On metallurgy, see Candice L. Goucher, "African Metallurgy in the Atlantic World," in Akinwumi Ogundiran and Toyin Falola, eds., *Archaeology of Atlantic Africa and the African Diaspora* (Bloomington, Ind., 2007), 277–291. On the porous borders of the pre-Columbian Taíno world, see Curet and Mark W. Hauser, eds., *Islands at the Crossroads: Migration, Seafaring, and Interaction in the Caribbean* (Tuscaloosa, Ala., 2011); Corinne L. Hofman and Anne van Duijvenbode, eds., *Communities in Contact: Essays in Archaeology, Ethnohistory and Ethnography of the Amerindian Circum-Caribbean* (Leiden, 2011).

5. Granberry and Vescelius, *Languages of the Pre-Columbian Antilles,* 41–43, 49–50. By 1450, Kalinagos from the Guianas populated the Lesser Antilles, adding another layer of language, history, and culture (ibid., 59). Quisqueya means "very mountainous" and is

Between 1492 and the 1530s, Taíno communities lived through every imaginable form of cultural change: agricultural, demographic, ecological, economic, legal, political, spiritual. By 1518, when Africans began to outnumber Taínos in La Española, changing the notion of what it meant to be Caribbean, the Indigenous population of the island had decreased from an estimated 250,000–500,000 in 1492 to 11,000. With this dramatic demographic and cultural shift, La Española truly became a New World—or, more specifically, "una nueva variante de sociedad colonial" (a new kind of colonial society). Before the arrival of Africans and Europeans, the island was neither old nor new; it was just a place with its own order.[6]

The Languages of Gold: Taínos and Colón

Panning for gold at night, as Colón reported, would make it difficult to see the metal, despite the glow of candlelight. It would be logical to align these periods of nocturnal mining with the cycles of the moon and to work when the moonlight was brightest. Although Colón shows no awareness of the ceremonial potential embedded in these practices, the communal nature of the activity and the spatiotemporal specificity he relayed suggest that rituals of gold collection had their own time, place, and season. Throughout the extended Caribbean, Indigenous goldworking communities harvested plants, honey, and beeswax at specific seasonal intervals in accordance with creation narratives and established traditions. For example, the U'wa people of northeastern Colombia relate that the world came into being when the Sun (Rukwa), a powerful deity in the masculine realm above, sent his daughters as bees to pollinate and flower the earth, a lower order associated with women. In compensation for their work, the daughter-bees received "tierra amarilla" (yellow earth), which was associated with gold metals, fructiferous seeds, and *raiya* (wealth / fertility). At the appropriate season, U'wa men harvest honey to continue this fertile, life-giving cycle, and they fashion beeswax into goods to trade with people from neighboring lands. According to anthropologist Ana María

---

composed of the root terms *kh,* "hard rock," *-khe-,* reduplication from the Honduran language of Jicaque-Tol, and *-ya,* "tree," derived from *yo* in Jicaque-Tol.

6. Jalil Sued Badillo, *El Dorado borincano: La economa de la Conquista, 1510–1550* (San Juan, 2001), 24. Demographic estimates of pre-Columbian Caribbean populations vary widely. For an excellent analysis of the strengths and limitations of various methodologies, see Karen F. Anderson-Córdova, *Surviving Spanish Conquest: Indian Fight, Flight, and Cultural Transformation in Hispaniola and Puerto Rico* (Tuscaloosa, Ala., 2017), 74–87. For archaeological methods, see L. Antonio Curet, *Caribbean Paleodemography: Population, Culture History, and Sociopolitical Processes in Ancient Puerto Rico* (Tuscaloosa, Ala., 2005), 47–61.

Falchetti, refining techniques like lost-wax casting connect metallurgical practices to the creation story.[7]

What Colón does seem to recognize, though, is that there is something new or different in Taíno metalworking traditions, relative to those known in Africa and Europe. To that end, he coins a novel expression in Spanish: "coger oro" (to gather gold), a fittingly colonial convergence of agricultural harvests, colonial appropriations, and sexual desire. One of the earliest lexical cases of "gathering wealth" occurred in 1505, when soldiers commanded by Governor fray Nicolás Ovando raided lands controlled by the cacique Higüey on La Española. After the invasion, treasurer Cristóbal de Santa Clara calculated a profit of 2,874 pesos and 9.5 grams of gold in "los esclavos e preseas que se cogieron a los indios que se rebelaron en la provincia de Higüey el año de 1505 e de cierto pan e ajes que se vendió a la gente que hizo la dicha guerra" (the slaves and jewels that were gathered from the Indians who rebelled in the province of Higüey in 1505, and from certain bread and chilis that were sold to the people who made the aforesaid war).[8]

By 1525, when the *vecinos* (landholders) of Concepción de La Vega, the primary mining town of La Española, petititoned the crown to reform the gold industry, "coger oro" (gathering gold or wealth from Indigenous people) had become the island's canonical expression of gold mining. At first glance, this expression seems to signal a new colonial regime of extractive wealth. Upon closer examination, we see how it also reflects Taíno understandings of the generation, collection, and use of golden metals.[9]

7. Ana María Falchetti, "La ofrenda y la semilla: Notas sobre el simbolismo del oro entre los Uwa," *Boletín Museo del Oro,* XLIII (1997), 2–37, esp. 7–9. I thank Diana Magaloni for sharing this article with me.

8. Juan Gil, "Las cuentas de Cristóbal Colón," in Gil and Consuelo Varela, eds., *Temas colombinos* (Seville, 1986), 44. For an analysis of Santa Clara's role in shaping gold reporting in these early years, see Esteban Mira Caballos, "La economía de la Española a través de las cuentas del tesorero Cristóbal de Santa Clara (1505–1507)," *Ibero-amerikanisches Archiv,* XXIV, nos. 3–4 (1998), 247–265.

9. "Petición de ciudad de la Concepción: Mercedes" (1525), 1–6v, Archivo General de Indias (hereafter cited as AGI), Patronato Real, 18, no. 1, ramo 4. One writer used the term "coger oro" in 1432, but 94 percent of the cases (seventeen out of eighteen authors) documented by the Real Academia Española appear after 1492 in texts written from or about the Americas. The anomalous document, not related to mining, was written by medieval notary Juan Péres d'Otalora, a native of the Basque town of Azpeitia, in a mix of Euskara and Spanish ("en guisa que le non mongue endo cosa alguna"). The next reference is Colón's, followed by chroniclers like Bartolomé de Las Casas, Oviedo, Francisco López de Gómara, and Antonio Herrera. Although it is possible that the phrase originated in Vizcaya, went unused for sixty years, and reemerged in the Caribbean at the moment of

To understand how Colón's neologistic turn of phrase seems to reflect Indigenous worldviews more than the admiral's particular kind of Spanish, we must understand the linguistic landscape of La Española in the pre-Columbian era. Taíno language data is highly fragmented. Only six complete sentences and a handful of phrases are known today. This linguistic rupture, which bears testimony to the sheer force and persistent legacies of colonialism, presents deep methodological challenges to our ability to understand Taíno knowledge production after 1492. In spite of the difficulty of rebuilding the lexicon from colonial sources, historical linguists like Julian Granberry, Gary S. Vescelius, Manuel Álvarez Nazario, and engineer / literary scholar Rafael García Bidó have assembled a corpus of approximately 1,500 Taíno terms, most of which are toponyms and proper nouns. By analyzing the prefixes, suffixes, and root terms embedded in these toponyms, mapping them onto geographic features, documenting migration histories and language contact through archaeological records, and comparing evidence from Antillean languages with larger inventories and living Native speakers (such as Warao and Arawakan languages), these researchers have provided crucial insights into the symbolic registers of pre-Columbian vocabularies in the Caribbean.[10]

Because of the value that Spanish writers placed on gold, metallic vocabularies provide some of the best—and, in certain cases, only—surviving testimony of pre-Columbian languages of the Antilles. For example, only one

---

colonial contact, the outlying case is likely a result of scribal error or language interference from Euskara. See Real Academia Española, Banco de datos, *Corpus diacrónico del español* (CORDE), s.v. "coger oro," http://www.rae.es. Searches with variant spellings, such as "coger el oro" (eleven documents), "coxer oro" (two documents), "coxer el oro" (one document), "cojer oro" (six documents), and "cojer el oro" (five documents) return the same results. Only Péres d'Otalora used the term before 1492; all of the remaining twenty-five documents deal with mining in the Americas. See *Labayru Hiztegia,* 2d ed., s.v. "mongue," https://hiztegia.labayru.eus. The Euskara verb *koxitu* means "take" (in Spanish, *coger,* also written as *coxer* in medieval and early modern orthography), and the noun *oro* means "all" (in Spanish, *todos*). See ibid., s.v. "oro" and "coger." Medieval contracts from southern Spain contain two examples of "coger azogue" (to gather mercury), both mentioning women. See "Traslado de la escritura de arrendamiento de los pozos de azogue de Almadén, otorgada por el maestre de Calatrava a favor del Rey Alfonso XI (vide *lámina* X.)," Mar. 13, 1348, and "Relación de los delitos cometidos por los arrendadores de la mina (vide *lámina* IX.)," Sept. 4, 1316, in A. Matilla Tascón, ed., *Historia de las minas de Almadén,* I, *Desda la época romana hasta el año 1645* (Madrid, 1958), I, 285–295, esp. 282, 289.

10. Granberry and Vescelius, *Languages of the Pre-Columbian Antilles,* 69–74, 97, 101–122; Manuel Álvarez Nazario, *Arqueología lingüística: Estudios modernos dirigidos al rescate y reconstrucción del arahuaco taíno* (San Juan, 1996); Rafael García Bidó, *Voces de bohío: Vocabulario de la cultura taína* (Santo Domingo, 2010).

word remains of the Ciguayo language: *tuob* (gold). The term was possibly derived from the proto-Chontal Mayan term *tun* (stone) and *-ob'* (pluralizer). Granberry and Vescelius consider Jicaque-Tol, the Honduran language that predated Taíno on the island, to be a more likely source, because Mayan languages generally follow a CVC syllabic structure (consontant + vowel + consonant), whereas *tuob* (or, phonetically, "twób") is CW (consonant + w). These phonologies and syllabic structures suggest deep language contact between Jicaque-Tol and pre-Columbian communities in Haiti / Quisqueya. Even with highly fragmented records, we are still able to understand something of the histories of migration and exchange that shaped the linguistic and cultural contours of the Caribbean before the arrival of Spaniards and Africans.[11]

According to Granberry and Vescelius, there were at least four languages spoken on Haiti / Quisqueya in 1492, each of which contained its own local forms and was derived from different origins (Map 2): Ciboney Taíno, an Arawakan language spoken in the far-western regions of Marién and Jaraguá and eastern Cuba; Macorís, a language thought to be of Waraoid origin, spoken in the northern part of the island; Ciguayo, perhaps derived from Taíno, Waraoid, or a combination of the two languages, spoken in a tiny sliver of the northeast; and Classic Taíno, an Arawakan language that was spoken in most of the island. Three languages had their own words for "gold": *nozay,* in Ciboney Taíno ("yellow pebble"?), *tuob,* in Ciguayo (heavy stone), the only word documented in the language, and *caona,* in Classic Taíno (gold). Macorís did not leave a lexical trace of "gold" in colonial records. Today, only one word is known in the Macorís language: *baeza* (no).[12]

All lexical expressions of "gold" contain information about the worldview of the linguistic communities from which they emerge. The Spanish noun *oro* stems from the Latin *aurum,* derived from the verb "burn," so named "after the color of fire." Spanish etymologies thus tell us about the movement of Latin to Iberia, a mining colony of the Roman empire, and how the material form of the object generates its name. In Haiti / Quisqueya, the term *caona* (pronounced phonetically as *kwaõna,* according to Bartolomé de Las Casas's notes) was formed by the prefix *-ka* (the), the root *wõ* (we), and the suffix *-na* (small). This Classic Taíno noun "has cognates in all the other Northern Maipuran Arawakan languages," such as the Island Karib term *kaouánam.* Moreover, it appears etymologically and conceptually related to *kawana* (small meeting place), as the two terms are composed of almost the same morphemic units. The idea of community is embedded in the Taíno expression for gold, much as Colón's

11. Granberry and Vescelius, *Languages of the Pre-Columbian Antilles,* 28–30.

12. Ibid., 14–15, 28–30, 31, 33, 34–35.

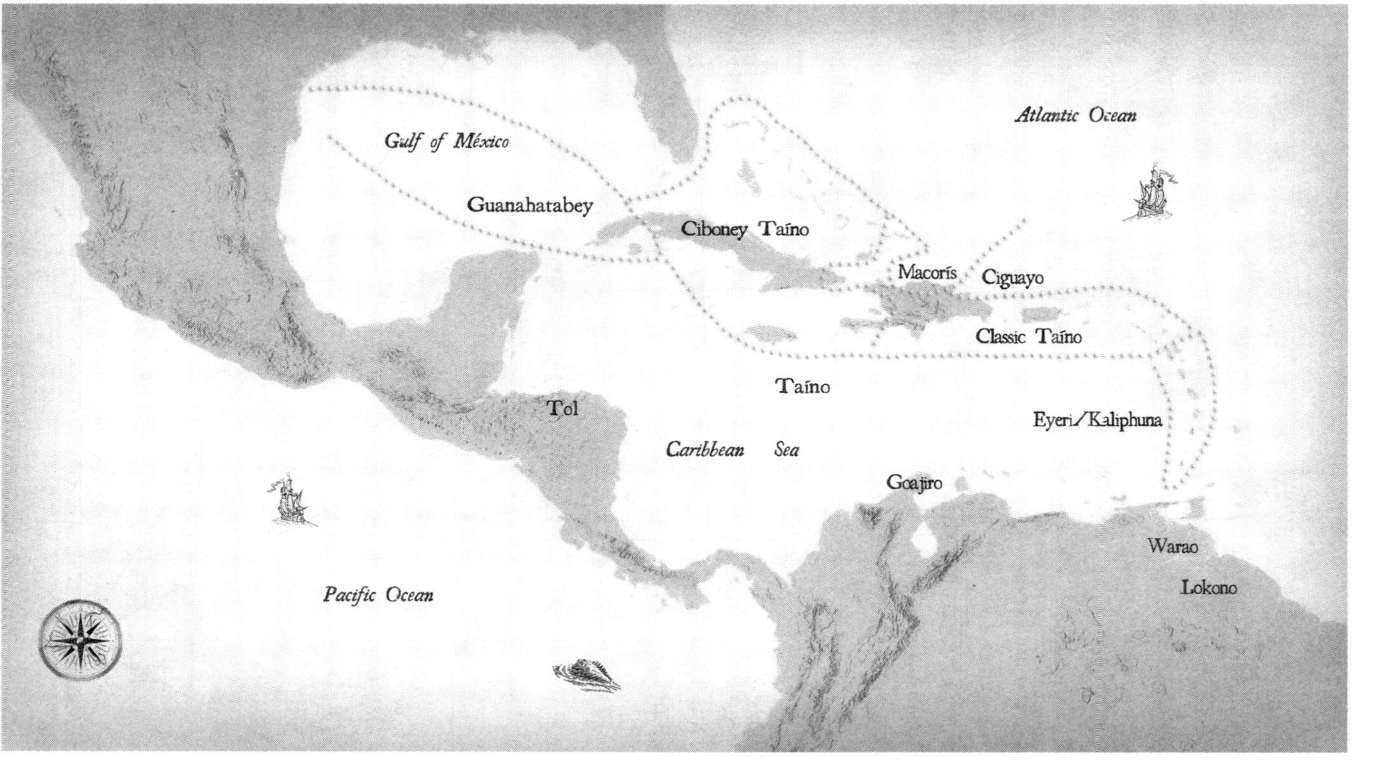

MAP 2. Language map of Haití / Quisqueya (La Española). Drawn by Lynn Carlson, GISP, Brown University, following Julian Granberry and Gary S. Vescelius, *Languages of the Pre-Columbian Antilles* (Tuscaloosa, Ala., 2004), with permission from the University of Alabama Press

description of communal rituals had suggested—whether the admiral knew it or not.[13]

Golden Cosmologies and Metalworking Traditions: Oviedo

We gain additional insight by combining language data with critical readings of historical and archaeological sources. Colonial writers are often silent on Indigenous knowledges, but some authors provide insight into Native metalworking traditions—even when they do not intend to. These voices include Colón, Las Casas, Catalán friar Ramón Pané, and, especially, royal refiner and natural historian Gonzalo Fernández de Oviedo y Valdés. In 1514, Oviedo was named as overseer of the gold refineries of Tierra Firme, and he departed for the Americas from Sanlúcar de Barrameda that year. In 1523, he took up the office in La Española, and he served in that capacity until 1532. These experiences allowed Oviedo to observe Indigenous metalworking communities in different areas of the Caribbean and to put their practices of gold mining and refining in dialogue with information about the animals, trees, plants, and stones of each region. He compiled this scientific data into a series of widely read natural histories that were published in 1526, 1535, and 1547. However, texts like Oviedo's must be read with great care before we can consider them as sources of ethnographic data. They require a methodology that combines scholarly practices of the disciplines we now divide into history, linguistics, and literature.[14]

According to Oviedo, Taíno miners observed an admirable reverence ("una notable religiosidad") in their preparations to extract gold, although he insists that these offerings were not made with the aim of spiritual perfection: "no para biē bivir ni quitarse de vicio semejante / sino pa cojer el oro" (not to live correctly or likewise free oneself from sin but rather to gather gold). Oviedo seems unaware that sacrificing personal pleasure was a crucial part of Taíno gold mining; to receive from the earth, one showed reverence for the blessing.[15]

Once Colón located the mines of the Cibao—meaning "land of stone," formed by the Taíno terms *siba,* "stone," and *-wo,* "land," closely related to *-wõ,* "gold," a valley of rich green lands and goldfields in the center of Haiti / Quisqueya—he, too, understood some of the ritual nature of metalwork in Taíno

13. Mohammad Diab, *Lexicon of Orthopaedic Etymology* (Amsterdam, 1999), 30; Granberry and Vescelius, *Languages of the Pre-Columbian Antilles,* 34, 101–102, 107.

14. José Amador de los Rios, "Vida y escritos de Gonzalo Fernández de Oviedo y Valdés," in Oviedo, *Historia general y natural de las Indias, islas y tierra-firme del mar océano,* 4 vols. (Madrid, 1851–1855), I, ix–cvii, esp. xxii.

15. [Gonzalo Fernández de Oviedo y Valdés], *La historia general delas Indias* (Seville, 1535), lxix.

communities. Before mining, men would separate themselves from women, echoing a practice relayed in a Taíno creation narrative that I analyze in Chapter 3. After this period of separation, male miners fasted and remained chaste for a few days, insisting, as Oviedo put it, "Quando se vian con la muger q̄ no hallavā el oro" (When they were seen with women that they did not find gold). When Colón learned of this ritual practice, he ordered colonists to observe the same ceremony. Believing that God's grace would shine more generously upon the penitent, the admiral prohibited anyone who had not confessed his sins or taken Communion from entering the goldfields. Spaniards refused, complaining that they were already dying of hunger, forced into abstinence by being far from "their women," and starved of spiritual sustenance, because the island's sole church was hardly open outside of Easter mass.[16]

Like Oviedo, Colón misunderstood the cosmological relationship between human activity, plants, and metals. Throughout the Americas, many Indigenous communities believed that gold grew like a plant or flower, with its own time for gathering. In diverse metalworking communities of the Caribbean, refiners added herbs to molten mixtures of gold and copper to impart an olfactory experience to *guanín* (gold-copper alloys). Such herbs enhanced the different textures and colors of gold and copper with a new scent, producing a rich sensory experience when viewers beheld metallic goods. In this way, guanín metals were not seen as works of art or modes of exchange, as they were in Europe, but as "spiritually active entities that maintained the world." Indigenous cosmologies were "reflected in the shiny objects they made" and reinforced through glittering proof of the human ability to transform matter. In other words, artisan labor made visible the "ephemeral sensations and esoteric knowledge" that Indigenous people throughout the Caribbean understood as the animating energies of the universe.[17]

Gold (caona, tuob, nozay) had a single hue, one texture, and no scent. Naturally occurring gold, as it was cast into molds and hammered into shape, amazed Spaniards for its unity of form and perfect sameness. But Taíno people

16. Granberry and Vescelius, *Languages of the Pre-Columbian Antilles,* 111, 113; Oviedo, *La historia general delas Indias,* lxix; José R. Oliver, "Gold Symbolism among Caribbean Chiefdoms: Of Feathers, *Çibas,* and *Guanín* Power among Taíno Elites," in Colin McEwan, ed., *Precolumbian Gold: Technology, Style and Iconography* (London, 2000), 196–219.

17. Nicholas J. Saunders, "Shimmering Worlds: Brilliance, Power, and Gold in Pre-Columbian Panama," in Saunders, John W. Hoopes, and Thomas Gilcrease, eds., *To Capture the Sun: Gold of Ancient Panama* (Tulsa, Okla., 2011), 79, 81, 95; Carmen Salazar-Soler, "Álvaro Alonso Barba: Teorías de la antigüedad, alquimia y creencias prehispánicas en las ciencias de la tierra en el nuevo mundo," in Berta Ares Queija and Serge Gruzinski, eds., *Entre dos mundos: Fronteras culturales y agentes mediadores* (Seville, 1997), 269–296.

valued resplendent metallic materials whose powerful sensory experiences revealed the fruits of human intervention, what archaeologist Nicholas J. Saunders calls "a multisensory world of phenomenological unity" that reflects and reveals a "holistic universe." In 1992, excavations in Maisabel, Puerto Rico, uncovered objects made of guanín. Chemical analysis revealed a blend of copper (Cu, 55 percent), gold (Au, 40 percent), and silver (Ag, 5 percent). This chemical signature points to human influence, because no naturally occuring metals have this particular composition. When objects were visibly unnatural, such as mixed metallic goods that combined distinct hues, textures, shines, scents, and sounds, Taínos celebrated them as expressions of artistic accomplishment that honored world-making, world-destroying spirits by giving form and experience to their otherwise invisible energies. Taínos called brasswares that arrived from Spain *turey* (sky / heavens), according to Las Casas, who translated the Indigenous concept into a Catholic frame with the Spanish term *cielo.* As these expressions and their culturally embedded meanings suggest, Taínos and Spaniards understood gold metals, and how to evaluate their meaning and worth, in radically different ways. Despite the deep ruptures of colonialism, some of these meanings are preserved in Taíno vocabularies.[18]

For Taínos, gold mining and refining occurred within a larger matrix of gendered social norms and cosmological principles of balance. When artists fashioned metals into sacred objects, they restored a sense of balance to the world by honoring the fruits of the earth. This is not to say that Taíno metalworking traditions were ecologically innocuous; after all, they demanded substantial amounts of water and charcoal to wash minerals and fuel fires. Rather, these practices occurred in a different context, on a different scale, and with a different sense of things than Spanish miners and metallurgists observed in their artisan labors.[19]

18. Saunders, "Shimmering Worlds," in Saunders, Hoopes, and Gilcrease, eds., *To Capture the Sun,* 81; Peter E. Siegel and Kenneth P. Severin, "The First Documented Prehistoric Gold-Copper Alloy Artefact from the West Indies," *Journal of Archaeological Science,* XX, no. 1 (1993), 68, 71, 76; Bartolomé de Las Casas, *Obras completas,* ed. Paulino Castañeda Delgado, III, *Historia de las Indias* (Madrid, 1994), 641. See also John K. Papadopoulos and Gary Urton, eds., *The Construction of Value in the Ancient World* (Los Angeles, 2012).

19. Richard Cooke et al., eds., "Who Crafted, Exchanged, and Displayed Gold in Pre-Columbian Panama?" in Jeffrey Quilter and John W. Hoopes, eds., *Gold and Power in Ancient Costa Rica, Panama, and Colombia: A Symposium at Dumbarton Oaks, 9 and 10 October 1999* (Washington, D.C., 2003), 91–158; Alice V. M. Samson et al., "Cavescapes in the Pre-Columbian Caribbean," *Antiquity,* LXXXVII (2013), which includes an online image gallery at http://antiquity.ac.uk/projgall/samson338. Daviken Studnicki-Gizbert's work on the environmental effects of mining in colonial Mexico suggests a promising avenue for

These divergent ways of evaluating the meaning and value of gold become apparent when we compare the first and second editions of Oviedo's natural histories. His first book, *De la natural hystoria de las Indias* (1526), celebrated the mastery of Indigenous metalworking traditions in places like Castilla del Oro ("Castile of Gold," present-day Panama and northern Colombia), where "han muchos tesoros de oro labrado / en poder delos indios q̄ se hā cōquistado" (there are many treasures of worked gold in the power of the Indians who have been conquered). Although most of this gold was copper plated *(encobrado),* Oviedo insisted that it was "muy bueno y es de xxii. q̄lates y dēde arriba" (very good and worth twenty-two karats and more). In contrast, by the time he finished his second, more extensive work, *Historia general y natural de las Indias* (1535), the royal refiner was forced to clarify what, exactly, he meant by "gold." Oviedo prefaced his second discussion by noting, "No hablo aqui en el oro que se ha avido por rescates: o enla guerra / ni enlo que de su grado los indios han dado en estas yslas o enla tierra firme: porque este tal Oro ellos lo labran e lo suelen mezclar con cobre y con plata: e lo abaxan segun quieren. E assi es de diferentes quilates e valores: mas hablo del oro virgen en quien la mano mortal no ha tocado o hecho estas misturas" (I do not speak here of the gold that we have through trade or war, nor that which is with or without the grade that the Indians of these islands or Tierra Firme have given it; because that kind of gold is what they work and they tend to mix it with copper or silver, and they debase it as they wish, and so it is different karats and values. Rather, I speak of virgin gold that no mortal hand has touched or introduced any such mixture). Oviedo's second work, later reprinted as the *Corónica delas Indias* (1547), deleted references to conquered peoples ("indios q̄ se hā cōquistado") and praise of Indigenous metalwork, replacing them with definitions of gold and descriptions of mining women. In 1526, Oviedo celebrated a shared sense of value in Indigenous and Spanish communities; by 1535, he insisted that Amerindian and Spanish gold were made of different matter, valued differently, and defined in different terms.[20]

Following Colón's promise of islands made of gold, the precious metal became what literary scholar Elvira Vilches eloquently calls "a synecdoche

---

analysis in other regions. See his "Exhausting the Sierra Madre: Mining Ecologies in Mexico over the *Longue Durée,*" in J. R. McNeill and George Vrtis, eds., *Mining North America: An Environmental History since 1522* (Oakland, Calif., 2017), 19–46.

20. [Gonzalo Fernández de Oviedo y Valdés], *Oviedo de la natural hystoria de las Indias* (Toledo, 1526), xlv–xlv(v); Oviedo, *Historia general delas Indias,* lxv. Even within Spanish systems, colonists developed different valuations. In Puerto Rico, alluvial gold was taxed more than gold mined on land in order to justify the time, risk, and expense of difficult extractions (Sued Badillo, *El dorado borincano,* 172).

for New World riches." Such golden islands went undiscovered, despite a centuries-long search for El Dorado (the Golden One). As seventeenth-century chroniclers like Juan Rodríguez Freyle and fray Pedro Simón eagerly pointed out, El Dorado was a Spanish mistranslation of Indigenous Andean political practices in central Colombia. There, newly named leaders dusted themselves with gold and traveled ceremoniously around the lake before ascending to political and spiritual power. Spanish speakers misunderstood the ritual and spent centuries searching for the so-called Golden One.[21]

As an economic engine, silver quickly replaced gold, which remained "the scarcer metal" for most of the hemisphere until the eighteenth century. Even in the sixteenth century, the Indigenous nature of American gold was a disruptive, destabilizing force in Spain. The arrival of New World gold upended markets in Spain, creating doubts about the nature of trust, credit, and value and sowing widespread confusion, as subjects could not conceive "how the value of gold and silver could ever fall when the whole country was reveling in a shower of gold."[22]

These were not mere economic valuations; the concept of value that Oviedo affirmed—which so thoroughly destabilized the Spanish economy and worldview—was a spiritual pronouncement on the state of human obligation to use the things of God's earth in a way that was right and just. In describing techniques used to pan for gold in La Española, Oviedo insists that his words honor the act of divine creation and serve as a source of true wisdom for his virtuous Catholic reader ("muchos virtuosos e catholicos esperaran esta lecion"), not

21. Colón, *Los cuatro viajes,* ed. Varela, 133 (Dec. 18, 1492); Elvira Vilches, *New World Gold: Cultural Anxiety and Monetary Disorder in Early Modern Spain* (Chicago, 2010), 29; Pedro Simón, *Primera parte de las noticias historiales de las conquistas de tierra firme en las Indias occidentales* (Cuenca, 1627), quoted in Juan Rodríguez Freyle, *Conquista y descubrimiento del Nuevo Reino de Granada,* ed. Jaime Delgado (Madrid, 1986), 15.

22. Vilches, *New World Gold,* 4, 31; John J. TePaske, *A New World of Gold and Silver,* ed. Kendall W. Brown (Boston, 2010), esp. 24, 42–48, 53, 69–78. The major exception is eighteenth-century Brazil; see A. J. R. Russell-Wood, "Technology and Society: The Impact of Gold Mining on the Institution of Slavery in Portuguese America," *Journal of Economic History,* XXXVII (1977), 59–83; C. R. Boxer, *The Golden Age of Brazil, 1695–1750: Growing Pains of a Colonial Society* (Berkeley, Calif., 1962), esp. 1–60; and Kathleen J. Higgins, *"Licentious Liberty" in a Brazilian Gold-Mining Region: Slavery, Gender, and Social Control in Eighteenth-Century Sabará, Minas Gerais* (University Park, Pa., 1999). On the importance of gold in local markets, see Zamira Díaz López, *Oro, sociedad, y economía: El sistema colonial en la gobernación de Popayán, 1533–1733* (Bogotá, 1994), 81–87, 193–203. On the scholarly imperative to analyze the gold industry as more than "labor" or "economics," see Sherwin K. Bryant, *Rivers of Gold, Lives of Bondage: Governing through Slavery in Colonial Quito* (Chapel Hill, N.C., 2014), 5–8.

like works based on medieval fantasy ("[los] libros mentirosos de amadís"). Translating the parable of the talents to the New World, Oviedo concludes the scene with a cautionary tale of human greed and environmental destruction:

> E assi como esta tierra nuestra madre universal se rompe e abre por diversas partes: e se acierta a topar en sus entrañas e interiores la vena del oro alos hombres: assi quando las yjadas dela psona đl guardador avariēto comiēçā a se đteriorar e rōper faziēdo el curso đ su vida: a ciertā a salir las monedas ocultas / đ q̄ nūca oso aprovechar se el miserable q̄ las ayūto. Quiero đezir q̄ he visto eñstas idias grādes allegadores đste oro / e por no lo despender bien / han acabado en mucha miseria e seles fue delas manos como rocio o sombra: e aun sus vidas tras sus dineros.

> And so as this earth (our universal mother) is broken and opened in sundry places, as men resolve to strike veins of gold in her entrails and innards, so, just as when a man's rib cage begins to deteriorate and break, and the jealous guardian of life appears to claim its victim, the coins that the poor thing hid and abstained from all his life never fail to appear. I mean to say that I have seen in these Indies great heapers of this gold, and in failing to spend it well, they have ended up in so much misery and it all slipped through their fingers, like morning dew or night shade, and even their lives have gone the way of this money.[23]

With these affirmations, Oviedo responds to authorities like Pliny the Elder, whose account of mining in antiquity famously insists, regarding the same "universal mother," earth, "The things that she has concealed and hidden underground, those that do not quickly come to birth, are the things that destroy us and drive us to the depths below; so that suddenly the mind soars aloft into the void and ponders what finally will be the end of draining her dry in all the ages, what will be the point to which avarice will penetrate." Oviedo, fashioning himself as the Pliny of the Indies, had a different influence in mind when he maintained that pure, noble gold was next to godliness: he derived his understandings of the purpose, worth, and manufacture of precious metals from Amerindian perspectives.[24]

According to him, gold exchanges fluctuated in La Española because "no saben todos el valor / đ cada maña dl oro" (not everyone knows the value of all these kinds of gold). On September 23, 1519, the Consejo de Indias therefore ordered that local officials appoint an assistant to the master refiner and that

23. Oviedo, *Historia general delas Indias,* lxiii(v).

24. Pliny the Elder, *Natural History,* trans. H[arris] Rackham (Cambridge, Mass., 1961), IX, 5.

all gold above half a peso be tried by the touchstone before it left the refinery. Lighter, unmarked gold, sent from Tierra Firme and the Antilles, should be weighed with official scales in Santo Domingo, not mining towns like La Vega or Buenaventura. Imperial officials attempted to standardize gold production by creating a new administrative post, moving certain functions from mining towns to the capital city, and specifying the tools to assay gold of different weights. What Oviedo suggested was a deeper kind of destandardization—a world in which the most noble, pure, and enduring metal no longer had a single definition, form, or value. Careful attention to Indigenous influences in the gold industry, even as they are mediated by colonial descriptions, reveals new insights into the cultural anxieties of the Spanish Siglo de Oro.[25]

In relaying these techniques as gatherings (coger) rather than using conventional terms of extraction or removal *(sacar),* Colón signaled that there was, indeed, something new to describe. Spanish writers soon began to talk of their own modes of mining in the same way, although they did not perform the same acts of worship. Oviedo's *Historia general y natural delas Indias* provides the most detailed account of gold mining in the early Americas, combining his eyewitness testimony ("he muchas vezes visto como se saca el oro e se labran las minas enestas Indias" [I have many times seen how gold is removed and worked in the mines of these Indies]) and reports from other miners ("e assi he entendido de quien lo ha cogido" [and so I have understood it from those who have gathered it]); in the *Natural hystoria,* he had emphasized experiential knowledge acquired with enslaved and coerced miners ("he fecho sacar oro para mi cō mis indios y esclavos" [I have removed gold for myself with my Indians and slaves]). The royal refiner uses neologisms from the Americas and conventional expressions from Spanish to address different geographies of minework and kinds of information: *sacar* and *labrar* refer to knowledge of mining that he observed "con mis indios y esclavos enla tierra firme / enla provincia e governacion de castilla del oro" (with my Indians and slaves on the mainland in the province and territory of Castilla del Oro), whereas *coger* glosses reports from fellow miners "en esta e otras islas" (in this and other islands).[26]

Mining Geographies and Taíno Toponyms

Although Oviedo insists in the *Historia general* that there is one "common art" of mining practiced throughout the Caribbean ("pues q̄ es comun el arte"), he

25. "Sobre el aquilatado del oro en La Española," Barcelona, Sept. 23, 1519, AGI, Indiferente, 420, legajo 8, fols. 144–145v, 1–1v.

26. Oviedo, *Historia general delas Indias,* lxiiii(v); Oviedo, *Natural hystoria,* xlv. The manuscript says "esta e otras yslas" instead of "estas y otras islas" (16).

uses different verbs to classify activities on the mainland and in the islands and to distinguish his personal experiences from secondhand reports. Space provides the organizing structure of his account, which delineates three gold mining areas in La Española: savannas, *arcabucos* (groves), and rivers. The ecological realities of island topographies dictated the mining methods and processes in each space. Notably, the *Natural hystoria* lists only two ways: "o lo hallā en çavana o enel rio" (they either find it in the savanna or in the river). Oviedo then adds that sometimes gold was found "enla tierra fuera del rio en lugares q̄ ay arvoles / e para lo sacar cortan muchos y grādes arvoles" (in the soil next to the river in places where there are trees, and to extract it they cut down many large trees). In the *Historia general,* Oviedo revised his assessment of the topographies of mining in the Caribbean, at once updating his information and more closely resembling Pliny's tripartite classification of methods used by Roman imperial miners in Spain. According to Pliny, "Gold in our part of the world—not to speak of the Indian gold obtained from ants or the gold dug up by griffins in Scythiae—is obtained in three ways: in the detritus of rivers ... by sinking shafts; or it is sought for in the fallen debris of mountains. Each of these methods must be described." Oviedo replaced the Indians of Southeast Asia with the indios of the Americas, a conflation that I examine in Chapter 4, through dialogues about iron written from Goa and Seville.[27]

The first two terms in Oviedo's topographic landscape, "savanna" and "arcabuco," were of Taíno origin, as he noted in the margins of the manuscript that he began between 1539 and 1546 in Santo Domingo and completed in Spain around 1548. Only "río" did not require an explanation, because he used the Spanish term instead of a Taíno designation for "river," such as *bō, no,* or *-ri-.* What Oviedo heard as "arcabuco" was probably a combination of the root *ara* (tree) and the suffix *-buko* (large area of land); today, the Real Academia Española lists it as of "unknown origin, or perhaps Taíno." *Sabana,* whose English version is "partly a borrowing from Latin" (after the term *zauana*) and "partly a borrowing from Spanish" (after the word *zavana*) is, in Taíno, *saba* (forested) + *-na* (small). It was either a linguistic coincidence that Spaniards and Taínos had the same term for "field," or "savanna" is one of many cases in which Indigenous vocabularies were so quickly incorporated into colonial speech and reported in imperial letters that early modern authorities had trouble distinguishing them from Castilian expressions. By 1604, *arcabuco* appears in bilingual dictionaries as a Spanish word, translated into French as *bocage espais*

27. Oviedo, *Historia general delas Indias,* lxiiii(v); Oviedo, *Natural hystoria,* xlv; Pliny, *Natural History,* trans. Rackham, IX, 51, 53; Kenneth W. Harl, *Coinage in the Roman Economy, 300 B.C. to A.D. 700* (Baltimore, 1996), 81–82.

(thick woods), into Latin as *Sylva densa* (dense forest), and into English as "a great thicket of high trees."[28]

The technologies to remove gold from rivers differed from those used in savannas and groves, suggesting how Taíno toponyms conveyed knowledge about physical spaces and extractive methods. Each mining area demanded different labor regimes. A comparison of Oviedo's first edition (1526), second edition (1535), and manuscript revisions (1539–1548) reveals how he edited his verbs to distinguish master from miner in savannas and arcabucos and to highlight the work of African and Indigenous mining women.

In the *Natural hystoria* (1526), plural verbs represent physical labor, and singular verbs convey analytical work, separating those who dig from he who decides: "Y seyendo en çavana limpiā primero todo lo q̄ esta sobre la tierra y cavan ocho / o diez pies en luengo e otros tātos / o mas / o menos en ancho segūal minero le parece" (And being in a savanna, they first clean all that is upon the surface of the earth and they dig eight or ten feet in length and an equal measure wide, more or less, according to what the miner deems fit). As Oviedo explains, "they" meant "indios y esclavos." In contrast, the *Historia general* (1535) relays embodied practices in savannas and groves from the perspective of the "hombre minero," reducing the plural verbs to third-person singular: "limpiā" (they wash, abbreviated for print with the *ā* character) becomes "limpia" (he washes) and "cavan" (they dig) becomes "cava con su gente" (he digs with his people).[29]

28. *Diccionario de la lengua española,* 23d ed., s.v. "arcabuco," https://dle.rae.es; Granberry and Vescelius, *Languages of the Pre-Columbian Antilles,* 69–70, 72; *Oxford English Dictionary,* s.v. "savannah"; *Diccionario muy copioso de la lengua española y francesa . . .* (Paris, 1604), s.v. "arcabuco"; John Minsheu, *Hēgemōn Eis Tas Glōssas Id Est, Ductor in Linguas: The Guide into Tongues . . . with Their Agreement and Consent One with Another, as Also Their Etymologies, That Is, the Reasons and Derivations of All or the Most Part of Wordes, in These Eleven Languages . . .* (London, 1617), s.v. "arcabuco." As Oviedo explains in his manuscript revisions, "Llaman Çabana los indios Como En otro lugar lo tengo dho las vegas e çerros e Costas de rriberas" (the Indians call "Savanna" what in another place I have said as plains and hills and riverbanks), whereas "El Arcabuso es bosquaje de En mōte Alto o En lo llano En fin todo lo q̄sta arbolado es Arcabuco" (An *arcabuco* is a grove in a high mountain or in a plain, in sum any sort of grove is an *arcabuco*); see "Natural y general hystoria de las Indias," ca. 1539–1548, MSS, HM177, 16v, Huntington Library, San Marino, Calif.

29. Oviedo, "Natural y general hystoria de las Indias," MSS, xlv(v); Oviedo, *Historia general delas Indias,* lxv. When Oviedo refers to "hombres mineros" (mining men), he defines them as "expertos en sacar Oro tienen cargo de algūa quadrilla de indios y esclavos" (experts in removing gold, in charge of a squadron of Indians and slaves, his own or others). In the *Historia natural,* the passage continues in the plural: "hasta un palmo / o dos de hōdo / e ygualmente sin ahondar mas / lavan todo aquel lecho de tierra q̄ ay enel espacio

Oviedo's manuscript begins with the same third-person singular perspective as the *Historia general,* following the view of the expert miner. But it quickly shifts into plural form to describe physical acts of digging and washing:

> Y Este tal minero, quando quiere dar Catas para tentar e buscar la mina q̄ ha de labrar, si las quiere dar en çavana o Arcabuso haze Assi: limpiā prmero todo lo q̄ esta sobre la tierra de Arboles o yerva o piedras e Cava Con su gente ocho o diez pies (y mas y menos en luengo y otros tantos, o lo q̄le paresçe en Ancho) no ahondando mas de un palmo, o dos, ygualmente: y sin Ahondar mas lavan todo Aq̄l lecho de t[ie]rra e Cantidad q̄ han Cavado.
>
> And this miner, when he wants to run a vein to test and look for the mine that will be worked, does it like so in a savanna or grove: first they clean everything that is on the surface of the earth of trees or plants or stones and he digs with his people eight or ten feet (and more and less across, and likewise in depth, or whatever he deems fit) without going any deeper than one or two feet, in the same way. And without digging down any further, they wash that entire bed of soil and all the dirt that they have dug up in the aforesaid space.

In marking physical and intellectual work in different ways, Oviedo's verbs place miners who dig ("indios y esclavos") or decide ("el hombre minero") into different racial categories and labor hierarchies.[30]

Oviedo's descriptions thus offer insights into the labor relationships, material practices, and technological ecosystems of alluvial mining relative to work in the goldfields. First, miners working in or alongside rivers had to stop or divert the water source. If working in a small body of water, such as a lagoon, they cleared the area using the same procedures as they did with tunneling through bedrock: "Labran y lavan aquella tierra del suelo y cogen el oro que enella hallan: segun se dixo de suso" (They work and wash that dirt from the ground, and gather the gold that they find in it, as has been said above). With rivers or ravines, they diverted the source entirely. Once the area dried out, what miners called *xamurado,* "que en lengua o estilo delos que son mineros platicos quiere dezir agotado. (Porque xamurar es agotar)" (which in the language or style of people fluent in mining means exhausted [because *xamurar* means "to exhaust"]), they could recover gold nuggets nestled among stones,

---

q̄ es dicho / e si en aquel peso que es dicho hallā oro siguenlo / e sino a hondana mas otro palmo ... e mas hasta q̄ poco a poco lavando la tierra llegan a la peña biva e si hasta ella no topan oro / no curan de seguirlo ni buscarlo mas allí" (lxv[v]).

30. Oviedo, "Natural y general hystoria de las Indias," MSS, 17.

concaves, and fissures. This hybrid term, *xamurar,* also written as *jamurar,* requires further consideration.[31]

The RAE defines *xamurar* (to bail out water) as Catalán in origin, derived from the term *eixamorar* (to dry). But the only two documented cases come from La Española. Two additional cases with the variant spelling *jamurar* likewise come from the Americas—one from La Española, recorded by Oviedo, and one from Colombia, noted by writer Juan de Castellanos. The verb first entered the Spanish lexicon in 1517, when Jerónimo de Agüero, a vecino of Santo Domingo who had lived on La Española for eight years, testified that "las mugeres preñadas ni paridas no trabajen en minas ni fasyendas, sy no fuere en las suyas propias a su voluntad" (pregnant women and new mothers do not work in mines or on haciendas other than their own and by choice), and "generalmente avemos visto quel mayor trabajo que los yndios tienen es en las minas. Es en tres cossas: en xamurar y de rrecoperar y rrebolver grandes piedras" (generally we have seen that the greatest work that the Indians have is in the mines. It's in three things: bailing water *[xamurar]* and picking up and then moving large stones).[32]

What Spanish speakers heard as *xamurar* and what Castilian dictionaries later traced to Catalán was probably a technical practice from the mining industry that was formed by the Taíno roots *xama* (bay of water) and *-wa* (verbalizer). As evidenced by the examples of arcabucos, sabanas, and bailing water from alluvial deposits, Indigenous topographies and techniques were so quickly incorporated into colonial mining lexicons that the Taíno roots of technical terms were forgotten. Attending to these terms, the contexts in which they appear, and their erasure into Iberian etymologies reveals how Indigenous men and women shaped the language of the gold industry.[33]

One final example stands out from Oviedo's account: "la batea," the device that miners—especially Indigenous and African women—used to wash metals in rivers and ravines. When he describes miners who use bateas, Oviedo begins his technical discussion with masculine forms ("estos" [these]) and transi-

31. Oviedo, *Historia general delas Indias,* lxvi.

32. *Diccionario de la lengua española,* 24th ed., s.v. "jamurar"; CORDE, s.v. "xamurar" and "jamurar." Agüero's testimony, which responded to the sixth question of the Hieronymite Interrogatory, is transcribed in full in Andreas Wesch, *Kommentierte Edition und linguistische Untersuchung der "Información de los Jerónimos": (Santo Domingo 1517)*... (Tübigen, 1993), 137. Colonial officials were instructed to "direis de mi parte A los dhos caçiques q̄ nra Voluntades q̄ ellos traten muy bien a los yndios" (say on my behalf to the aforementioned *caciques* that it is our will that they treat the Indians very well) ("Registros: Instrucciones," May 3, 1509–Sept. 13, 1565, AGI, Indiferente, 415, legajo 2).

33. Granberry and Vescelius, *Languages of the Pre-Columbian Antilles,* 102, 113.

tions into feminine referents, although he does so in different ways in his published accounts and manuscript revisions. His most extensive natural history, *La historia general delas Indias* (1535), affirms, "Estos que lavan / por la mayor parte son mugeres indias" (These who wash / Are generally Indian women). In the manuscript, Oviedo updates his assessment to mark the presence of African women: "son mugers Indias o negras" (they are Indian or black women). In both editions, Oviedo doubly signals women's work with feminine endings ("indias," "negras") and the noun "mujeres" (women).[34]

In all of his texts, Oviedo plays with novelty in two ways: by invoking newness and by showing continuity with the past. First, he shows that the masculinist terms of the mining industry did not reflect practices in the Caribbean and that he had to modify them. Second, he describes a set of techniques, tools, and gendered labor domains that are decidedly not new. There is a curious amount of ink spilled on a time-honored technology, especially for a writer who was so eager to convey the richness and novelty of the plants, animals, metals, and customs of the Americas rather than to echo the accounts of other writers that he consolidated technical information into the book of deposits "por no lo repetir despues en otro lugar" (to avoid repeating it elsewhere). Readers of Strabo and Pliny were familiar with the methods of mineral washing that Oviedo explains in vivid detail, and women had mined for mercury in the Spanish mine of Almadén since the medieval era. Oviedo did not need to dedicate such attention to mineral washing, yet that is precisely what he did. For that, it deserves consideration.[35]

In book 3 of Strabo's *Geography,* one of Oviedo's influences, the Greek geographer praises the mineral and agricultural wealth of Turdetania, later called Andalusia, the land that the Catholic kings reconquered from the Moors in 1492 and the point of departure for most ships heading to the Americas. Strabo notes, "Neither gold, nor silver, nor yet copper, nor iron, has been found anywhere in the world, in a natural state, either in such quantity or of such good quality." These natural blessings lead him to celebrate human ingenuity, as he observes how "gold is not only mined, but is also washed down . . . by the rivers and the torrents" in mountainous terrains, whereas in arid regions, intricate canals "flood the waterless districts by conducting water thither, and thus

34. Oviedo, *Historia general delas Indias,* lxv(v); Oviedo, "Natural y general hystoria de las Indias," MSS, 18.

35. Oviedo, *Historia general delas Indias,* lxiiii(v); "Escritura de arrendamiento de los pozos de azogue del Almadén, otorgada por el maestre de Calatrava a favor de unos mercaderes genoveses," Mar. 26, 1399, in Tascón, ed., *Historia de las minas de Almadén,* I, 305–310, esp. 307.

they make the gold-dust glitter; and they also get the gold out by digging pits, and by inventing other means for washing the sand; and the so-called 'gold-washeries' are now more numerous than the gold-mines." Perhaps because they were such well-known techniques, Strabo spends the rest of the passage explaining silver refining by fire rather than gold washing in rivers. By 25 CE, gold panning and washing were familiar technologies, undeserving of treatment in Strabo's seventeen-book compilation of the regions of the world and the human knowledges that unlocked their resources.[36]

Likewise, Pliny's *Natural History* explains a variety of extractive technologies in rapt detail, although he, too, is uninterested in panning or washing. In breathless fashion, Pliny narrates how miners in Spain blasted through mountains to create channels (*"corrugi,* a term derived I believe from *conrivatio,* a uniting of streams of water") to transport gold from the bowels of the earth to streams for washing. Others diverted those rivers "by man's agency to run where there is no place for a man to plant his footsteps," digging out spaces that were two hundred feet wide and ten feet deep. Into these man-made openings, miners placed five-yard-long sluices to capture gold nuggets that flowed from fresh mountain springs. This last method, which occurred at a scale whereby "the workman hewing the rock hangs suspended with ropes, so that spectators viewing the operations from a distance seem to see not so much a swarm of strange animals as a flight of birds," led to massive erosion and ecological destruction in ancient Iberia. As Pliny puts it, "The earth carried along in the stream slides down into the sea and the shattered mountain is washed away; and by this time the land of Spain owing to these causes has encroached a long way into the sea." Such risk was offset only by the "pure gold" that came "straight away" from the mines, requiring no form of refining or metallurgical processing.[37]

By contrast, the scale of washing gold in the New World was much smaller. Whereas Pliny stands at a distance, Oviedo zooms in to detail the spatial relationship of people and place. He describes minute actions, like miners' carefully turning their wrists and shifting their balance on wet rocks, to emphasize skills that artisans developed as they worked on land and in rivers. After narrating the extractive techniques used in these spaces, Oviedo turns to the

36. E. Capps, T. E. Page, and W. H. D. Rouse, eds., *The Geography of Strabo,* trans. Horace Leonard Jones, II (London, 1932), 39–41 (3.2.8).

37. Pliny, *Natural History,* trans. Rackham, IX, 57, 59, 61. For help with Latin language terms, I thank Karen S. Myers and John D. Dillery in the Department of Classics at the University of Virginia.

practice shared by miners in savannas, arcabucos, and rivers: mineral washing in *bateas* (sifters).

Women, Men, and the Taíno Roots of Mining Tools

Although the word *batea* existed in Spanish before 1492, it was unrelated to mining. It was a verb conjugated as an *-ar* paradigm and used almost exclusively in baptismal ceremonies like those documented in Alfonso X's *Primera partida* (undated), an anonymous interpretation of the New Testament (ca. 1260), Juan Manuel's *Libro del caballero y del escudo* (1326), and Martín Pérez's *Libro de las confesiones* (ca. 1312–1317). The Real Academia Española traces the roots of *batea* to Arabic Spanish (*árabe hispanico*), derived from *baṭíḥa,* but it does not document any association with mining or refining in the Spanish lexicon before 1492. In the Caribbean, where speakers of Arawakan languages classified hollowed-out objects like baskets, houses, and canoes as grammatically feminine, the term becomes a feminine noun rather than an *-ar* verb. As we have seen with *coger oro* and *xamurar,* only in the Antilles does *la batea* first appear in Spanish in connection with gold refining. In an industry composed largely of Native women and men—and, later, African and Indigenous miners—we should not be surprised to find that Indigenous ideas and grammatical genders are embedded in colonial mining vocabularies.[38]

Oviedo's was not the first report on gold mining to use the feminine noun *batea.* In 1517, imperial officials explained to newly installed Hieronymite governors how "los tales yndios, en espeçial los desta ysla Española, asy henbras como varones" (the aforesaid Indians, especially those of this island of Española, women as well as men), could, under Spanish rule, continue to "bevir politica mente, sabiendo adquerir por sus manos de qué se mantengan agora, sacando oro por su batea, o fasyendo conucos" (live as a political body, knowing how to secure with their own hands the ways in which they currently maintain themselves, by mining for gold with their *batea* or making *conucos* [mounds of soil for growing root vegetables]). The expression from this legal order, called "Instrucción a los padres de la Orden de San Jerónimo," was repeated in the list of questions *(interrogatorio)* that the friars put that year to La Española's longest-standing vecinos as they investigated the state of Indigenous commu-

38. Álvarez Nazario, *Arqueología lingüística,* 50; CORDE, s.v. "batea," 191 cases found in 84 documents. The RAE dates Martín Pérez's confessional book as ca. 1500, but here I follow the dates suggested in the new critical edition: Pérez, *Libro de las confesiones: Una radiografía de la sociedad medieval española,* ed. Antonio García y García, Bernardo Alonso Rodríguez, and Francisco Cantelar Rodríguez (Madrid, 2002).

nities, visited mining regions, and determined whether and to what extent Native peoples were "capable" of living independent of Spanish governance.[39]

It did not take long for *la batea* to circulate in other parts of the Spanish-speaking Americas or to be received as a Spanish word. In his 1571 *Vocabulario en lengua castellana y mexicana,* fray Alonso de Molina translated the "Spanish" term "batea para lavar oro" (*batea* used to wash gold) into Nahuatl as *teocuitlapaconi.* This word is related to a variety of specialized terms for gold and goldworking, such as *teocuitla cocoualoni* ("moneda de oro" [gold coin]) and *teocuitla cuicuiloa* ("labrar algo de sinzel, o dorar algo el pintor o dorador" [to work something with a chisel, or for a painter or goldsmith to make something gold]). Molina also offered the variant terms *quauhapaztli* and *quauhxicalli,* related to *quauhapipilhuaztli* ("canal de madera" [wooden canal]), *quauhaquia* ("plantar arboles, o estacas de olivas" [to plant trees or olive tree stakes]), and *quauhatlapalli* ("hoja de arbol" [tree leaf]), suggesting the kind of discursive and conceptual overlap in agricultural and metallic vocabularies that we see in Taíno languages. In the Nahuatl section of the dictionary, Molina listed *teocuitlapaconi* as "batea o cosa semejante para lavar oro" (*batea,* or similar thing to wash gold), perhaps indicating something less than equivalence in the translations.[40]

A close look at Oviedo's description of the mining device and the specific geographies in which it was used allows us to appreciate how the Taíno knowledges embedded in the term were omitted from written records when *la batea* was traced to Spanish etymologies. According to Oviedo, there were three stages of excavation in savannas and on land; the final stage, mineral washing, was also how miners panned for gold in rivers and ravines. On land, the first group of miners removed small samples of soil; a second group then brought the samples to the nearest available water source. There, "las indias e indios lavadores" (female and male Indian washers) washed the samples to determine whether there was enough gold to continue digging or whether the crew should move to a new site. Oviedo explained in his manuscript that, in this

39. CORDE, s.v. "batea." On the Hieronymite Interrogatory, see Anderson-Córdova, *Surviving Spanish Conquest,* 39–40. Eva Bravo-García and María Teresa Cáceres-Lorenzo find earlier dates in Juan Ponce de León's letter to the crown of 1509, which includes the words *bohío, conuco, batea, cacique,* and *caribe.* See Bravo-García and Cáceres-Lorenzo, *La incorporación del indigenismo léxico en los contextos comunicativos canario y americano (1492–1550)* (Bern, 2011), 67.

40. Alonso de Molina, *Vocabulario en lengua castellana y mexicana y mexicana y castellana,* ed. Miguel León-Portilla, 4th ed. (Mexico City, 1970), s.v. "batea para lavar oro," "teocuitla cocoualoni," "teocuitla cuicuiloa," "quauhapipilhuaztli," "quauhaquia," and "quauhatlapalli."

group, "Estos q̄ lavā por la mayor pte son mugers Indias o negras porq̄ el offiçio del lavar es de mas Importançia e mas sçiente y de menos trabajo q̄ el escopetar ni q̄ acarrear la tierra-" (They [masculine] who wash are generally Indian women or black women; because the office of washing is more important and requires greater knowledge and less work than excavating or transporting the soil). Writers in Mexico and the Andes echoed Oviedo's idea that women were better suited for mineral washing and sorting than were male miners, because they had the patience and dexterity for such tasks. One writer, projecting his vision for a new mining community of autonomous enslaved Africans and families in the Andean foothills of Cocorote, Venezuela, made a similar argument about black women's abilities to grind and sort copper before the metal was treated by male refiners.[41]

Once washers finished their tasks and relayed their opinions, miners from the second group of go-betweens returned to the site with new information and empty bateas, as Oviedo explains in an aside, "que son cierto instrumento con que la dicha tierra se lava" (which are a certain kind of instrument with which they clean dirt). In his manuscript revisions, Oviedo added bateas to the list of mining expenses: "La Costa grande q̄ En ello se pone de bastimentos e otros Aparejos Asi Como đlas Compras delos esclavos y herramientas y bateas y otras Cosas" (the great cost required in food and other devices such as the purchases of slaves and tools and bateas and other things). In 1535, Oviedo listed only "las compras delos esclavos: y herramientas / y otras cosas" (the purchase of slaves and tools and other things). His explanation in both versions is nuanced, technical, and grounded in material practices that he admires. Oviedo chronicles, in a passage worth quoting in full, how

> estas mugeres o lavadores estan assentados orilla del agua / e tienen las piernas metidas enel agua hasta las rodillas o quasi / segun la dispusicion del assiento e del agua / y tienen enlas manos sendas Bateas asidas por dos asas o puntas que tienen para asideros. Y despues que enla Batea tienen la tierra que se les trae dela mina para lavar la / mueven la Batea a balances tomādo agua dela corriente con cierta maña o bayben: que no

41. Oviedo, *Historia general delas Indias,* lxv(v); Oviedo, "Natural y general hystoria de las Indias," MSS, 18; García de Llanos, *Diccionario y maneras de hablar que se usan en las minas y sus labores en los ingenios y beneficios de los metales* (1609), ed. Rose Mary Buchler, Gunnar Mendoza, and J. V. Murra (La Paz, 1983), 97–98; Juan Ordóñez Montalvo, *Arte o nuevo modo de beneficiar los metales de oro y plata y de plata con ley de oro, por azogue . . .* (Mexico City, 1758), 24; Juan de Cárdenas, *Problemas y secretos maravillosos de las Indias . . .* (1591) (Valladolid, 2003), 90; Manuel Gaytán de Torres, *Relacion, y vista de ojos . . .* ([Havana], 1621), 5v.

> entra mas cantidad de agua dela que el lavador quiere: e con la mesma maña y arte y en continente que toman el agua la vazian por el otro lado e la echan fuera: e tanta agua sale quanta entra sin que falte agua dentro: mojando e deshaziendo la tierra. E assi la tierra se va a bueltas del agua que se despide dela Batea: e robaba poco a poco la tierra llevando la tras si el agua: como el Oro es pesado va se siempre al hondo o suelo dela Batea. E como queda de todo punto la Batea sin tierra: e queda el Oro limpio: pone lo el lavador a parte e torna a tomar mas tierra e lava la segun que es dicho ec. E assi continuando esta manera e lavor cada uno delos que lavan saca al dia lo que dios es servido segun a el plaze sea la vētura del señor delos indios e gente que en tal hazienda y exercicio se ocupan.

> these women, or washers, are seated at the water's edge, with their legs submerged in the water up to their knees, or thereabouts, according to the disposition of the land and the water. And they hold in their lands their own bateas, made with two handles or points which they grip; and after the batea is filled with the soil that was brought to them for washing from the mine, they move the batea back and forth, taking water from the current with such skill and facility and sway, that no more water enters the device than what the washer wants. And with the same skill and art, and as soon as it takes water, they empty it on the other side and they cast it aside; and just as much water enters as leaves, so that the soil is always damped and breaking apart. And so the clumps of dirt separate from the water and are dismissed from the batea; and so as the soil is robbed bit by bit, one piece following another into the water, the gold sinks to the bottom or base of the batea, because it is heavy. And once the batea has no dirt, and only clean gold, the washer sets it aside, and takes a second round of dirt, and washes it according to what has been said, etc. And so continuing this way and work, each of those who wash produce in a day what God is served, according to what pleases Him and what is the fortune of the lord of the Indians and the people who are occupied in such estate and exercise.

These coordinated movements combine strength and precision, as mining women balance their hands and feet in moving water, rotating a handheld device in flowing currents without losing precious metal. The passage also reveals a spatially organized form of gender complementarity, as women (in water) and men (on land) coordinate the extraction and cleaning of metals to determine their next steps as a group. Oviedo notes, in meticulous detail, the small-scale movements and motions of skilled miners, the tools they use in their trade, and the collaborative efforts of women and men as they labor in different ecological spaces.[42]

But Oviedo bookends the passage with two curious expressions that seem to undercut the material he presents. First, although he insists that most of the mineral washers are women ("mujeres indias o negras"), Oviedo defaults to a variety of masculine pronouns ("lavadores," "el lavador," "los que lavan") to describe the role. Doing so throws his opening line into confusion: we begin with women ("estas mujeres") and quickly revert to type with universal pronouns. The modern edition of his work regenders the adverb: "Estas mujeres o lavadores estan assentados orilla del agua." Oviedo's struggle to reconcile the default masculine pronouns of mining speech with the practices that he observes in La Española are writ large in his grammatically gendered nouns, pronouns, and adverbs. Second, although Oviedo explains that women perform these tasks because they require more knowledge ("sçiente") and less labor ("trabajo") than do other forms of mine work, his prose enacts the physical feats, such as balance, strength, and coordination, that are required to sort and wash metals throughout the day; in industries like mining and refining, knowledge is part and parcel of embodied labor.[43]

At first glance, Colón's report of "gathering gold" ("coger oro") does not seem to contain any information on Taíno metalworking technologies, traditions, or the kinds of customs—social, spiritual, cultural—that circumscribe human-metallic relationships in the technical arts. But when we situate the expression coined in La Española alongside other historical sources, a fuller vision of Taíno metallic cultures emerges. By correlating fragments of linguistic data with historical reports on mining in pre-Columbian and early colonial communities of the extended Caribbean, we see how Indigenous and Afro-Indigenous ideas, bodies, and skilled technical practices were embedded in various keywords of the colonial Spanish gold industry. In this way, colonial lexicons and their spatiotemporal specificities reveal traces of subaltern miners whose contributions are not often acknowledged in early American mining and metallurgy.

42. Oviedo, *Historia general delas Indias,* lxv(v), lxvi; Oviedo, "Natural y general hystoria de las Indias," MSS, 16. According to CORDE, only one writer in the recorded history of the Spanish language has used the term *escopetar:* Oviedo, first in 1526 and again as he revised the text in the following decades. See CORDE, s.v. "escopetar."

43. Oviedo, *Historia general delas Indias,* lxv(v); Oviedo, "Natural y general hystoria de las Indias," MSS, 18; Oviedo, *Historia general y natural de las Indias,* ed. Juan Pérez de Tudela Bueso (Madrid, 1959), 161.

2 : VISUAL LANGUAGES OF SPACE AND PLACE

Scholars once spoke of the nearly immediate and almost-complete collapse of Taíno communities in La Española. New archaeological research focusing on gender, class, and household unit analysis, however, shows that we have overlooked greater histories of continuity, adaptation, and accommodation. Even in goldfields and refineries, where colonial Iberian customs were perhaps most deeply imprinted upon the island's landscape, archaeological and historical records provide testimony of Taíno influences throughout the first half of the sixteenth century. In these formative decades, as Spanish officials planned new mining towns, gold refineries, and labor systems, their designs incorporated Amerindian ideas about space, place, and time. (By the late 1520s, "Amerindian" was synonymous with "Afro-Indigenous" in mining communities of La Española, as West African miners from Mina, a center of gold-mining expertise, outnumbered Indigenous miners and refiners.) A reading of the visual and spatial languages of archival reports, maps, and plans, juxtaposed with historical analysis of labor and gender systems, provides new insight into the Taíno and Afro-Taíno cosmologies and technologies that helped to shape the gold industry in the early colonial Caribbean. The published versions of these works often erased Afro-Taíno traces, suggesting how early modern print culture manufactured a specific image of colonial mining—one that wiped away the messiness of imperial debates about metalworking cultures and Afro-Indigenous contributions to the colonial gold industry.[1]

People and Place: Villas, Reducciones, and Mineros

A painted manuscript map of La Española, made around 1508 by Spanish mariner *(piloto)* Andrés Morales or copied from his work, shows how the min-

1. "Capítulos que llevó Gonzálo Fernández de Oviedo a Su Majestad," Sept. 28, 1535, AGI, Santo Domingo, 77, ramo 4, no. 88, cited in Esteban Mira Caballos, *El indio antillano: Repartimiento, encomienda, y esclavitud (1492–1542)* (Seville, 1997), 154; Kathleen Deagan, "Reconsidering Taíno Social Dynamics after Spanish Conquest: Gender and Class in Culture Contact Studies," *American Antiquity*, LXIX (2004), 597–626, esp. 602; Pauline Kulstad-González, "Striking It Rich in the Americas' First Boom Town: Economic Activity at Concepción de La Vega (Hispaniola), 1495–1564," in Pedro Paulo A. Funari and María Ximena Senatore, eds., *Archaeology of Culture Contact and Colonialism in Spanish and Portuguese America* (New York, 2015), 313–337, esp. 314–315.

ing, refining, and shipping of gold informed the spatial organization of life on La Española within the first decades of colonial rule. The map was inserted between the cover and first page of Italian humanist Pietro Martire d'Anghiera's *De orbe novo* (1516), prefaced with a letter to the "candide lector" by Spanish grammarian Elio Antonio de Nebrija, who famously declared in 1492 "que siempre la lengua fue compañera del imperio" (that language was always the companion of empire).[2]

The map is a stunning portrait of imperial aspirations, geographic facts, and Indigenous histories. It plots fifteen Spanish settlements, illustrated with castles and cathedrals that are more reminiscent of *El Cid* than any buildings in La Española at the time. Many of them float in gravity-defying ways: some stand upright, facing the viewer, whereas others rest on their sides, towers pointing west, and one lies upside down. Five cathedrals form a vertical axis that runs from Puerto de Plata ("Portys Argentu") in the north to Santo Domingo in the south, connected by the mining towns of La Vega and Buenaventura, home to the island's two gold refineries. The fort of Bonao is strategically placed between them. The largest feature of the built environment is the mass of structures in San Juan de la Maguana, the ancestral home of the *cacique* Caonabo, whose name means "Possessor of Gold" (composed of the roots *ka-*, a prefix that attributes the rest of the sentence to the subject, *wõ*, "gold," *n*, an empty morph, perhaps designed to facilitate pronunciation, and *-abo*, "in possession of"). Caonabo's lands are nestled among verdant spaces that coil into mountains as if they were made of ribbon, interlaced with windy blue rivers rich in alluvial gold. The lush green hues of the interior regions throw into sharp relief the yellow-hued port cities that dot the island's edges. These sand-dusted spots mark points of connection in an Atlantic world where gold from the Americas, some fifteen years after Colón's landing, took pride of place among commercial and economic possibilities.[3]

2. Pietro Martire d'Anghiera, *De orbe novo* (Alcalá, 1516) (this copy, and the manuscript map enclosed within it, are now housed at the Biblioteca Universitaria di Bologna, Collezioni speciali, Raro D 26); Antonio de Nebrija, *Gramática de la lengua castellana* (1492), ed. Antonio Quilis (Madrid, 1980), 1. Toward the end of the year, the crown raised Morales's salary to 25,000 *maravedíes* in recognition of his service; see "Nombramiento de Andrés Morales," Madrid, Oct. 25, 1516, AGI, Indiferente, 419, legajo 6, fols. 547v–548. On translation and empire, see Miguel Ángel Esparza Torres, *Las ideas lingüísticas de Antonio de Nebrija* (Münster, 1995), esp. 78–96, 123–124.

3. Julian Granberry and Gary S. Vescelius, *Languages of the Pre-Columbian Antilles* (Tuscaloosa, Ala., 2004), 94; Kulstad-González, "Striking It Rich in the Americas' First Boom Town," in Funari and Senatore, eds., *Archaeology of Culture Contact and Colonialism*, 317. Rafael García Bidó translates Caonabo as "hombre de oro"; see his *Voces de bohío: Vocabulario de la cultura taína*, 2d ed. (Santo Domingo, 2014), 51.

FIGURE 2. Andrés Morales, Map of La Española (1508). Courtesy of the Biblioteca Universitaria di Bologna, Collezioni Speciali, Raro D 26 (3)

The map's combination of cartographic forms—real places (mountains, bodies of water, towns), spatial concepts (distance between points, architectural orientation), and spatial imaginations (castles in a colony where there were none)—is what Edward W. Soja would later theorize as the tripartite nature of spatiality. For Soja, "Firstspace" is a "perspective and epistemology, fixed mainly on the concrete materiality of spatial forms, on things that can be empirically mapped," whereas "Secondspace" represents "ideas about space, in thoughtful re-presentations of human spatiality in mental or cognitive forms." "Thirdspace," perhaps Soja's most important contribution to modern spatial thinking, covers "journeys to 'real-and-imagined' (or perhaps 'realand-imagined'?) places." Although Soja was originally arguing for a "critical cultural studies" approach to space, one less bounded by the divisions of traditional academic disciplines like architecture, geography, and urban planning, his theories explain the interlocking spatialities of Morales's map. The colonial vision projected on the map—informed equally by mountain topographies and a jagged, detailed coastline (Firstspace), Spanish redistricting of Indigenous people and places (Secondspace), and geographic imaginaries (Thirdspace)—reveal the visual interplay of these three ways of conceiving and conveying space on a painted, two-dimensional map. Here, I distinguish "space" from "place," following geographer Yi-Fu Tuan's argument that "what begins as undifferentiated space becomes place as we get to know it better and endow it with value." As we will see with labor groups in mining communities, physical and symbolic concepts of space and place were understood in relational terms.[4]

The fifteen sites plotted on the map were termed *villas* by Governor Nicolás Ovando, who designed each settlement with a specific purpose in mind, such as access to labor, natural resources, and transit routes. La Vega, Buenaventura, and San Juan de la Maguana were selected for their proximity to gold deposits, whereas Vera Paz and Salvaleón de Higüey were built atop ancestral Taíno settlements. The remaining villas—Puerto Real and Lares de Guahaba in the northwest, Salvatierra de la Sabana and Yáquimo in the southwest, Puerto

4. Edward W. Soja, *Thirdspace: Journeys to Los Angeles and Other Real-and-Imagined Places* (Cambridge, Mass., 1996), 10–12; Yi-Fu Tuan, *Space and Place: The Perspective of Experience* (Minneapolis, 1977), 6. For Tuan, "Place is security, space is freedom: we are attached to the one and long for the other" (3). The idea of "freedom" is difficult to locate on colonial maps, but the larger distinctions have been instrumental to my own thinking about space and place. See also Setha M. Low and Denise Lawrence-Zúñiga, eds., *The Anthropology of Space and Place: Locating Culture* (Malden, Mass., 2003); Daniel Nemser, *Infrastructures of Race: Concentration and Biopolitics in Colonial Mexico* (Austin, Tex., 2017).

de Plata on the north coast, Santa Cruz in the east, Santo Domingo and Azua in the south—were port cities necessary to ship and receive goods. Only Santiago was not located on the coast, although, as a site equidistant between La Vega and Puerto de Plata, it helped to form a chain of Spanish settlements stretching north-south across the island.[5]

The cartographic vision depicted in Morales's map reveals more than just imperial spatial power; the map also suggests how environmental realities and Indigenous histories shaped early Spanish settlements. Colonial agents surveyed gold deposits and studied the chiefdoms with the largest concentrations of people, such as the region ruled by Caonabo; they understood that these were the signs of leaders who could organize resources and command large groups of laborers. Local officials developed policies about free, enslaved, and coerced labor based on their readings of Taíno social structures, which influenced Spanish, African, and Indigenous labor dynamics and household compositions before, during, and after the first gold boom. To comprehend these changes, we need to know what Taíno life looked like before 1492.[6]

In the pre-Columbian era, Taínos sorted themselves into three main social classes. At the very top were caciques as well as *cacicas* (female chiefs). Next were an elite group of medical healers *(behiques)* and elders renowned for their wisdom; this class was called *nitaínos* (literally, "His goodness," formed by the possessive *ni* and the noun *taino,* or "good"). Colón arrived without any knowledge of the language, yet within two and half months he understood the difference between caciques and nitaínos, indicating that such social statuses were well defined. Members of the third group were *naborías* (commoners), whose name "literally translates as 'the remainder' or 'what is left'" (following the terms *-bori* [work], *-borí* [native people, home people], and *-boriya* [worker]). As these names suggest, Taíno hierarchies were relational and mutually constitutive. One group could not exist without the others, and all were necessary for community life.[7]

5. Karen F. Anderson-Córdova, *Surviving Spanish Conquest: Indian Fight, Flight, and Cultural Transformation in Hispaniola and Puerto Rico* (Tuscaloosa, Ala., 2017), 36–37; Luis Arranz Márquez, *Repartimientos y encomiendas en la Isla española: El repartimiento de Alburquerque de 1514* (Santo Domingo, 1991), 98.

6. Kulstad-González, "Striking It Rich in the Americas' First Boom Town," in Funari and Senatore, eds., *Archaeology of Culture Contact and Colonialism,* 314–319.

7. Granberry and Vescelius, *Languages of the Pre-Columbian Antilles,* 104, 111; Cristóbal Colón, *Los cuatro viajes: Testamento,* ed. Consuelo Varela (1986; rpt. Madrid, 2011), 143 (Dec. 23, 1492); José R. Oliver, "Gold Symbolism among Caribbean Chiefdoms: Of Feathers, *Çibas,* and *Guanín* Power among Taíno Elites," in Colin McEwan, ed., *Precolumbian Gold: Technology, Style, and Iconography* (London, 2000), 207 ("the remainder"). Some scholars

Spaniards grasped distinctions within Taíno society, although men like Colón and Ovando took different approaches in commandeering Native peoples' land, labor, and knowledge. Colón sought strategic partnerships with elites to facilitate his collection of tribute goods, following the extractive model of the Portuguese *factoría* system in West Africa. Ovando reconfigured the island's sociocultural and physical landscape by reducing diverse chiefdoms into villas and estates controlled by Spanish landholders. He forced compliance by burning leaders alive or hanging them to death. Colón approved of intermarriage as a strategy to create alliances; Ovando worked to ensure that Taína women could not receive or transmit inheritances through marriage.[8]

Ovando and Colón's tactics in managing people and land reflect changes in Spanish law regarding Indigenous people's status as well as ongoing debates about coerced and enslaved laborers of Indigenous and African descent. In the summer of 1502, fray Ovando arrived in La Española with some 2,500 men—eight times as many Spaniards as were then living on the island. The next year, he began a series of military campaigns against Native people in the southern half of the island, from the western *cacicazgos* (chiefdoms) of Jaraguá to the eastern realms of Higüey. As he claimed, confiscated, and conquered people and territories, he gave them to soldiers and officials as rewards, extending what had been a localized, informal system of *repartimiento* (distribution of laborers) to the entire island. These rewards went disproportionately to Spaniards who were already established in the colony. In turn, they leased lands and laborers to new Spanish arrivals, many of whom worked Indigenous miners to death. With rampant disease, chronic food shortages, massive losses of life,

argue that there were two groups—elites and non-elites—rather than three; all agree that it is difficult to reconstruct Taíno social orders with colonial sources. See Deagan, "Reconsidering Taíno Social Dynamics after Spanish Conquest," *American Antiquity,* LXIX (2004), 600; Lynne Guitar, "No More Negotiation: Slavery and the Destabilization of Colonial Hispaniola's Encomienda System," *Revista interamericana,* XXIX (1999), http://cai.sg.inter.edu/revista-ciscla/volume29/guitar.pdf. Guitar cites Esteban Mira Caballos, "El sistema laboral indígena en las Antillas (1492–1542)," in Julián B. Ruiz Rivera and Horst Pietschmann, eds., *Encomiendas, Indios, y Españoles* (Münster, 1996), 20–27; and Roberto Cassá, *Historia social y económica de la República dominicana* (Santo Domingo, 1993), I, 53. For an analysis of different interpretative frameworks, see Anderson-Córdova, *Surviving Spanish Conquest,* 20–23. I thank Nico Wey Gómez for helping me to see Colón as a careful observer of language.

8. Kathleen Deagan and José María Cruxent, *Columbus's Outpost among the Taínos: Spain and America at La Isabela, 1493–1498* (New Haven, Conn., 2002); Arranz Márquez, *Repartimientos y encomiendas,* 26–27, 110; Frank Moya Pons, *Después de Colón: Trabajo, sociedad, y política en la economía del oror* (Alianza, 1987), 32–38; Guitar, "No More Negotiation," *Revista interamericana,* XXIX (1999).

and deep debts held by newly arrived colonists, by 1503, there were serious doubts about the sustainability of the imperial enterprise.[9]

The Catholic monarchs responded by authorizing colonists to appropriate Indigenous peoples' knowledge, labor, and resources. New legal conditions recognized Amerindians as full human beings who were subjects equal to property holders *(vecinos)* and residents *(moradores)* and, thus, obliged to serve the common good. In December 1503, "Doña Ysabel por la grā[cia] đ dios" (Queen Isabel by the grace of God) declared that all "yndios vezinos e moradores đ las yslas española fuese libres e no sujetos a servidumbre" (Indians, property holders, and residents of the islands of Las Española be free and not subject to servitude), citing the dangerous "liberty" *(libertad)* with which Indigenous wage laborers fled to the countryside, remaining outside the realm of Christian influence. To prevent such flight, and so that the colony would be "cultivated and peopled" ("se labre e pueble"), Isabella I ordered Spaniards to pay wages to workers, reward caciques with servants, and observe religious feast days. By recognizing the rights of Indigenous miners as Spanish subjects, the law bound Taínos to systems of imperial governance, political economy, and social organization.[10]

At the same time that imperial councillors redefined the legal status of Indigenous miners, they debated whether and how to enslave African miners. As these deliberations unfolded across Caribbean settlements and Spanish cities, including Seville, Madrid, Medina del Campo, Burgos, Monzón, and Barcelona, they united different Iberian linguistic communities and cultural traditions into a shared and often uneasy imperial position. In creating policies that were variously enforced and ignored by colonial agents, Spanish officials determined who would mine and where they would live.

Before La Española sent its first shipment of gold to Seville, and before Colón finished his final voyage, imperial officials evaluated the possibility of replacing Indigenous miners with enslaved Africans—but only those who knew Spanish and Catholic doctrine *(ladinos)*. In 1501, the crown instructed fray Ovando, still in Spain at the time, to give passage to Iberian-born Africans. Ovando complained that they understood Iberian norms too well and easily created alliances with Amerindians in lands beyond Spanish rule. Although imperial officials and local administrators aimed to generate colonial wealth, they held different beliefs about the role of coerced labor in reaching their goal. In 1503, the crown reversed its policy and prohibited *negros ladi-*

9. Moya Pons, *Después de Colón,* 15–17, 33–34.

10. "Orden de apremio a los indios de La Española," Medina del Campo, Dec. 20, 1503, AGI, Indiferente, 418, legajo 1, fols. 121v–122, esp. 121v.

nos from entering the territory, but the instructions were vague enough to be flexibly interpreted. The next year, Fernando II ordered officials from the Casa de la Contratación to relieve those who "andan en las minas" (go about the mines) by sending all of the people, animals, and goods that Ovando had requested: ten pairs of bellows (two forged by blacksmiths), two dozen pickaxes ("picayos") like those from Extremadura, an equal number of flat-bottomed vessels to separate gold and silver ("redomas"), a good measure of reagents ("aguafuerte"), one expert in underground tunnels ("un tonelero"), twenty enslaved Africans "para andar en nras obras" (to serve in our works), and "bestias de carga para llevar los bastimos delos q̄ andan en las mynas por q̄ los q̄ agora enllas se gastan los llevā onbres A cuestas y no pueden llevar tanto q̄baste pa mantenymo de todos" (beasts of burden to carry the supplies of those who serve in the mines, because at present they are carried by men with great difficulty, and they wear out quickly and cannot carry enough to maintain everyone).[11]

In 1505, fray Ovando requested the same supplies, and officials once more promised that the fleets were on their way, stocked with "fuelles e Aguas e otros e otras co qe aveys enbiado đ pedir" (bellows and reagents and these and other things that you have written to request). At the same time, following the death of Isabella I, the crown ruled that negros ladinos could enter the colony, overturning the policy of 1503. That year, seventeen enslaved African miners disembarked in La Española. By 1506, the crown changed its policy on enslaved miners again, this time prohibiting "criados entre moros" (servants among the Moors) from setting foot on the island. A mere three years later, in 1509, when Diego Colón replaced fray Ovando as governor, the crown once again reversed course. This time, the policy deemed that La Española would accept no "moros, ni herejes, ni judíos, ni reconciliados, ni personas nuevamente convertidas a nuestra santa fe, salvo si fueren esclavos negros que hayan nacido en poder de cristianos nuestros" (moors, nor heretics, nor Jews, nor reconciled people, nor they who have recently converted to our holy faith, unless they be black slaves who were born into the rule of our Christians).[12]

11. Carlos Larrazábal Blanco, *Los negros y la esclavitud en Santo Domingo,* 2d ed. (Santo Domingo, 1998), 17–18; "Orden de compra de fuelles," Medina del Campo, May 10, 1504, AGI, Indiferente, 418, legajo 1, fols. 130v–131.

12. "Respuesta a carta del Comendador Mayor de Alcántara," Toro, Mar. 5, 1505, AGI, Indiferente, 418, legajo 1, fols. 148v–149; Anderson-Córdova, *Surviving Spanish Conquest,* 36–37; Larrazábal Blanco, *Los negros y la esclavitud en Santo Domingo,* 18–19. Elite mining families complained that the lack of refining tools undercut gold production. Doña María Niño de Ribera, mother of Pedro Niño de Conchillos y Ribera, *fundidor y marcador* of Tierra Firme and wife of Aragonese politician Lope de Conchillos, petitioned about the

Amid the constant push and pull of competing imperial agendas in the 1510s, the first enslaved African miners arrived in La Española, ostensibly in response to fray Ovando's request for laborers, pack animals, and mining tools. This is one of many moments in which Spanish administrators interpreted colonial petitions in ways that favored the crown's interests. By the 1520s, African gold miners outnumbered those of Indigenous descent. A sustained look at the records chronicling these demographic, labor, and cultural changes reveals the Spanish empire's unsteady, chaotic approach to managing gold mining in the Caribbean.[13]

With Isabella's cédula of 1503, fray Ovando's ad hoc distribution of laborers (repartimiento) became the official institution of the *encomienda*. In Spain, the encomienda system distributed land, but the colonial repartimiento distributed labor—even to migratory colonists, although they received fewer laborers than landholders did. As labor, rather than just land, became a crucial source of New World wealth, imperial officials resolved to restrict the spaces of colonial life and metallic production. To centralize tribute collection and facilitate conversion efforts, religious leaders and local officials created settlements that "reduced" people from diverse Native communities into a single place. Although such displays of spatial power seem to suggest Spanish dominance over people and land, new work in historical geography finds that, in much of colonial Latin America, *reducciones* were sites of "entangled spatiality of power struggles" where nuanced, competing, local interests defied binary divisions like "Indigenous" or "European." In 1517, the first reducciones were officially declared in La Española. Before that, concentrations of relocated Indigenous peoples were called *mineros* (miners / mineral sources), blurring the line between human beings, labor, and land as key sources of colonial wealth.[14]

Just as reducciones (or mineros) and repartimientos reconfigured the spa-

---

lack of basic tools like crucibles *(crisoles)*, weights *(marcas)*, and stamps *(cuños)*. See "Crisoles para la fundición de Panamá," Medina del Campo, Jan. 31, 1532, AGI, Panama, 234, legajo 5, fols. 11v–12. Las Casas records a meeting of doña María and royal councillor don García de Padilla in *Obras completas*, ed. Paulino Castañeda Delgado, III–V, *Historia de las Indias* (Madrid, 1994), V, 2197.

13. Anderson-Córdova, *Surviving Spanish Conquest*, 74–87.

14. Moya Pons, *Después de Colón*, 34–35, 38, 44; Jail Sued Badillo, *El dorado borincano: La economía de la Conquista, 1510–1550* (San Juan, 2001), 45; Arranz Márquez, *Repartimientos y encomiendas*, 76; Heidi V. Scott, "A Mirage of Colonial Consensus: Resettlement Schemes in Early Spanish Peru," *Environment and Planning D: Society and Space*, XXII (2004), 885–899, esp. 895; Nemser, *Infrastructures of Race;* Esteban Mira Caballos, "La primera utopía americana: Las reducciones de Indios de los Jerónimos en La Española (1517–1519)," *Jahrbuch für Geschichte Lateinamerikas*, XXXIX (2002), 9–35, esp. 9.

tial dynamics of Native communities, so did colonial policies alter the temporal cycles of life in La Española. The repartimiento of 1514 specified that tribute laborers mine for part of the year *(la demora)* and spend the rest of their time farming in their villages. These provisions built from the informal method that Ovando had long practiced on the island. At first, Ovando's system divided the year equally, as Taíno men spent six months in the goldfields and six months in their villages; by 1510, as colonists demanded greater amounts of Indian labor, time in the villages was reduced to four months. Under this revised time frame, wealthy, well-connected *encomenderos* enjoyed even greater benefits of Indigenous labor, whereas colonists with small stakes stopped mining for gold. Fray Ovando's repartitions of life and land in 1502, repeated in 1506 in what historian Frank Moya Pons called a "re-repartimiento," were the root of the general repartimiento of 1514. By then, Spanish officials had secured permission to import greater numbers of enslaved Africans directly to mining districts and to relocate Indigenous people from neighboring Caribbean islands to the goldfields.[15]

In remapping Indigenous spaces, arranging agricultural seasons around gold mining, and introducing new populations of miners from different parts of the island as well as other regions, Ovando created alliances where none had existed. At first, these alliances facilitated gold production, as output increased during fray Ovando's governorship; over time, they became sites where miners organized to disrupt gold production. For example, the cacique who inspired his community to rise up against Christian slaveholders in 1519, known in Spanish archives as don Enrique Yndio and in colonial chronicles as Enriquillo, was relocated from the southwestern district of Jaraguá (present-day Haiti) to the villa of San Juan de la Maguana (present-day province of San Juan, Dominican Republic). Enrique was one of the most powerful leaders on the island, for he was the nephew of cacica Anacaona, whose name is composed of the roots "flower" and "gold"; his relocation came about following Ovando's brutal retaliation for an uprising, for which Ovando hanged Anacaona to death.[16]

15. Guitar, "No More Negotiation," *Revista interamericana,* XXIX (1999); Irving Rouse, *The Tainos: Rise and Decline of the People Who Greeted Columbus* (New Haven, Conn., 1992), 154; Deagan, "Reconsidering Taíno Social Dynamics," *American Antiquity,* LXIX (2004), 601–602; Moya Pons, *Después de Colón,* 47. Puerto Rico saw similar concentrations of power; see Sued Badillo, *El Dorado borincano,* 45.

16. Nicholas J. Saunders, "'Shimmering Worlds': Brilliance, Power, and Gold in Pre-Columbian Panama," in Richard G. Cooke et al., eds., *To Capture the Sun: Gold of Ancient Panama* (Tulsa, Okla., 2011), 80 (Saunders argues that Anacaona's name reflects "the spiritual and creative power of light" that Indigenous people ascribed to resplendent golden

Upon their relocation, Enrique and 35 other caciques became part of a new community of 1,529 Taínos held in encomienda by 27 Spaniards. An additional 469 commoners *(naborias)* were distributed to seventeen colonists in the villa. With this regrouped population, Enriquillo led a revolt that lasted until the 1530s, establishing a model of prolonged rebellion that inspired women and men from coerced and enslaved communities across the island. These practices of regrouping, following forced relocations and distributions of labor in new spaces, represent what historian Lynn Guitar identifies as an "extension of the traditional Taíno ways," following what seem to be established survival strategies and population management techniques that allowed Taíno communities to respond to ecological disruptions or political chaos.[17]

In congregating Indigenous and African people from different traditions and social ranks, Spanish colonial redistricting generated sites of resistance, giving place to an Afro-Indigenous culture that came to define the island—and, in many ways, the whole of the Caribbean. Afro-Taíno *cimarrones* (communities of enslaved people who had escaped from European rule) developed survival strategies that were animated by and "derived from their traditional ancestral knowledge"—what artist, educator, and healer Margaret Mitchell Armand identifies as a shared "spiritual worldview, ancestral reverence, respect for nature and environment, reverence for their traditional ways, a spirit of tolerance." Running away, burning crops, participating in uprisings, concealing medical knowledge, taking one's own life, consuming abortifacients, intermarrying, introducing matrilineal Taíno lifeways into colonial homes, sharing technologies, and complying with orders to labor in plantations and goldfields—these were some of the many strategies that Indigenous, African, and Afro-Indigenous people employed in their responses to colonial rule in the Caribbean. Each response was rooted in a particular spatial reality.[18]

---

objects whose energies connected this plane of existence with ancestral realms); Bidó, *Voces de bohío,* 12–13; Granberry and Vescelius, *Languages of the Pre-Columbian Antilles,* 116–117.

17. Rouse, *Tainos,* 154–155; Joaquín F. Pacheco, Francisco Cárdenas, and Luis Torres de Mendoza, eds., *Colección de documentos inéditos relativos al descubrimiento, conquista y colonización de las posesiones españolas en América y Oceanía, sacados, en su mayor parte, del Real Archivo de Indias,* I (Madrid, 1864), 196–207, hereafter cited as *DII,* cited in Guitar, "No More Negotiation," *Revista interamericana,* XXIX (1999); letter to Carlos V, June 6, 1534, AGI, Santo Domingo, 77, cited ibid. For descriptions of Enriquillo's revolt, see [Gonzalo Fernández de Oviedo y Valdés], *Historia general y natural delas Indias* (Seville, 1535), lv–lvi; Las Casas, *Obras completas,* ed. Delgado, V, 2302–2316. Las Casas disagrees with Oviedo in book 3 (chaps. 142–147) and with Oviedo and Gómara (chap. 160).

18. Candice L. Goucher, "African Metallurgy in the Atlantic World," in Akinwumi Ogun-

Before the arrival of Spaniards and Africans in La Española, Taínas were largely responsible for the management of land, shaping farming techniques, foodways, and perhaps even controlling "access to military and political power through matrilineage." Under the colonial system, elite Taínas continued to use matrilineage to protect their children in an ever-shifting world. After 1492, their strategies were less about spatial control of land than about creating biopolitical alliances across ethnic and linguistic groups. In the 1520s, Taínas, including women whose families had remained in their ancestral homes and those who were forcibly relocated, married Spaniards, Africans, Taínos, and non-Taínos willingly and unwillingly. They became part of a female population that included Africans, Arawaks, Kalinagos, Lucayas, Mayas, and a range of Indigenous communities from the extended Caribbean (present-day Colombia, Venezuela, the Guayanas, and Brazil). Intermarriage with Spanish colonists was a strategy that elite Taínas employed to protect their children from encomienda service; the children of these unions, unlike those born to enslaved African women, were exempt from tribute labor. In 1514, 40 percent of Spanish men acknowledged marriages to Taínas, mostly cacias from the nitaíno class. In mining towns, the rate was even higher: half of the vecinos of La Vega were married to Taína elites.[19]

The terms that classify miners and mining communities provide insights into the workings of the Spanish empire on and underneath the ground. As colonial officials created new labor systems in La Española, they retained the names of some groups, such as *naborías,* a term they exported to Mexico to classify miners in Zacatecas, but they redefined the members according to

---

diran and Toyin Falola, eds., *Archaeology of Atlantic Africa and the African Diaspora* (Bloomington, Ind., 2007), 277–291; Margaret Mitchell Armand, "Taíno Resistance (1492–1519)," in Junius P. Rodríguez, ed., *Encyclopedia of Slave Resistance and Rebellion* (Westport, Conn., 2007), 498–503, esp. 500–501. For an excellent analysis of Taíno responses, see Anderson-Córdova, *Surviving Spanish Conquest,* 30–33, 58–72. Oviedo describes Indigenous women's consumption of "una yerva con que muevē por estar desocupadas para su libidne" in his *De la natural hystoria de las Indias* (Toledo, 1526), xiii. Las Casas explains these choices in terms of the repartimiento; see *Obras completas,* ed. Delgado, IV, 1347.

19. Deagan and Cruxent, *Columbus's Outpost among the Taínos,* 32; Anderson-Córdova, *Surviving Spanish Conquest,* 134–149; "Licencia para comprar indios a los portugueses," Barcelona, Jan. 9, 1520, AGI, Indiferente, 420, legajo 8, fols. 177–178, cited in Guitar, "No More Negotiation," *Revista interamericana,* XXIX (1999); Arranz Márquez, *Repartimientos y encomiendas,* 72; Rouse, *Tainos,* 158; Kulstad-González, "Striking It Rich in the Americas' First Boom Town," in Funari and Senatore, eds., *Archaeology of Culture Contact and Colonialism,* 327. The Taínas forced to relocate came from other parts of the island, as well as neighboring islands like Cuba, Jamaica, and Puerto Rico.

utility for metallic production. Pre-Columbian nitaínos included elders who transmitted ancestral knowledge to the next generation, but the only elites who mattered in colonial gold districts were those who could organize large workforces. Colonial officials thus removed healers and elders from the nitaíno category, leaving only caciques. Next, they divided the commoner class into two categories, at once expanding the range of non-elites and more carefully defining their obligations: forced laborers (*indios repartidos,* or *encomendados*), who corresponded to the geographic limits of a traditional *cacicazago* (chiefdom) and who were thus distributed by caciques in mining districts, and servants (naborías), who worked in private households and on farms. Colonial-era naborías were drawn from African, Taíno, and various Indigenous communities, especially Kalinago and Lucayo populations. Legally, naborías of Kalinago and Lucayo ancestry could not be sold as slaves, but many were anyway.[20]

The Spaces of Gold Refining

As Spanish officials layered labor frameworks atop existing Taíno social classes and colonists incorporated elements of Native gender and family structures into their own households, so, too, did they follow Indigenous spatialities in plotting gold districts—often without noting the influence. In 1515, Diego Velázquez de Cuéllar, governor of Cuba, built a refinery in the southeastern town of Santiago, which he named as the island's capital. Following Velázquez's model, conquistador Pánfilo de Narváez requested permission to build a refinery in the town of Trinidad, the island's geographic center. The crown agreed, as long as the new refinery was identical to the facility in Santiago. At first glance, it seems that the two-part distribution of smelting houses in Cuba imitated the system in La Española, which divided gold production between La Vega and Buenaventura. But there was a deeper influence at work. According to archaeologist Irving Rouse, the spatial relationship of Santiago to La Española "reflects the Spanish view that Cuba was peripheral to Hispaniola, as it had been during Taino time." During the pre-Columbian period, Taíno leaders from more densely populated Haití / Quisqueya expanded their chiefdoms by establishing commercial ties with people in what is now the city of Santiago de Cuba. In other words, after twenty-three years of Spanish pres-

20. P. J. Bakewell, *Silver Mining and Society in Colonial Mexico: Zacatecas, 1546–1700* (Cambridge, 1971), 124; Kulstad-González, "Striking It Rich in the Americas' First Boom Town," in Funari and Senatore, eds., *Archaeology of Culture Contact and Colonialism,* 314–315; Guitar, "No More Negotiation," *Revista interamericana,* XXIX (1999).

ence, the relationship between La Española and Cuba remained similar to that which had existed under Taíno sovereigns.[21]

By the late 1520s and early 1530s, officials selected sites using other criteria—namely, the ability to defend gold refineries from attacks by Africans, Amerindians, and Europeans. In 1521, after some debate, officials in Panama convinced the crown to relocate the smelting house from Darién to Panama City, following La Española's lead. In 1511, the refinery of Santo Domingo had been moved to Buenaventura for defensive reasons. By comparing the shifting language of spatial thinking in colonial instructions, royal decrees, and mining protocols between these two points—that is, the 1510s and the 1530s—we can better understand the nuanced, often contingent planning of early colonial goldworks in the Caribbean and where African and Amerindian agencies influenced the design of the colonial gold industry.[22]

Throughout the 1510s, Indigenous precedents shaped the design of gold refineries and the plotting of mining towns. In 1511, officials in Puerto Rico were charged with building a refinery to relieve miners of the inconvenience of traveling to La Española. Some of these local designs, reinforced by cédulas, incorporated Indigenous ideas of space and technology. In January 1513, Cuban officials received permission to build "un buhio p[ara] q̄ este la casa de la dha fundçō" (a bohío for the aforesaid refinery) so that newly appointed overseer and mint master *(veedor y marcador mayor)* Hernando de Vega would enjoy "el buē uso y exerçicio del dho offo" (good use and exercise of the aforesaid office).[23]

As the cédula makes clear by juxtaposing *bohío* and *casa de fundición,* the two buildings were not the same. They were made of different materials, in different ways, with different cultural meanings. Taíno-style bohíos (Figure 3) were circular, thatched-roof houses made of rounded sticks that were bound with *bejuco* (a vinelike climbing plant), whereas Spanish refining houses were

21. "Orden a Diego Velázquez," Zaragoza, July 11, 1518, AGI, Indiferente, 419, legajo 7, fol. 136; Rouse, *Tainos,* 156–158; Granberry and Vescelius, *Languages of the Pre-Columbian Antilles,* 35–47; Sued Badillo, *El Dorado borincano,* 17.

22. AGI, Panama: "Respuesta al tesorero Alonso de la Puente," Aranda, Aug. 2, 1514, 233, legajo 1, fols. 185–186; "Ordenanzas para la fundición del oro en Tierra Firme," Barcelona, Sept. 14, 1519, fols. 259–261; "Casa de fundición en Panamá," Burgos, Sept. 6, 1521, fols. 291–291v; "Traslado de la fundición del oro a la ciudad de Panamá," Vitoria, Feb. 20, 1524, fols. 366v–367. AGI, Indiferente: "Merced a Diego Colón," May 24, 1511, 418, legajo 3, fols. 65–65v.

23. AGI, Indiferente: "Orden a Juan Ponce de León," Seville, Feb. 26, 1511, 418, legajo 3, fols. 52–53v; "Orden a Miguel de Pasamonte," Tordesillas, July 25, 1511, 418, legajo 3, fols. 138v–139; "Orden a Diego Velázquez," Valladolid, Jan. 26, 1513, 419, legajo 4, fol. 72.

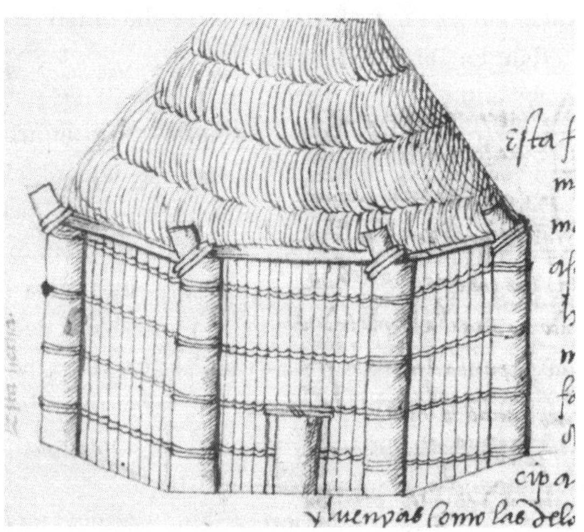

FIGURE 3. Bohío (detail). In Gonzalo Fernández de Oviedo y Valdés, "Natural y general hystoria de las Indias," 1539–1548, HM177, 3v. The Huntington Library, San Marino, Calif.

square. (In some parts of Tierra Firme, colonial writers observed square dwellings; see Figure 4, below.)[24]

These spatial differences go beyond style. Architecture heightens human awareness "by creating a tangible world that articulates experiences," affecting the lives of people who inhabit the built environment. The bohío's circular structure reflected and refracted Taíno cosmologies, communicating symbolic registers of cultural values. The largest Taíno communities in La Española, like those in Cuba and Puerto Rico, were arranged in concentric circles that were organized around a central plaza; round houses were microcosms of this larger order. Archaeological evidence suggests that plazas often included a court for playing *batey,* a ceremonial ballgame that resembles the cosmic ballgame de-

24. When bohío was exported to other regions of the Americas, it meant *casa de paja,* not a round building. See García de Llanos, *Diccionario y maneras de hablar que se usan en las minas y sus labores en los ingenios y beneficios de los metales* (1609), ed. Rose Mary Buchler, Gunnar Mendoza, and J. V. Murra (La Paz, 1983), 97–98; Las Casas, *Obras completas,* ed. Delgado, V, 1867. Pedro Cieza de León repeats the definition ("una casa o bohío de paja") in his *Obras completas* (1553–1584), ed. Carmelo Sáenz de Santamaría, II, *Las guerras civiles peruanas* (Madrid, 1991), 515. In Oviedo's manuscript, the text wraps around the image of the bohío, which appears in the top left-hand corner of the page, suggesting that he sketched it before writing the description. Oviedo's marginal gloss, "Esta hecha," suggests that a version of the image had already been printed. The rectangular house, also marked "Esta hecha," appears in the center of the page between two marginal glosses, including "otra manera de Casa."

FIGURE 4. Caney (detail). In Gonzalo Fernández de Oviedo y Valdés, "Natural y general hystoria de las Indias," 1539–1548, HM177, 4. The Huntington Library, San Marino, Calif.

scribed in Mesoamerican texts like the *Popol Wuj* and documented by colonial observers throughout Central and South America. According to Oviedo, large viewing stations were created on the outskirts of towns so that people could watch the game from afar.[25]

Such designs are rooted in the sacred. The architecture of bohíos and the design of towns organized around batey make visible a cosmology that extends beyond the visible plane of this world. Through the ritual enactment of the ballgame, players and observers connected our world to the lands of ancestral spirits. The spatial organization of community life epitomized a cosmology grounded in what archaeologist Peter E. Siegel calls "a concentric model of the universe," in which the earthly realm (our world) is nestled between the celestial world above (the heavens) and a watery world beneath (the oceans). These three planes are connected by the kinds of subterranean spaces that Catalán friar Ramón Pané recorded in an origin story analyzed in the next chapter.[26]

25. Tuan, *Space and Place,* 102, 108; Oviedo, *Historia general delas Indias,* lviii–lviii(v). Smaller settlements, particularly in the eastern regions controlled by the cacique Higüey, were organized along perpendicular streets, forming a cross in the middle. Las Casas suggested that they were designed "para pelear, porque sin ellas no se pudieran menear, según los montes son espesos y las rocas o peñas y piedras que hay también muy ásperas, aunque llanas" (*Obras completas,* ed. Delgado, IV, 1358).

26. Marcio Veloz Maggiolo, "The Daily Life of the Taíno People," in Fatima Bercht et al., eds., *Taíno: Pre-Columbian Art and Culture from the Caribbean* (New York, 1997), 37; Ricardo E. Alegría, "An Introduction to Taíno Culture and History," ibid., 29. See also Gerardo Reichel-Dolmatoff, *Goldwork and Shamanism: An Iconographic Study of the Gold*

The materials used to build bohíos merited attention from colonial writers because they differed from those used in Spanish constructions. According to Oviedo, bejucos were flexible, strong, and resisted rot; they were ideal building materials, able to join reeds, canes, and wood as effectively as ropes made of animal skin *(cuerdas)* and nails made of iron *(clavos)*. The sap, which Indigenous and Spanish residents in La Española used as a purgative, had excellent medicinal properties. African and Afro-descendant healers in seventeenth-century Colombia used bejucos for a variety of treatments, including dental pains, cleaning mouth sores, and venereal diseases. These remedies suggest how knowledges of organic matter circulated within the connected communities of what historian Pablo F. Gómez calls "Atlantic healing systems." The selection of materials to build family dwellings and gold refineries reflected deep knowledges and skilled techniques that were required to transform trees, plants, and metals for human use; in healing and home design, these materials and ways of knowing represented physical, epistemological, and spiritual sources of community building.[27]

By the end of the century, writers read plants like bejucos as revelations of the Book of Nature that foretold undesirable paths of mixed-race colonies. In a *relación* to Felipe II, *licenciado* Juan de Echagoyán, *oidor* (judge) of the Real Audiencia of Santo Domingo, argued that bejucos epitomized the island's unnerving body politic. When cut and washed, their veins were fashioned into "cabestros muy lindos y blancos" (very pretty and white bridles), but when heated, the same white veins produced "un agua que es admirable betumen para teñir de negro, que es señal de poca justicia" (an admirable tar to dye things black, which is a sign of little justice). The hard, white exterior of the vine belied its liquid, black essence, emblematizing colonial racial anxieties about life in the New World. The colony's "so-called rivers of gold" ("ríos . . . llamados de oro") created a similarly suspect culture of sin and irreverence with their free-flowing wealth. As Echagoyán explained in a paragraph-long sentence, to understand the secular state of things in La Española ("del estado de la gente seglar"), one had to decipher its landscape: "Como no hay minas de oro sino lavaderos, y como el cobre está asimismo en la superficie de la tierra, es la causa de que la dicha ciudad y isla todos los árboles, como ser muy poderosos, no entra en la tierra el cuerpo de ellos, salvo que juntas con la superficie de la

---

Museum of the Banco de la Republica (Bogotá, 2005), 43; Peter E. Siegel, "Ancestor Worship and Cosmology among the Taíno," in Bercht et al., eds., *Taíno,* 106–111, esp. 109.

27. Oviedo, *Historia general delas Indias,* lxviii–lxviii(v); Pablo F. Gómez, *The Experiential Caribbean: Creating Knowledge and Healing in the Early Modern Atlantic* (Chapel Hill, N.C., 2017), 81–84; for recipes involving *cañafístola,* see ibid., 118–123.

tierra tienen muchas raices" (Because there are no gold mines, but only washing stations, and also because copper is likewise on the surface, in the aforesaid city and island, all of the trees, even though they are quite powerful, do not have trunks that enter into the soil, but rather have many roots that rest upon the surface of the earth). For Echagoyán, social disorder was geographically foreordained, for nothing was as it should be: copper and gold were superficial, and native plants blurred the line between white and black.[28]

Other officials, like Hieronymite friars Luis de Figueroa, Illdelfonso de Santo Domingo, and Bernardino de Manzanedo, tied colonial economic problems to Spanish abuses of Indigenous people, and they explained their arguments with metaphors that were likewise inspired by the natural world. In January 1518, the friars requested "negros bozales" to replace Indigenous miners because "al tiempo que los castellanos entraron en esta isla, habia muchos millares é aun cientos de miles de indios en ella, é por nuestros pecados dióse en ellos tanta prisa que al tiempo que llegamos aquí, que há poco mas de un año, los que hallamos eran tan pocos, cuanto es el redrojo que queda en los árboles despues de cogida la fruta" (at the time that the Spaniards entered this island, there were many thousands and even hundreds of thousands of Indians here, and because of our sins, they have been given such haste that when we arrived here, a little more than a year ago, we found that they were so few in number that they are like the tiny shoot that remains on a tree after its fruit is picked). The Hieronymite friars saw the expansion of African slavery as a solution to a problem created by Europeans in La Española, and they naturalized the story of Taíno collapse through symbolic language. Whereas Echagoyán read the landscape as a sign of natural ills, the friars' agricultural language legitimized their call for Africans to people the land. That year, in August, Holy Roman Emperor Carlos V instructed officials at the Casa de la Contratación in Seville to allow Lorenzo de Gornod (Gorrevod), governor of Bresse (France) and baron

28. Juan de Echagoyán, "Relación de la isla Española enviada al Rey D. Felipe II por el licenciado Echagoian, oidor de la Audiencia de Santo Domingo," *DII* (1864), I, 9–35, esp. 14, 27, 28. The undated letter references the earthquake that destroyed La Vega on Nov. 2, 1564, and orders sent by Juan de Ovando of "vuestro Consejo de Inquisicion, y vuestro visitador en el de Indias," who served as president from 1571 to 1575 (10, 30), providing a rough date of 1568, when Echagoyán was in Madrid after being removed from his post. See Águeda María Rodríguez Cruz, *Historia de las universidades Hispanoamericanas* (Bogotá, 1973), 368; and Héctor Martínez Fernández, *Historia de la comunicación social dominicana, 1492–1844* (Santo Domingo, 1999), 95. Compare this with Oviedo's concern that La Española had no underground mining: "Los indios no sabiã cojer sino selo hallavã encima dela trra," *Historia general delas Indias*, xvii. It is possible that miners only knew techniques of placering and panning or that they hid knowledge of sacred metals from colonists.

of Montenay, to import four thousand enslaved Christian African women and men to Española ("xipanos los dhos negros y negras").[29]

As colonial officials and imperial agents changed policies for enslaved and coerced laborers in mines and refineries, they also altered the architectures of such spaces, articulating a spatial dialectics of people, peopling, and the built environment. In 1531, Oviedo, serving as royal refiner in Tierra Firme, reported that Panama's refinery had burned to the ground "por ser de paja" (because it was made of straw). One year later, the crown authorized local officials to dispense with thatched-roof models and build a refinery with stone, brick, and mortar—although they were advised to do so at the lowest possible cost. Unlike bohío-style refineries proposed for Cuba in the 1510s, this refinery was part of a larger complex, including a church and a fortress, all built by Native men. In early 1533, builder Pedro de Villafranca received permission to travel to the Indies with his wife and three eligible daughters, along with four or five married men to administer the complex. Upon arriving, he would receive an encomienda of ten or twelve Indigenous servants. A cédula drafted on March 8 made clear why the refinery's material conditions were of such urgency: African and Afro-Panameño communities had organized to resist Spanish rule, and the city's orientation on the Pacific Ocean left it vulnerable to attacks from rival empires. Gold production on the isthmus was spatially conjoined with Spanish fears of uprisings by enslaved communities, defense from pirates, and the spiritual and institutional extension of Catholic doctrine.[30]

29. Figueroa and Santo Domingo, "Al Emperador Carlos V—Los Padres Gerónimos, de Santo Domingo, à 1518," *DII* (1864), I, 298–304, esp. 300; "Licencia de cuatro mil esclavos a Lorenzo de Gornod," Zaragoza, Aug. 18, 1518, AGI, Indiferente, 419, legajo 7, fols. 735–735v; Larrazábal Blanco, *Los negros y la esclavitud en Santo Domingo,* 28.

30. AGI, Panama, 234, legajo 5: "Construcción de una casa de piedra para fundición," Medina del Campo, Apr. 25, 1532, fol. 24v; "Que Pedro Villafranca tenga la fortaleza de Panamá," Medina del Campo, Dec. 22, 1532, fols. 83v–84v; "Naborías para Diego y Miguel Pérez de Villafranca," Madrid, Feb. 16, 1533, fols. 93v–94; "Edificación de una casa fuerte para fundición," Zaragoza, Mar. 8, 1533, fols. 100v–101; "Fortaleza de Panamá," Zaragoza, Mar. 8, 1533, 101v–102. Villafranca's main qualifications seem to be his ability to people the colony and enlist support from his brother, Francisco Pérez de Lezcano, who became the archpriest of Panama in 1526 and later canon *(deán);* see "Arciprestazgo de Panamá a Francisco Pérez de Lezcano," Seville, May 3, 1526, AGI, Panama, 233, legajo 2, fols. 145–145v. Oviedo argues that a properly thatched roof made of *corbana (Canella alba), guayacán (Guaiacum),* or what Spaniards called *madera prieta* (blackwood) provided better protection from the elements than those in Spain, although the thatchings and posts had to be replaced every two or three years. Oviedo's official reports omitted these positive assessments of Indigenous technologies; see "Natural y general hystoria de las Indias," ca. 1539–1548, MSS, HM177, 4 (libro 6, capítulo 1), Huntington Library, San Marino, Calif.

The rhetorical binding of gold production and defensive designs in Panama represented a distinct change from the spatialities of gold refining in the Antilles. Before the conquests of Mexico and Peru, the crown often asked officials in La Española and Puerto Rico to expand the range of functions that were performed in smelting houses instead of building new facilities. In 1512, when the treasurers of la Cruzada (the Crusade), a Catholic institution composed of a council and a tribunal that reported to the Consejo de Indias, complained of difficulties in collecting taxes from colonists in La Española, Fernando II ordered local officials to find a place in the refinery where members of the Crusade could place "una mesa pa dar las dhas bulas y Recibir los Juros dellas" (a table to dispatch the aforesaid bulls and receive the testimonies thereof). In 1528, Carlos V—anxious at the limited state of Spanish governance and the economic potential in the western Puerto Rican mining town of San Germán, where gold production had stopped after a series of French attacks and uprisings by enslaved Native people—insisted that the refinery be rebuilt with a room for council meetings ("que en ella se pudiese hazer cabildo"). The crown's repurposing of gold refineries into new assemblages of colonial power, from councils to Crusades, reveals how imperial and local officials negotiated diverse spatial dialectics in the Caribbean, incorporating Native architecture, designing buildings around African uprisings, and restructuring administrative operations without introducing material changes.[31]

In contrast, officials in Panama had been prohibited from conducting meetings or discussing judicial matters in the smelting house of Castilla del Oro as early as 1519, although the factor (fiscal administrator) was allowed to live there while performing duties associated with his post. This policy remained in place until 1538, when imperial officials conceded that the judges of the newly created Real Audiencia de Panamá could convert a royal manor *(solar),* located near the port, into its administrative home. The first floor was to be made into a chamber *(aposento)* for smelting; the building's proximity to the port meant that the site, which already hosted judicial quarters and a refinery, could also serve as a fortress staffed with soldiers. In the early sixteenth century, refineries in the Antilles were physical spaces that consolidated the production, collection, and distribution of colonial wealth with the secular and spiritual administration of colonial affairs, whereas in Panama such operations were

31. "Orden a Diego Colón," Burgos, May 22, 1512, AGI, Indiferente, 418, legajo 3, fols. 294v–295; "Informe sobre la casa de fundición y cabildo de la villa de San Germán," Monzón, June 6, 1528, 421, legajo 13, fol. 151v. San Germán was moved by decree to the northwest region of Rincón. See Francisco Lluch Mora, *Fundación de la villa de San Germán en las Lomas de Santa Marta* (Mayagüez, 1971), 1–2.

kept separate. By the late sixteenth century, however, offices of accountants, archives, and gold counters were merged into single spaces throughout the extended Caribbean region.[32]

Managing Miners through Law and Image

In this uneven effort to control colonial subjects and increase gold output, imperial councillors confronted their inability to manage local officials, and local officials confronted miners who did not comply with orders. In 1523, authorities in Cuba and Puerto Rico had to be told to open their refineries; in 1524, Carlos V ordered the governor of Jamaica not to interfere in gold refining. The next year, councillors reminded the governors of La Española, Puerto Rico, Cuba, and Jamaica that it was illegal to refine metals outside of royal smelting houses. At the start of the gold boom, in 1503, smelting houses in La Española were scheduled to be open four times a year; six years later, officials processed gold whenever miners arrived at the refineries. By 1514, reports of illicit metalworking in the Caribbean had reached Spain, and colonial officials were again instructed to fine miners who refined gold ("muelen oro") in their homes or outside of authorized spaces. By expanding the times of gold refining from four times a year to on-demand services, imperial administrators sought to restrict the spaces of metalworking activities. Women and men defied attempts to consolidate gold production in royal refineries; they refined metals on small scales in their homes, knowing that local merchants would accept gold dust as payment for goods and services.[33]

There was no single, stable imperial position regulating the people or places of the gold industry during these early years. In some regions, such as Mexico, Cuba, and La Española, the crown rewarded wealthy elites with contracts to

32. AGI, Panama: "Que no se haga audiencia en la casa de fundición," Barcelona, June 29, 1519, 233, legajo 1, fol. 239; "Que el factor pueda residir en la casa de fundición," Barcelona, June 17, 1519, 233, legajo 1, fol. 233v; "Casa de la Audiencia en Panamá," Valladolid, May 13, 1538, 235, legajo 6, fols. 218v–219; "Edificio para la contaduría de Cartagena," Monzón, [1585?], 237, legajo 12, fol. 41.

33. AGI: "Real Cédula al gobernador de la isla de Santiago," Burgos, May 7, 1524, Contratación, 5787, no. 1, legajo 1, fol. 26v; "Utilización de la casa de fundición de Puerto Rico," Valladolid, June 5, 1523, Indiferente, 420, legajo 9, fols. 133v–134; "Real cédula a los gobernadores, alcaldes, aguaciles y otras justicias de las islas Española, San Juan, Cuba y Santiago," Toledo, Nov. 24, 1525, Indiferente, 420, legajo 10, fols. 170–170v; "Orden para labrar el oro en Santo Domingo," Valladolid, Aug. 14, 1509, 418, legajo 2, fols. 42v–43; "Real Cédula a Don Diego Colón y a los jueces y oficiales de la Isla Española," Valbuena, Oct. 19, 1514, 419, legajo 5, fol. 279. On underreporting of gold, see John J. TePaske, *New World of Gold and Silver,* ed. Kendall W. Brown (Boston, 2010), 46–48, 53.

reprocess *relaves* (gold particles that remained after the first round of washing) and *escobillas* (a mixture of dust and gold found on the floor of the refinery after smelting). In other areas, most notably Guatemala, Panama, and Peru, such licenses were prohibited. There, the crown insisted that the fruits of the mines be applied to care for injured miners: proceeds from relaves and escobillas were used to operate hospitals. In Peru, patients were disproportionately miners hurt while working underground or sick from exposure to toxic reagents like mercury. These regional differences in public policies epitomize the Spanish empire's uneven approach to managing gold production in the New World. Part of this disparity was surely driven by the novelty of attempting to organize a large-scale, transatlantic, extractive industry around dynamic organic material in the early modern era.[34]

Another, equally important part of Spain's difficulties can be traced to non-Spanish actors. As we have seen, the key words of colonial labor structures indicate how officials repurposed Indigenous social hierarchies into their own systems of distribution. Visual and spatial analysis of towns selected for refineries (such as Santiago de Cuba, Trinidad, La Vega, Buenaventura, San Germán, Darién, and Panama) and the designs of refineries positioned there (whether Taíno-inspired bohíos or military defenses against Afro-Panameños) reveals Indigenous and African agencies' influence upon the path of the gold industry. Although histories of American gold have often emphasized the ways in which imperial Spain forced its might into the mineraled bowels of the New World, my close reading of texts from the crucial first years of Spanish settlement suggests a more nuanced story of colonial power. Attending to the spatiotemporal

34. Mexico: Charles I, "Reissue of a Merced to Diego de Carvajal for the Sweepings and Washings of Gold and Silver from Smelters in New Spain," 1534, MS 1225, Edward E. Ayer Digital Collection, Newberry Library, Chicago. The license stopped at Guatemala, where Isabella I authorized officials to use escobillas and relaves from gold, silver, and "any other metal" to fund hospitals. Cuba and La Española: "Merced escobilla y relaves: Juan López de Calatayud: Cuba," Monzón, June 1, 1528, AGI, Patronato Real, 177, ramo 7, no. 1; "Real Provisión a Juan López de Calatayud, argentier real, concediéndole la merced de la escobilla y relaves de las casas de fundición de oro que hay y hubiere en adelante en la Isla Fernandina, por renuncia a su favor del gentilhombre Juan de Vinancuyt," Monzón, July 1, 1528, AGI, Indiferente, 421, legajo 13, fols. 228–229. The Real Academia de la Historia digitized the Calatayud family tree: http://bibliotecadigital.rah.es/dgbrah/i18n/consulta/registro.cmd?id=49725. Guatemala, Panama, and Peru: "Que los oficiales no tengan a su cargo la escobilla del oro," Monzón, June 5, 1528, AGI, Panama, 234, legajo 3, fols. 132v–133v; "Escobilla y relaves a los hospitales de Tierra Firme," Medina del Campo, Dec. 19, 1531, AGI, Panama, 234, legajo 5, fols. 8v–9v; "Concesión a hospitales del Perú: Escobilla y relaves," Toledo, July 26, 1529, AGI, Patronato Real, 28, ramo 42.

dialectics of mining communities in the sixteenth-century Caribbean makes clear that Indigenous and African miners influenced the plotting of Spanish goldworks. Colonists followed Indigenous architecture, geography, and technologies, and they designed refineries in response to the agencies of women and men who resisted colonial rule. These visual and spatial stories, viewed critically, highlight the roles of subaltern miners in the design of the early colonial gold industry.

In turn, an analysis of the printed forms of images from these texts explains how published records omit the traces of subaltern miners. Oviedo is the paramount example of such erasure. His first publication, *De la natural hystoria de las Indias* (1526), contained four images: a *hamaca* (hammock), an unnamed tree that grew along the banks of the river Cuti in Colombia, sticks to spark fire, and a leaf from the plantain tree. His second book, *La historia general delas Indias* (1535), expanded the visual scope to include twenty-seven images. The eighth chapter, which deals with plants, contains the most images; nine plates convey plantain leaves, higüero *(Crescentia cujete),* cacti *(cirios),* guiabara *(Coccoloba uvifera),* copey *(Clusia major),* guanábano *(Annona muricata),* mamey *(Pouteria sapota),* and pitahaya (dragon fruit). The Book of Deposits, dedicated in part to mining, was not far behind. This sixth book contained six images: two houses (bohíos and caneys), a hatchet, a canoe, hands grasping fire-starting sticks, and three miners enclosed within a single frame. The final edition published in Oviedo's lifetime, *Corónica delas Indias* (1547), reprinted the images from 1535 with notable differences—especially in his depictions of miners, who became thinner, less connected to each other's work, and less identifiable by jewelry and status.[35]

Although the 1547 images were ostensibly copies of the plates from 1535, their notable changes communicate different messages about Taíno metalwork. By comparing graphic registers across print and manuscript editions, we see how early modern print culture influenced European ideas about Amerindian goldwork. African and Afro-Indigenous miners were central to the physical planning of the gold industry, but the mechanics of publishing removed traces of their presence. Although the historiography has traditionally emphasized origins and originality in early modern artwork, new research on copies shows that "recycled images performed overlooked but important tasks for epistemology: prints enabled the rise of observation and conditioned

35. Oviedo, *De la natural hystoria de las Indias,* xvii(v), xxxix(v), xli, xlii(v); Oviedo, *Historia general delas Indias,* lviii(v), lix, lxi–lxi(v), lxvi, lxxxi, lxxxiii–lxxxiv(v), lxxxv(v), lxxxvi, lxxxvi(v).

FIGURE 5. Manuscript depiction of gold mining (detail). In Gonzalo Fernández de Oviedo y Valdés, "Natural y general hystoria de las Indias," 1539–1548, HM177, 16v. The Huntington Library, San Marino, Calif.

it by providing parameters for visual investigation." Within genres like natural history, travel writing, and zoology, art historian Stephanie Leitch argues, "images were particularly invested in verifying knowledge—their repetition through copies served to habituate the viewer's eye." Oviedo's images were not true copies; as such, they offer different kinds of instruction and epistemology than those that Leitch locates in copies of Albrecht Dürer's rhinoceros, a widely circulated image that traveled through genres and across time in early modern Europe, "even becoming a functionary of natural history." For Dürer, graphic evidence helped to verify information in works by different authors; specific details conveyed in each iteration underwrote the scientific authority of the image and its copies. Oviedo's images, recirculated in works by the same author, undercut many of his prose distinctions, such as different mining environments and the roles of mining women.[36]

In Oviedo's manuscript portrayal of gold mining (Figure 5), read from left to right like words on a page, one sees three distinct, partially clothed male figures, each of whom illustrates a different method of gold mining. By now, Oviedo's Spanish readers would have learned of different mining methods for

36. Stephanie Leitch, "Dürer's *Rhinoceros* Underway: The Epistemology of the Copy in the Early Modern Print," in Debra Taylor Cashion, Henry Luttikhuizen, and Ashley West, eds., *The Primacy of the Image in Northern European Art, 1400–1700* (Leiden, 2017), 241–255.

goldfields, groves, and rivers; the image places alluvial mining alongside land-based excavations. The first man, to the viewer's left, holds an empty *batea* at waist level, gripping the handles of the device with both hands; his arms reach to his sides to accommodate the large, round tool as he stands in the current of knee-high water. (See Chapter 1, above, for an analysis of bateas.) His hair is secured with a ponytail, and he looks straight ahead, making eye contact with the viewer. Because of the position of his batea, none of his clothing is visible to the reader, other than a two-ringed necklace with small, decorative pieces placed in a pattern along the cord. The second man, wearing a loincloth, hoists a full batea above his head, indicating the procedural nature of mine work; he shows the second stage in gold panning. Standing upon two rocks, delicately balanced on the river bed, he grips each handle from below, arms bent at the elbow, and cuts a solid, rectangular figure through the center of the frame. He, too, looks straight ahead, though his hair falls loosely around his face.

The third man, to the viewer's right, planted solidly on the ground, holds a long hoe in both hands; he is not panning, but his gaze, directed over his right shoulder toward the other miners, connects him to the collective work. A much smaller batea, relative to the tools used by miners who pan for gold, rests upon a rock near his left foot. He leans over his knee, back bent, as he breaks up the topsoil with a *coa,* a tool repurposed from agricultural work. The name of the device, described by Las Casas as "unos palos tostados que usan por azadas" (burned sticks that they use as hoes), was perhaps derived from the Taíno root *kō-,* "planting."[37] This visual depiction of the instrument hints at practical transfers from agriculture to mining and conveys symbolic domains of Taíno cosmology, which understands gold metals as part of a continuum of dynamic material. The miner's batea rests upon the river embankment, empty. He is the heaviest man, and he wears only a three-part headdress; his strategically placed coa hides his genitals from the viewer. The largest feather, placed in the center of the head ornament, stands straight up, whereas the smaller feathers fall to either side. This three-part, asymmetrical pattern of the headdress resembles a Yaguajay statuette recovered from the Chorro de Maita complex in present-day Holguín, Cuba. Like the first miner's necklace, this headdress, which appears prominently against the plain background of the image, conveys the third miner's high status within Taíno social orders. These icono-

37. Las Casas, *Obras completas,* ed. Delgado, IV, 995; Granberry and Vescelius, *Languages of the Pre-Columbian Antilles,* 71. For an excellent synthesis of Taíno agriculture, including an analysis of limited colonial sources, see Anderson-Córdova, *Surviving Spanish Conquest,* 18–20.

FIGURE 6. Depiction of gold mining. In [Gonzalo Fernández de Oviedo y Valdés], *La historia general delas Indias* (Seville, 1535), libro 6, capítulo 8, fol. lxvi. RB 55597 ANAL. The Huntington Library, San Marino, Calif.

graphic features represent gold mining as the work of skilled laborers who harvest gold for reasons beyond currency or coinage: gold is part of a social fabric and spiritual body. Oviedo carefully described women's work in prose, but Indigenous and African women miners are entirely absent from the visual story. As we see below, they do not appear in any of the printed works, either.[38]

In a marginal gloss along the right-hand column, Oviedo classified the manuscript sketch as a "Pintura đla mina e del lavar đl oro" (painting of the mine and of the washing of gold). Along the left-hand column, writing vertically, he noted, "Es hecha. mas no tan biē como aquí esta" (It's done. But not as good as it is here). He seems to refer to the woodcut image that was published in the 1535 edition of the *Historia general delas Indias,* which modified the manuscript drawing in several ways (Figure 6).

Some of the differences between the manuscript sketch and the printed image were aesthetic, such as filling in the frame with solid black lines and inserting a floral garland along the left and right borders. Three other differences undercut the content that Oviedo had so painstakingly described. First,

38. The artifact was photographed by Cuban archaeologist Orencio Miguel Alonso and appears as part of the author's collection, in Alonso, "Discovery of a Pre-Columbian Gold Figurine in Cuba," *American Antiquarian,* XV (1950), 340. A smaller version of the image is available from the Museo Indocubano Baní at https://www.ecured.cu/Museo_Indocubano_Baní.

FIGURE 7. Depiction of gold mining. In Gonzalo Fernández de Oviedo y Valdés, *Corónica delas Indias* (Salamanca, 1547), libro 6, capítulo 8, fol. lxvi. RB 55600 ANAL. The Huntington Library, San Marino, Calif.

the printed version fills in the manuscript's empty background with various kinds of tree ferns, collapsing Oviedo's distinctions between mining in groves *(arcabucos),* fields *(sabanas),* and rivers. There is no blank space in the printed edition. Second, all three bateas, still of different sizes, are empty, erasing the relationship between miners who formed a productive chain; instead, they are connected by their gazes. The second and third men look to their right, and the first miner looks to his left, glancing toward them. The miner in the center, now thicker around the middle, balances his batea on his head, arms hoisted straight up, cutting a softer figure than he had in the sketch. Third, the material cultures change notably. The jewelry that the first and third miners wore in the manuscript sketch is removed from the printed scene. The first miner still wears his hair in a ponytail, but his necklace is gone, as is the third miner's headdress.

The final image printed during Oviedo's lifetime appeared in a book that was published twelve years after the *Historia general.* The *Corónica delas Indias* (1547) used a different title and was recast as a different genre, but it contained the same prose content as the 1535 edition. The image, once more, changed dramatically (Figure 7). Here, the scene is encased in a decorative, ribbon-like border that surrounds the rectangular image. The solid black border from the 1535 edition becomes a raised frame that adds perspective to the image, which is now missing a row of rocks along the bottom edge to generate space for these more elaborate iconographic details.

Within the image, key details about the miners and their work also change. The muscular, stocky men of the first illustration become nymph-like, as the lean miner in the middle dances along the riverbank with an empty batea on his head. His hands are placed delicately on either side, his arms are raised gracefully to encircle the device, and his eyes glance upward. A large tattoo in the shape of an "X" is marked upon his left upper thigh, visible just below his loincloth. The first miner's marks of social distinction, his necklace and ponytail, are gone, and the third miner's headdress has not reappeared. He now stands with his backside to the viewer, eyes turned toward the land and the task at hand, all connection with the group effectively severed. Only the first miner makes eye contact with another person—the viewer. Whereas the bateas formed a point of connection between the first and second miners in the 1535 edition, and their varying dimensions conveyed information about mining in rivers and on land in the manuscript sketch, all three devices here are the same size.

Each version of the image removes essential details about Taíno technical knowledges and social status. The manuscript image depicts miners with different kinds of jewelry and hairstyles, suggesting that men of different social statuses and aesthetic traditions engaged in a collective mining of gold, including caciques, for whom metallic objects contained and conveyed sacred and secular powers. The published images emphasize labor, not lives. Oviedo's eyewitness testimony certified details in his natural history, but the images that accompanied his work undermined much of what he wrote. To understand the complexities of Taíno gold mining and metalworking practices as they are mediated through Spanish-language documents and European graphic traditions, we must juxtapose our analysis of textual languages with those of the visual.

This chapter has therefore examined manuscript illustrations and woodcut engravings, alongside evidence of labor, design, and demographics culled from colonial letters, maps and plans, and printed accounts, in order to read Indigenous, African, and Afro-Indigenous spatial presences and absences in the gold industry of the colonial Caribbean. Instead of seeing Taínos as a people whose way of life collapsed upon the arrival of Spaniards and Africans, we instead learn how the mechanics of print culture, from colonial reports to imperial interlocutors and networks of printers and publishers, fashioned a narrative of Indigenous absence in the first half of the sixteenth century. Interpreting those images alongside the technical prose that they supposedly explain, and situating such prose within a wider web of spatial thinking that colonial officials developed in response to Indigenous and African agencies, provides a fuller image of the Spanish empire and its extractive economies. In such an image, early modern Spain is contingent, negotiated, and uneven in its initial essays into New World mining and refining. And subaltern miners are the ones crucial to the plotting of community life, the design of metalworking districts, and the physical infrastructure of the gold industry.

3 : SEASONS OF GOLD

In 1525, Pedro López de Mesa, a *vecino* of Concepción de La Vega, La Española, traveled to Spain to petition the crown to alter the season of gold refining in his town. Little is known of López de Mesa. He had lived in the mining town long enough to have received, per the island's first *repartimiento* in November 1514, an encomienda of fifty-eight workers: thirty-six men and thirty-two women, as well as five elders, five children, and two servants *(naborías),* all ruled by *cacica* María de Luna. La Vega, which was controlled by the cacique Guarionex at the time of Cristóbal Colón's landing, is located in the heart of the region known as the Cibao ("land of stone"). In the valley where key rivers converged, arable lands that Spaniards later put to agricultural use were dotted with gold mines. These include Pueblo Viejo, currently the fifth largest gold mine in the world.[1]

In the early sixteenth century, gold was refined in November or December, depending on when local officials initiated smelting, which lasted for thirty days. According to López de Mesa, this was a poor time to run the refinery *(casa de fundición):* heavy, year-end rains flooded the road to Santo Domingo, and miners could not buy or sell goods to residents of the booming port city. Miners and their families were near ruin, because "no solian entender en otras granjerías salvo en cojer oro" (they did not tend to understand any trade other than gathering gold).[2]

1. "Las cosas que Pedro Lopez de Mesa habrá de pedir á Su Majestad en favor de la ciudad de la Concepcion de la Isla Española, para su poblacion (Patronato, número 4, estante 1, cajón 1, legajo 18)," in Joaquín F. Pacheco, Francisco Cárdenas, and Luis Torres de Mendoza, eds., *Colección de documentos inéditos relativos al descubrimiento, conquista y colonización de las posesiones españolas en América y Oceanía, sacados, en su mayor parte, del Real Archivo de Indias,* I (Madrid, 1864), 456–469, hereafter cited as *DII;* "Repartimiento de la Isla Española," ibid., 50–236, esp. 68; Vilma Benzo de Ferrer, *Pasajeros a la Española: 1492–1530* (Santo Domingo, 2000), 515, no. 3027; Julian Granberry and Gary S. Vescelius, *Languages of the Pre-Columbian Antilles* (Tuscaloosa, Ala., 2004), 111, 113; "The Top 10 Gold Producing Mines in the World," *Business Insider,* Sept. 10, 2016. López de Mesa's manuscript, "Petición de ciudad de la Concepción: Mercedes," (1525), held at Archivo General de Indias (hereafter cited as AGI), Patronato Real, 18, ramo 4, no. 1, fols. 1–6v, includes council notes. In this chapter, I cite the published account in *DII* and supplement from the manuscript when necessary.

2. "Las cosas que Pedro Lopez de Mesa habrá de pedir," *DII,* 462.

This phrase, "coger oro," coined in November 1492 when Colón learned how Taínos mined for gold, was central to López de Mesa's proposal to reform La Vega's economic and community life (see Chapter 1, above). It appears twenty-four times, in various forms, throughout his five-folio petition ("coger oro," "se cogia oro," "se deja de cojer," "que no cojen oro," "paguen del oro que cogieren," "poco oro que agora se coje," "se darán en cojer oro," "con ellos cojan oro," "llevará del oro que cogieren," "para donde lo hay que se coja," "los que lo han cojido é cojen," "los que lo cojian," "é muchos no lo cojerian"). By juxtaposing the visions of gold articulated in Taíno creation myths and López de Mesa's proposal, we can see that the phrase "coger oro" provides crucial evidence of Indigenous influences in the colonial gold industry. It grabbed the attention of imperial reviewers, earning a notably different reception at council relative to the rest of the petition (Figure 8). Imperial officials were unimpressed with most of López de Mesa's twenty-seven ideas, marking requests for tax holidays (nos. 3, 5, and 7) and public notaries (no. 19) as "no puede ser" (this cannot be / we will not allow this), setting aside matters that had been discussed elsewhere (nos. 4, 12, 14, 15, 18, 19), and doodling in the margins (nos. 6, 13, 16, 25). In another document, gathered by imperial historian Juan Bautista Muñoz as part of his sweeping *Historia del nuevo mundo* (1793), council members summarized the ten-page petition in a scant three sentences, showing what they thought of these ideas.[3]

But they underlined one passage almost in its entirety, with seven dashes drawn vertically along the left-hand side. In his ninth point, López de Mesa claimed that, by moving the season of smelting from November or December to June (which officials glossed as "July" before correcting it in the margins), miners could harvest *cañafístola (Cassia fistola),* a medicinal plant that some Indigenous communities in Yucatán and Central America call "lluvia de oro" (golden rain). As López de Mesa put it in overlapping terms of gold mining and agricultural husbandry, "si la fundicion se hiziese en el tiempo de la cosecha de cañafístola, los vezinos de la ciudad recibirian mucho provecho . . . é la ciudad quedaria proveida, é al tiempo que se coje es muy buen tiempo, que es verano" (if smelting were done when we harvest cañafístola, the property holders of the city would receive great profit . . . and the city would be provided for, and its

3. Cristóbal Colón, *Los cuatro viajes: Testamento,* ed. Consuelo Varela (1986; rpt. Madrid, 2011), 90 (Nov. 12, 1492); "Parece del mismo tiempo otra instruccion o Memorial de peticiones al rei que la Ciudad de la Concepcion dio a Pero Lopez de Mesa su Procurador en Corte," in Roberto Marte, ed., *Santo Domingo en los manuscritos de Juan Bautista Muñoz* (Santo Domingo, 1981), 276, tomo A/105, fol. 56. I thank Barbara Fuchs for suggesting the second interpretation of "no puede ser."

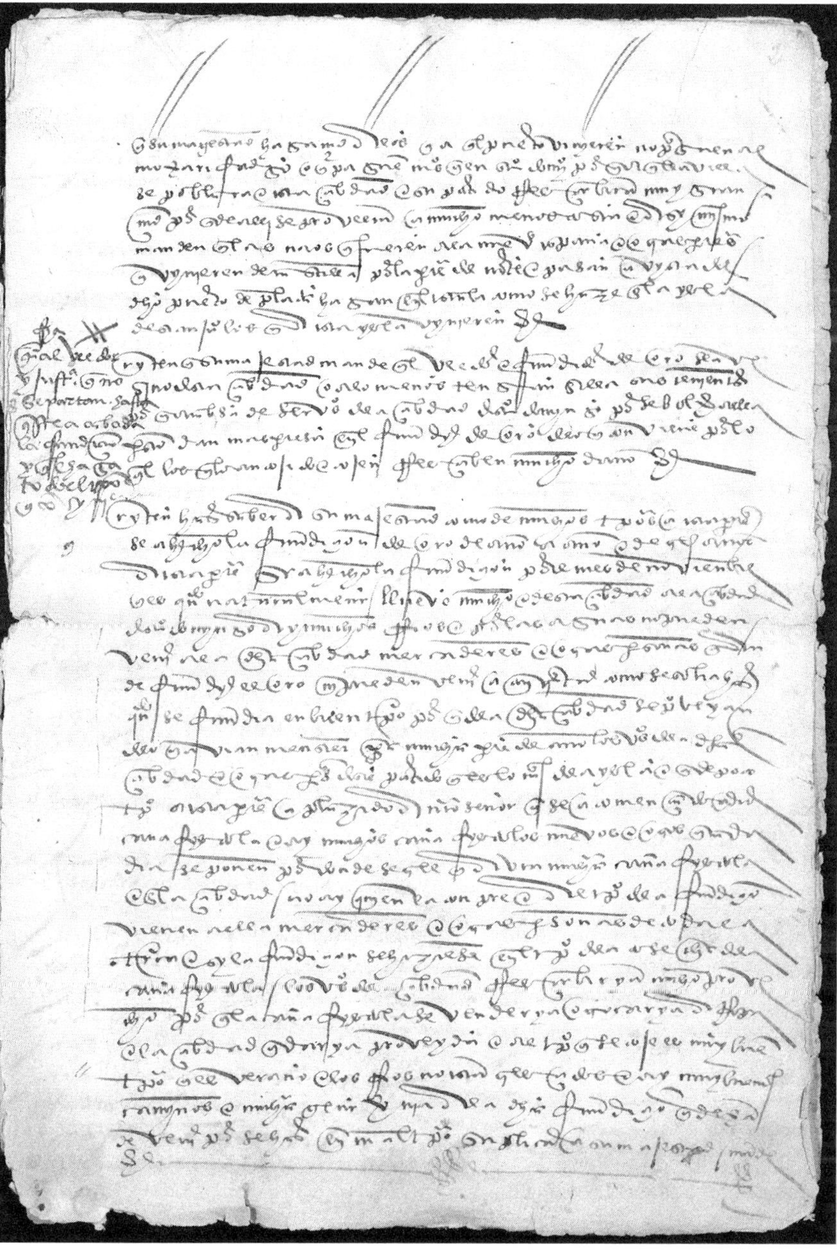

FIGURE 8. "Petición de ciudad de la Concepción: Mercedes." 1525. Archivo General de las Indias, Patronato Real, 18, ramo 4, no. 1, fols. 2–2v. Reproduced with permission of the Ministerio de Educación, Cultura y Deporte

harvest season is a very good season, summer). These lines explode imperial fantasies of a golden age of permanent bloom in the Americas and, instead, insist upon seasonal ecologies for gold metals and fragrant, yellow-leafed plants. There were two varieties of cañafístola in La Española, one native to the region and one Spanish strand introduced during the rule of the Hieronymite friars (1516–1519). According to Oviedo, the plant was an excellent purgative, and the imported stock grew so well that boats returned to Spain loaded with sugar, cañafístola, and animal hides.[4]

In August 1525, the crown ordered a review of López de Mesa's proposal. Two months later, the Consejo de Indias officially changed the season of gold refining in La Vega to the month of June. A separate *cédula,* written on the same day, ordered colonial officials to be present at the refinery when miners arrived with their harvests of gold. This chapter analyzes the language and logic of López de Mesa's proposal to show how Indigenous ideas of human, plant, and metallic relationships, as well as broader cosmological principles of time, the seasons, and cultural genesis, influenced the vision of goldwork that López de Mesa articulated on behalf of the vecinos of La Vega.[5]

Reading Taíno Cosmologies in Imperial Archives

There are at least four reasons why the crown's enthusiastic response to the petition is striking and why the ideas expressed within the proposal seem to undercut imperial efforts to extract wealth from the New World. First, colonial reports and climate data gathered from the nineteenth century through the present day indicate that the dry season on the island runs from Novem-

4. Narciso Souza Novelo, *Plantas melíferas y poliníferas que viven en Yucatán,* ed. Alfonso Barrera Vázquez and Victor M. Suárez Molina (Mérida, Yucatán, 1981), 21; J. Alberto Arellano Rodríguez et al., *Nomenclatura, forma de vida, uso, manejo y distribución de las especies vegetales de la península de Yucatán* (Mérida, Yucatán, 2003), 330; "Las cosas que Pedro Lopez de Mesa habrá de pedir," *DII,* 460; [Gonzalo Fernández de Oviedo y Valdés], *La historia general delas Indias* (Seville, 1535), lxxviii(v). I cite this edition unless Oviedo's manuscript or first edition (*Oviedo de la natural hystoria de las Indias* [Toledo, 1526]) differs significantly. The *DII* transcript reads, "porque la cañafístola se venderia otro (1) . . . é la ciudad quedaria proveida," signaling a manuscript tear. The authors offer "tanto más" as one possibility (460). My reading of AGI, Patronato Real, 18, ramo 4, no. 1, fol. 2, suggests "porque la cañafistola se venderya o tomarya A RRto" (because cañafístola could be sold or taken as rent).

5. AGI, Indiferente, 420, legajo 10: "Informe sobre la petición de Pedro López de Mesa," Toledo, Aug. 18, 1525, fols. 74v–75; "Real cédula a los oidores de la Audiencia de La Española . . . ," Toledo, Oct. 13, 1525, fols. 120–120v; "Real cédula al veedor de las fundiciones de la Isla Española y justicia de la ciudad de la Concepción . . . ," Toledo, Oct. 13, 1525, fol. 118v.

ber through May. The rainy season includes the hot, summer months of June, July, and August, the official start of the Atlantic hurricane season. In other words, López de Mesa argued to move gold refining to the beginning of hurricane season in a country that is positioned in the central path of summer storms in the Caribbean. He did so at a time when two devastating hurricanes were within living memory, one of which destroyed the island's other refinery, located in Buenaventura (present-day Villa de Altagracia), just outside of Santo Domingo.[6]

Second, this change would disrupt the logistics of transoceanic crossings. Passenger logs from Spain and records from colonial refineries suggest that ship captains often timed their departures to coincide with periods of refining in the Caribbean, promising sailors an immediate source of income upon making land. In these early years, imperial officials enacted policies about refining in Iberia that were designed to promote colonial gold production. Beginning in 1505, refiners in Seville were authorized to process gold from the Indies wherever they could find space in the city. The crown enacted this policy at the beginning of the gold boom in La Española—a surge that was directly tied to fray Nicolás Ovando's brutal attacks on Native sovereigns and his remapping of community life. In 1503, one year after Ovando arrived in the colony, refiners in Santo Domingo sent their first gold shipments to Seville: 5,292 pesos. The next year, they sent almost eight times as much: 39,985 pesos. Between the years of 1505–1509, Spanish officials received an annual average of 43,491 pesos, with significant fluctuations: 47,984 pesos in 1505, 35,800 pesos the next year, and 44,000 pesos in 1507. The same amount arrived in 1508, alongside 16,000 pesos of gold from Puerto Rico. Production in La Española peaked in 1512, when miners sent an astounding 72,013 pesos, approximately 33 percent more gold than they had sent in a single year. The following year, officials in Seville recorded 43,845 pesos, more or less the customary amount. By 1520, the boom in La Española was over, although production increased in Puerto Rico and Cuba. With the arrival of enslaved African miners at the end of the decade, La Española's gold output increased once more, although production did not return to peak levels. Even during the bust years, however, gold played a central economic role in La Vega, which served as La Española's primary refinery through the 1540s. Amid these cycles of boom and bust, ship captains timed arrivals in La Española to provide incentives to would-be colonists, and

6. Francisco Álvarez Leal, *La República dominicana,* trans. Manuel García Cartagena (Santo Domingo, 2014), 21 (first publ. as *Le République dominicaine* [Paris, 1888]); Development Assistance Research Associates (DARA) Climate Vulnerable Forum, *Climate Vulnerability Monitor* (Madrid, 2010), 194; Oviedo, *Historia general delas Indias,* lix(v)–lx(v).

the crown supported the production of colonial wealth by expanding the times and spaces of smelting in Spain.[7]

Third, whereas the mountains surrounding the Cibao are rich in gold, the valley has high-quality land and ample rivers that create favorable conditions for a variety of crops, including monoculture commodities like sugar, cotton, and tobacco. In 1506, La Vega became the site of the first experiments in sugar cultivation on La Española, followed quickly by tobacco and cotton. The first sugar trials produced only molasses, but by 1512, miners began processing it with the same pressing devices that Taína women used to remove toxic juices from cassava roots, which they then made into bread *(cazabe)*. By repurposing agricultural tools and Indigenous women's technical knowledge, miners in La Vega refined sugar into the crystalline substance that we know today, and they exported their model of extractive plantation agriculture throughout the hemisphere.[8]

The gold industry played an important role in this process, as local officials redeveloped gold infrastructure to help in such projects. In 1521, the crown authorized gold refineries to be used to "fundir y labrar las las pieças de cobre q̄ fueren menester pa los dhos yngenios de açucar qto vtra voluntad fuere" (smelt and make the copper goods that are necessary for the aforesaid sugar

7. Jalil Sued Badillo, *El Dorado borincano: La economía de la Conquista, 1510–1550* (San Juan, 2001), 48; "Orden para labrar el oro de Indias," Segovia, Sept. 15, 1505, AGI, Indiferente, 418, legajo 1, fols. 183v–184; Francesco D'Esposito and Auke P. Jacobs, "Auge y ocaso de la primera sociedad minera de América: Santo Domingo, 1503–1520," *Nuevo mundo–Mundos neuvos* (October 2015), pars. 31–32, https://journals.openedition.org/nuevomundo/67723; Pauline Martha Kulstad-González, "Striking It Rich in the Americas' First Boom Town: Economic Activity at Concepción de La Vega (Hispaniola) 1495–1564," in Pedro Pablo A. Funari and María Ximena Senatore, eds., *Archaeology of Culture Contact and Colonialism in Spanish and Portuguese America* (New York, 2015), 313–337, esp. 328, 331–335; Carlos Larrazábal Blanco, *Los negros y la esclavitud en Santo Domingo,* 2d ed. (Santo Domingo, 1998), 34. Records of gold production in La Española before 1520 are lost; only documents of shipments received in Seville remain. Shipping records from La Española between 1504 and 1514 suggest that all of the gold that was registered in Santo Domingo arrived in Spain. Small discrepancies—such as in 1509, when Capitán Diego Rodríguez de Grajeda received 10,000 pesos and delivered 9,999 pesos, 12 granos, or 1510, when pilot Cristóbal Vibas received 6,000 peso of gold in La Española and delivered 6,003 pesos and 2 tomines—are attributable to errors of measurement or differences in the scales rather than intentional underreporting. The real fraud was in never reporting gold to colonial officials. See Juan Gil, "Las cuentas de Cristóbal Colón," in Gil and Consuelo Varela, eds., *Temas colombinos* (Seville, 1986), 1–75, esp. 35–42.

8. Kulstad-González, "Striking It Rich in the Americas' First Boom Town," in Funari and Senatore, eds., *Archaeology of Culture Contact and Colonialism,* 329.

refineries in whatever amount you determine). Gold refining did not operate separately from plantation agriculture or copper manufacturing; a change in the timing of one industry would affect the others. The cédula does not specify how these copper wares would be used within sugar plantations, although it seems reasonable that some metal intended for sugar boilers might have been made into artillery to fight against African and Indigenous people who coordinated large-scale rebellions in sugar plantations *(ingenios)* and gold refineries across the island. By 1521, don Enrique / Enriquillo's long-term revolt was well under way, and Afro-Taíno cimarrones reclaimed lands outside of Spanish control, establishing new communities in the northern, eastern, and southwestern corners of the island. Although López de Mesa argued for the expansion of slavery in La Vega, requesting that four hundred Africans be brought to the town and distributed among its twenty vecinos, he did not ask to increase the scale of profitable monocultures like tobacco, sugar, or cotton. Instead, he sought to synchronize gold refining with the harvest of a fragrant, yellow-hued laxative that was worth no more than 4 *ducados* per quintal (one hundred pounds), according to Oviedo, in a colony whose annual trade he estimated to be 2,250,000 ducados. López de Mesa's petition was at odds with colonial economic interests, including those of slaveholders and plantation owners.[9]

Fourth, although gold production in La Española had declined in the early 1520s, following promising news of mineral-rich lands in Mexico, the island remained central to the mining, refining, and shipping of gold within the Spanish empire. Soon after Hernán Cortés conquered the Mexica imperial capital of Tenochtitlán in 1521, he established a refinery on his estate in Coyoacán (a neighborhood of Mexico City). Almost immediately, he learned that none of Moctezuma's golden objects could serve as coins because they contained too much copper—what Cortés called "betún" (bitumen) and Nahua speakers called "tepuzque." Bernal Díaz del Castillo alleged that Cortés's failures with coinage proved that he defrauded soldiers of metallic spoils. This was certainly possible, although the mixed-metallic content of the stolen objects can also be

9. "Licencia para fundir piezas de cobre en La Española," Burgos, Apr. 11, 1521, AGI, Indiferente, 420, legajo 8, fol. 285; Lynne Guitar, "No More Negotiation: Slavery and the Destabilization of Colonial Hispaniola's Encomienda System," *Revista interamericana,* XXIX (1999), http://cai.sg.inter.edu/revista-ciscla/volume29/guitar.pdf; Guitar, "Boiling It Down: Slavery on the First Commercial Sugarcane Ingenios in the Americas (Hispaniola, 1530–45)," in Jane G. Landers and Barry M. Robinson, eds., *Slaves, Subjects, and Subversives: Blacks in Colonial Latin America* (Albuquerque, N.M., 2006), 39–82, esp. 49–50; José Amador de los Ríos, "Vida y escritos de Gonzalo Fernández de Oviedo y Valdés," in Oviedo, *Historia general y natural de las Indias,* ed. Juan Pérez de Tudela Bueso (Madrid, 1959), ix–cvii, esp. xci–xciin, citing fols. xlii–xliii of the 1535 edition.

traced to Indigenous metalworking traditions. In the time of emperor Axayacatl (ca. 1469–1481), the Mexica collected bells as tribute from communities in western Mexico. Although colonial reports sometimes describe these objects as "golden," material and chemical analysis suggests that they are often mixed-metallic alloys that contain various amounts of copper, silver, arsenic, tin, and sulfur. By combining these elements, refiners created a variety of metallic goods, from axes and bells to hooks, needles, and sheet metal, whose finished forms conveyed different sounds, colors, and textures. Mexica agents and refiners in Michoacán were not melting these objects for coin; they valued sensory elements of metallic goods in ways that Cortés, who needed pure metals for coinage, did not.[10]

Despite the early promise of Cortés's conquest, the first results from the refineries of New Spain did not suggest fruitful returns. The first shipment was sent on January 3, 1526, but without protocols *(ordenanzas)* regulating processes in the refinery, gold production was uneven. In 1532, Sebastián Ramírez de Fuenleal, serving as president of the Audiencia of New Spain, visited the casa de fundición in Mexico City. He remarked on the widespread state of disorder and shortage of basic materials like crucibles *(crisoles)* and bellows *(fuelles),* in place of which "se funde el oro con indios soplando con unos cañutos de caña" (gold is refined by Indians who breathe into cane rods). In light of these shortcomings, payments in copper-gold *tepuzque* continued to be made to university officials, religious orders, and private pilots in Mexico and the Philippines throughout the sixteenth century. The lack of standardized currency in Spain's North American and East Asian colonies even led writers there and in other regions, such as Peru, to publish mathematical manuals and assay tables that explained how to convert imperial monetary units like *maravedis,* ducados, and pesos into local forms of exchange, such as gold from China and pesos de tezpuque and cacao beans in Mexico.[11]

10. Román Beltrán Martinez, "Primeras casas de Fundición," *Historia mexicana,* I (1952), 372–394, esp. 375, 377; Bernal Díaz del Castillo, *Historia verdadera de la conquista de la Nueva España,* 2 vols. (Madrid, 1933), II, 160, quoted ibid., 377; Dorothy Hosler, *The Sounds and Colors of Power: The Sacred Metallurgical Technology of Ancient West Mexico* (Cambridge, Mass., 1994), 227–251, esp. 243–248.

11. Beltrán Martinez, "Primeras casas de Fundicion," *Historia mexicana,* I (1952), 385, 386; "Mandamiento del Consejo de Indias a Hernando de Ochoa," Valladolid, Oct. 16, 1554, AGI, Indiferente, 425, legajo 23, fol. 109 (3); "Mandamiento del Consejo de Indias a Sebastián de Portillo," Valladolid, Oct. 24, 1554, AGI, Indiferente, 425, legajo 23, fols. 110v–111; "Real cédula a la Audiencia Real de Nueva España," Toro, Jan. 18, 1552, AGI, Mexico, 1089, legajo 4, fols. 464v–465; "Real cédula a la Audiencia de México y oficiales reales," El Escorial, Apr. 24, 1573, AGI, Mexico, 1090, legajo 7, fols. 190–191v; "Real cédula a lo oficiales

Hence, when López de Vega submitted his proposal, the Caribbean was still the main and most important source of American gold. For an empire dedicated to the production of colonial wealth and the extraction of precious metals, it was indeed a curious decision to rearrange the gold industry in the only populated refining town in La Española to accommodate a purgative plant whose harvest cycle aligns with the hurricane season. Any one of these four economic and environmental reasons should have been enough for the crown to reject the proposal submitted by the vecinos of La Vega. At the very least, López de Mesa's proposal of 1525 makes little sense from a Spanish perspective. Yet it passed almost immediately.[12]

At the same time, the idea to harvest gold in the early summer season, as if it were a yellow plant ("coger oro," "coger cañafistola"), makes a lot of sense from the viewpoint of Taínos in La Española. Their cosmologies might well have influenced López de Mesa's proposal—especially regarding relationships between animal, botanical, metallic, and human life.[13]

Gold and Guanín: Taíno Beliefs of Power, Culture, and Becoming

One crucial source in the study of Taíno metallic cosmologies is the creation narrative that speakers of Classic Taíno relayed to Catalán friar Ramón Pané in 1498, when he lived in the goldfields ruled by cacique Guarionex. The narrative's own history indicates the difficulty of deciphering elements of Taíno cosmovision from colonial sources; it was related in Classic Taíno to a priest who had studied Macorís, spoken in a different part of the island. Pané, in turn, documented the tale in Spanish, his second language. The story was first published in an Italian-language translation of Fernando Colón's history of his father, printed in Venice as the *Historie del S.D. Fernando Colombo* (1571).

---

reales de México," El Escorial, Apr. 24, 1573, AGI, Mexico, 1090, legajo 7, fols. 191v–192v; "Merced de pesos de tepuzque y arroz a jesuitas de Filipinas," Alcalá de Henares, Jan. 26, 1585, AGI, Filipinas, 339, legajo 1, fols. 315–315v; Elvira Vilches, "Trade, Silver, and Print Culture in the Colonial Americas," *Journal of Latin American Cultural Studies,* XXIV (2015), 315–334; Bruce Stanley Burdick, *Mathematical Works Printed in the Americas, 1554–1700* (Baltimore, 2009), 48–54.

12. Luxury items dated from 1520 to 1550 suggest that declining gold production did not affect colonists' standards of living; see Kulstad-González, "Striking It Rich in the Americas' First Boom Town," in Funari and Senatore, eds., *Archaeology of Culture Contact and Colonialism,* 327–328.

13. See Pablo F. Gómez, *The Experiential Caribbean: Creating Knowledge and Healing in the Early Modern Atlantic* (Chapel Hill, N.C., 2017), 95–117, for an insightful study of Afro-descendant healers who "smelled herbs" in order to know their virtues and hidden workings.

There are multiple layers of linguistic translation, cultural interpretation, and material remediation embedded in the story, as it moved from oral relation to written work and between and among Indigenous and European languages. Yet, for all of the interpretative difficulties that the text presents, it remains one of the only sources testifying to Taíno beliefs about the sacred and the material.[14]

According to the story that Taínos in La Vega relayed to Pané, the first people of the island were created in a cave called Cacibajagua (opening [*ka,* top / junction, and *siba,* stone] + *jagua* tree, used as a black dye in body painting). This cave was located in Caonao ("place of gold"), in the center of the island. One day, some of these first people went outside to fish; when they returned to the cave, the entrance had been sealed shut. They were turned by the Sun into trees called "jobos" *(Spondius mombin).* However, the people inside the cave remained alive. This was the first transformation of the Taíno people.[15]

Later, one of these men, Guahayona, sent another to look for an herb to wash himself; this man, Yahubaba, was turned into a hummingbird and never returned, forcing Guahayona to exit the cave. He took all of the women with him to "coger el digo" (gather the herb), promising that they could return to their families once they had collected the plant. In addition to women from his part of the cave, he took all of the women from cacique Anacacuya ("Central Star," derived from the Arawak terms *ánnaka,* center, and *cuya* or *cuyhuya,* star) and threw the cacique into the water. Linguistic anthropologists believe that Anacacuya's name refers to the North Star, which Taínos associated with the Ursa Major constellation because two stars in Ursa Major point toward the North Star. When observed from the Caribbean, Ursa Major dips below the horizon between the months of April and August, effectively marking the beginning of the rainy, hurricane season. Evidence from Mesoamerican texts suggests that neighboring pre-Columbian communities likewise associated strong hurricane winds with Ursa Major.[16]

Guahayona's action against Anacacuya is not a mere assertion of power

14. Ramón Pané, *Relación acerca de las antigüedades de los Indios* (ca. 1498), ed. José Juan Arrom (Mexico City, 2001), xviii–xxiii.

15. Ibid., 5–6 (see n. 10 for "Caciba"); Granberry and Vescelius, *Languages of the Pre-Columbian Antilles,* 71–72.

16. Pané, *Relación acerca de las antigüedades de los Indios,* ed. Arrom, 7, 10–11. On the unidentified "digo" plant and its resemblance to Andean coca, according to Las Casas, see 39–40n. In the *Popol Wuj,* the K'iche' deity Juraqan (*jun,* one + *raqan,* foot), or "huracán" in Spanish, is part of the creator force Uk'u'x Kay (Heart of Sky). See "Juraqan," in *Multepal Project at the University of Virginia,* Dept. of Spanish, Italian, and Portuguese, http://multepal.spanitalport.virginia.edu/node/11.

over the population. As José Juan Arrom argues in his multidisciplinary study of Taíno linguistics, material cultures, and literary traditions, following anthropologist Sebastián Robiou-Lamarche, the hero is displacing the old order and asserting his role as the new North Star. Guahayona will soon complement his command of navigation and astronomy with dominion over earth and fire, as metals and plants enter the story, suggesting that his power comes from the ability to connect his knowledge of the earth, sea, and sky.[17]

After arriving at the place of herbal gathering, Guahayona forbade the women from his community and Anacacuya's land from returning to their husbands. Instead, he left them on an island where they were the only inhabitants—becoming an island of women, called Matininó (without fathers). He placed their children in a ravine far away. The children soon grew hungry and cried out for their mothers, yelling "toa, toa," (water, water). For this, they were transformed into frogs, called *tona*. In this way, the men were forever separated from the women, and all biological traces of the first generation were erased from the Taíno world. This was the second transformation of the Taíno people.[18]

Whereas the Sun was responsible for the first transformation, rainfall, water, and the arrival of the spring season occasioned the second. As archaeologist José Oliver explains, "Ordinary time, the rhythm of the seasons, is established," and the division of the sexes marks a new social order, "the rule of exogamy."[19]

17. José Juan Arrom, "The Creation Myths of the Taíno," trans. William A. Christian, Jr., in Fatima Bercht et al., eds., *Taíno: Pre-Columbian Art and Culture from the Caribbean* (New York, 1997), 68–79, esp. 76; Sebastián Robiou-Lamarche, "Astronomy in Taíno Mythology," *Archaeoastronomy,* XII (1984), 110–115.

18. Pané, *Relación acerca de las antigüedades de los Indios,* ed. Arrom, 8–9. Many people thought that Matinino was a real place, including modern scholars who equated it with Martinique; see Carl Ortwin Sauer, *The Early Spanish Main* (Berkeley, Calif., 1966), 302. A cédula decreed in Burgos on Dec. 23, 1511, authorized colonists to enslave Caribs from "las islas de San Bernardo e isla Fuerte y en los puertos de Cartagena e islas de Baru y la Dominica y Matiniño y Santa Lucía y San Vicente y la Asensión y la isla de los Barbudos y Tabaco y Mayo, donde estaba una gente que se llaman los caribes." See "R. Provision que los Indios Caribes se Puedan Tomar por esclavos," in Richard Konetzke, ed., *Colección de documentos para la historia de la formación social de Hispanoamérica, 1493–1810,* I (Madrid, 1953), 31–33, doc. 12. However, Indigenous people of Martinique call their island Ioüanacaera (island of iguanas) in Kalinago, bearing no relation to "Matininó"; see Raymond Breton, *Dictionnaire caraïbe-français,* ed. Julius Platzmann (Leipzig, 1892), 78, cited in Pané, *Relación acerca de las antigüedades de los Indios,* ed. Arrom, 5n.

19. José R. Oliver, "Of Feathers, *Çibas,* and *Guanín* Power among Taíno Elites," in Colin McEwan, ed., *Precolumbian Gold: Technology, Style, and Iconography* (London, 2000), 196–219, esp. 209–211. The Kogi people of present-day Colombia also associate women with

The Taíno story does not relay a single act of creation from a world of nothingness *(ex-nihilo)* like the story of Genesis that informed Catholic worldviews. This is a tale about processes of creation that unfold over time and in response to new conditions—a cosmology of balance and becoming. Objects recovered from pre-Columbian communities suggest that gold metals were used as mediating forces between the sacred and the earthly, from one people to another. Archaeologists believe that Taínos affixed gold to spatulas used in ritual purging and added golden items to art and jewelry as "points of articulation between inside-outside," such as the mouth, a site of ingestion (food) and expulsion (speech, vomit). Gold metals allowed access to these "contrasting domains" because they emerged with the creation of the Taíno way of life. Whereas Spaniards celebrated the possibility of perpetual summer in the New World, the Taíno story cautions that, in a world without seasons, there was only social chaos, agricultural confusion, spiritual disorder, and speech without sense.[20]

Guahayona's journey did not end with the second transformation of the Taíno people. He continued westward to the land of Guanín, the Taíno term for copper-gold alloy (see Chapter 1). In the story, gold and women are linked with the east and the lower order; guanín and men are associated with the west, a higher order. This may also suggest why Taínos in Cuba pointed Cristóbal Colón eastward to find the gold that he sought. As we saw in Chapter 1, the admiral took this information literally and sailed southeast in November 1492 toward the place where he was told, through signs *(señas),* that "la gente d'ella coge el oro con candelas de noche en la playa y después con martillo diz que hazían vergas d'ello" (the people of that place gather gold by candlelight at night along the beach, and then it is said that they hammer it into sheets).[21]

On his way toward the land of guanín, Guahayona finds a woman floating in the middle of the ocean; she turns out to be Guabonito, one of the Taína women whom he had left behind when he brought them to Matininó. Here, Pané worried that he had recorded the story out of order, writing, "Creo que

---

frogs. According to the story, the first wife of the Sun was a toad, but she was banished from the community for being unfaithful. Today, frogs are understood as symbolic embodiments of culturally defined dangerous aspects of femininity; see Gerardo Reichel-Dolmatoff, *Goldwork and Shamanism: An Iconographic Study of the Gold Museum of the Banco de La República, Colombia,* trans. Jimmy Weiskopf (Bogotá, 2005), 115–122.

20. Oliver, "Of Feathers, *Çibas,* and *Guanín* Power among Taíno Elites," in McEwan, ed., *Precolumbian Gold,* 204.

21. Colón, *Los cuatro viajes,* ed. Varela, 90. On Oct. 13, 1492, one day after making landfall, Colón was told to sail southeast to find gold: "al Sur y al Sudeste y al Norueste; y qu'estas del Norueste les venían a combatir muchas vezes—, y así ir al Sudueste a buscar el oro, y piedras preçiosas" (62).

pongo primero lo que debiera ser último y lo último primero, pero todo lo que escribo así lo narran ellos, como lo escribo, y así lo pongo como lo he entendido de los del país" (I think I put first what should have gone last and the last first, but everything that I write is how they tell it, as I have written here, and so I put it as I have understood it from the people of this land). But this passage reinforces the connection of women-water (linked with gold and the east) and men-land (associated with copper-gold alloys and the west), two key sites of natural knowledge and cosmological principles of ecological balance and gender complementarity. Pané's reluctance to intervene in the story allows us to have some confidence in reading it for evidence of Taíno cosmology: all colonial works require cautious interpretation, but texts that impose their own order are especially difficult to decipher. As anthropologist Mercedes López Baralt observes, Pané wrote what he heard, as it was told to him and he understood it, without changing the story to cohere with his sense of things.[22]

Immediately upon reuniting with Guabonito, Guahayona looks for somewhere to wash himself, because his skin shows signs of syphillis ("aquellas llagas que nosotros llamamos mal francés"). Some scholars interpret the venereal disease as part of the incest taboo, whereas others suggest that the physical revelation of bumps on the skin "was metaphorically used by the Taíno to express an extraordinary, numinous condition intimately associated with gold," such that Guahayona "wrestled from the divine . . . sacred emblems of chiefly power: *cibas, guanín,* and metallic feathers," translating "the power and knowledge that comes from what is esoteric and remote" into performances of political and social power on earth. In either reading, archaeological evidence reinforces the story's suggestion that guanín, more than gold, emerged in a multisensory assemblage of symbolic objects that caciques wore to display masculine, chiefly power in a matrilineal society.[23]

Guabonito responds to these changes, written on the body, by putting Guahayona into quarantine *(guanara).* After enough time passes, he asks for permission to leave, and she grants it. In his emergence, Guahayona takes a new name, Albeborael Guahayona. Guabonito, whom some scholars read as his sister, gives him objects that signify his new status as cacique: "muchos guanines y muchas cibas" (many guanín metals and *cibas* [stones]) to adorn his ears and arms. The origin of these metals is intimately familiar: Guabonito, Al-

22. Mercedes López-Baralt, *El mito taíno: Levi-Strauss en las Antillas* (Río Piedras, 1985), 37–41; Pané, *Relación acerca de las antigüedades de los Indios,* ed. Arrom, 13.

23. Pané, *Relación acerca de las antigüedades de los Indios,* ed. Arrom, 11; Oliver, "Of Feathers, *Çibas,* and *Guanín* Power among Taíno Elites," in McEwan, ed., *Precolumbian Gold,* 211.

beborael Guahayona, and his father, Hiauna, who does not call his son by the name he took as a cacique but Híaguaili Guanín (son of Hiauna), the name he is known by thereafter. Oliver, who has written extensively on the metallic symbolism of the story, concludes that guanín metals are "the product of a fusion . . . of 'sibling' metals."[24]

When Guahayona violates the incest taboo without punishment from the gods, he defeats the old social order and instantiates a new kind of world. This world has already been changed once in ecological terms, with the development of wet and dry seasons; it was transformed a second time, in social terms, with the separation of women and men. In this third incarnation, environmental and cultural transformations fuse into a world with a new leader, family line, and metallic material. The hero becomes a chief of this society, and his power—both divine favor from the otherworld and political leadership in this realm—is signified through shiny objects that reflect the fruits of human agencies and knowledges that are required to transform matter in diverse ways, such as alloying gold and copper metals and creating pendants from stones and shells.

Archaeologists working in Nariño, Colombia (on the border with present-day Ecuador), have excavated hummingbird-shaped earspools made of gold-copper alloys, suggesting that pre-Columbian metalworking communities created material cultural forms from guanín metals to reinforce their visions of the shiny, resplendent feathers of the hummingbird (called *guaní* in Ciboney Taíno). These objects were designed to be "viewed with awe, smelled pungently, tasted strongly and distinctively, and touched in order to be able to grasp and sense the power and knowledge" of other spiritual realms.[25]

Metallic objects were not just representations of knowledge—they were knowledge itself. Linguistic evidence reinforces the cosmological vision that is told in the story. Guahayona's guanín ear spools are called *taguagua,* which shares the same root as the *tagua-tagua* plant *(Passiflora foetida),* a stinky

24. Pané, *Relación acerca de las antigüedades de los Indios,* ed. Arrom, 12; Oliver, "Of Feathers, *Çibas,* and *Guanín* Power among Taíno Elites," in McEwan, ed., *Precolumbian Gold,* 199, 203, 211, 213–214. In some parts of Cuba, *guanara* is a kind of dove *(paloma)* that lives only in the mountains, whereas, in the Arawakan language of Wayuu, it means "sickness" (11n). Similar stories of life-creating, incestuous relationships are documented by Breton among Kalinagos on Dominica, Walter Roth among Arawaks and Guaraos in mainland South America, and Neils Fock among Waiwai communities of the Amazon. The name Híaguaili remains undeciphered; *híali* means "He-who-has-been-made-brilliant" in Island Karib (13n).

25. Reichel-Dolmatoff, *Goldwork and Shamanism,* 133; Oliver, "Of Feathers, *Çibas,* and *Guanín* Power among Taíno Elites," in McEwan, ed., *Precolumbian Gold,* 211.

FIGURE 9. Pre-Columbian earspool of a hummingbird *(guaní)* made of gold-copper alloy *(guanín)*. Recovered from the Nariño region of Colombia. Museo del Oro, calle 16, no. 5–41, Bogotá, Colombia

flower native to the Caribbean whose yellow-orange fruit becomes red when fully ripe. Another fragrant yellow flower, one that is now used in African diasporic medicine in the Caribbean, bears an equally strong association with guanín metals: the *guanina* flower, formerly classified as *Cassia occidentallis* and now classified as *Senna occidentallis*. In Cuba, guanina is used to treat a variety of aliments—including several that are related to eyesight, such as pain, itchiness, redness, and sensitivity to light. As a healing remedy, the yellow petals are applied to what Oliver called "points of articulation."[26]

The Taíno narrative explains the origin of a people and place in which

26. Oliver, "Of Feathers, *Çibas*, and *Guanín* Power among Taíno Elites," in McEwan, ed., *Precolumbian Gold*, 211; Dalia Quiros-Moran, *Guide to Afro-Cuban Herbalism* (Bloomington, Ind., 2009), 323.

golden metals, animals with shiny feathers, and odorous, medicinal, yellow plants form part of a new world of rainy seasons and gendered domains. These details may, by now, sound familiar: they resemble Pedro López de Mesa's proposal to synchronize the harvesting of gold metals and yellow cañafístola leaves during the rainy season in La Vega in 1525.

Sensing Metals in Europe and the Americas

Even when we account for the long history and continued importance of alchemical thinking and sensory experiences in vernacular scientific traditions of early modern Spain, the ideas articulated in López de Mesa's proposal—and the points of the petition that imperial officials so eagerly responded to—are difficult to trace to European origins. This is not to say that the kinds of sensory data and material transformations that figure so centrally in the story were unknown to Spanish writers or metalworkers, just that they were understood differently.

For one, scent plays different roles in Taíno and Spanish mining systems. According to Andalusian priest and metallurgical writer Álvaro Alonso Barba, who spent the majority of his life in the Andes, most metals "no tienen buen olor, ni buen sabor generalmēte ... por la sulfareidad que a todos acompaña, aunque el oro huele, y sabe bien, por su excelentissimo temperamento, o por lo menos no sabe, ni huele mal" (generally do not have a good scent, nor a good taste ... because of the sulfurity that accompanies them, although gold smells and tastes good, because of its excellent temperament. Or at least it doesn't taste or smell bad). Other authors, such as Bernardo Pérez de Vargas, writing from Madrid, provided an index of metallic scents and tastes: sulfur was "salado" (salty), whereas "hot" metals like gold and copper were "agudo" (sharp) in taste and "hediondos" in smell (penetratingly unpleasant). Barba and Pérez de Vargas use scent as a way of gathering information about metals; for Taínos, metals were knowledge, and animate matter communicated its insights through sensory forms.[27]

Additionally, European concepts of alchemical conversion—informed by a long history of translation from Greco-Roman antiquity and the medieval Middle East and circulated within universities that drew from a shared natural history curriculum, whether taught in Paris or Padua—were different from

27. Alvaro Alonso Barba, *Arte de los metales en que se enseña el verdadero beneficio de los de oro, y plata por açogue....* (Madrid, 1640), 21v; Bernardo Pérez de Vargas, *De re metalica: En el qual se tratan muchos y diversos secretos del conocimiento de toda suerte de minerales, de como se deven buscar ensayar y beneficiar, con otros secretos e industrias notables ...* (Madrid, 1569), 25v.

the ways in which Amerindian communities understood the borders of plant, mineral, animal, and human life. In an undated letter to Protestant reformer Samuel Hartlib, included in Hartlib's *Legacy of Husbandry* (1655), English projector Gabriel Plattes promises to show Hartlib's readers in four parts "how Minerals may be turned into vegetables; the second, how vegetables may be turned into Minerals; the third, how animals may be turned into vegetables back again; the fourth, how those vegetables may be turned into Minerals." Plattes insists that, in this four-part series of transformations, one should not believe that "the whole substance is changed" but only "a share thereof." Even the most alchemically minded European practitioners, such as Hartlib's network of correspondents in the early modern Atlantic world, held different ideas about the transmutability of form than did Indigenous miners and metalworkers in the Caribbean.[28]

As we saw in the creation myth recorded by fray Pané, Taínos trace the origin of their people, way of life, and time itself to the emergence of stunning golden objects, metal-like feathers, and fragrant, yellow plants. This understanding of an interconnected world of animate, sensory-rich animal forms, metals, and plants also shaped Taíno metalworking practices. These practices are thought to have originated in Colombia, where artisans used methods like lost-wax casting, hammering, and embossing to manufacture objects that circulated throughout the Antilles, including artifacts made in the shape of hummingbirds, frogs, and jaguars, as well as elaborate, multi-headed birds and human-animal hybrids formed of intricate geometric features, such as circular, rectangular, and petaloid shapes. Although they used similar animal iconographies and geometric motifs, these communities would have interpreted, in their own, symbolic ways, what archaeologist Warwick Bray calls the "belief-systems encoded in metal objects."[29]

28. Edward Grant, *A History of Natural Philosophy: From the Ancient World to the Nineteenth Century* (Cambridge, 2007); Gabriel Plattes, "Certain Notes, and Observations concerning Setting of Corn, and the Great Benefit Thereof: Together with Several Experiments and Improvements Imparted by Gabriel Plats to Mr. Hartlib," in Samuel Hartlib, ed., *Legacy of Husbandry . . .*, 3d ed. (London, 1655), 184–216, esp. 214; Reichel-Dolmatoff, *Goldwork and Shamanism.* See also William R. Newman, *Atoms and Alchemy: Chymistry and the Experimental Origins of the Scientific Revolution* (Chicago, 2006); Marcos Martinón-Torres, "Some Recent Developments in the Historiography of Alchemy," *Ambix,* LVIII (2011), 215–237.

29. Marcos Martinón-Torres et al., "Metallic Encounters in Cuba: The Technology, Exchange, and Meaning of Metals before and after Columbus," *Journal of Anthropological Archaeology,* XXXI (2012), 439–454, esp. 439, 447–449; Warwick Bray, "Metallurgy and Anthropology: Two Studies from Prehispanic America," *Boletín Museo del Oro,* XLII (1997), 37–55,

According to Spanish colonial reports and ethnographic data from goldworking centers in Colombia, metallurgists used a plant *(hierba)* to create guanín, called *tumbaga* in Colombia. Standing over open flames, after enough time had passed for gold and copper metals to become liquid—no small feat, given their different melting points—metalworkers stirred the botanical element into the molten mixture. Colonial writers were unable to identify the substance; as Oviedo lamented, "Yo he visto la hierba, e indios me la han enseñado; pero nunca pude por halagos ni de otras formas sacar dellos el secreto" (I have seen the herb, and Indians have shown it to me; but I could never extract the secret from them, whether by flattery or other means). Some archaeologists now believe that the plant was *Costus spicatus,* an oxalis-rich plant native to lowland tropical regions in South America. Oxalic acid is the main ingredient in distilling solutions in which metalworkers immersed gold-copper goods before refining them in oxygen-less ovens to separate gold and copper layers of mixed-metallic objects. As these examples of sensory properties, physical conversions, and herbal mixtures suggest, metals and plants played different symbolic and material roles within Amerindian and European goldworking practices.[30]

Tracing Taíno Cosmologies in Printed Translations

There is no perfect correlation between the story that Pané recorded in La Vega in 1498 and the vision of metallic, botanical, and human life that López de Mesa put before imperial officials nearly thirty years later. The complex layers of translation and print history of Pané's text and the nature of oral traditions mean that such equivalence is impossible, especially in a place like La Vega, where crucial demographic and cultural changes transformed mining districts of La Española in the first twenty-odd years of colonial life.

Specifically, we must consider the changing Afro-Indigenous demographics of La Vega between 1498 and 1525, and the ways in which new communities of African, Indigenous, and European storytelling traditions would have come

esp. 37. See also Roberto Valcárcel Rojas et al., "Oro, *guanínes* y latón: Metales en contextos aborígenes de Cuba," *El caribe arqueológico,* X (2007), 116–131.

30. Oviedo, *Historia general y natural delas Indias,* lxvii(v); William C. Root, "Pre-Columbian Metalwork of Colombia and Its Neighbors," in Samuel K. Lothrop et al., eds., *Essays in Pre-Columbian Art and Archaeology* (Cambridge, Mass., 1961), 242–257, 252, cited in Burton L. Gordon, *Chemical Arts and Technologies of Indigenous Americans* (Oxford, 2009), 147. On the relationship between creation narratives and goldwork in the U'wa community of northeastern Colombia, see Ana María Falchetti, "La Ofrenda y la Semilla: Notas sobre el simbolismo del oro entre los Uwa," *Boletín Museo del Oro,* XLIII (1997), 2–37, esp. 7–9. I thank Diana Magaloni for sharing this article with me.

into contact in the mining town. In 1509, some two hundred vecinos lived in La Vega; by the middle of the next decade, there were eighty-two property-holders in the town. Passenger lists suggest that almost none of the vecinos were skilled miners. Between 1492 and 1519, only forty-four mining professionals, including miners, washers, and silversmiths, traveled from Spain to the Americas. In ten of those twenty-eight years, not a single miner made the trip; in ten other years, only one or two crossed the Atlantic. By 1525, twenty vecinos remained in La Vega, a decline of 77 percent in ten years and 90 percent from the end of fray Ovando's governorship. Buenaventura was by now abandoned *(despoblada),* and Spanish residents of Lares de Guahaba and Yáquimo had been relocated to Puerto Real (present-day Cap-Haïtien) and Santa María del Puerto (present-day Arrondissement de Jacmel). As Spanish and Taíno populations declined in mining communities across the island, enslaved African women and men from Elmina arrived at La Española in greater numbers. Almost immediately, gold production increased notably. In 1531, La Española produced 13,995 pesos of gold; two years later, five hundred enslaved African miners generated an astounding 70,000 pesos of the precious metal.[31]

The changing labor dynamics of goldfields and refineries influenced every aspect of life within mining districts—commercial transactions, marriage, children, food, clothing, language, religion—and would surely have influenced the kinds of stories that circulated in La Vega. Attending to the demographic realities of La Vega at the time of López de Mesa's proposal allows us to understand how Taíno ideas—even when mediated by multiple layers of linguistic, written, and cultural translation—might have influenced Spanish visions of goldwork. To conclude this part on gold, I review the print history of Pané's manuscript and new research on Taíno life to suggest why the creation story that Pané recorded, when juxtaposed with evidence from imperial archives, can be used to document Taíno influences in the sixteenth-century gold industry of La Española.

Sometime in the summer of 1498, Pané delivered his manuscript to Cristóbal Colón, who was set to return to Spain. Nothing more was known of the text until excerpts appeared in chapters 120, 166, and 167 of Las Casas's *Apolo-*

31. D'Esposito and Jacobs, "Auge y ocaso de la primera sociedad minera de América," *Nuevo mundo-mundos neuvos* (October 2015), pars. 18, 35; Kulstad-González, "Striking It Rich in the Americas' First Boom Town," in Funari and Senatore, eds., *Archaeology of Culture Contact and Colonialism,* 317; Sauer, *Early Spanish Main,* 67–68, 200; Ida Altman, "Towns and the Forging of the Spanish Caribbean," in Kimberly Lynn and Erin Kathleen Rowe, eds., *The Early Modern Hispanic World: Transnational and Interdisciplinary Approaches* (New York, 2017), 23–44, esp. 24, map 1; Blanco, *Los negros y la esclavitud en Santo Domingo,* 34.

gética historia de las Indias (ca. 1527–1560). The story was recorded in full—and in full justification of Colón's actions—in the *Historia del Almirante don Cristóbal Colón,* composed by Fernando Colón in the late 1530s but published much later. The Taíno creation story first appeared in print in Alfonso Ulloa's Italian-language translation of Fernando Colón's work, *Historie del S.D. Fernando Colombo . . . et dello scoprimento, ch'egli fece dell' Indie occidentali, dette Mondo nuovo, hora possedute dal Sereniss; Re Catolico* (1571). This version remained the only known edition of the Taíno story until the 1970s, when José Juan Arrom back-translated the text into Spanish. Using insights from colonial sources, historical linguistics, and archaeological records, Arrom corrected Italianized words like "conichi," "iobi," and "guica" for the Taíno terms *conucos* (agricultural mounds), jobos (the tree that bears yellow fruit), and *yuca* (cassava roots).[32]

Using Arrom's work as a base text, anthropologists and literary scholars compared the story that Pané recorded with creation narratives from Indigenous communities in Central America, South America, and the Caribbean. In the mid-twentieth century, folklorist Douglas MacRae Taylor conducted oral histories with speakers of Island Karib in Belize and Kwéyòl Donmnik in Dominica. Then he compared them with the origin stories of Kalinagos in Dominica as they had been recorded by Dominican friar Raymond Breton. Accounting for change and continuity over time, as well as deep layers of fragmentation produced by the institution of slavery, Taylor found that almost all of the stories relayed to him by community elders revealed a preoccupation with regulating gender roles and matrilocal family structures that form the core of socioeconomic life in Kalinago communities. "Fragmentary as they are," Taylor concluded, "the stories recorded below bear out this view to a remarkable extent."[33]

Historians have not often searched for evidence of Taíno influences and agencies in the gold industry, and we have largely overlooked storytelling tra-

32. Alfonso Ulloa, *Historie del S.D. Fernando Colombo . . . et dello scoprimento, ch'egli fece dell' Indie occidentali, dette Mondo nuovo, hora possedute dal Sereniss. Re Catolico* (Venice, 1571), 127v, 131, 138v; Pané, *Relación acerca de las antigüedades de los Indios,* ed. Arrom, 6, 16, 34. Arrom explains his methodology in "Estudio preliminar," xx–xxv. See 18n (Bayamanaco / Bassamanaco), 38n (Faraguuaol / Baraguabael), and 44n (Giovanni di Agiada / Juan de Ayala) for examples of how Arrom uses phonetic and morphosyntactic analysis to decipher source terms in Taíno and Spanish.

33. Douglas Taylor, "Tales and Legends of the Dominica Caribs," *Journal of American Folklore,* LXV (1952), 267–279, 268; R. P. Raymond Breton, *Dictionnaire caraibe-français,* ed. Julius Platzmann (1665–1666) (Leipzig, 1892).

ditions as archives of knowledge. World historian David Abulafia characterizes Taíno origin stories as tales that "were not located in past time, but were timeless metaphors." Scholarship has, with good reason, focused on the brutal asymmetries of colonial power and gendered violence that led to Taíno demographic and social collapse under colonial rule. In this historiographic mode, Taínos are, as Abulafia writes, "a vanished people" who held "a rather small" view of an "island world . . . surrounded by the waters, and they did not look beyond it."[34]

However, this older, historiographical assumption overlooks key research from archaeology, anthropology, and literary studies—fields whose methods help us to interpret fragmented colonial archives. By tracing the flows of jadeite and metallic goods, archaeologists like L. Antonio Curet, Mark Hauser, Corinne Lisette Hofman, and Anne van Duijvenbode have shown how migration and exchange with Mesoamerican and South American communities shaped the development of Taíno societies long before 1492. Along similar lines, López Baralt follows oral histories to identify points of correspondence and divergence between the Taíno creation story and those of Indigenous communities in Venezuela, Colombia, and the Guayanas, considered the most likely points of departure for Taíno migrants in the pre-Columbian era. She concludes that Pané's work, however fragmentary, maintains core elements of Taíno mythology and culture.[35]

As these studies indicate, the pre-Columbian Taíno world was never self-contained; it was a continual negotiation of change and continuity. After 1492, and throughout the critical first decades of Spanish colonial rule, as African, Amerindian, and European peoples became "African" rather than "Elmina" or "Ndongo," "Indian" rather than "Maya" or "Mexica," and "European" rather than "Basque" or "Andaluz," Taínos continued to create and preserve forms of social organization, material culture, and storytelling traditions in new demographic and cultural contexts. On a more localized scale, archaeologists like Kathleen Deagan, who uses gender, class, and household-unit analysis as frames to understand Taíno matrilineal social structures in La Española, have

34. David Abulafia, *The Discovery of Mankind: Atlantic Encounters in the Age of Columbus* (New Haven, Conn., 2008), 137–138.

35. L. Antonio Curet and Mark W. Hauser, eds., *Islands at the Crossroads: Migration, Seafaring, and Interaction in the Caribbean* (Tuscaloosa, Ala., 2011); Corinne L. Hofman and Anne van Duijvenbode, *Communities in Contact: Essays in Archaeology, Ethnohistory, and Ethnography of the Amerindian Circum-Caribbean* (Leiden, 2011); López-Baralt, *El mito taíno,* 41. The original Spanish reads, "Una porción de mitología taína, que, aunque fragmentaria, todavía conserva el sentido de totalización de lo fundamental de su cultura."

found greater evidence of cultural continuity, rather than rupture or collapse, within Taíno households after 1492.[36]

Narrative reframing was surely one of these responses, although, with only six full sentences remaining of the Taíno language, it is hard to use written sources to prove how stories circulated within mining communities. However, by locating elements of Taíno worldviews in colonial documents, we can see how Indigenous ideas of mining temporalities and the relationship of plant, mineral, and human life could have influenced Spanish proposals to reshape the goldworks of La Vega. What is more, recall that imperial officials acted upon this proposal after only one day's review at council. The language of colonial reports and the materiality of manuscript records suggest that Spanish-speaking officials incorporated elements of Taíno origin stories and cosmologies into the new colonial order. In so doing, Indigenous miners articulated ideas that were legally enacted in Spain's oversees empire.[37]

Compared with European accounts of the time, there are few documentary accounts of Taíno peoples' experiences of Spanish colonialism, as told in their own words. Colonial archives are fragmented, asymmetrical, and incomplete. But new research has deepened our understanding of these crucial first years of conquest and colonization. In place of a historiography of extinction and collapse, scholars across the disciplines now analyze Afro-Taíno and Spanish accommodations of a new kind of world.

By taking continuity, rather than collapse, as our departure, we can see how and when Taíno visions of gold, time, and the cosmos contributed to the design of the gold industry in La Vega. When we read stories like the one Pané recorded alongside archival documents, and when we do so while attending to layers of literary translation and the mediating influences of print culture, we gain new access to Taíno worldviews and a new understanding of how Taíno metalwork and metallic cosmologies informed colonial approaches to mining and metallurgy.

Taken together, the three chapters that comprise "Gold" used methods drawn from history, linguistics, literary studies, and visual analysis to identify the influences of Amerindian, African, and Afro-descendant miners, includ-

36. For a historiography of Taíno collapse, see Kathleen Deagan, "Reconsidering Taíno Social Dynamics after Spanish Conquest: Gender and Class in Culture Contact Studies," *American Antiquity,* LXIX (2004), 597–626, esp. 601–603.

37. Granberry and Vescelius, *Languages of the Pre-Columbian Antilles,* 97; "Real cédula a los oidores de la Audiencia de La Española . . . ," Toledo, Oct. 13, 1525, AGI, Indiferente, 420, legajo 10, fols. 120–120v; "Real cédula al veedor de las fundiciones de la Isla Española y justicia de la ciudad de la Concepción . . . ," Toledo, Oct. 13, 1525, ibid., fol. 118v.

ing Afro-Indigenous people, in the gold industry of the extended Caribbean region during the early sixteenth century. Put simply, colonial mining methods in the Americas had Indigenous and African roots. Gold refineries in La Española bore the imprint of Taíno architecture, whereas smelting operations in Panama were designed to withstand attacks from Afro-Panameños. Chapters 1 and 3 documented the linguistic footprints and cosmological beliefs of subaltern miners as recorded in archival documents, manuscripts, printed books, and origin stories that moved between the spoken, written, and printed word. Chapter 2 provided evidence of Taíno and Afro-Taíno influences in mining towns, variously called *villas, reducciones,* and *mineros,* and then emphasized the erasure of African and Indigenous mining women from printed images. In small mining communities like La Vega, where Taínos outnumbered colonists, Indigenous worldviews shifted the seasons of gold refining, aligning Taíno visions of cosmological unity and cultural continuity with Spanish imperial gold production. When viewed in the light explored in these chapters, using linguistics, visual analysis, and literary studies, the gold metals that crossed the Atlantic and gave rise to Spain's Siglo de Oro look quite different than the historiography suggests. The story of colonial gold cannot be imparted without centering the ideas and histories of Indigenous and African miners—even, and especially, when our sources silence their contributions.

Iron

4 : IRON, INDIOS, AND IBERIAN SCIENCE IN DIALOGUE

Of the four major metals that circulated within the interconnected economies of the Old World—gold, silver, copper, and iron—only iron was not used as money, whether the coins, bars, and bullion of global commerce (gold and silver) or the many forms that enabled local transactions (copper). Because Spanish ironworks were among the most celebrated of early modern Europe, Iberian imperial agents did not need to travel to Africa or the Indies to gain access to raw materials or knowledgeable experts. Instead, European smiths often visited Spain to learn from Iberian practitioners; one late-seventeenth-century Swedish book on iron mining devoted nearly 13 percent of its text (twelve of ninety-six folios) to an analysis of Spanish technologies in the northern regions of Catalonia and Vizcaya.[1]

Iberian literatures about iron thus look quite different from narrative treatments of gold, copper, and silver. Although the mining and refining of iron ores in the Americas played virtually no role in the sixteenth or seventeenth centuries, the idea of iron in the Indies—that imaginative geography that connected Asia and the Americas—influenced Spanish and Portuguese thinking about colonization and colonial life. The two chapters in this part analyze iron metals as they were understood by dominant imperial voices and the authors who answered them. By interpreting the range of social and scientific meanings that writers in Europe, Asia, and the Americas layered into their descriptions of iron objects and minerals, these chapters show how networks of informants, authors, translators, and printers shaped early modern understandings of Amerindian and South Asian communities.

Most of the chapters in this book combine methods from literature, linguistics, and history, including the visual analysis of art history, to unearth the contributions of under-studied agents in the history of mining and metallurgy in the early Americas. This part provides an important balance to the chapters on gold, copper, and silver, both by extending the plane of analysis to imperial ideologies about the Indies and by providing texture to the idea of Europe that is presented throughout the book. My focus on Indigenous and African knowl-

1. Gunner Pipping, ed., *Iron and Steel on the European Market in the 17th Century: A Contemporary Swedish Account of Production Forms and Marketing* (Stockholm, 1982), fols. 12–15, 22–29.

edges can imply that these ways of knowing stand in opposition to European knowledge systems. "Europe," as we know, is as much of a contested, internally ridden category as are the terms "Indigenous" and "African." As literary scholar Walter Mignolo reminds us, there are many kinds of Europes. The Europe of early modern Atlantic empires is not the same as the "colonial Europe" of Ireland and southern Italy. Nor is "Portugal" equivalent to "Spain," even though they are often collapsed into a single category of "Iberian." The differences within Iberian scientific writing, especially the reception histories of Portuguese- and Spanish-language dialogues about the East and West Indies, provide critical context for this book's discussion of Iberian literatures and its focus on the Americas.[2]

Medical Dialogues and the Nature of Iberian Empires

Unlike their pursuit of gold, Portuguese and Spanish writers were interested in colonial iron as *materia medica,* the plants, herbs, minerals, and stones that healers used to prepare medicines. In emphasizing iron as a site of healing rather than a source of military might, late-sixteenth-century writers used the production and communication of natural knowledge in the East and West Indies to challenge imperial voices that had dominated the first half of the century, including Cristóbal Colón, Hernán Cortés, and the men who retold their conquests, such as Cortés's secretary, Francisco López de Gómara. These writers staged their interventions on "Indian" materia medica in a particular literary form: the dialogue, studied here in the works of Sephardic physician García d'Orta, who wrote from the Portuguese colony of Goa about Iberian and South Asian healing practices, and Dr. Nicolás Monardes, who wrote from Seville about New World materials and Old World methods. Both authors had studied similar medical programs in Spain; d'Orta attended university in Salamanca and Alcalá de Henares, where Monardes also took his degree in medicine.[3]

Although d'Orta's dialogue treats a variety of plants and stones where Monardes focuses exclusively on iron, the difference would not have seemed

2. Walter D. Mignolo, *The Darker Side of Western Modernity: Global Futures, Decolonial Options* (Durham, N.C., 2011), 110. On critical discussions of Iberian science, see, for instance, José Ramón Marcaida, "Afterword: #IberianScience," *Early Science and Medicine,* XXI (2016), 273–276.

3. Juan Pimentel and Isabel Soler, "Painting Naked Truth: The *Colóquios* of Garcia da Orta (1563)," *Journal of Early Modern History,* XVII (2014), 101–120; C. R. Boxer, *Two Pioneers of Tropical Medicine: Garcia d'Orta and Nicolás Monardes* (London, 1963); Francisco Guerra, "Nicolás Bautista Monardes: Su vida y su obra, ca. 1493–1588," in Modesto Bargalló, ed., *Diálogo del hierro y de sus grandezas* (Mexico City, 1961).

so great at the time. Deep patterns of alchemical thinking and experiential practice in the vernacular sciences—which included mining, metallurgy, and medicine—compelled early moderns to perceive plants, stones, and metals as part of a richly symbolic web in which artisan labor unlocked the mysterious forces of animate bodies, linking things like "vermilion, the color red, blood, mercury, gold, and lizards." Such modes of thinking influenced definitions of the mineral realm, which included all "naturally occurring, nonliving, solid objects on the globe (and in some systems, fluids)," as well as scientific approaches to the topic. Early modern mineralogy encompassed most "of what is now geology—crystallography, mineralogy, petrology, and paleontology—as well as interpenetrating much of the domain of chemistry." When mineralogy split into three branches in the eighteenth century, these fields became discrete areas of study that "closely approximate the scope of modern geology: oryctognosy (the identification and classification of minerals), mineral geography (the distribution of rocks and minerals), and geognosy (the formation and history of rocks and minerals)." The sixteenth-century line between matter and spirit, and plant and mineral, was not what is today—or even what it was in the 1700s.[4]

Such lines were even less clear in dialogues that blended past and present, fact and fiction, and Christian and non-Christian knowledges from the early modern Atlantic and Pacific worlds. These combinations of knowledge systems were inherent in the literary conventions of the Renaissance dialogue as it was formed in antiquity and refashioned over time. The printed, manuscript, and visual sources studied in Part 1 provided testimony of metalworking practices, spaces, and tools that joined Indigenous, African, and Iberian ways of knowing, although there is nothing innately hybrid about those texts or genres. These chapters build from that work to show how d'Orta and Monardes voiced arguments about medical knowledge and imperial structures within a genre whose conventions foregrounded issues of hybrid epistemologies and scientific communications.

D'Orta's *Colóquios dos simples e drogas e cousas medicinais da India* (1563) features two main interlocutors: Orta, a Portuguese physician stationed in Goa, and Ruano, a visiting Spanish medic. In Orta's salon and its adjacent garden ("horta"), and in the homes of patients, Orta and Ruano dialogue with di-

4. Pamela H. Smith, "Vermilion, Mercury, Blood, and Lizards: Matter and Meaning in Metalworking," in Ursula Klein and E. C. Sparry, eds., *Materials and Expertise in Early Modern Europe: Between Market and Laboratory* (Chicago, 2010), 29–49, esp. 33, 47 (alchemical thinking); Rachel Laudan, *From Mineralogy to Geology: The Foundations of a Science, 1650–1830* (Chicago, 1987), 21.

verse community members, including Malupa, an Indian physician ("fisico de Guoa"), who praises Orta's knowledge of Christian, Islamic, and Jewish medicine; *licenciado* Dimas Bosque, a physician whose prefatory letter praises the author's language ("na lingoa purtuguesa"), genre ("a modo de dialogo"), and truthful ways ("puras verdades cõ puro estillo") of treating topics not often covered in medical works; Orta's servant Antonia, who acts as a physician's assistant in the colloquy on hemp; Paula de Andrade, a wealthy *mestiça* who is poisoned with datura herb *(Datura stramonium)* by a female servant ("negra da casa") who robs her; and André Milanês, a stonesmith who appears in the colloquy on ivory to entertain rather than instruct ("não faz para fisica se não para pasatempo"). The domestic setting, which includes plentiful meals prepared with local fruits, vegetables, and herbs, allows Orta to display his hospitality, command of servants, and knowledge of local ingredients. He does so over the course of fifty-three colloquies and a list of errata that is longer than some of the chapters. The cost of printing this list suggests that d'Orta was commited to correcting the information he presented in his book. As the interlocutors converse in Orta's home, which, in real life, was located on the Rua dos Namorados in the center of the city, the dialogue shows how medicine both crosses and reinforces social, ethnic, and racial lines in Goa and how the genre intermixes dramatic interludes and gossipy asides with serious transmissions of scientific and medical knowledge.[5]

There is less dramatic staging in Monardes's *Diálogo del hierro, y de sus grandezas* (1574) because the interlocutors take refuge indoors to escape the midday sun of Seville. (Somehow, it is not as hot in Goa.) Like the speakers in d'Orta's dialogue, which literary scholar Ralph Bauer identifies as "Monardes's immediate inspiration," the interlocutors are drawn from real life, and they interweave conversational pleasantries into their discussions of iron as a remedy for melancholy, infertility, and the founding of New World colonies. The primary speaker, called Doctor, is a physician from Seville; his interlocu-

5. [García d'Orta], *Colóquios dos simples e drogas e cousas medicinais da India: Reprodução facsimilada da edição impressa em Goa em 10 de abril de 1563; comemorando o quarto centenário da edição original . . .* (1563) (Lisbon, 1963), 88, 207, 217v–224v (Bosque), 23–25v (Antonia), 81–83 (Andrade); Hugh Glenn Cagle, "The Botany of Colonial Medicine: Gender, Authority, and Natural History in the Empires of Spain and Portugal," in Sarah E. Owens and Jane E. Mangan, eds., *Women of the Iberian Atlantic* (Baton Rouge, La., 2012), 174–195, esp. 183; Teresa Nobre de Carvalho, "A Behind-the-Scenes Glimpse into the Princeps Edition of *Colóquios dos Simples* (Goa, 1563)," *Early Science and Medicine,* XXI (2016), 232–251; Palmira Fontes da Costa, "Geographical Expansion and the Reconfiguration of Medical Authority: Garcia de Orta's Colloquies on the Simples and Drugs of India (1563)," *Studies in History and Philosophy of Science,* XLIII (2012), 74–81, esp. 76.

tors are visitors from the iron-rich regions of northern Spain. The two-day discussion explores the efficacy of iron medicines in intimate ways (inside the womb, in the blood) and on larger levels of the body public, wherein iron metals are used in battle, to bind the enslaved, and as they "defienden la justicia, conservan las republicas" (defend justice and conserve republics), including "ciudades, y los campos y desiertos" (cities, towns, and the wilderness). Monardes's interlocutors contrast iron's sociomedical values and public virtues with those of other metals, especially gold. According to Pliny, one of his many cited authorities, "Con el Hierro y no con el Oro se defiende la patria . . . por el Hierro es tenida y acatada la justicia, y mediante el se castigan los malos y se conservan los buenos" (with iron and not with gold the homeland is defended . . . with iron all is held in justice, and through it wrongs are punished and good acts are conserved).[6]

As we saw in the first part of this book, the possibility of uncovering large stores of gold, understood as a synonym for wealth, motivated the first Spanish imperial extractions in the Americas. Against that hegemonic hallucination, Monardes's imagined interlocutors insist that the world and its powerful empires have it wrong. While humans flock to fantasies of gold, celebrating holders of precious metals for their riches and justifying this praise with scientific classifications about the purity and *limpieza* of gold ("el metal mas puro y limpio de todos"), classical philosophers like Socrates warned that gold and silver are of no use to wise men. Monardes's speakers thus tout the virtues of iron for a life well lived—artisan labor to create materials for daily life, commercial trades for goods and services free from greed, and medical healing that keeps the human body well balanced.[7]

In their quasi-imagined dialogic personas, d'Orta and Monardes use medical goods like iron metals, healing stones, and plants to voice real questions about scientific knowledge, communication, and the nature of early modern Iberian empires. They did so precisely at a time when Asians and Amerindians of different ethnicities were defined in some of the same terms: "indio," for one, was a "homogenizing label that constituted difference based on unequal power relations" and was central to the strategies of "colonial governance,"

6. [Nicolás] Monardes, *Diálogo del hierro, y de sus grandezas, y como es el más excelente metal de todos, y la cosa más necesaria para servicio del hombre, y de las grandes virtudes medicinales que tiene* (Seville, 1574), 175–184, esp. 165, 179v; Ralph Bauer, "The Blood of the Dragon: Alchemy and Natural History in Nicolás Monardes's *Historia Medicinal,*" in John Slater, Maríaluz López-Terrada, and José Pardo-Tomás, eds., *Medical Cultures of the Early Modern Spanish Empire* (Burlington, Vt., 2014), 67–88, esp. 84.

7. Monardes, *Diálogo del hierro, y de sus grandezas,* 159v–161v.

including "comparative knowledge of slavery, labor extraction, and belonging," as historian Nancy E. van Deusen argues. In this way, early modern Spaniards collapsed diverse populations in Central and South America into a single label, then conflated that label with equally diverse East Asian peoples. The erasure of important within-group differences in the Americas, and the discursive merging of Amerindian and Asian communities, is one of the many ways in which colonial vocabularies reinforce Spanish imperial policies and practices.[8]

To understand how d'Orta and Monardes intervene in Renaissance debates about knowledge production within Iberian imperial frameworks, we must first know something about the writers they respond to. I begin that work by analyzing colonial reports that bemoan the lack of iron mining and refining in the Americas, which the authors interpreted as a proxy for Amerindian intellectual and social simplicity. To canonical imperial writers, iron signified superior weaponry, technology, and civilization; iron metals were visible data that allowed insight into non-European histories and cultures. D'Orta and Monardes interpret plants, stones, and metals as evidentiary nodes, but they reach different conclusions about observable data in science and medicine. The literary space of the dialogue allows them to challenge dominant visions of knowledge and conquest and to safely distance themselves from the ideas that they present. The second part of the chapter analyzes the generic conventions of the Renaissance dialogue as it emerged as a key site for reconciling different kinds of knowledges. This literary history suggests why the genre appealed to writers like d'Orta, Monardes, and physician Georgius Agricola, "the 'father of mineralogy'" and author of a Latin-language dialogue on scientific transmissions.[9]

This chapter thus establishes the context for the next, a study of how d'Orta's and Monardes's dialogues were shaped by generic and linguistic translation: d'Orta's dialogue was recast as a natural history, whereas Monardes's work circulated in its original form. These different receptions produced divergent interpretations of Lusophone and Hispanophone treatments of iron metals, scientific communications, and medical knowledge. D'Orta's incorporation of Indian and South Asian knowledges was translated out of the literary record; Monardes's engagement with New World materia medica remained intact. Tracing the erasure of Indian epistemes from d'Orta's *Colóquios dos simples* while

8. Nancy E. van Deusen, *Global Indios: The Indigenous Struggle for Justice in Sixteenth-Century Spain* (Durham, N.C., 2015), 11.

9. George Rapp, *Archaeomineralogy* (Berlin, 2009), 12.

comparing it with the reception history of Monardes's *Diálogo del hierro* allows us to document how subaltern ways of knowing from diverse colonial contexts informed imperial scientific writing. It also puts pressure on the category of "Iberian scientific writing" by revealing how the dominant imperial languages of Iberian scientific communications—Portuguese and Spanish—influenced modes of literary translation, genre, and circulation in different ways.

Forging Conquests: Iron Metals and the Reading of Civilization

Iron metals and minerals are native to the Americas, and they were fashioned into a variety of wares in the pre-Columbian era. However, because Indigenous communities did not use iron in the same ways that Europeans knew and expected—namely, in ferrous metallurgy to produce weapons—many colonial writers concluded that Native people had no knowledge of iron. Well through the twentieth century, mining historians agreed with these assessments, citing reports from fray Pedro Simón in Nueva Granada and José de Acosta in Peru to confirm the absence of iron metallurgy. Geography played an important role in shaping these early reports. The richest iron deposits in the Americas are found in sites that Europeans did not immediately explore, such as northern and northwestern Mexico (the present-day states of Nuevo León, Coahuila, and Durango, known in the colonial era as Nueva Vizcaya), the western Andes (Valle Ingenio in Peru and Antofogasta in Chile), and northern Brazil (home to the world's largest iron mine, Carajás, in the state of Pará).[10]

But records from Mesoamerica, a region that early writers did know, confirm the presence of iron in pre-Columbian communities and its diverse uses. Iron communicated spiritual principles and cultural beliefs, not in ferrous

10. Modesto Bargalló, *La minería y la metalurgía en la América española durante la época colonial: Con un apéndice sobre la industria del hierro en México desde la iniciación de la Independencia hasta el presente* (Mexico City, 1955), 36; Scott E. Simmons and Aaron N. Shugar, *Archaeometallurgy in Mesoamerica: Current Approaches and New Perspectives* (Boulder, Colo., 2013), 4; Ezequiel Ordoñez, "Iron Resources of the Republic of Mexico," *Engineering and Mining Journal,* XC (1910), 665–667; John M. Guilbert and Charles F. Park, Jr., *The Geology of Ore Deposits* (New York, 1986), 563–565; Kevin J. Vaughn et al., "Minería de hematita en la costa sur del Perú: Investigaciones arqueológicas en Mina Primavera," *Chungara,* XLV (2013), 131–142; Arthur A. Bookstrom, "The Magnetite Deposits of El Romeral, Chile," *Economic Geology,* LXXII (1977), 1101–1130; Zara Gerhardt Lindenmayer, Jorge Henrique Laux, and João Batista Guimarães Teixeira, "Considerações sobre a origem das formações ferríferas da formação Carajás, Serra dos Carajás," *Revista brasileira de geociências,* XXXI (2001), 21–28; Elizabeth Dore, "Environment and Society: Long-Term Trends in Latin American Mining," *Environment and History,* VI (2000), 1–29, esp. 18–20.

metallurgy, but in artisan traditions, like painting and mirror making. Anthropologist Davide Domenici's team performed research on Mayan and Mexica codices using noninvasive chemical analysis, revealing important differences in the meaning-shaping materials that artists used to paint-write codices. In the Mayan region, artist-authors used hematite (Fe_2O_3), an oxidized iron mineral, to represent materials like blood, stones, and rain in deep-red tones. In this way, the material source of the red color reinforces the symbolic cosmological relationship between earth and sky. In Yukatek, the word for red is *chak,* closely related to the name of the rain deity, Chaak. In contrast, painter-writers in the central Mexican valley, including Mixtecs and Mexicas, used red pigments that were derived from flowers or cochineal *(Dactylopius coccus).* They represent speech acts with flower petals, reinforcing a culturally specific connection between matter, color, and language that distinguishes the material conditions and symbolic registers of plant-derived painted works in central Mexico and mineral pigments used in the Mayan region. Among Nahua-speaking communities, red is linguistically and symbolically associated with wisdom. The linguistic practice of *difrasismo* yokes two terms to convey metaphorical concepts like "wisdom," which is formed by the Nahuatl terms *in tlilli* (black ink) and *in tlapalli* (red ink). Pre-Columbian writer-painters working in different linguistic and cultural traditions harnessed technologies of pigment production from plants and minerals to convey locally specific associations and concepts—even that of knowledge itself.[11]

Material cultural analysis of mirrorwork provides additional insight into the artistic use of iron metals in pre-Columbian Mesoamerica. From Nahua, Otomí, and Tolteca cities in Teotithuacán, Zacatecas, and central Mexico to Mayan communities of central Guatemala, northeast Honduras, and eastern and southern Costa Rica, iron pyrites were used as jewelry that conveyed political and social status and mirrors that revealed connections to ancestral spirits. A sixth-century mirror from Teotihuacán shows how Tolteca artisans polished the surface of a single sheet of iron pyrite to set in relief mythological figures like Jaguar Gods, Maize Deities, and emblems of the afterlife. Religious leaders hung iron-ore mirrors from their necks and wore them upon

11. D. Buti et al., "Non-Invasive Investigation of a Pre-Hispanic Maya Screenfold Book: The Madrid Codex," *Journal of Archaeological Science,* XLII (2014), 166–178; Davide Domenici et al., "La cochinilla en la pintura de códices prehispánicos y coloniales," in Miguel Ángel Fernández Félix, ed., *Rojo mexicano: La grana cochinilla en el arte* (Mexico City, 2017), 88–99. See also "Chak" and "camino rojo" in *Multepal: A Thematic Resource Collection of the Popol Wuj,* available at http://multepal.spanitalport.virginia.edu/node/16 and http://multepal.spanitalport.virginia.edu/node/736.

FIGURE 10. "Mirror with Mythic Jaguar." Teotihuacán, 500–600 CE. Iron pyrite, jade, shell, magnetite or ilmenite, and spondylus shell. 19.1 cm. The Art Institute of Chicago / Art Resource, NY. Accession number ART538291

their backs as divinatory mechanisms to perceive what could not be seen by human eyes (Figure 10).[12]

In extending the plane of human understanding, these mirrors were thought to reconcile oppositional energies. Iconographic representations in codices, sculptures, and stonework associate mirrors with fire (because of

12. Achim Lelgemann, "Pre-Hispanic Iron-Ore Mirrors and Mosaics from Zacatecas," in Emiliano Gallaga M. and Marc G. Blainey, eds., *Manufactured Light: Mirrors in the Mesoamerican Realm* (Boulder, Colo., 2016), 161–178; Carrie L. Dennett and Marc G. Blainey, "Reflecting on Exchange: Ancient Maya Mirrors beyond the Southeast Periphery," ibid., 229–254; Karl A. Taube, "The Iconography of Mirrors at Teotihuacan," in Janet Catherine Berlo, ed., *Art, Ideology, and the City of Teotihuacan* (Washington, D.C., 1992), 169–204 (Tolteca mirror). The Art Institute of Chicago holds a variety of pyrite objects from pre-Columbian Mesoamerica, including Mixtec discs (ca. 1400–1500) that overlay shell and turquoise on iron pyrite bases and Mexica masks (ca. 1350–1521) and pectorals (ca. 1350–1521) that use iron pyrites to convey physical eyes and symbolic visions of creator deities. Some artifacts are available at "Arts of the Americas," Art Institue of Chicago, http://www.artic.edu/aic/collections/amerindian.

their ability to reflect light) and water (because their smooth surfaces resemble standing pools). Several objects from Teotihuacán link pyrite mirrors with the iconography of netted disks and spider webs to other woven goods, perhaps indicating gender complementarity with textiles that were woven by women and shieldlike mirrors that were used by men. As anthropologist Nicholas Saunders argues, iron-ore mirrors "were not the vanity mirrors of European tradition, but magical scrying mirrors wielded to give access to and power over the supernatural realm." As far south as the Andes, shiny, reflective objects worked by human hands, including those fashioned from pyrites and shells, converted "ephemeral sensations and esoteric knowledge" into "an artifactual trace in the archaeological record." Throughout the hemisphere, Indigenous artisans worked with iron ores and pyrites in ways that reflected local ways of knowing, realizing the power of material goods to convey ideas, beliefs, and wisdom that connected human existence with otherworldly knowledge.[13]

A few technological and labor dynamics may explain why iron mirrors became such high-status objects in Mesoamerica. A team of experimental archaeologists led by Emiliano Gallaga scanned a pyrite mirror with an electron microscope to determine how artisans would have made the object. The team recreated the mirror using only lithic tools and pre-Columbian materials: basalt metate, river stones, stone hammers, sand, water, and quartz. They estimate that artisans would have spent 800–1,200 hours to produce one plain mirror. Adorning mirrors with obsidian, shells, copper, gold, and turquoise required additional time, suggesting why iron-ore mirrors were originally limited to elite politicans and spiritual leaders. However, by the time of the Spanish conquest, pyrite mirrors appeared in central Mexican markets, suggesting that they had lost their elite status and had become part of popular habits of consumption in some regions of Mesoamerica. These findings belie the arguments of sixteenth-century writers about the absence of iron. Indigenous Mesoamericans used iron metals and minerals to create culturally, economically, and spiritually meaningful goods and objects. What Indigenous communities did not do was use iron in the same ways as Europeans, which would explain Spanish chroniclers' conclusions.[14]

When colonial writers did not see traces of iron weapons, men like Colón fashioned the absence of the metal into evidence of a New World of paradise.

13. Nicholas J. Saunders, "Shimmering Worlds: Brilliance, Power, and Gold in Pre-Columbian Panama," in Saunders, John W. Hoopes, and Thomas Gilcrease, eds., *To Capture the Sun: Gold of Ancient Panama* (Tulsa, Okla., 2011), 79–113, esp. 81, 92.

14. Gallaga M., "Introduction," "How to Make a Pyrite Mirror: An Experimental Archaeology Project," in Gallaga M. and Blainey, eds., *Manufactured Light,* 17–18, 28–31.

In this way, iron—like skin color—became a visible fact upon which early moderns founded their conclusions about the ethos of conquest and the colonization of knowledge. In our own time, books like Jared Diamond's popular account, *Guns, Germs, and Steel: The Fates of Human Societies,* and folkloric compilations for young readers, such as *Jade and Iron: Latin American Tales from Two Cultures,* suggest that iron metals continue to be read as signs of cultural development and markers of human difference.[15]

In his letter to royal scribe Luis de Santángel, Colón narrates the teeming, untapped wealth of the New World with polysyndetic trains of nouns: islands brim with "canpiñas grandíssimas, e ay miel i de muchas maneras de aves y frutas muy diversas. En las tierras ay muchas minas de metales y ay gente *instimabile numero"* (the greatest champaigns, and there is honey and so many kinds of birds and diverse fruits. In these lands there are many mines of metals and people beyond measure). In contrast to the accumulative logic with which he represents the land ("and . . . and . . . and"), Colón describes people in terms of lack: they cannot be qualified ("instimabile numero"), do not wear clothing, and "no tienen fierro ni azero ni armas, ni son para ello," because "sus azagayas son unas varas sin fierro" (they do not have iron nor steel nor weapons, nor are they given to such things; their lances are thin sticks without iron). Golden objects that adorned Indigenous bodies emblematized the possibilities of colonial wealth; iron metals suggested advanced metallurgical technologies, sophisticated civilization, and high levels of social organization. Colón interpreted the absence of iron tools as evidence of primitive underdevelopment and an easy route to conquest.[16]

Throughout his diary, Colón analyzes other ostensibly observable data, especially skin color, to make sense of a place for which he has no reference, despite his study of "pinturas de mapamundos" *(mapamundi)* beforehand. One day after noting the lack of iron in the Caribbean, Colón remarks on the

15. Jared Diamond, *Guns, Germs, and Steel: The Fates of Human Societies* (1997; rpt. New York, 2005); Patricia Aldana, ed., *Jade and Iron: Latin American Tales from Two Cultures,* trans. Hugh Hazelton (Toronto, 1996).

16. Consuelo Varela and Juan Gil, eds., *Cristóbal Colón: Textos y documentos completos; Nuevas cartas,* 2d ed. (Madrid, 1992), 60 (Oct. 11, 1492), 221–222 (Santángel). By the mid-1520s, officials in Santo Domingo affirmed that "en essa Isla ay mineros y venas de hyerro en mucha cantidad" (in this island there are mines and veins of iron in great amount). In a letter of Nov. 9, 1526, Carlos V (1500–1558) turned the colonial discourse of wonder against local officials and criticized them for not investigating the mines, writing, "Estoy maravillado de vos otros no lo aver fecho" (I am amazed that you have not done it). See "Respuesta a los oidores y oficiales de Santo Domingo," Nov. 9, 1526, Archivo General de Indias (hereafter cited as AGI), Indiferente, 421, legajo 11, 300–303, esp. 300.

skin color of Native Americans, finding them "ninguno prieto, salvo color de los canarios" (not black, but rather the color of Canary Islanders). He justifies his conclusion with latitudinal logic: "ni se deve esperar otra cosa, pues está Lestegüeste con la isla del Fierro en Canaria, so una línea" (nor should one expect any other thing, for this island lies on an East-West line with the Island of Iron in the Canaries). Two weeks later, he modified his claim, reporting that the people were "de muy buen acatamiento ni muy negro[s] salvo menos que Canarias" (of very good reverence and not very black, but less than Canary Islanders). Within two months, he pronounced that Indigenous caribeños were "cuasi tan blancos como en España, porqu'esta tierra es harto fría y la mejor que lengua pueda dezir" (almost as white as the people of Spain, because this land is extremely cold and the best that a human tongue can express). By his third voyage, Colón developed his own vocabulary to convey color. Although he first described the people of Trinidad in terms of negation ("No eran tan baços como otros, antes más blancos que otros que oviese visto en estas Indias"), he concluded that the appropriate designation was "de color india" (Indian-hued). Mid- and late-sixteenth-century writers, including López de Gómara, d'Orta, and Monardes, readily interpreted the use of iron metals as a proxy for the state of cultural and human development in a particular and particularly non-European region, and often did so with color vocabularies that echoed the language of Iberian ideas about purity and *limpieza de sangre;* Colón's words, on the other hand, suggest that the ideological connection between iron metals and degrees of blackness already held great purchase by the late fifteenth century.[17]

These passages on iron metals and skin color are bookended by emphatic insistence that they contain Colón's own words: "Dize aquí el Almirante," "dize él," "Estas son sus palabras" "Todas son palabras del Almirante," "Todo esto dize el Almirante" (Here the admiral says . . . he says . . . These are his words . . . All these are the words of the admiral). As literary scholar Margarita Zamora shows, such phrases underscore the mediated nature of the text and the role of Colón's editor, Bartolomé de Las Casas, in undercutting the admiral's reading of material facts as evidence of civilization or barbarity. He often does so by structuring sentences around the word "although" *(aunque).* For example, on December 26, 1492, following the Christmas celebration, Colón reported that people used bows and arrows "sin hierro" (without iron) and that they

17. Cristóbal Colón, *Los cuatro viajes: Testamento,* ed. Consuelo Varela (1986; rpt. Madrid, 2011), 61 (Oct. 13, 1492), 77 (Oct. 24), 89 (Nov. 6), 127 (Dec. 16), 255 (1498–1500). On latitudinal thinking, see Nicolás Wey Gómez, *The Tropics of Empire: Why Columbus Sailed South to the Indies* (Cambridge, Mass., 2008), 293–333.

offered no memory of metals other than gold and copper—"aunque cobre no avía visto sino poco el Almirante" (although the admiral had seen only a little copper). On January 15, 1493, Colón reaffirmed that "no tenían hierro ni otro metal que se oviese visto, aunque en pocos días no se puede saber de una tierra mucho, así por la dificultad de la lengua, que no entendía el Almirante sino por discreçión, como porque ellos no saben lo qu'él pretendía" (they did not have iron, nor had they seen any other metal, although it is difficult to know much about a land in just a few days, both because of the difficulty of the language, which the admiral did not understand, and because of the discretion that they showed, because they did not know what he aimed to do). Here, Las Casas engages in what literary scholar Stephen Greenblatt calls "dialogical disavowal," named in part because writers of Renaissance dialogues, including d'Orta and Monardes, so often employed the tactic. By throwing into relief Colón's limited, third-person perspective, Las Casas repeats the admiral's conclusions and distances himself from them, marking a critical separation between his role as an editor and his participation in the narrative justification of conquest and colonization of the Indies.[18]

Both Colón and Hernán Cortés equated Spanish supremacy with the command of iron weapons, used against people who lacked iron. Cortés detailed, in his longest missive from Mexico, how he defeated the armies of Mexica sovereign Moctezuma with day-long attacks by "a half dozen fireshots, five or six arquebuses, forty crossbows, and thirteen calvary." Iron weapons were central to the torture and dismemberment of prisoners in Cempoala (designed to "show them who we were") and to Cortés's forming strategic alliances with Mexica rivals, especially soldiers from Tlaxcala, Cholula, and Huachinango.[19]

Whereas Las Casas sowed doubt into Colón's reports, López de Gómara gave narrative coherence to these early assessments about iron. López de Gómara bundled Colón's words with Cortés's exploits, retelling the conquest of Taíno and Mexica communities at a notable historiographic and geographic distance. By combining the rhetorical techniques of accumulation and reported speech, López de Gómara relayed that the Catholic kings hung on

18. Margarita Zamora, *Reading Columbus* (Berkeley, Calif., 1993); Colón, *Los cuatro viajes,* ed. Varela, 149, 171; Stephen Greenblatt, *The Swerve: How the World Became Modern* (New York, 2012), 222.

19. Hernán Cortés, "Segunda carta-relación de Hernán Cortés, al Emperador Carlos V, Segura de la Frontera, 30 de octubre de 1520," in Manuel Alcalá, ed., *Cartas de relación,* 24th ed. (Mexico City, 2013), 37–121, esp. 38, 45, 47, 110. Cortés begins the letter by lamenting the loss of his original account of the events of the conquest, and asking the crown to forgive his omission of key facts—establishing the reconstructed and purposeful nature of his missive.

Colón's every word, "maravillãdose de oyr que los Indios no teniã vestidos, ni letras ni moneda, ni hierro, ni trigo, ni vino, ni animal ninguno, mayor que perro" (marveling to hear that the Indians did not have clothing, nor letters, nor currency, nor iron, nor wheat, nor wine, nor any animal larger than a dog). López de Gómara similarly defined Amerindian bodies through negation: "q̄ ni fuessen blancos, ni negros, ni loros, sino como tiriciados o membrillos cochos" (and they were not white, nor black, nor brown *[loros],* but rather like yellowed ones or cooked quinces).[20]

The term *loro,* as it shifted from a color classification into a marker of enslavement in the early modern era, deserves special attention. Its meaning as a color signifier of brownness stems from the Latin horticultural term *laurus* (laurel), so named in Spanish, according to the Real Academia Española, because of its dark-colored leaves and fruit. Modern historians translate the term as "laurel" or "green-brown" to convey colonial officials' descriptions of enslaved peoples. Multilingual lexicographers like Antonio de Nebrija, working in Spanish and Latin, and fray Pedro de Alcalá, working in Spanish and Arabic, defined *loro* as "entre blanco e negro" (between black and white) and "que tira a negro" (which turns toward black), and they offered different translations for the two definitions: *fuscus* (fuscous, or of a dark hue) and *luridus* (sallow, or yellow-brown), in Latin, and *ḳamrĭ* and *borgŏċi* in Arabic, also transcribed as *khamrī* (wine-colored, or خمري) and *burghuthī* (flea-infested, or برغثي). "Flea-infested" seems unrelated to the color terms of colonial writers, but medieval authorities listed *burghuthī* as a synomyn of *ṭuḥla* (ash-hued, or طحلة), following a metaphorical tradition that extended the medical meaning of *ṭuḥla* into symbolic realms of color. Linguist Ivan Sivkov identifies this as "the color of the spleen *(lawn aṭ-ṭiḥāl)* or the color between that of dust and whiteness, with a little blackness *(lawn bayna-1-ġubra wa-l-bayāḍ bi-sawād qalīl),* like the color of ashes *(lawn ar-ramād)* or a color between that of dust and blackness, with a little whiteness *(lawn bayna-1-ġubra wa-s-sawād bi-bayāḍ qalīl)* and its derivatives." Late-sixteenth-century lexicographers like Richard Percivale preserved Nebrija's and Alcalá's translations of *loro* as burgundy / wine-colored and yellow-brown, equating it with color signifiers like the Latin *fuscus* and the English "dun" (dingy brown, gray-brown).[21]

20. Francisco López de Gómara, *Primera y segunda parte de la Historia general de las Indias: Con todo el descubrimiento y cosas notables que han acaecido donde que se ganaron ata el año de 1551* (Zaragoza, 1553), xxii, 21v–22.

21. *Diccionario de la lengua española,* 23d ed., s.v. "loro," https://dle.rae.es; van Deusen, *Global Indios,* 9, 171; Elio Antonio de Nebrija, *Vocabulario español-latino* (Salamanca, [1495?]), 123; Pedro de Alcalá, *Vocabulista arávigo en letra castellana: En arte para ligera-*

By the seventeenth century, the word meant much more. As Córdoba-born physician Francisco del Rosal explained, *loro* shifted from a category of Roman slave to a mixed-race person:

> *Loro* llamaban al esclavo, que agora decimos *Mulato,* no bien negro, del Latino *Lora,* que es agua a pie, o vino segundo, que tiene este color, al qual decía el Latino *Luridum,* y nosotros *Clarete.* Ultra de esto llamó el Romano *Lorarios* a los esclavos antiguos y mas honrados porque castigaban a los demás, de *Loro,* que es la correa o azote. De aquí, pues, llamando al esclavo Loro, decimos *Loro* al Papagayo, como quando dicen, *¿Cómo estas, Loro?* como cautivo, que a los demás Animalejos habladores llamaron por el nombre de Mozos ò criados, como Urracas, Catalnillas, Perico Rey, Martín, Marta, y otros. B. Marquesota.
>
> *Loro* is what they used to call slaves, for which we now say *Mulato,* not full black. Derived from the Latin *Lora,* which means dirty water or old wine, because it has this color, for which they once said *Luridum* in Latin, and *Clarete* in Spanish. Beyond this, the Romans called the slaves of antiquity *Lorarios,* and they were the most honored because they punished the others, who were called *Loro,* which means belt or whip. From there, that is, in calling the slave Loro, we say *Loro* for parrot, as when someone says, What's up, Loro, to prisoners, just as we say that the other talking animals are lackeys or servants, such as the magpie, Peruvian parrot, yellow-headed Amazon, bronze-winged parrot, Santa Marta parakeet, and others. S(ee) Marquesota

Here, the term *marquesota,* a collar or "señal que se echaba al cuello al esclavo" (sign thrust upon the neck of the slave), derived from *marca* (seal / stamp), acts metonymically. Spanish speakers transferred the chains worn by the enslaved into a term that denoted enslaved status. Rosal added, "Y de allí quedó llamar a los perrillos *Marqués* y *Marquesilla,* dandoles nombre de esclavos ò criados, como se dice en la palabra Loro. De donde, convirtiendo a los esclavos llamaron *Perros,* como se nota en el Alfabeto 3º" (And thus it resulted that little dogs were called *Marquis* and *Little Marquesa,* and these names were given to slaves or servants, as is said under the entry for Loro. From there, it was converted to slaves who were called *dogs,* as is noted in the third alpha-

---

mente saber la lengua aráviga (Granada, 1505), 321; *Oxford English Dictionary,* s.v. "fuscous," "sallow"; Ivan Sivkov, "Etymology of Arabic Terms Denoting Internal Body Parts," *Romano-arabica,* XVI (2016), 269–279, esp. 273; Richard Percivale, *Bibliothecae Hispanicae Pars Altera: Containing a Dictionarie in Spanish, English, and Latine* (London, 1591), 117. I thank Nasser Meerkhan and Andrea Pauw for helping me with the Arabic translations.

bet). English lexicographer John Minsheu traced a more straightforward path, defining *marquesota* as "ore of lead," after the iron-leaden ores used to make chains.[22]

According to the RAE, the term *roro,* used in the Caribbean to mean "parrot," provided the linguistic and conceptual link from the classification of enslaved peoples in antiquity to colonial chains and captive talking birds. In this way, the Latin and Caribbean roots of the word—the one grounded in horticultural taxonomy, the other in animal vocabularies—converged to produce a critical term of racial and ethnic classification in the Spanish empire: *loro,* the skin color that observers ascribed to Indians in the Americas and South Asia.[23]

As López de Gómara worked through a range of color terms before settling on his food-inspired classification of Indigenous bodies, "tiriciados o membrillos cochos," he also relayed natural historical information on La Española, including the material cultures (clothing, houses, metals) and customs of the country (devil worship, female doctors). He concluded the section with what its people lacked: letters, ways of measuring, and currency, "aunque avia mucho oro, plata, y otros metales" (even though there was a lot of gold, silver, and other metals). Having thus distinguished between natural wealth (metals) and cultural deficiency (coinage), the list ended definitively: "ni conocian el hierro" (nor do they know of iron). Unlike Colón or Cortés, López de Gómara did not read iron metals as evidence of civilization; for him, material cultures evidenced the newness of the Americas, as understood through Spanish eyes: "Todas sus cosas son tan diferentes delas nuestras quanto la tierra es nueva para nosotros" (Everything of theirs is so different than ours that the land is en-

22. Francisco del Rosal, "Origen y etymología de todos los vocablos originales de la Lengua Castellana . . . ," 1611, 396 ("loro"), 416 ("marquesota"), MS 6929, Biblioteca Nacional de España; John Minsheu, *Hēgemōn Eis Tas Glōssas Id Est, Ductor in Linguas: The Guide into Tongues . . . with Their Agreement and Consent One with Another, as Also Their Etymologies, That Is, the Reasons and Derivations of All or the Most Part of Wordes, in These Eleven Languages . . .* (London, 1617), s.v. "marquesota." The term *catalnilla* appears in book 8, chap. 21 of El Inca Garcilaso de La Vega's *Primera parte de los Comentarios reales* (Lisbon, 1609), 219, but I have not found modern vernacular names. See Manuel Alvar Ezquerra, *Vocabulario de indigenismos en las crónicas de Indias* (Madrid, 1997), 95.

23. *Diccionario de la lengua española,* s.v. "loro." Taíno and Arawak dictionaries list *hiwaka* and *korlijaka* for "parrot." See Julian Granberry and Gary S. Vescelius, *Languages of the Pre-Columbian Antilles* (Tuscaloosa, Ala., 2004), 119; "The Story of the Founder of the Medicine-Art," in Claudius Henricus de Goeje, *The Arawak Language of Guiana* (Munich, 2011), 296, story no. 212, lines 92–100. In the uncanny genealogy of colonial misunderstanding, Taínos gave parrots *(papagayos)* to Colón and his men because they seemed so interested in the birds. See Colón, *Los cuatro viajes,* ed. Varela, 123 (Dec. 13, 1492).

tirely new to us). For the next fifty years, this newness inspired Christian thinkers to question whether Native Americans were human beings in the same way—and with the same degrees of humanity—as the people of Asia, Africa, and Europe formed the nations of the world.[24]

In the concluding chapters of his 225-chapter volume, López de Gómara synthesized his thoughts regarding skin color and liberty in the Indies, the customs of Canary Islanders, and the greatness of Spaniards. As he acknowledged that all of humankind descends from Adam and Eve, the chronicler celebrated God's providence in creating diversity, "casi por grados, porque ay hombres blancos de muchas maneras de blancura: y bermejos de muchas maneras de bermejura: y negros de muchas maneras de negrura: y de blanco va a bermejo por descolorido, y ruuio: y a negro por ceniçoso, moreno, loro, y leonado, como nuestros Indios" (almost by degree, because there are many different manners of whiteness among white men; and different rednesses among red men; and different blacknesses among black men: and a white man tilts toward red when stained and blonde; and he tilts toward black when ashy, brown *[loro]*, dun, and leopardine, like our Indians). Even along the shared latitudes of the torrid zone, people are "blancos en Sevilla, negros enel cabo de Buena esperança, y castaños en el rio de la Plata, estando en yguales grados de la Equinocial" (white in Seville, black in the Cape of Good Hope, and brown in River Plata, being in equal degrees from the equatorial line).[25]

This color variation violates the assumptions of latitudinal logic, as Colón had cited it, which supposed that all inhabitants of the tropics—whether in Africa, Asia, or any part of the world—shared a similar degree of blackness, "y no lo sean los q̄ biven de baxo la mesma Zona en Mexico, Yucatán, Quauhtemallan . . . y otras tierras del Peru, que tocan enla misma Equinocial" (but this is not true of those who live under the same zone in Mexico, Yucatán, Guatemala . . . and other regions of Peru, located along the same equatorial line). Skin color signals difference, but not suitability for enslavement, which is instead figured by cultural practices like sodomy, idolatry, and cannibalism. As he justified the subordination of people in two Atlantic world regions, López de Gómara reported that, on the island "El Hierro" (Iron), canarios, much like

24. López de Gómara, *Primera y segunda parte de la Historia general de las Indias,* 36. Compare with José de Acosta's marshaling of biblical silences into evidence of shared human ancestry in *Historia natural y moral de las Indias, en que se tratan las cosas notables del cielo, y elementos, metales, plantas, y animales dellas: Y los ritos, y ceremonias, leyes, y govierno, y guerras de los Indios* (Seville, 1608), 56–72, esp. 61.

25. López de Gómara, *Primera y segunda parte de la Historia general de las Indias,* 277–277v.

Caribs, practiced polygamy, worshipped idols, and lacked iron ("No tenian hierro, que tambien era gran falta"). On the same page, he repeated the point a final time—"careciesen de fuego, hierro, letras, y bestias de carga" (they lack fire, iron, letters, and beasts of burden)—to show that material records provided historical testimony: these absences proved that no Christian had touched the land until the Spaniards arrived. Colón observed matters firsthand and drew conclusions about customs; López de Gómara practiced a kind of armchair archaeology in which he read reports on material cultures and organized them into broader arguments about what is new (America), what is old (Canary Islands), and what they share in common. In repackaging Colón's early reports into stylized accounts with narrative cohesion, López de Gómara became part of a group of writers who marshalled what they believed to be observable social factors, especially skin color and the use of metals, into evidence that justified conquest and domination.[26]

What Colón, Cortés, and López de Gómara worked through in these early letters was an ideological formation that preoccupied the Spanish empire and its legal theorists, economic apologists, and religious officials throughout the colonial period. Some historians, such as James H. Sweet, argue that this is the moment in which skin color became a determinative marker of enslaved status and that these early comparisons of caribeños to canarios tapped into a long Iberian tradition in which "those who were naturally suited for slavery were individuals who were 'the color of Canarians.'" Other scholars, such as Mignolo, argue that Colón's hierarchies were racist, in the fifteenth-century Iberian sense of the term, which prioritized religious difference over physical features and devaluated the humanity and knowledges of those marked as "other," in whichever shapeshifting terms were used to mark difference at a particular moment. For such scholars, slavery was not yet, and not only, tied to skin color.[27]

26. Ibid., 277v–278, 286v. López de Gómara also writes, "Es mucho de maravillar, que estando tan cerca de Africa, fuesen de diferentes costumbres, traje, color, y religion, que los de aquella tierra: no se si en lengua, porque Gomera, Telde, y otros vocablos assi, ay en el reyno de Fez, y de Benamarin" (It is a great wonder that being so close to Africa, the customs, dress, color, and religion here are so different from that land: and I do not know about the language, because Gomera, Telde, and other similar words exist in the kingdom of Fez, and that of Benamarin) (286v).

27. James H. Sweet, "The Iberian Roots of American Racist Thought," *William and Mary Quarterly,* 3d Ser., LIV (1997), 143–166, esp. 165–166; Walter Mignolo, "Hermenéutica de la democracia: El pensamiento de los límites y la diferencia colonial," *Tabula Rasa,* IX (2008), 39–60, esp. 44; Mignolo, *Local Histories/Global Designs: Coloniality, Subaltern Knowledges, and Border Thinking* (Princeton, N.J., 2012), 13–15.

The texts considered here suggest that sixteenth-century conquistadores, and the writers who brought narrative order to their words, considered skin color as one of a number of visible facts that evidenced intangible truths about a place and its people. Whether or not color was an absolute marker of humanity, it, like iron objects and metallurgical technologies, was evaluated with a determined degree of materiality.[28]

In Dialogue with the Chroniclers: García d'Orta and Nicolás Monardes

Some authors disagreed with Colón and López de Gómara about the nature of observable data and the place of iron metals within imperial history. García d'Orta, writing from his clinic in the colony of Goa, presented South Asian interpretations that linked iron—not gold—to the seat of paradise. Iron metals in the Spice Islands evidenced deep Christian histories that predated Portuguese imperial intrusion. Monardes, whose dialogue began outside of the Casa de la Contratación, the Spanish seat of institutionalized scientific inquiry and knowledge production about the Americas and the Asia-Pacific region, rejected the idea that metals could be known or categorized based on their external forms. He argued for metallic monogenesis, or the belief that all metals derived from a single origin, and he insisted that whatever visible difference existed between iron, "negro y feo" (black and ugly), and gold, "puro y limpio" (pure and clean), was of little matter to scientists and physicians.[29]

Whereas the lack of iron in the West Indies led Colón to read the land as paradise, Orta's South Indian collaborators, as voiced by Ruano and Orta in the *Colóquios dos simples,* believed the opposite: the presence of iron, rather than gold, was evidence of a promised land. The interlocutors represent different Iberian empires and different approaches to medical and scientific knowledge. Ruano is a book-wise Spanish doctor and a somewhat clueless speaker who asks more questions than he answers and argues generally in favor of ancient Greek and Roman authorities. Some scholars believe that Ruano represents Orta's alter ego, whereas others see him as an "everyman" character

28. For an excellent overview of the ideological underpinnings of enslavement in the New World, including the relationship between the Canary Islands and the Caribbean, see Herbert S. Klein and Ben Vinson III, *African Slavery in Latin America and the Caribbean,* 2d ed. (New York, 2007).

29. Monardes, *Diálogo del hierro, y de sus grandezas,* 161v, 162v; and see Antonio Barrera-Osorio, *Experiencing Nature: The Spanish American Empire and the Early Scientific Revolution* (Austin, Tex., 2006). On the relationship between the Casa de la Contratación and Portugal's Armazéns da Guiné e Índia, see Henrique Leitão and Antonio Sánchez, "Zilsel's Thesis, Maritime Culture, and Iberian Science in Early Modern Europe," *Journal of the History of Ideas,* LXXVIII (2017), 191–210, esp. 202–203.

("Ruano" / "Fulano," or What's His Name). Orta is a wise Portuguese physician who has traveled extensively through South Asia and spent enough time in Spanish medical schools to know that "não ousaria de dizer cousa algũa cõtra Galeno, e cõtra os Gregos" (one does not dare to say anything against Galen or the Greeks). His horticultural name ("horta") clearly takes after the author, d'Orta, and his impressive colonial garden.[30]

The *Colóquios dos simples* is organized alphabetically ("pello a b c"), using Portuguese vernacular names for South Asian materia medica, such that the interlocutors review aloe in the second colloquy and proceed to ambergris in the third. This unorthodox organization of spoken words may be one of d'Orta's many techniques to appeal to readers in Portugal and the colonies. As historian Hugh Cagle argues, alphabetic organization by Portuguese common names allowed merchants, medical practitioners, and members of the court to find information easily. It also enabled d'Orta to make language a central aspect of scientific debates, as the interlocutors deliberate whether something ought to be called "canela" ("cinnamon spice" / *Cinnamomum zeylanicum*), "cassia lignia" ("Chinese cinnamon" / *Cinnamomum cassia*), or "cinamomo" ("true cinnamon tree" / *Cinnamomum verum*). This structure occasions playful moments of self-referentiality and meta-analysis in the spirit of humanist scholar Desiderius Erasmus, who dedicated an entire dialogue to "The Usefulness of *Colloquies*" ("De utilitate Colloquiorum"). Nearing the end of their discussion of lacre (29th colloquy), Ruano notes that iron-derived minerals and plant-based resins are both called "samge de drago" (dragon's blood); Orta reminds him, "Jà reprovei isso" (I already set that in its place). Here, Orta refers to their earlier debate, where he dismissed Avicenna's idea that dragon's blood could replace lacre as an intervention to stop hemorrhage ("he mezinha estitica"). Orta breaks the fourth wall with an overt reference to the audience's reading of the dialogue, reminding his readers of the constructed, highly mediated nature of his discussion on nomenclature. (Monardes makes the same move, as I discuss in Chapter 5.) With moments like these, the *Colóquios dos simples* intersperses discussions of weighty scientific matters involving the naming of iron minerals and plant-based medicines in different historical moments and imperial contexts with a winking nod to its early modern readers.[31]

30. Monardes, *Diálogo del hierro, y de sus grandezas,* 130v; Pimentel and Soler, "Painting Naked Truth," *Journal of Early Modern History,* XVII (2014), 109; Clements R. Markham, trans. and ed., *Colloquies on the Simples and Drugs of India by Garcia da Orta* (1913; rpt. Delhi, 1979), xiin.

31. [D'Orta], *Colóquios dos simples,* iv–2, 124v, 126; Hugh Cagle, "Cultures of Inquiry, Myths of Empire: Natural History in Colonial Goa," in Palmira Fontes da Costa, ed., *Medi-*

In the final lines of the colóquio, Ruano listens attentively as Orta reports what Indians tell him of Ceylon, the land of "os negros" (the blacks). This vision of a promised land differs substantially from the fantasies that Portuguese colonists projected onto tropical regions: "Tē linho, e ferro, e entre os negros qua dizē os indios ser ho parayso terreal" (There is flax and iron in the land of the blacks [the people of Ceylon], which the Indians say makes it the earthly paradise). This idea was reinforced by Edenic footprints imprinted upon the landscape: "e fabulam que hūa serra que ahi a muyto alta (que chamã ho pico dadam) e dizē q̄ esta ally apegada dadam, e outras fabullas muyto mayores que por tais volas conto" (and they fabulate that there is a mountain there, very tall, which they call the Peak of Adam, where there are Adam's footprints, and they say other fables even greater than these, which I tell because that's how they are). Instead of reinforcing Colón's version of an American Eden with islands, gold, and eternal bloom, Orta links black iron metals and fibrous linseed with earthly paradise and Adamic ancestry.[32]

This vision of Ceylon departs from those articulated by other scientific writers, such as Ptolemy, Pomponius Mela, and early modern authors who reinterpreted ancient cartographies. In one sixteenth-century compilation of a printed edition of Mela's *Libri de situ orbis* (1518) and manuscript maps based on Ptolemy's *Geographia,* now held at the Newberry Library, a reader marked the center of "Tabrobana Insula" (modern-day Sri Lanka) as an important source of botanical and mineral wealth (Figure 11). The reader, presumably the same person who annotated the first part of the book, copied Ptolemy's affirmation that "nascit apud hos oriza, mel, zingiber, beryllus hyacinthus, et universorum metallorū genera, auri et argēti et aliorum" (there grow rice, honey, ginger, beryl, amethyst, and all kinds of metals are generated, gold and silver

cine, Trade, and Empire: Garcia de Orta's "Colloquies on the Simples and Drugs of India" (1563) in Context (Burlington, Vt., 2015), 107–128, esp. 113–116.

32. [D'Orta], *Colóquios dos simples,* 64. When Ruano asks why Orta does not speak of "os negros" mentioned by Avicenna, he replies, "Os negros nã osha ahi nē sã outros se nã os indios, e porq̄ sã mais negros q̄ todos" (There are no blacks here, for they are no other than the Indians, but are called as such because they are darker than the rest) (148v). Las Casas amended Colón's version of Eden to align with the topographies of Genesis 2:10–14 (KJV). According to the Dominican friar, paradise contains a river that waters the garden, forks into the four cardinal points, and leads to land rich in gold, fine resins, and precious stones. See Bartolomé de Las Casas, *Obras completas,* ed. Paulino Castañeda Delgado, IV, *Historia de las Indias* (Madrid, 1994), 1078–1106. I thank Nicolás Wey Gómez for pointing me to this passage. In this chapter and the following, I use "Ceylon" to refer to colonial-era descriptions of the present-day island of Sri Lanka; I use the modern name when referring to the island more generally.

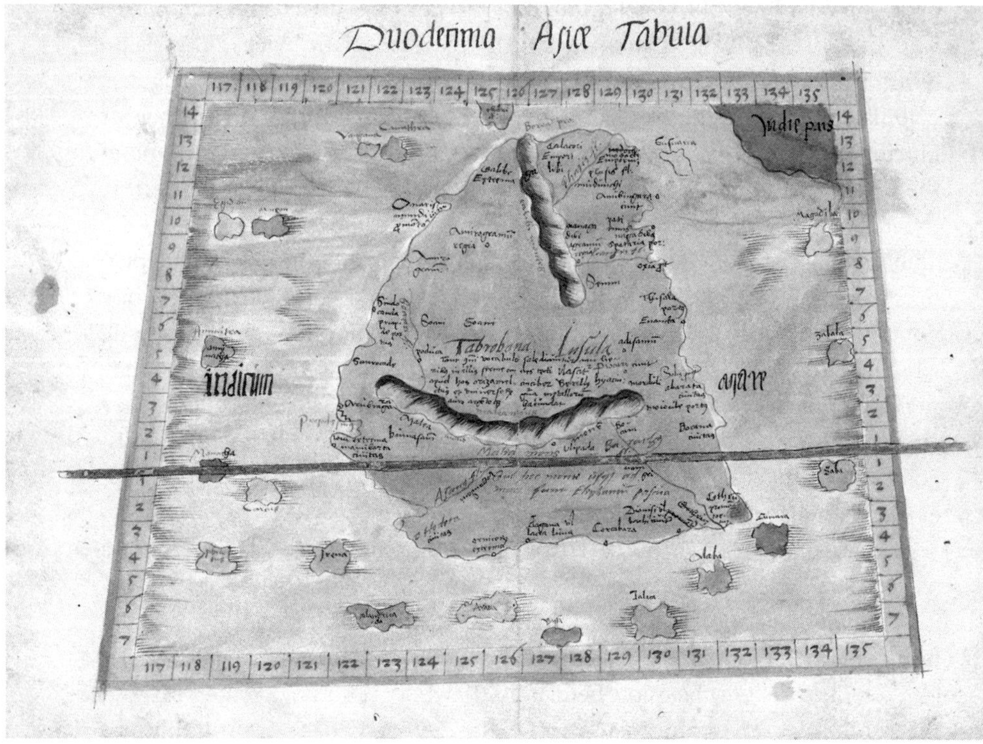

FIGURE 11. Early-sixteenth-century manuscript map of Ceylon (Sri Lanka), "Duodecima Asiae Tabula," based on Ptolemy's *Geographia.* The Newberry Library, Chicago, Ayer Collection, #6.P9 M5 1518

and others). The comment appears firmly in the center of the island, just above a stunning equatorial line painted in gold leaf. Unlike d'Orta's text, which foregrounds Indian and South Asian beliefs about iron and paradise, this painted map gives pride of place to imperial European fantasies of gold in the tropics.[33]

Orta's vision also puts him at odds with Iberian imperial authors like Spanish jurist Alonso de Zuazo and the premier poet of the Portuguese empire, Luis de Camões. Zuazo conceded the site of earthly paradise to Asia and argued

33. Manuscript maps derived from an early-sixteenth-century edition of Ptolemy's *Geographia,* ca. 1518, Ayer Collection, Vault 6.P9 M5 1518, Newberry Library, Chicago. The legend appears in the twelfth map of Asia ("Duodecima Asiae Tabula"), following Claudio Ptolomeo's *Geographiae universalis, vetus et nova complectens* (Basel, 1545), 136. The map is reproduced, with annotations in a different hand, as "Duodecima et ultima asye Tabula" in Edward Luther Stevenson, ed. and trans., *Claudius Ptolemy: The Geography* (1932; rpt. New York, 1991), n.p. The description appears on 158–159.

for America's worth in medicinal virtues, citing goods like brazilwood, guayacan, canafistula, and unnamed fruits. Camões, whose ode to dom Francisco Coutinho, conde do Redondo and viceroy of India, prefaced the *Colóquios dos simples,* echoes Orta in repeating Ceylonese claims to Adamic origins: "Os naturaes o tem por cousa santa, / Pela pedra, onde está a pegada humana" (The natives hold it as a sacred fact, / That the stone is where mankind first tracked). However, book X of Camões's *Os Lusíadas* goes on to survey colonial possibilities from the Pacific to the Antarctic, whereas d'Orta's colloquy comes to a definitive end, giving narrative weight to South Asian spiritual beliefs.[34]

D'Orta's refashioning of iron-flaxen paradise occured at a key moment in Iberian ideas of the Indian Ocean world. These visions were shaped by new knowledges learned in the colonies and fanciful, untried imaginings. Since the twelfth century, medieval rulers had been captivated by the legend of Prester John, a Christian priest who presided over the marvelous riches of the East. By the thirteenth century, Prester John had become a political office, rather than a single person, that governed the lives of Christian converts in East and Central Asia, the Middle East, and North Africa. By the fourteenth century, the legend moved to Ethiopia, where, in the fifteenth century, Portuguese imperial expansion helped to solidify its imagined place as a haven for Christian refugees from Islam.[35]

Early modern Portuguese sailors stretched this haven into Atlantic geographies by arguing, with competing classical and medieval sources, that the Senegal River was a tributary of the Río de Oro, a branch of the Nile River, which flowed through Prester John's kingdom. After fifty years of trading for

34. Alonso de Zuazo, "Primera carta del licenciado Zuazo a Su Majestad, sobre la necesidad del buen gobierno de las Indias, para conservarlas," *Cartas y memorias (1511–1539)* (Mexico City, 2000), 56–80, esp. 63–64, 68–69. The quotation begins by citing Adam's exit from the "Campo de Amanciena," next to his native city of Hebron. I cannot find a reference for this place in other sources, although in Franciscan friar Juan Peñalver's reading of Isaiah 17, "Damascena" appears as a toponym for "gran parte de la Syria"; see Peñalver, *Historia cronológica del pueblo de Dios desde Adan hasta Jesu-Christo: Y descripción de la tierra que habitó el mismo* (Alcalá, 1793), 287. For Camões, see his *Os Lusíadas* (1572), livro X, canto CXXXVI, quoted in [García da Orta], *Colóquios dos simples e drogas da Índia: Reprodução em fac-símile da edição de 1891 dirigida e anotada pelo Conde de Ficalho,* 2 vols. (Lisbon, 1987), I, 233. D'Orta is believed to have traveled with Governor Martim Afonso de Sousa to Ceylon at least twice, in 1537 and 1538.

35. Keagan Brewer, *Prester John: The Legend and Its Sources* (Burlington, Vt., 2015), 1–4, 213–227. For an insightful analysis of the spatial dynamics of the legend and its Habsburg imperial circulations, see Carina L. Johnson, *Cultural Hierarchy in Sixteenth-Century Europe: The Ottomans and Mexicans* (New York, 2011), 145–154.

gold, ivory, and enslaved peoples, Portuguese writers revised their beliefs about the region's good health and great wealth. By the sixteenth century, as Cagle shows, the land "beyond the Senegal" was seen as a place of "debilitating illness and death." In the midst of this imperial reimagining of biblical paradise on Earth, and while addressing the metal that was perhaps most deeply associated with violence of conquest, d'Orta's dialogue voiced Indian visions of a black-green utopia whose iron-flaxen contours clashed starkly with European imaginations of the tropics. Without comment or correction, the *Colóquios dos simples* placed South Asian assessments of tropical matter and material cultures in conversation with changing Portuguese ideas of paradise, medicine, and climate.[36]

Monardes, too, writes back against traditional imperial readings of metals. His target is, not the fantasy of a golden paradise, but rather the science of metals. The interlocutors of his *Diálogo del hierro*—the Doctor, a *sevillano* physician, and Burgos and Ortuño, two subjects from iron-rich Basque country—represent three scientific ways of knowing. The Doctor speaks for traditional, humanist medical knowledge. Burgos stands in for the practice of medicine among the Spanish public. He traveled from his apothecary shop to marvel at wealth from the Indies held in the Casa de la Contratación, the source of Spain's imperial power ("por do tienen el imperio y mando en el mundo"). He is probably based on one of Monardes's correspondents, Bernardino de Burgos, "varon docto y experto en su arte" (learned man and expert in his craft), who provided samples of sulfur ("sulfuro vivo") and a sweet-smelling wood from Puerto Rico ("palo aromatico") for Monardes's *Historia natural.*[37]

In the *Diálogo del hierro,* Burgos and the Doctor retire to the comfortable home of Burgos's fellow Basque, Ortuño, an expert blacksmith whose walls are adorned with iron, "el verdadero Oro y Plata, sin el qual no podriamos bivir, ni los hombres podrian exercitar sus artes y officios" (the true gold and silver, without which we could not live, nor could man exercise his arts and offices). The physical staging complements Monardes's careful act of naming: Ortuño is "an ancient Basque noble lineage whose name derives etymologically from the Latin roots fortuna (fortune) and hortus (garden), thus evoking the idea of empirical knowledge and the manipulation of nature by art and linking his art

36. Hugh Cagle, "Beyond the Senegal: Inventing the Tropics in the Late Middle Ages," *Journal of Medieval Iberian Studies,* VII (2015), 197–217, esp. 200–202.

37. Monardes, *Diálogo del hierro, y de sus grandezas,* 158–159; Acosta, *Historia natural y moral de las Indias,* 37v–39. See also Josep Lluís Barona and Xavier Gómez Font, eds., *La correspondencia de Carolus Clusius con los científicos españoles* (Valencia, 1998), 128.

in alchemy to Monardes's own of botany or exotic horticulture." Erasmus's *De rebus ac vocabulis* (Things and Names, 1527) reminded dialogists of the difference between being something and being called it. In naming his interlocutor Ortuño (fortune / garden), an echo of Orta (garden), Monardes nods to García d'Orta and to intersecting vernacular scientific knowledges.[38]

When Burgos insists that iron and gold are fundamentally different, the Doctor launches into a five-page monologue on metallic monogenesis. In his thorough review of the literature, the Doctor brings into dialogue a variety of scholarly voices. He begins with the great alchemical thinkers of medieval Iberia and the Middle East—such as Ibn Sīnā / Avicenna, Abu Mūsā Jābir ibn Hayyān / Gerber, Raymundo Lullio / Raimundus, Arnaldo de Villanova / Arnaldus de Villa Nova—courses through church fathers like Saint Augustine of Hippo, and concludes with diverse traditions of antiquity, including pre-Socratics (Anaxagoras, Democritus), classical Greek writers (Aristotle, Plato, Democritus), Roman imperial historians (Pliny), and collective authorial identities, like "the Astrologists" and Hermes Trismegistus, author of the *Corpus Hermeticum.* With this presentation of various scientific voices, language communities, ethnic groups, religious affiliations, and knowledge-generating traditions, the Doctor lays out the dominant view of minerogenesis and gives voice to scholarly disputes. In this way, his speech shows points of overlap and disagreement among the alchemical thinkers whose traditions form the heart of early modern medical understandings of iron.[39]

The dominant alchemical consensus, borne out in the works of writers like Gerber and Paracelsus, is that all metals are created from a single origin. The Doctor phrases the mercury-sulfur thesis in familial terms, with "el Açufre como padre, y el Azoge como madre" (Sulfur as the father, and Mercury as the mother). As the father's heat crystalizes the mother ("se fermēta yquaja el Azogue"), her congelations give form to the metals that grow in the earth's entrails. Over time, the children develop into different kinds of metals, "y q̄ dela pureza destos dos principios vienen a ser unos mas excelentes q̄ otros" (and from the purity of these two principles some come to be more excellent than others).

38. Monardes, *Diálogo del hierro, y de sus grandezas,* 160; Bauer, "Blood of the Dragon," in Slater, López-Terrada, and Pardo-Tomás, eds., *Medical Cultures,* 85; Smith, "Vermilion, Mercury, Blood, and Lizards," ibid., 43–48; Daniela Bleichmar, *El imperio visible: Expediciones botánicas y cultura visual en la ilustración hispánica* (Mexico City, 2016); Clement Salaman et al., *The Way of Hermes: New Translations of The Corpus Hermeticum and the Definitions of Hermes Trismegistus to Asclepius* (London, 1999).

39. Monardes, *Diálogo del hierro, y de sus grandezas,* 160v–162v.

He concludes, "El Hierro se haze y cria de los mismos principios y materia que se hacen el Oro y Plata y los demas metales" (Iron is made and grows from the same origins and matter from which gold, silver, and other metals are made). After giving equal time to alchemical practitioners who believe in the transmutation of metals and writers who insist that such conversions are impossible, the Doctor submits, "Solo Dios lo sabe q̄ dio a naturaleza ciertas leyes y modos para condensar y hazer los metales, con la mixtion y forma q̄ fue servido" (Only God knows, for He gave to Nature certain laws and modes to condense and make metals, with the mixture and form in which He is served).[40]

This appeal to divine wisdom does not settle the question of the origin of matter; it serves as a transition into the next group of authorities, church fathers. After presenting Saint Augustine's views on the generation of metals, juxtaposting the ideas of pagan, Islamic, and Christian natural philosophers, the Doctor endorses the traditional mercury-sulfur thesis ("la opinion comun"). He does so, not because it is necessarily correct, but because it provides the line of best fit for questions that are otherwise impossible to resolve. Monardes thus uses the conventions of the dialogue—namely, the presentation of alternative viewpoints regarding the mercury-sulfur thesis—to challenge rigid binaries of learning and doing, pagan and Christian, black-ugly and gold-pure.[41]

The Doctor is not wrong; at the atomic level, "all the metals share a common electronic structure such that outer valence electron orbitals, typically the *s* orbitals, are unfilled." Modern scientific explanations of metallic structures suggest how we define expertise today. In the same way, the Doctor's expression follows conventional early modern Iberian religious and racial classifications. For, as much as he challenges the logic of marking difference from data that can be observed through the senses, the Doctor adheres to a con-

40. Ibid., 161, 162–162v. On the mercury-sulfur thesis, see Walter Pagel, *The Smiling Spleen: Paracelsianism in Storm and Stress* (Basel, 1984), 30, 40–41; Carmen Salazar-Soler, "Álvaro Alonso Barba: Teorías de la antigüedad, alquimia y creencias prehispánicas en las ciencias de la tierra en el nuevo mundo," in Berta Ares Queija and Serge Gruzinski, eds., *Entre dos mundos: Fronteras culturales y agentes mediadores* (Seville, 1997), 269–296, esp. 272.

41. Monardes, *Diálogo del hierro, y de sus grandezas,* 162; Smith, "Vermilion, Mercury, Blood, and Lizards," in Klein and Sparry, eds., *Materials and Expertise,* 40–41; Daniela Bleichmar, "Books, Bodies, and Fields: Sixteenth-Century Transatlantic Encounters with the New World *Materia Medica,*" in Londa Schiebinger and Claudia Swan, eds., *Colonial Botany: Science, Commerce, and Politics in the Early Modern World* (Philadelphia, 2005), 83–99. See also Brian W. Ogilvie, *The Science of Describing: Natural History in Renaissance Europe* (Chicago, 2008); Justin E. H. Smith, *Nature, Human Nature, and Human Difference: Race in Early Modern Philosophy* (Princeton, N.J., 2015), esp. 70–91.

ventional early modern lexicon of religioracial terminology: "que no difiere el Hierro del Oro en mas, q̄ ser el Oro hecho de sus principios limpios y puros, por do es lucido, resplandeciente y hermoso, y el Hierro por ser hecho de principios gruessos y impuros es feo negro y obscuro, como aqui lo vemos" (thus it is that iron and gold do not differ in any way other than that gold is made from clean and pure principles, which makes it lucid, resplendent, and beautiful, and iron, because it is made of gross and impure principles, is ugly, black, and dark, as we see here). Monardes draws on classical theories of minerogenesis, but he conveys them in the polemical terms of early modern racial and ethnic classifications.[42]

Iron, Indios, and Racial Classifications

When Monardes wrote these words in 1574, black skin was linked to enslavement in the Americas and to deep histories of inferiority and ugliness in Europe. Between 398 and 405 CE, when St. Jerome took up the task of rendering the Hebrew Scriptures into Latin, he mistranslated the Queen of Sheba's assessment of her entwined blackness and beauty. As historian Kate Lowe argues in her reading of Canticles 1:4 (Song of Solomon 1:5), in the line that we now know as "I am black but beautiful," Jerome replaced the Hebrew word "ו" (and) with the Latin term *sed* (but), such that the translation read "Nigra sum set formosa" (I am black but beautiful) instead of "Nigra sum et formosa" (I am black and beautiful). It is doubtful that the patron saint of translation misunderstood the Hebrew meaning of "ו"; it is more likely that he saw "an opposition between 'black' and 'beautiful.'" Saint Jerome's mistranslation imparted into the phrase "a newly adversarial nature" that was readily "adopted as a linguistic and cultural formulation" throughout Europe and colonial communities in Asia and the Americas.[43]

Historian Michel Pastoureau charts a different linguistic genealogy, although he arrives at a similar conclusion. Because speakers of ancient languages developed color terms that included "texture, density, brilliance, or

42. Monardes, *Diálogo del hierro, y de sus grandezas,* 162v; P. Geoffrey Feiss, "The Geology and Science of Gold," in Richard F. Knapp and Robert M. Topkins, eds., *Gold in History, Geology, and Culture: Collected Essays* (Chapel Hill, N.C., 2001), 33–42, esp. 34. See also Ralph Bauer, *The Alchemy of Conquest: Science, Religion, and the Secrets of the New World* (Charlottesville, Va., 2019).

43. Kate Lowe, "The Global Consequences of Mistranslation: The Adoption of the 'Black but . . . ' Formulation in Europe, 1440–1650," *Religions,* III (2012), 544–555, esp. 545–546; Sweet, "Iberian Roots," *WMQ,* 3d Ser., LIV (1997), 145–146, 165–166. Augustine argues that these lines epitomize Christian reading practices. See Saint Augustine, *On Christian Doctrine,* trans. D. W. Robertson, Jr. (Indianapolis, 1977), 106–107.

luminosity" as well as tone, Hebrew and Greek color lexicons were richer than those of Latin, producing "irresolvable difficulties for translation." By the late fifteenth century, with the spread of movable type and European imperialism, "black entered a new phase of its history." Polychromatic medieval manuscripts were replaced by printed books and woodcut engravings whose circulation "led to black and white becoming colors 'apart,'" inspiring "profound transformations in the domain of color sensibility." One fifteenth-century work that was given greater purchase in a post-Gutenberg world was Franciscan friar Juan de Dueñas's six-part *Espeio de consolacion de tristes.* Originally printed in Burgos in 1540, it was reprinted some forty-nine times before the turn of the century. Dueñas's reconciliation of classical paradigms and Christian parables associates the immutable properties of blackness ("es imposible, segun via humana, el negro mudar la pelleja") with evil characters in the book, such as "el Etiopio tan feo y negro" (the Ethiopian, so ugly and black).[44]

The conceptual link between blackness and ugliness was deeply entrenched in European imaginations. At times, artists even mapped physical and metaphysical darkness onto the undesirable properties of iron metals. In the medieval era, writers like Chrétien de Troyes, author of the late-twelfth-century romance *Perceval; ou, Le conte du Graal,* invoked the trinity of blackness, iron, and horrid appearance to describe the ugliest woman ever seen, whose "neck and hands were blacker than the blackest of metals." Joseph Beaumont personified cruelty in his *Psyche; or, Loves Mysterie in XX Canto's, Displaying the Intercourse betwixt Christ and the Soule* (1648), as a woman "whose Heart was harder than / Her knotty *Crocodiles* black iron Skin."[45]

The symbolic association of blackness and undesirability is even clearer in medical literatures, where observable, physical properties are taken as symptoms that reveal inner conditions. For example, English writer Robert Burton uses "black" as a synonym for "frightful" in his reinterpretation of Avicenna's description of a hybrid state of madness and melancholy, producing a nonsensical diagnosis. According to Burton, Avicenna calls the condition "cutubuth," variously spelled as "cucubut" and "kutubut," derived from the Arabic *al-qutrub.* Other writers preferred "Lycanthropia," "Lupinan insanium," and

44. Michael Pastoureau, *Black: The History of a Color* (Princeton, N.J., 2008), 27, 114, 120; Juan de Dueñas, *Espeio de consolacion de tristes* (Toledo, 1589), part 1, 100, part 2, 65; Alexander S. Wilkinson, ed., *Iberian Books: Books Published in Spanish or Portuguese or on the Iberian Peninsula before 1601* (Leiden, 2010), 183–185. I thank Nancy Marino for help with these sources.

45. Pastoureau, *Black,* 80; Joseph Beaumont, *Psyche; or, Loves Mysterie in XX Canto's, Displaying the Intercourse betwixt Christ and the Soule* (London, 1648), 354.

"Wolfe madnesse," but all agreed that the condition was marked by "a pale, blacke, ugly, and fearfull looke."[46]

For a patient to be simultaneously "pale" and "black" is a remarkable form of color transformation—unless "black" no longer refers to color and instead means "ugly," "dreadful," or "revolting." This is precisely how Burton interprets the term, unlike Avicenna, for whom "If the complexion is pale and the hair scanty, there is seldom any excess of black bile." Burton claims that, for Avicenna, the signs of melancholy and madness, "which are in the brain," are written on the body as blackness: "Melancholiacs show the same color of the head, face, and eyes and the same blackness and thickness of hair and head"; "The signs of melancholy are . . . the body's blackness, its dryness, . . . the multitude of body hair, its powerful blackness."[47]

Blackness, for Avicenna, was part of a humoral *(akhlat)* color cosmology whose remedies shaped early modern beliefs about the medicinal properties of iron to cure melancholic and splenetic diseases. As Monardes's Doctor explains, following Avicenna's classification of iron as cold and dry in book 1, part 2 of the Persian physician's *Canon of Medicine (al-Qānūn fī'l-tibb),* iron produces a drying effect upon the body. Iron grindings were mixed with vinegar to cure Saint Anthony's Fire (madness), applied to the skin with wool or cotton strips to remedy all manner of women's fluxes, and distilled into tonics that were administered to spelenetic patients or anyone suffering from poor organ function, for "se engendra el apetito, conforta el Higado, y los demas miembros interiores" (it encourages appetite, comforts the kidneys, and the rest of the internal organs). But that is as far as the link between iron and melancholy went in Avicenna's work. Blackness, on its own, was no uglier than other color signifiers, like yellow pus, turbid blood, or urine "the character of milk." Burton's citation of Avicenna suggests the opposite—that a pale complexion is as symptomatic as a "blacke, ugly, and fearfull looke."[48]

46. Robert Burton, *The Anatomy of Melancholy What It Is: With All the Kindes, Causes, Symptomes, Prognostickes, and Severall Cures of It . . .* (Oxford, 1621), part 1, §1, 13; Antonius Deusingius, *Disputatio medica de lycanthropia . . .* (Groningen, 1654), n.p.; Gerardus Cremonensis, *Liber canonis totius medicinae* (Lugdunum, 1522), 150v. I thank Jessica Wolfe and Taneen Maghsoudi for help with these sources.

47. Avicenna, *The Canon of Medicine (al-Qānūn fī'l-tibb),* ed. Laleh Bakhtiar (Chicago, 1999), 281; Jennifer Radden, *Melancholic Habits: Burton's Anatomy and the Mind Sciences* (New York, 2017), 19–22. There is no complete, modern English-language edition of the passage that Burton cites, but Marin Eisner's (1999) partial translation of Avicenna's *On Black Bile and Melancholia* is reprinted in Radden, *The Nature of Melancholy: From Aristotle to Kristeva* (New York, 2000), 75–78, esp. 77.

48. Monardes, *Diálogo del hierro, y de sus grandezas,* 175v–178; Avicenna, *Canon of Medi-*

By repurposing terms like "limpio y puro," "negro y feo," Monardes responds to the lexicon of medical authorities from Greco-Roman antiquity and the medieval Middle East, as they were recast over time and in translation. More pointedly, he answers the language that sixteenth-century Iberian writers used to mark colonial difference, placing his discussion of the origins, genesis, and generation of metals in dialogue with larger debates about language, bloodlines, and purity. He suggests, like other thinkers of the era, that blackness is undesirable; but he argues, against Colón and López de Gómara, that observable properties like color do not reveal the true nature of matter. Monardes's Doctor argues for the value of theoretical frameworks that have been transmitted from the greats and remade over time. He insists that this genealogy of knowledge—rather than observational data alone—provides proper insight into organic matter. In other words, Monardes pushes back against those dominant imperial voices to suggest that physical objects like iron metals cannot be taken as proxies for the culture and civilization of a particular place. True knowledge of a place and its people, especially regarding medical practices that were at once intensely personal and a matter of public health, must be combined with deep study of medical texts and traditions from different linguistic communities and world regions—especially scientific voices who disagree with each other, and those who reinterpreted ancient medical theories in their own historical moments.

D'Orta and Monardes speak through interlocutors whose arguments about iron and Indios point to deeper debates about knowledge-making power, medical applications, and the nature of Iberian empires in the sixteenth century. By invoking the quasi-fictional space of the dialogue to stage real questions about earthly ideals, evidence, and the limits of sensory observation, these author-physicians center questions of language, scientific communications, and social polemics that were born of European colonialism in Asia and the Americas. While New World conquerors looked to physical evidence like iron metals and skin color to interpret signs of human civilization, d'Orta and Monardes offered other ways of reading the Book of Nature and non-Christian communities. For d'Orta, this meant presenting Indian beliefs about iron and paradise without accommodating them to dominant Portuguese expectations of the tropics or coloniality, as had Camões. For Monardes, it involved defining knowledge as a combination of experience and mastery of textual transmis-

---

cine, 32–40, 346–347. On Atlantic contexts, see James H. Sweet, *Domingos Álvares, African Healing, and the Intellectual History of the Atlantic World* (Chapel Hill, N.C., 2011), 115–121; Lady Anne Wallis Blencowe, *The Receipt Book of Mrs. Ann Blencowe, A.D. 1694* (London, 1925), 43.

sions. In contrast to conquerors like Colón, whose single-minded pursuit of gold was by then infamous, Monardes esteemed the virtues of iron, the basest of metals, in intimate acts of medical healing and communal levels of the body politic. Although they combined insights from India and the Americas in similar ways in their dialogues, d'Orta's and Monardes's works were received in very different ways. That history of reception and mistranslation is the subject of the next chapter.

5 : EARLY MODERN DIALOGUES AND COLONIAL KNOWLEDGES

Both García d'Orta and Nicolás Monardes determined that the dialogue was the most appropriate way to convey divergent medical and scientific opinions about plants, metals, stones, and simples. But when their works were translated by other early modern authors across Europe, only Monardes's *Diálogo del hierro, y de sus grandezas* (1574) continued to circulate in its original form, in this case among Anglophone (1580) and German-speaking (1615) audiences. In the hands of Flemish botanist Charles de l'Écluse, known by his Latinized pen name, Carolus Clusius, d'Ortas's *Colóquios dos simples* (1563) became a Latin-language natural history whose generic conversion eliminated some of the core features of the original dialogue, including key scenes where interlocutors evaluated competing authorities and evidentiary forms to show readers how and why they reached a particular conclusion.[1]

This chapter presents defining features of the early modern dialogue, including the genealogies of medical and scientific writers in which d'Orta and Monardes so carefully positioned their works. It examines how the re-genreing of the dialogue through translation affected d'Orta's argument about the role of firsthand experience in acquiring and communicating medical, scientific, and mineralogical knowledge. In contrast, Monardes's points about the medical properties and public virtues of iron went unchanged. Although this chapter's geographical focus takes us away from the Americas and the methods derive from fields like the history of the book rather than linguistic and literary analysis, the emphasis on reception histories shows patterns of erasure that we have seen in Part 1 ("Gold") and will revisit in Part 4 ("Silver"). Whereas those sections focus on the silencing of Indigenous and African influences in the technical arts, this chapter shows how early modern print culture subjected the ideas of a Goa-based Portuguese medical expert to similar mechanisms of erasure when his work was returned to Europe.

1. [García d'Orta], *Colóquios dos simples e drogas e cousas medicinais da India* (1563) (Lisbon, 1963); [Nicolás Monardes], *Primera y segunda y tercera partes de la historia medicinal de las cosas que se traen de nuestras Indias occidentales que firven en medicina: Tradtado de la piedra Bezaar, y de la yervea Escuerçonera; Diálogo de las grandezas del Hierro, y de sus virtudes medicinales, tratado de la nieve y del bever frio . . .* (Seville, 1574), 175–184.

Defining a Genre, Reconciling Knowledges

In the first half of the sixteenth century, dialogues transmitted moral, ethical, and philosophical principles that were rehabilitated from classical forms into Christian parables; by the end of the century, the dialogue had become a significant genre in the transmission of natural philosophical ideas. Despite its importance in early modern scientific communications, there are few studies of technical or medical dialogues in this fundamental moment of transition. This lacuna stems, in part, from the complex nature of the early modern dialogue—a form that was not tied to content. Virtually any aesthetic mode, such as theater, philosophy, science, or classroom lessons, could be staged as a dialogue.[2]

The subjects of dialogues ranged from serious fictions that imagined alternative models of human society, such as Thomas More's *Utopia* (1516) and Miguel de Cervantes's *Coloquio de los perros* (ca. 1613), to didactic works of grammar and language acquisition, such as instructor William Stepney's seven Spanish-English dialogues (one for each day of the week, and an additional eighth work for commercial transactions) or, not to be outdone, Peter (Pierre) Erondell's series of thirteen French-English dialogues. The dialogue was a popular form through which to treat a variety of subjects in different ways, ranging from nonfiction prose on moral philosophy, politics, and religion to bantering songs about gender and the strife of married life.[3]

2. R. W. Serjeantson, "Proof and Persuasion," in Katherine Park and Lorraine Daston, eds., *Early Modern Science,* vol. III of *The Cambridge History of Science* (Cambridge, 2006), 132–174, esp. 166; Francisco Calero, *Los diálogos (Linguae latinae exercitatio) de Juan Luis Vives* (Valencia, 1994), 3. See also Reijer Hooykaas, "Science in Manueline Style: The Historical Context of João de Castro's Works," in Armando Cortesão and Luís de Albuquerque, eds., *Obras completas de João de Castro,* IV (Coimbra, 1982), 231–426, esp. 394. I thank Edward Collins for the reference.

3. Thomas More, *Utopia: A Revised Translation, Backgrounds, Criticism* (1516), trans. and ed. Robert M. Adams, 2d ed. (New York, 1992); Miguel de Cervantes Saavedra, *El casamiento engañoso y el coloquio de los perros: Novelas ejemplares* (ca. 1613) (Madrid, 1912); William Stepney, *The Spanish Schoole-Master: Containing Seven Dialogues, According to Every Day in the Weeke, and What Is Necessarie Everie Day to Be Done* . . . (London, 1591); [Pierre] Erondell, *The French Garden: For English Ladyes and Gentlewomen to Walke in . . . Being an Instruction for the Attayning unto the Knowledge of the French Tongue: Wherein for the Practise Thereof, Are Framed Thirteene Dialogues in French and English, concerning Divers* . . . (1605; rpt. London, 1621) (language learning); Antonio de Torquemada, *Jardín de flores curiosas* (1570), ed. Giovanni Allegra (Madrid, 1982); Thomas Nash, *Quaternio; or, A Fourefold Way to a Happie Life: Set Forth in a Dialogue betweene a Countryman and a Citizen, a Divine and a Lawyer* (1633; rpt. London, 1636); [John Echard], *Mr. Hobbs's State of Nature Considered, in a Dialogue between Philautus and Timothy: To Which Are Added*

Within colonial contexts, the dialogue served as an influential mode of Christian doctrinal writing. In 1524, when twelve Franciscan missionaries arrived in New Spain, Hernán Cortés arranged meetings with political and spiritual leaders from the court of Cuauhtémoc, the reigning lord of Tenochtitlán and son-in-law of deposed leader Moctezuma. To instruct Indigenous leaders in the ways of the Catholic faith, and to do so without printed materials in Nahuatl, missionaries adopted a conversational mode of instruction that they called *coloquios.* In the Andes, religious writers used the artifice of the dialogue to voice their concerns about the treatment of Indigenous people; in the conversational give-and-take between colonial officials and Indigenous chiefs, presented in interpolated lines of Spanish and Quechua, readers were forced to consider both perspectives. Such efforts were not limited to colonial Latin America. Puritan missionaries like John Eliot also wrote dialogues to aid in conversion efforts in seventeenth-century Massachusetts, for there was no manner "more familiar, then by way of Dialogues" to explain English church doctrine to Algonquian communities.[4]

Writers of dialogues explicitly positioned their works within a critical gene-

---

Five Letters from the Author of the Grounds and Occasions of the Contempt of the Clergy (London, 1672) (moral philosophy); Thomas More, *A Dialogue of Cumfort against Tribulation, Made by the Right Vertuous, Wise and Learned Man, Sir Thomas More . . .* (Antwerp, 1573); Walter Raleigh, *The Prerogative of Parlaments in England: Proved in a Dialogue (pro and contra) betweene a Councellour of State and a Justice of Peace . . . Dedicated to the Kings Majesty, and to the House of Parlament Now Assembled . . .* (Hamburg, 1628) (politics); Henoch Clapham, *Errour on the Right Hand, through a Preposterous Zeale: Acted by Way of Dialogue* (London, 1608); Ant[onio] de Molina, *A Treatise of Mental Prayer . . . Togeather with a Dialogue of Contrition and Attrition* (Saint-Omer, 1617) (religion); *Haec-Vir; or, The Womanish-Man: Being an Answere to a Late Booke Intituled Hic-mulier; Exprest in a Briefe Dialogue betweene Haec-Vir the Womanish-Man, and Hic-Mulier the Man-Woman* (London, 1620); *A Way to Wooe a Witty Wench; or, A Dialogue between Two Lovers Who Meeting One Day . . .* (London, 1674–1679) (gender).

4. Juan Guillermo Durán and Rubén Dario García, "Los 'coloquios' de los 'Doce Apósteles' de México: Los primeros albores de la predicación evangélica en el nuevo mundo," *Teología: Revista de la facultad de teología de la Pontificia universidad católica Argentina,* XXXIV (1979), 131–185, esp. 131–133, 142; Bernardino de Sahagún, *Coloquios y doctrina cristiana: Con que los doce frailes de San Francisco, enviados por el papa Adriano VI y por el emperador Carlos V, convirtieron a los indios de la Nueva España, en lengua mexicana y española,* ed. Miguel León Portilla (Mexico City, 1986); Ana Vian Herrero, ed., *El indio dividido: Fracturas de conciencia en el Perú colonial; Edición crítica y estudio de los "Coloquios de la verdad" de Pedro de Quiroga* (Madrid, 2009), 381; John Eliot, *Indian Dialogues, for Their Instruction in That Great Service of Christ, in Calling Home Their Country-Men to the Knowledge of God, and of Themselves, and of Jesus Christ* (Cambridge, 1671), A3.

alogy of other dialogists. The conventions of the dialogue—especially its persuasive aim, informational content, playful tone, and thin line between fiction and nonfiction—were shaped in antiquity by writers like Cicero, Plato, and Aristotle, and they were rehabilitated by early church fathers, medieval scholastics, and sixteenth-century humanists like Saint Augustine, Francesco Petrarca, and Desiderius Erasmus. For example, Petrarch's imagined dialogue with Augustine (Augustinus) regarding the source and nature of happiness employs techniques that the author (Franciscus) learned "from Cicero, who in turn had learned it from Plato." To avoid "inserting 'I said' and 'he said' too often," Petrarch writes their names as "Aug." and "Fr." so that, per Cicero's advice, "'the discussion may seem to be carried on in person by those who were present.'" Sometimes, as when Augustinus explains his methods of right reading, he sounds like the author of *Doctrina christiana* and *De civitate Dei contra paganos.* At other times, the fictional interlocutor is substantially graver than Augustine—even to the point of silliness. When Augustinus begins to taxonomize natural philosophical ideas into Aristotelian definitions "because although this 'desire' is but a single word, it consists of innumerable elements," Franciscus replies simply, "You frighten me." The gap between Augustine the author and Petrarch's Augustine epitomizes the early modern dialogue: a hybrid space of historical actors and literary imagination in which different ways of knowing—spoken and written, classical and Christian, philosophical and prophetic—are evaluated with serious play.[5]

The author who best defined the early modern dialogue and its spirit of serious play was the Dutch humanist Erasmus. Some four years after its first print run in 1518, until the final "authorized" text was issued in 1533, Erasmus's *Familiarium colloquiorum formulae* (Familiar Patterns of Conversation) was reissued at least thirty times; it was expanded, reworked, and republished no fewer than nine. If a canonical model of dialogic writing existed in the early modern era, it was Erasmus's blend of pedagogy and play and his use of the genre to invite readers to interrogate the border between the two—indeed, to interrogate the nature of category making itself. When Philecous (Fond of Hearing) of "Alcumista" ("Alchemy," 1524) says that Lalus (Talkative) is "describing a rhetorician to me, not an alchemist," and when the interlocutors Eutrapelus (Witty) and Fabulla (Fond of Talk) of "Puerpera" ("The New Mother," 1526) use Aristotelian terms of generation and corruption to analyze the merits of

5. David Marsh, *The Quattrocento Dialogue: Classical Tradition and Humanist Innovation* (Cambridge, Mass., 1980), 1–3; Francesco Petrarca, *My Secret Book,* ed. and trans. Nicholas Mann (London, 2016), 3, 9, 35, 143. The Latin text is printed on verso pages; English translations are on recto pages.

breast-feeding, they gesture to the artificial nature of epistemological categories and the porous borders of science and society. Scientific writers were drawn to these kinds of serious jests and to other features of Erasmus's work, such as his use of multiple languages, diverse female characters, and debates about the relationship of language to knowledge, as seen in dialogues like "Virgo μισόγαμος" ("The Girl with No Interest in Marriage," 1523), "Senatulus, sive Γυναικοσυνέδριον" ("The Council of Women," 1529) "De rebus ac vocabulis" ("Things and Names," 1527), and "Synodus grammaticorum" ("A Meeting of the Philological Society," 1529).[6]

Medical and scientific dialogues, including those published before and after Erasmus's major works circulated in Europe, varied widely in length, language, and subject matter. Humanist Fernán Pérez de Oliva's *Dialogus inter siliceum, arithmeticam et famam* (1514) covered two folios; fray Juan de Pineda's *Diálogos familiares de la agricultura cristiana* (1589) spanned more than five volumes. They were received differently when read privately versus aloud and in groups. In one case, Galileo Galilei's metallurgical dialogue *Il Saggiatore* (The Assayer, 1623) was voiced by the scientist's well-connected broker, Giovanni Ciampoli, at the dining table of Pope Urban VIII. The dialogue was well received. The author's other works, most notably the *Dialogo sopra i due massimi sistemi del mondo* (Dialogue concerning the Two Principal Systems of the World, 1632), were not so fortunate as to be performed by such entertaining intermediaries, who could have disposed audiences to accept their novel content.[7]

6. Jessica Wolfe, *Homer and the Question of Strife from Erasmus to Hobbes* (Toronto, 2015); Craig R. Thompson, ed., *Collected Works of Erasmus: Colloquies,* 2 vols. (Toronto, 1997), I, xxiv–xxvii, "Alchemy," 547, 553n, "New Mother," 590–618.

7. Virginia Cox, *The Renaissance Dialogue: Literary Dialogue in Its Social and Political Contexts, Castiglione to Galileo* (Cambridge, 1992), 5; Adrian Johns, *The Nature of the Book: Print and Knowledge in the Making* (Chicago, 1998), 26–29; Galileo Galilei, *Dialogue concerning the Two Chief World Systems, Ptolemaic and Copernican,* trans. Stillman Drake (Berkeley, Calif., 1953); and, for an alternative translation, Galilei, *Dialogue on the Great World Systems: In the Salusbury Translation,* ed. Giorgio de Santillana, 3d ed. (Chicago, 1964). Other notable early modern scientific dialogues include João de Castro, *Tratado da sphaera, por perguntas e respostas a modo de dialogo* (Lisbon, [1537?]); Pedro Mexía, *Los dialogos o coloquios del magnifico caballero Pero Mexia coronista de Su M . . .* (Seville, 1548); John Levett, *The Ordering of Bees . . . Set Forth in a Dialogue, Resolving All Doubts Whatsoever* (London, 1634); J. H., *Astronomia Crystallina; or, A New and Clear Way to Know and Perceive All the Motions of the Heavens, and also the Motion of the Earth Plainly, as through a Crystal-Glass . . . Whereunto Is Now Added a Postscript by Way of Dialogue, between the Author and Two Grand Objectors . . . ,* 2d ed. (London, 1676); W[illiam] Simpson, *Philosophical Dialogues concerning the Principles of Natural Bodies . . .* (London, 1677); Thomas Emes,

Erasmus's colloquies, in their multilingual combinations of ancient and modern and their voicing of different ways of knowing, became touchstone texts for the scientific writers who followed him, from Galileo in Italy and Pineda in Spain to diverse authors in Germany. These writers included Freiburg-based physician, mining engineer, and astrologer Ulrich Rülein von Kalbe, whose dialogue between an expert miner and his student, *Ein nützlich Bergbuchleyn* (A Useful Book on Mining, 1500), considered "the earliest known printed book of mining," circulated in no fewer than ten different editions before 1540; and physician Georgius Agricola, the "father of mineralogy," whose 1530 dialogue begins with a letter signed by Erasmus. Agricola's knowledge of metals came from his nearly thirty years of treating miners at clinics in Jáchymov (1527–1530), nestled in the Ore Mountains of the present-day Czech Republic, and Chemnitz (1530–1555), present-day state of Saxony, then the center of German mining activity.[8]

Agricola is best known for his *De re metallica* (1556), a twelve-book compilation of mineralogical theory, mining practice, and metallurgical techniques, accompanied by some three hundred woodcut images that required nearly twenty years to prepare; but medical writers were drawn to his other works. Most notably, Agricola's Latin-language dialogue *Bermannus, sive, de re metallica* (1530) reconciles divergent scientific approaches and forms of communication. It was a precedent for the dialogues of d'Orta and Monardes. Within forty years of its original publication, *Bermannus* was published in at least five editions in three cities by three different houses, with and without other books on metals.[9]

A Dialogue between Alkali and Acid: Containing Divers Philosophical and Medicinal Considerations . . . Being a Specimen of the Immodest Self-Applause, Shameful Contempt, and Abuse of All Physicians, Gross Mistakes and Great Ignorance of the Pretender John Colbatch (London, 1699).

8. Jesús Gómez, *El diálogo en el Renacimiento español* (Madrid, 1988), 15; Warren Alexander Dym, "Alchemy and Mining: Metallogenesis and Prospecting in Early Mining Books," *Ambix*, LV (2008), 232–254, esp. 238–239; Georgius Agricola, *De re metallica* (1556), trans. Herbert Clark Hoover and Lou Henry Hoover (New York, 1950), vii–ix. Erasmus's letter is dated Feb. 18, 1529.

9. The first translation into a European vernacular was a German volume of 1778 that took great license with the text. The first complete translation was Friedrich August Schmidt's volume of 1806; translations in Czech, French, Hungarian, and Italian were not published until the second half of the twentieth century. See Friedrich August Schmidt, *Georg Agrikola's Bermannus: Eine Einleitung in die metallurgischen Schriften desselben* (Freyburg, 1806); Georg Agricola, *Bermannus aneb rozmluva o hornictví*, ed. Jan Reiniš (Prague, 1957); Agricola, *Bermannus (le mineur): Un dialogue sur les mines*, ed. Robert Halleux and Albert Yans (Paris, 1990); Agricola, *Bermannus avagy beszélgetés az ásványok cso-*

The choice of Latin as a vehicle of expression in *Bermannus* is as important as it is ironic. Over the course of some 131 folios, the three interlocutors—Bermannus, the eponymous everyman, Nicolaus Ancon, an expert in Arabic medicine, and Joannes Naevius, a specialist in Greek and Latin peripatetic philosophy—debate the merits of firsthand experience in mining and print-based medical knowledge that is susceptible to mistranslation. Bermannus argues that, without understanding how minerals look underground, healers cannot make sense of the confusing color vocabularies inherited from antiquity and the medieval era. The black minerals that Albertus Magnus calls "pyrites" (iron pyrite, FeS_2) in Latin are also the white material that the Greeks call "marchasita" (marcasite, FeS_2). Bermannus concludes, as would Monardes forty years later, that the external forms of stones, metals, and minerals are misleading ("et profecto multa alia sunt quae persaepe specie fallunt"); thus, vocabularies based on visible properties like color are inaccurate. He then shows how such inaccuracies were compounded by a history of mistranslation, as when Pliny, writing about Galicia and Portugal, conflated lead (Pb) and galena (PbS) because the sulfide had the same color as the metal; later, Dioscorides mistranslated Pliny's confusion, producing a vocabulary that obscured material facts and proved impossible to interpret. By the end of the dialogue, Bermannus, speaking with great conviction in Latin, convinces Ancon and Naevius to abandon Latin as the language of scientific and medical communications. As he inveighs against the lexical corruptions of the greats, the miner reveals himself to be an excellent student of antiquity. In this way, the dialogue offers a specific definition on early modern epistemology, suggesting that true scientific knowledge is the domain of those who can situate their book learning within practical contexts. More playfully, it uses a Latin-language debate to argue against Latin-language discussions of scientific matters.[10]

---

dálatos világáról . . . , ed. László Zsamboki and Péter Tóth (Miskolc, 1994); Paolo Macini and Ezio Mesini, *De re metallica: Con in appendice il De amantibus subterraneis; Bermannus, ovvero Un diálogo sul mondo minerale* (Bologna, 2003). The many editions of Agricola's *Bermannus* include works published by Hieronymus Froben (Basel, 1530); Hieronymus Gormontius (Paris, 1541), who bound the dialogue to works by Albertus Magnus and Ramón Llull; Froben (Basel, 1546), which included Agricola's *De natura fossilium* and a Latin-German glossary prepared by Petrus Plateanus; Erasmus's correspondent and Agricola's friend from Jácymov, Valentini Papae (Leipzig, 1546); and a final work issued by Froben (Basel, 1568).

10. Agricola, *Bermannus,* ed. Halleux and Yans, 39, 41, 53–55 (fols. 13, 15, 44–46, 59–60). The text is printed on facing pages in French (recto) and Latin (verso), with folio signatures from the original and page numbers of the modern edition. I cite in both formats so that

As these examples suggest, early modern dialogues were serious and playful, learned and bawdy, secular and sacred, long and short. Their interlocutors, who could be human or nonhuman, spoke in one language or in many. They often debated the merits of language itself. Some dialogues, such as those written by ancient philosophers like Plato, were what literary scholar Virginia Cox calls "meticulously crafted dramas of persuasion," whereas others staged "threadbare," "half-hearted," or "formulaic" literary representations of oral transmissions, sometimes with an interlocutor who resembled the author. With its combination of instruction and entertainment, pagan and Christian knowledges, and conventions from antiquity that were reinterpreted in the Renaissance, the early modern dialogue was known as an "awkwardly hybrid genre," one whose form converted issues like knowledge and communication into central thematic devices.[11]

Sixteenth-century scientific works, including natural histories and tomes like Agricola's *De re metallica,* adopted authoritative voices often phrased in the third person and intercut with first-person corrections, using evidence that was based on deep study and seasoned experience. Authorial attempts to persuade readers were incorporated into the information that such texts conveyed. In contrast, dialogues placed the element of persuasion on center stage, forcing readers to reflect on the manner and mode of transmission, often without pedantic intervention by the author. By juxtaposing competing evidentiary forms and sources of knowledge, early modern dialogues invited readers into the process of evaluating evidence and rhetorical forms. They became what Cox identifies as both "symptoms of an unease with the conventions which govern the transmission of society within a society" and a mode of remedying such problems by better understanding the language and logic of such arguments.[12]

For example, when Monardes's Doctor cites Galen to support the claim that iron is both a "hot" and "cold" metal, the *Diálogo del hierro* shows how medical expertise is used to justify two contrary positions at the same time. The Doc-

---

readers can compare them with the German-language translation, Agricola, *Bermannus: Oder Über den Bergbau; Ein Dialog,* ed. and trans. Helmut Wilsdorf, Hans Prescher, and Heinz Techel, vol. II of *Ausgewählte Werke* (Berlin, 1955).

11. Cox, *Renaissance Dialogue,* xi, 2. By the eighteenth century, Anthony Ashley Cooper, third earl of Shaftesbury (1671–1713), argued that monologic efforts to persuade readers of an author's opinion violated the genre's intellectual purpose. See Cooper, *Characteristics of Men, Manners, Opinions, Times, Etc.,* ed. John M. Robertson, 3 vols. (1757; rpt. London, 1900), II, 338, cited ibid., 4–5.

12. Cox, *Renaissance Dialogue,* 5–7.

tor, invited by Burgos and Ortuño to review the state of the field, initially puts forth the argument that iron is cold. His first authority is Galen, who affirms that all metals are naturally dry ("todos los metales de su naturaleza son secos, y assi tienen gran virtud y fuerça dessecar"). Because iron behaves like stones, which are cold and dry ("fria y seca"), analogically the two must contain the same properties. After presenting two pages' worth of experts—including Andalusian Muslim natural philosophers Abū al-Qāsim Khalaf ibn al-Abbās al-Zahrāwī al-Ansari (Albucasis) and Abū l-Walīd Muḥammad Ibn' Aḥmad Ibn Rushd (Averroes), Persian physician Ibn Sīnā (Avicenna), German-born Dominican friar Albertus Magnus, and Italian doctor Antonio Musa Brassavola—Burgos asks the Doctor for evidence that supports the competing position. The Doctor once more begins with Galen, affirming that, for the Greek physician, "los metales tienen mucha substancia de fuego mezclada con las demas" (metals have a great degree of fiery substance mixed with the rest). He presents many of the same sources, such as Avicenna (twice) and Albertus Magnus, and remarks on the effects of iron in the body—opening veins, promoting blood flow (including menstruation), and "consuming superfluous humidity in the stomach" to support the idea that iron is a "hot" metal.[13]

At this point, the Doctor steps out of his narration to comment on the changes that he observes in the faces of his interlocutors, bringing the fictional exchange to life for his readers, much as d'Orta did in his discussion of iron-based resins. Burgos confirms that this new information has caused him to rethink his assumptions about the nature of metals, agreeing with the Doctor that the question will remain unresolved until experts who write about iron can better understand its "complexion" ("que complexion tenia"). As we saw in the last chapter, early moderns understood that the composition (or "complexion") of iron consisted of two contrary elements, sulfur (S) and mercury (Hg), what the authorities call the "father" and "mother" of minerogenesis. The Doctor concludes that iron is both hot and cold, because it has the "complexion and temperature" of both metallic materials ("la cōplexiō y tēperatura, q̄ participle de entrābas calidades"). When Monardes presents these competing views on humoral principles, as when d'Orta shares South Asian beliefs about iron and earthly paradise, the authors allow the interpretations to speak for themselves without overt intervention.[14]

In this way, the dialogue functioned as a genteel space for the presentation and reconciliation of divergent views. D'Orta's and Monardes's dialogues, in

13. [Monardes], *Primera y segunda y tercera partes de la historia medicinal,* 169–171.

14. Ibid., 171–171v.

accordance with these conventions, communicated this spirit of civility by balancing thoughtful conversation on important matters with small talk about the weather in Seville, playing games of chess that epitomize larger political processes in India, and discussing elephant hunts in such breathlessly naturalistic detail that readers feel as if they, too, are participating in the kill. By talking about lunch and planning time for rest, d'Orta and Monardes write human bodies, daily experience, and leisure time into the printed form of the dialogue. Through the genre and its history as a platform for scientific communication, they refine base metals like iron into subjects that suit humanist aesthetics and enable seriously entertaining debates about language and knowledge. In the hands of New World conquerors, the absence of iron metals and ferrous metallurgy justified theories of European supremacy. In the dialogues of d'Orta and Monardes, iron became a tool for talking about the machinery of Iberian empires, modes of information gathering, and the transmission of medical and scientific knowledge—especially those ideas and practices that were perfected by people in the "Indian" lands colonized by Spain and Portugal.[15]

Lost and Retained: D'Orta and Monardes in Translation

The *Diálogo del hierro* was not Monardes's first dialogic work. In 1536, the young physician had written a brief Spanish-language dialogue on global pharmacological traditions that were then used in Spain, featuring Nicolao, a physician and a precursor to the Doctor of the *Diálogo del hierro,* and Ambrosio, an apothecary. Monardes's father, Dr. Juan Bautista Monardes, wrote the Latin-language prologue to the work, which was published in Seville as the *Dialogo llamado pharmacodilosis o declaracion medicinal.* As he shaped his career as a medical writer, Monardes expanded into other forms of scientific writing. His major work began as a natural history of American *materia medica* that was edited, expanded, retitled, and republished several times. The first edition was published by sevillano printer Sebastián Trujillo in 1565. The work, *Dos libros: El uno trata de todas las cosas q̄ traē de n-ras Indias occidētales, que sirven al uso de medicina,* contained twenty-five chapters in book 1 and two in book 2. Four years later, the text was issued by another sevillano publisher, Hernando Díaz, who combined some of book 1's chapters on similar materials, such as resins (anime, copal, and liquidambar oil) and stones (bloodstone, or heliotrope, and jade). Book 1 of Díaz's volume held twenty-one chapters,

15. Ibid., 168–168v; [d'Orta], *Colóquios dos simples,* 35–35v, 87v–88v. On the strategic use of contradictory ideas, see Vittorio Hösle, *The Philosophical Dialogue: A Poetics and a Hermeneutics,* trans. Steven Rendall (Notre Dame, Ind., 2012), 49.

whereas the two chapters in book 2, "Bezoar Stones" and "Black Salsify," went unchanged. In 1571, Monardes published his thoughts on snow and the properties of cold beverages as a stand-alone volume, *Libro que trata de la nieve, y de sus propielades: Y delmodo que se ha de tener, en el bever enfriado cō ella.*[16]

Finally, in 1574, Monardes converted the work from a two-part book to a three-part medical history that included illustrations and letters from the Americas, as well as multiple genres like books *(libros),* treatises *(tratados),* and a Latin-language prologue addressed to Pope Gregory XIII. Book 1 contained the same information as the 1565 and 1569 volumes; book 2 included thirteen new chapters on materia medica such as tobacco, dragon fruit, and ambergris, along with the letter of soldier Pedro de Osma y de Xara y Zejo, signed from Lima on December 26, 1568. Book 3 began with a letter, addressed to Cristóbal de Rojas y Sandoval, archbishop of Seville, and accompanied by a wealth of new material: thirty-five new chapters, many treating matter that was explicitly marked as American in origin ("Canela de nuestras Indias" [Cinnamon of Our Indies], "Ruybarbo de Indias" [Rhubarb of the Indies]), curious ("La fruta que se cria debaxo de tierra" [The Fruit That Grows Underground], "El bitumen que se saca debaxo de tierra" [The Bitumen That Is Extracted Underground]), or mystical ("El árbol que muestra si uno a de morir, o vivir" [The Tree That Shows if Someone Will Live or Die]). The work concluded with the same treatises on bezoar stones and black salsify, now paired with a dialogue on iron and the book on snow and cold beverages. Monardes published his masterpiece as *Primera y segunda y tercera partes de la historia medicinal de las cosas que se traen de nuestras Indias occidentales que sirven en medicina Tratado de la piedra Bezaar, y dela yerva Escuerçonera* (1574).[17]

In 1569, Clusius published his Latin-language edition of Monardes's *Dos libros,* including the letter from Osma in Peru. Because the 1569 edition did not include Monardes's dialogue, we cannot compare Clusius's handling of d'Orta's *Colóquios dos simples* and Monardes's *Diálogo del hierro.* What we can see from Monardes's print history is his ability to position different forms of medical writing within the same literary markets. With these works, Monardes

16. [Nicolás Monardes], *Dialogo llamado pharmacodilosis o declaraciō medicinal . . .* (Seville, 1536); *Dos libros: El uno trata de todas las cosas q[ue] trae[n] de n[uest]ras Indias Occide[n]tales, que sirven al uso de medicina . . .* (Seville, 1565); Monardes, *Dos libros, el uno que trata de todas las cosas que traen de nuestras Indias occidentales, que sirven al uso de la medicina . . .* (Seville, 1569); Monardes, *Libro que trata de la nieve, y de sus propielades: Y delmodo que se ha de tener, en el bever enfriado cō ella . . .* (Seville, 1571).

17. [Monardes], *Primera y segunda y tercera partes de la historia medicinal,* along with the letter of soldier Pedro de Osma y de Xara y Zejo, signed from Lima on Dec. 26, 1568.

reveals himself to be an astute observer of the role of genre within scientific communications.[18]

García d'Orta was not as prolific a writer as Monardes. To appreciate the Portuguese physician's preference for the dialogue, we must look for clues in the text itself. Two examples of exchanges between Orta and Ruano in the *Colóquios dos simples* will demonstrate why the dialogue was so crucial to the work's dissemination of medical and scientific information. In colloquy 50, on *espiquenardo* (spikenard, *Nardostachys jatamansi*), Ruano asks Orta whether it is true that there are two kinds of "spodio": one that was known to Arab authorities as a silicon-like concretion found in Asian bamboo trees and one described by Greek writers as pulverized zinc oxide (ZnO). This question couches Orta's know-it-all-ness as the polite fulfillment of his friend's request for information. Orta explains that there is only one spodio, the resin from Asia. Greeks called the mineral compound "pōfolix," meaning anti- or artificial spodio. According to him, authors who insist that there are two kinds of spodio—such as Italian-born and Toledo-trained Gerardus Cremonensis, who translated many of Avicenna's works—see difference where they ought to find similarity. As Orta concludes, although spodio appears in different forms, "não seia mais deferente do que he branquo cõ preto" (the difference is not greater than it is with white and black). Color properties distinguished human beings in Goa ("os Indios") and Ceylon ("os negros"), but Orta, like Monardes's Doctor, does not find color to be a scientifically meaningful way of marking difference in plant or mineral bodies.[19]

Ruano ignores this point and instead takes issue with Cremonensis's mistranslation of "spodio," illustrating why the dialogue, with its built-in tangents and exchanges, was such an attractive platform for d'Orta. Ruano asks Orta whether it is wrong that such a skilled translator would confuse the names.

18. Nicolo Monardes, *De simplicibus medicamentis ex occidentali India delatis, quorum in medicina usus est,* trans. Clusius (Antwerp, 1574).

19. [D'Orta], *Colóquios dos simples,* 193–193v. Agricola reaches a similar conclusion. Although I have not found evidence that d'Orta or Monardes owned copies of Agricola's *Bermannus,* Monardes does cite Agricola's medical works in his treatise on the bezoar stone (*Primera y segunda y tercera partes de la historia medicinal,* 142v). Despite being placed on the *Index of Banned Books,* many German scientific materials made their way to the peninsula, often by way of Italian booksellers. In contrast to the Roman Inquisition, Spanish censors removed offending passages and allowed the rest of the book to circulate. See Henry Kamen, *The Spanish Inquisition: A Historical Revision* (London, 1997), 103–136; and Klaus Wagner and Manuel Carrera, *Catalogo dei libri a stampa in lingua italiana della Biblioteca Colombina di Siviglia* (Modena, 1991). I thank James Ameland, Clive Griffin, LuAnn Homza, and Pepé Pardo Tomás for help with these sources.

Orta replies that it makes sense, given that the name means something very different from how it appears in the source text ("Não se aq̃lle nome não sinificar outra cousa muyto deferẽte no pareçer"). In such cases, when correcting the translation would lead to fewer errors in medical practice, Orta approved of a translator's intervening into the material. Unlike Erasmus, who was most concerned with the gap between names and things, Orta takes issue with physicians who fail to consider the origins of their sources and then compound print-based errors in their practice of medicine. The way to fix these errors is, not to avoid Greek-, Latin-, or Arabic-language works, as it was for Agricola's Bermannus, but rather to understand the histories of diverse linguistic and epistemological traditions in translation. As Orta explains, Cremonensis's contemporary in Toledo, 'Abd al-Raḥmān ibn Muḥammad Ibn Wāfid (Serapio), follows Avicenna and calls the resin "tabaxir," as it was known in the Middle East ("toda ha Arabia, e turquia, e persia"). But "tabaxir" was mistakenly pronounced as "babaxir," meaning "congealed liquid" ("cumo") or "humidity" ("humidade"). Without technologies to navigate the globe and enable universal communication, no one knew to correct these errors. The colloquy thus ends with a prescription for right reading: in Greek texts, understand that "spodio" means "metal" ("do espodio verdadeiro de metal"); with Arabic authors, interpret it as the resin that comes from India ("que levareis da India"); and with Latin writers, know that it refers to external appearance ("se ha meezinha q̃ se ha de tomar por dentro ou per forma"). Orta's grouping of medical authorities into ethnolinguistic categories and his instructions on how readers ought to treat each author are not just part of a linguistic ecumenicalism that resolves the problem of mistranslated works from antiquity. They also reflect the unique position of Portuguese scientific writers to gather information from local experts using their empire's modern navigational technologies and to communicate these knowledges through print on a global scale.[20]

Ruano misses the point completely, as d'Orta shows in the forty-third colloquy on precious stones. Here, the Spanish visitor to Goa asks whether the navigational powers of magnets or lodestones ("pedra de çevar") are diluted by Asian diamonds and whether this is why Portuguese use wooden fasten-

20. [D'Orta], *Colóquios dos simples,* 193v–194, 195, 196. The passage also sets up one of the text's many joking moments of self-referentiality, explicitly reminding readers that this is a staged conversation. In colloquy 44, when Ruano asked why some writers in the Levant call diamonds "ferrugezi," whereas Persians say "esmeralda" and Indians say "Pachee," Orta reminds him, "Aveis de saber que P. e F. no Arabio sam letras muyto hirmam (como jà outras vezes vos dixe)" (You must know that P. and F. are close cousins in Arabic, as I have already told you before [167v]).

ers instead of iron nails. Orta replies sharply that they generally sail on ships with iron nails ("ha mais navios de preguos de ferros que de pao") but replaced some with wood in the Maldive Islands to reduce shipping costs. Ruano pushes on, repeating what he heard about magnets' drawing ore out of iron mines, invoking the common wisdom of "what they say" ("Dizē tambē"); Orta insists anew, "Nã ha tal cousa porq̄ ēcabos deferētes se criã.s.ōde nã ha ferro" (There's no such thing because they grow in different points, some where there is no iron). Ruano tries a third time, noting that an unnamed French philosopher says the weight of a magnet remains constant in the presence of iron. This time, Orta draws on his experience: "O cōtrario disto espremētamos jà eu, e algũas pessoas por isto nã vos maravilheis porq̄ nã açertam ē todas as cousas os homēs" (On the contrary, we experimented with this already, I with some others, but you should not wonder at it because few things that men say are true). When Ruano inquires about the maddening properties of magnets, Orta quickly refutes the claim. Local people say no such thing, and, to the contrary, they use magnets for medical advantage: "Tēse cà açerqua dos gētios q̄ comida em pouca cātidade os faz não em velheçer, e o cōserva em sua moçidade, e por tāto el Rey de çeilã velho mādava fazer panellas desta pedra pa lhe fazerē đ comer nellas" (Among the Gentiles it is said that eating a small amount protects against aging and preserves their youth, and for that reason the old king of Ceylon ordered that they prepare small loaves made of the stone for him to eat). Ruano asks incredulously, "Como sabeis isto?" (How do you know this?), enabling Orta to show how he uses military and scholarly information networks to learn about the people and plants of India. Orta acquired this information from Jewish philosopher Isac do Cairo, a skilled interpreter who collaborated with Portuguese agents in India and traveled to Portugal to report on the death of Sultan Badur.[21]

Each time Ruano offers information culled from European sources, Orta refutes the claims, either with book learning or his own experience. The back-and-forth of ideas highlights the difference between the two Iberian doctors, one a visiting Spaniard and the other a Portuguese colonist who resided in Goa. When Ruano reveals that his source on Indian diamonds is the Spanish chronicler Francisco de Támara, better known for his work on Peru, Orta replies, "Pois Françisco de tamara queria cōtar fabulas q̄ as cōtara das suas indias, e não das nossas" (Well, if Francisco de Tamara wants to tell tales, he should tell them about his Indies, not ours). The conventions of the dialogue emphasize Orta's position within South Asian information networks and Por-

21. Ibid., 164–164v. See Juan Pimentel and Isabel Soler, "Painting Naked Truth: The *Colóquios* of Garcia da Orta (1563)," *Journal of Early Modern History,* XVIII (2014), 107.

tuguese maritime channels, both of which afford key insights into the scientific, medical, and technological properties of metals and stones—insights that were not available to the dialogue's Spanish interlocutor.[22]

In these exchanges, Ruano and Orta do not just talk about what they know; they also ask each other how they know what they know. Time and again, Ruano cites European authorities like Brassavola and Spanish medical writer Andrés Laguna, best known for his illustrated commentary of Dioscorides's *De materia medica,* published in Spanish as *Pedacio Dioscorides Anazarebo* (Antwerp, 1555 / Salamanca, 1566). Orta refutes these sources with Indian information on metals and stones and with things he observed through experience—both of which stress the accomplishments of the Portuguese empire and the scientific writers who served it.

And yet, as much as the fictional Orta believes in the power of new technologies to disseminate medical knowledge to a wide community of readers and practitioners, early modern translations of the *Colóquios dos simples* suggest that the problem of language as it was staged in the work went unresolved in real life. As we have seen, Carolus Clusius's Latin translation converted the text into a natural history. Other translators, working from Clusius's edition, followed in kind. Like the aforementioned silencing of Indigenous and African mining and metallurgical knowledges from Latin American works that were printed in Spain, here we see a similar dynamic unfolding in northern European treatments of d'Orta's dialogue and its diverse Indian informants from Goa.

The shift from dialogue to natural history caused three major changes in the text. First, it obscured d'Orta's critical self-positioning within a genealogy of dialogists who foregrounded issues of scientific communication and invited readers to evaluate different kinds of evidence and ways of knowing. Second, it erased the performative roles of South Asian interlocutors like Malupa, the physician from Goa, Antonia, the servant who assists Orta in his clinic, Paula de Andrade, the unwed *mestiça* who is robbed by her servant, and André Milanês, the stonesmith. Historian Hugh Cagle argues that figures like Antonia were not incidental to the text. As we follow her presence and information shared in colloquies on *bangue* (cannabis), *açafram* (saffron), *pateca* (watermelon), and tamarind, "the example of Antonia demonstrates how the violence and compromise inherent in colonialism and colonial science combined to give individual women in Iberian colonies a distinctive hand in scientific

22. [D'Orta], *Colóquios dos simples,* 163. See Mário Farelo, "Garcia de Orta, the Faculty of Medicine at Lisbon, and the Portuguese Overseas Endeavor at the Beginning of the Sixteenth Century," *Journal of Medieval Iberian Studies,* VII (2015), 218–231.

transformation." Finally, the shift from dialogue to natural history collapsed crucial differences between Spanish and Portuguese knowledge networks. By flattening epistemological debates between Orta and Ruano into straightforward conclusions, Clusius's translation occasionally contradicts the information that d'Orta presents about plants, stones, and metals.[23]

It is hard to consider Clusius's *Aromatum, et simplicium aliquot medicamentorum apud indos mascentium historia* (1567) as a "translation" of *Colóquios dos simples.* Clusius's version rearranged the order of the source text, divided it into two books, separated colloquies into discrete chapters, added woodcut illustrations, and—most important—converted the dialogue into a natural history. In a word, Clusius produced an entirely new book.

In *Colóquios dos simples,* Orta and Ruano clearly play different roles in asking questions, presenting evidence, and resolving doubts. They also make jokes, talk politics, and break bread together, sometimes converting the experience of eating into modes of information gathering. For example, the 28th colloquy, featuring Ruano, Orta, Antonia, and a military captain who delivers samples of jangomas from Bombay, deals with four fruits: jaca (*Artocarpus integrifolia,* jackfruit), jambolan *(Syzygium cumini),* jambos *(Jambosa malaccensis),* and jangomas *(Flacourtia jangomas).* Orta and Ruano try only the jackfruit. As they eat it, Ruano tries to reconcile his book knowledge of the fruit, which has a watery but good taste ("aquoso . . . ho sabor he muyto bom"), with the experience of tasting a local variety in Goa. He remarks that the smell and appearance remind him of just-sprouted gall nuts, which are called "the fruit of the oak" in Spain ("pareçe como hũas bugualhas grandes quando sam novas [a que chamamos maçaas de cuquo]"). Ruano ends his line by asking Orta what the fruit is called in India. Eating is a way for the interlocutors to exchange scientific information and communicate it to their readers. By presenting different kinds of information, based on fruits that Orta and Ruano do or do not taste, the *Colóquios dos simples* reveals the value of firsthand experience in transmitting locally gathered knowledge through print.[24]

The 28th colloquy prefigures the gustatory dialogue of the 36th, when Ruano tries a local watermelon, "de cà chamamos pateca" (which we call *pateca*), which differs in size and color from the fruits called "samdias" (watermelon, *sandía*) in Spain. The visiting Spaniard acquires the fruit from one of Orta's market women ("hũa vossa cõpradeira"), but he finds himself deceived by its

23. Hugh Glenn Cagle, "The Botany of Colonial Medicine: Gender, Authority, and Natural History in the Empires of Spain and Portugal," in Sarah E. Owens and Jane E. Mangan, eds., *Women of the Iberian Atlantic* (Baton Rouge, La., 2012), 174–195, esp. 185–186.

24. [D'Orta], *Colóquios dos simples,* 121v.

taste. Ruano had asked whether it would be good, and the market woman had answered yes. He found it unsatisfactory, having the taste of mud ("sabor da lama"). As Orta explains, invoking the voice of colonial authority, matters of perception are decidedly local. It's not that the taste is bad but that the market woman "falou vos segundo seu gusto" (spoke to you according to her taste). Orta's assessment of local preferences, perceptions, and tastes echoes his ecumenical prescription for a right reading of ancient authorities. Rather than a single, dogmatic position, Orta's comments show the value in multiple evidentiary nodes and modes of interpretation.[25]

Clusius modifies the 28th colloquy in three main ways, disrupting the relationship between scenes of eating that unfold across various colloquies. First, he divides the four fruits into separate chapters on jackfruit, jambolões, jambos, and jangomas. Second, he conflates Ruano's observations with Orta's answers. Third, by eliminating conversational exchanges among the Iberian and Indian characters, he compresses the dialogic process of knowledge making into a single moment of textual communication. As he converted the dialogue into a natural history, Clusius equated Ruano's remark about the resemblance of jambos and gall nuts with Orta's ideas about botanical matter. He then corrected the statement in a footnote, marked with an asterisk, revealing that he interpreted the fictional Orta as the real-life author García d'Orta. Clusius's version of the line reads: "Vel, vet verius dicam, similis est hic fructus magnis Gallis * recentibus (quas poma de Cuquo nuncupamus)" (Or, put more properly, this fruit is similar to large, fresh Gallis * [which we name fruits of oak]). In the footnote, he takes issue with d'Orta's classification of the fruit and insists: "Nisi noster Auctor Gallasillas maiores, quae in Robore passim per Hispaniam et Lusitaniam nascuntur, intelligat per Bugualhas grandes, quid fibi velit, ignorare me fateor" (But unless our Author means large *Gallasillas,* which are called oak in all of Hispania and Lusitania, here written as large *Bugualhas,* I profess to ignorance of what he wishes to say).[26]

Of course, when Clusius says that he cannot understand what the author means or why he would say such a thing, it is because neither the author (d'Orta) nor the interlocutor who voices his experience (Orta) actually

25. Ibid., 142–143. Hugh Cagle interprets the market woman as Antonia in *Assembling the Tropics: Science and Medicine in Portugal's Empire, 1450–1700* (New York, 2018), 119.

26. Carolus Clusius, trans. and ed., *Aromatum, et simplicium aliquot medicamentorum apud Indos nascentium historia: Ante biennium quidem Lusitanica lingua per dialogos conscripta, D. Garcia ab Horto, proregis Indiq medico, auctore; Nunc verò primùm Latina facta, et in epitomen contracta à Carolo Clusio Atrebate* (Antwerp, 1567), book 2, 232.

made these claims in the dialogue. The idea was Ruano's, the fictional character charged with marking the limits of Spanish knowledge in India by asking questions that only Orta, as a Portuguese colonist living in Goa, could answer. By combining conversational exchanges with expository prose and collapsing Spanish and Portuguese interlocutors into a single Iberian scientific voice, Clusius overlooks the role of imperial rivalry in d'Orta's gathering and communication of information.

In a similar way, d'Orta's dialogue showed how diverse Indian characters, including market women, Hindu and Islamic physicians, and male servants who sought medical treatments, shaped the colonial scientific knowledge that circulated in the text. In the 54th colloquy (erroneously marked "53" in the first print run), on turbit *(Ipomoea turpethum),* Ruano asks Orta about his knowledge of the plant, which, when dried, can be used as a purgative. He inquires specifically about Orta's sources: "Antes que vos tragua os ditos dos escritores Gregos, e latinos modernos quero que me diguaes como soubestes isto que me dizeis" (Before you treat the sayings of Greek writers, and modern Latins, I want you to tell me how you came to know all this that you say to me). Orta replies that he learned about the plant and the drying technique from a woman in a bazaar in the city of Diu, when he accompanied de Sousa on an expedition to build a fortress. These exchanges show how the collection and communication of colonial scientific information were bound up with Portuguese imperial military movements. Such passages also reveal gender-inclusive traditions of harvesting knowledge of plants and minerals, Indian women's commercial roles, and Orta's respect for knowledge transfers of all kinds—so long as they were useful and held up to trial, as the market woman's method of preparing turbit must have done to be endorsed by medical authorities like Malupa. None of these interlocutors or their perspectives appears in Clusius's natural history translations. The erasure of dialogic exchanges and performative elements in the *Colóquios dos simples* silences a range of colonial and South Asian voices, as well as critical sources of information on materia medica. As we saw with the reprinting of Oviedo's manuscript illustration of Taíno gold miners in Chapter 2, here the mechanics of print culture, especially genre and translation, lock together to omit Indian, non-Christian ways of knowing from scientific communities in early modern Europe.[27]

In fact, only one translation of d'Orta's work retained the text's dialogic origins, although Spanish royal physician Juan Fragoso translated from Clusius's *Aromatum, et simplicium* rather than d'Orta's *Colóquios.* The resulting work

27. [D'Orta], *Colóquios dos simples,* 205, 206v.

was a dialogue (or "discurso") in name only: *Discursos de las cosas aromaticas, arboles y frutales, y de otras muchas medicinas simples que se traen de la India oriental, y que sirven al uso de medicina* (1572). Fragoso's Spanish-language discourse is organized alphabetically, such that there are thirteen entries under "A," six under "B," and so on. Because Fragoso translated the Latin-language names into Spanish, the *Discurso* departs from the order of Clusius and d'Orta. For example, d'Orta's colloquy on cinnamon *(canela)* appears as the fifteenth conversation, but it is the twenty-first entry in Fragoso's work. None of the distinguishing features of d'Orta's dialogue, such as the performative staging of community life or Orta and Ruano's competing perspectives on metals, plants, and stones, appears in Fragoso's translation.

Instead, the treatise, written in the third person, intermixes passages from Clusius with Fragoso's own ideas. Whereas d'Orta's colloquy on cinnamon presents Indian ideas on iron and earthly paradise, Fragoso's discourse cites the work of his patron, Dr. Ortega, which was based on Mexican sources that dealt with the spice. Fragoso then mentions specimens gathered by colonial agents in Quito before abruptly going back to the source text: "Bolviendo ala isla de Zeylon donde se dixo cogerse la buena canela, tienen porsi los Indios estar los campos Elysios: y que en un monte alto de alli, que llaman la cumbre de Adam, se veē las pisadas por donde el anduvo" (Returning to the island of Ceylon, where they say the good cinnamon is gathered, the Indians understand the Elysian Fields to be; and that in a tall mountain, named the Peak of Adam, there one can see the footsteps of where he walked). Fragoso fuses the biblical idea of paradise with the classical vision of Elysian Fields, following Clusius's translation ("Elysios Campos") of what d'Orta said Indians called "ho parayso terreal" (the terrestrial paradise). In this translation of a translation, cinnamon, not iron, is associated with sacred landscapes and earthly paradise.[28]

In this way, Fragoso's text marks a decided departure from d'Orta's dialogue and from the works of writers like Bartolomé de Las Casas, who insisted that classical and Christian toponyms for paradise were not synonymous. As Las Casas told it, Colón had discovered, "no los campos elísios como los gentiles, sino, como católico, el terrenal paraíso" (not the Elysian Fields of the Gentiles, but rather, as a Catholic, the earthly paradise). Fragoso's equating of pagan Elysian Fields with Catholic visions of Eden removes the Indian voices who first articulated this vision of iron-laden paradise. The epistemological conse-

28. Juan Fragoso, *Discursos de las cosas aromaticas, arboles y frutales y de otras muchas medicinas simples que se traen de la India oriental, y que sirven al uso de medicina* (Madrid, 1572), 72v, 73–73v; Clusius, *Aromatum, et simplicium,* I, 81; [d'Orta], *Colóquios dos simples,* 64.

quences of Clusius's decision to recast d'Orta's dialogue as a natural history echoed throughout the genealogy of Spanish- and Italian-language editions.[29]

Elsewhere in the text, Fragoso's points of reference seem to come from Monardes's *Primera y segunda y tercera partes de la historia medicinal* rather than d'Orta's *Colóquios dos simples* or Clusius's *Aromatum, et simplicium.* The opening discourse on amber retains Clusius's annotation on the resin's New World origins ("genus ex America"), but instead of referencing Mexico, as Clusius does, Fragoso follows Monardes in his note on bitumen in Cuba and the coast of La Florida. He returns to Clusius's passage on New Spain and the Nahuatl term for amber, "Ocosotl" in Clusius and "Ocoçol" in Fragoso, in the middle of his discourse. Whereas Cluisus concludes his discussion of Mexican amber with a footnote on its variations and etymologies ("quam Mexicana historia describit in hunc modum"), Fragoso courses through ancient Egypt and ends with medical citations from Laguna, by way of Italian physician Pietro Andrea Gregorio Mattioli and "el q llaman de don Juan de Granada" (the one they call don Juan de Granada), the inventor of a balsam that cured ulcers *(llagas)* and abscesses *(postemas).* This represents one of many times in which Fragoso incorporates references that were not in the source text, such as Agricola's classification of bitumen. In other words, even though Fragoso preserves the spirit of a dialogue (in title, at least), he also incorporates his own references, citations, and ideas, gathered from his study of European sources. Fragoso's edition of d'Orta is yet another interpretation of the *Colóquios dos simples*—one that reflects the state of medical knowledge in Spain, channeled through French natural history writing, as much as it conveys information on Portuguese India.[30]

29. Bartolomé de Las Casas, *Obras completas,* ed. Paulino Castañeda Delgado, IV, *Historia de las Indias* (Madrid, 1994), 1090.

30. Clusius, *Aromatum, et simplicium,* 13; compare Fragoso, *Discursos des las cosas aromaticas,* 4v–6v, with Monardes, *Primera y segunda y tercera partes de la historia medicinal,* 10–11v. Granada's balsam was approved by physicians in Córdoba on April 25, 1570 (11v–12). "Ocoçol" is how Monardes wrote the term for amber in 1565 (bvii[v]), 1569 (C), and 1574 (8). For secondary sources that treat d'Orta and Monardes, see Palmira Fontes da Costa, "Geographical Expansion and the Reconfiguration of Medical Authority: Garcia de Orta's *Colloquies on the Simples and Drugs of India* (1963)," *Studies in History and Philosophy of Science,* XLIII (2012), 74–81, esp. 77; and Conde de Ficalho's (1837–1903) annotations to the *Colóquios dos simples e drogas da India por Garcia da Orta,* 2 vols. (Lisbon, 1891–1892), I, 198n ("cassia fistula"), II, 206–207n ("diamante"), 237–239n ("pedra bezar"), 271n ("raiz de China / guaiacam"), 405n ("rosas persicas"). On Juan Granada de Consesuegra, see Jesús Domínguez Aparicio and Santiago Domínguez de Castro, *Leganés en el Archivo Histórico de Protocolos: Colección documental (siglos XVI–XVIII)* (Madrid, 2007), 52–54. I thank Pablo Gómez for the reference.

Other translators likewise declined to consult d'Orta's dialogue as their source text and instead based their editions on Clusius's *Aromatum, et simplicium.* Italian physician Annibale Briganti linked his prose translations of d'Orta's *Colóquios* and Monardes's *Primera y segunda y tercera partes de la historia medicinal* in a work that was published as *Due libri dell'historia de i semplici, aromati, et altre cose, che vengono portate dall'Indie orientali, pertinenti alla medicina* (1576). Briganti's translation follows Clusius to the letter, including the botanist's objection to the comparison of jambos and gall nuts: "Se questo nostro auttore per Bugualbas non intende quelle galle grandi, che per tutta Spagna, e per Portogallo nascono nelli roueri, io non saprei, che altro possa egli intendere" (If our author does not mean that large gall nut when just born, found in all of Spain and Portugal, when he says *Bugualbas,* I do not know what other thing he understands). Briganti's translation circulated widely in Italy. Soon after the first print run, the book was reissued in 1582, 1589, and 1597 by rival printers stationed in the city of Venice. (See Appendix 1 for a comparison of chapter titles in d'Orta, Clusius, Fragoso, and Briganti.)[31]

In 1578, a work that verified information from d'Orta's dialogue was published in Spain. It did not reach Italy until 1585, after Briganti's translation had proved that Italian readers would buy books on South Asian materia medica. The first edition of Portuguese soldier-physician Cristóvão da Acosta's *Tractado delas drogas, y medicinas en las Indias orientales, con sus plantas dibuxadas al bivo por Christoval Acosta medico y cirujano que las vio ocularmente* (Treatise of the Drugs and Medicines of the West Indies, with Their Live Plants Drawn by Cristóbal Acosta, Physician and Surgeon Who Saw Them with His Own Eyes), published in Burgos by royal printer Martin de Victoria, included the author's portrait and Latinized pen name, Christophorus Acosta Africanus. The edition and its market-friendly title highlighted the author's eyewitness testimony, illustrations of live plants, and confirmation of material presented by d'Orta.

The text itself departs from the structure of d'Orta's *Colóquios dos simples.* Unlike d'Orta, da Acosta begins the treatise with cinnamon because "tanta confusion ha havido entre los Sabios antiguos" (it has caused such confusion

31. Annibali Briganti, trans., *Due libri dell'historia de i semplici, aromati, et altre cose, che vengono portate dall'Indie orientali, pertinenti alla medicina* (Venice, 1576); Briganti, trans., *Due libri dell'historia de i semplici, aromati, et altre cose; che vengono portate dall'Indie orientali pertinenti all'uso della medicina . . .* (Venice, 1582), "Della historia de I simplici, aromati, et alter cosec che vengono portate dall'Indie orientali . . . ," book 2, 218; Briganti, trans., *Dell'historia de i semplici aromati, et altre cose, che vengono portate dall'Indie orientali pertinenti all'uso della medicina* (Venice, 1597); and see Angela Nuovo, *The Book Trade in the Italian Renaissance,* trans. Lydia G. Cochrane (Boston, 2013), 184–188.

among the wise ancients). Da Acosta agrees with d'Orta that the best, most fragrant, and most medically useful cinnamon comes from Ceylon and that other products, known as *canela* (cinnamon) or *cassia lignea* (Chinese cinnamon), can also be used in medicine. He cautions patients to beware the practices of unscrupulous medics and apothecaries who sell inferior *cassia* strands as if they were the true cinnamon.[32]

Although da Acosta adds some of his own commentaries, he follows d'Orta precisely in other passages, such as the one on iron and Ceylon, writing, "Tiene lino, y hierro. Los naturales desta isla fabulā, diziēdo: que aquel es el parayso terrenal, porque esta alli una muy alta sierra, a que llaman, el Pico de Adan y dizen ellos, que alli esta en el alto el pie de Adan figurado, y otras fabulas, que ellos al mismo tono dizen . . . y los Jogues (q̃ son los pereginos, que andan haziendo penitencia, de unas partes a otras) la princípal romeria suya es aquel Pico" (They have flax and iron. The natives of this island fabulate, saying: that there is the earthly paradise, because of a very tall mountain there, which they call Adam's Peak, where Adam's footprint is marked at the top, and other such fables that they say in the same tenor . . . and for the yogis [who are their pilgrims who go making pennance from one part to another] that Peak is their main point of pilgrimage). Instead of reporting things "because that's how they say them" ("que por tais volas conto"), as d'Orta had done, da Acosta strategically invokes his eyewitness experience to cast doubt on Ceylon's place in Christian history and to reinforce its place in South Asian spiritual traditions, such as yoga. To those who told him of a burning bush at the top of the mountain, da Acosta declares, "Yo no lo vi, y a los que me lo affirmarom lo remitto" (I did not see it, and I refer the matter to those who told me of it).[33]

In 1582, Clusius translated da Acosta's treatise into Latin and sold the book, from Antwerp, under two different titles. Both titles mentioned d'Orta's influence: *Christophori a Costa, medici et cheirurgi aromatum et medicamentorum in orientali India nascentium liber . . . quae à Doctore Garcia de Orta in hoc genere scripta sunt* and *Aromatum et medicamentorum in orientali India nascentium liber. . . quae à Doctore Garcia de Orta in hoc genere scripta sunt.* However, the 1585 Italian-language translation, which was based on Clusius, removed d'Orta's name from the title: *Trattato di Christoforo Acosta africano medico, et chirurgo della historia, natura, et virtu delle droghe medicinali, et*

32. Christobal Acosta, *Tractado delas drogas, y medicinas de las Indias orientales . . . en el qual se verifica mucho de lo que escrivio el Doctor Garcia de Orta* (Burgos, 1578), 1, 5, 10.

33. Acosta, *Tractado delas drogas,* 16; compare with *Trattato di Christoforo Acosta africano medico, et chirurgo della historia, natura, et virtu delle droghe medicinali, et altri semplici rarissimi . . .* (Venice, 1585).

altri semplici rarissimi: Che vengono portati dalle Indie orientali in Europa: Con le figure delle piante ritratte, et disegnate del vivo poste a' luoghi propii, nuovamente recato dalla spagnuola nella nostra lingua.[34]

French translators like Antoine Colin continued to cite d'Orta in the titles of their works, but they interpreted his name literally, writing "M. Garcie du Jardin" and thus obscuring the author's identity. Colin's *Des drogues et medicaments qui naissent aux Indes* (1602) was not the first instance where Francophone audiences encountered d'Orta's and Monardes's works. In 1584, botanist Geoffroi Linocier published his *L'histoire des plantes, traduicte de Latin en François,* which advertised its use of visual and alphabetic information extracted from Dioscorides (by way of Mattioli), García d'Orta and Monardes (by way of Clusius), and Conrad Gessner (by way of Jean Liébault). An expanded second edition, printed in 1620, included botanical information from Virginia. None of the Latin-, Spanish-, Italian-, or French-language translations retained d'Orta's use of diverse Indian characters or Iberian imperial rivalries to collect or report on scientific and medical information. In this way, the nuanced and competing views that characterized the *Colóquios dos simples* were eliminated from the editions that circulated in Europe. These omissions included serious medical debates, such as treatments for hemorrhaging that were transmitted from Greek and Arab authorities and tested in clinics, spiritual beliefs about iron and paradise, and moments from daily life, like the taste of a fruit, that allowed glimpses into the complex power structures and gender systems of colonial Goa.[35]

In contrast to the re-genreing of d'Orta's dialogue into prose natural histories, Nicolás Monardes's *Diálogo del hierro* was consistently translated as a dialogue in different European readership communities. In 1580, John Frampton, having already published an English-language edition of the *Historia medicinal* under the title *Joyfull Newes out of the Newfound World* (1577), translated the *Diálogo del hierro* as *The Dialogue of Yron, Which Treateth of the Greatnesse*

34. Carolus Clusius, *Christophori a Costa, medici et cheirurgi aromatum et medicamentorum in orientali India nascentium liber: Plurimum lucis adferens iis quae à Doctore Garcia de Orta in hoc genere scripta sunt* (Antwerp, 1582); Clusius, *Aromatum et medicamentorum in Orientali India nascentium liber: Plurimum lucis adferens iis quae à Doctore Garcia de Orta in hoc genere scripta sunt* (Antwerp, 1582); Acosta, *Trattato di Christoforo Acosta africano medico et chirurgo.*

35. Anthoine Colin, trans., *Traicte de Christophle de la Coste medicine et chirugien des drogues et medicaments, qui naissent aux Indes* (Lyon, 1602); Geofroy Linocier, trans., *L'histoire des plantes, traduicte de Latin en françois: Avec leurs pourtraicts, noms, qualitez et lieux où elles croissent . . .* (Paris, 1584); Linocier, *L'histoire des plantes . . . ,* 2d ed. (Paris, 1620).

Thereof, and How It Is the Most Excellent Metall of All Others, and the Thing Most Necessarie for the Service of Man: And of the Greate Medicinall Vertues Which It Hath; An Eccho for the Doctor Monardus Phisition of Sevill. In his Englishing of the text, Frampton even translated the original publication markers that appeared at the foot of the page: "In Sevill in the House of Alonso Escrivano." Notably, Norton replaces Escribano's distinctive printer's mark—"a female, witchlike figure with sagging breasts devouring two snakes that she appears to have stolen from Hermes's caduceus"—with a cherub emerging from an ornately carved bookholder, surrounded by blooming flowers. Through translation, Monardes's iconographic reminder of the dialogue's alchemical theories of metallic transformation came to emblematize angelic investigations into natural knowledge.[36]

In the second edition of *Joyfull Newes,* Frampton bound his *Dialogue of Yron* to his translation of Monardes's work on the bezoar stone and black salsify, which he published as *A Booke Which Treateth of Two Medicines Most Excellent against All Venome, Which Are the Bezaar Stone, and the Hearbe Escuerconera . . . Newly Complyed by Doctor Monardes of Sevill, 1574, Translated out of Spanish into English, by John Frampton, 1580* (1596). Frampton preserved the generic forms of each part of Monardes's medical history. Within the *Dialogue of Yron,* his versions of the Doctor, Burgos, and Ortuño occupy the same roles as they did in the source text.

The same was true of German-language editions of Monardes's dialogue. One year before defending his thesis on epilepsy at the University of Basel, medical doctor Jeremias Gesner ("Jeremiam Gesnerum") used Clusius's translation to produce his *Ein nützlich und lustig Gespräche, Von Stahl und Eisen: Darinnen dieser Metallen Würdigkeit und Artzney Tugenden angezeiget werden.* Gesner credited both Monardes ("Medico D. Nicolao Monardo") and Clusius ("Carolum Clusium") on the title page, and he marked the interlocutors, "Burgus," "Ortunnus," and "Doctor Monardus," in the margins throughout, dispensing with the separation between Monardes's fictional Doctor and the author-physician. Gesner also added Clusius to the authorities mentioned in the text, such that the Flemish botanist's ideas on medical simples and com-

36. John Frampton, trans., *Joyfull Newes out of the Newfound World, Wherein Are Declared the Rare and Singular Vertues of Divers and Sundrie Herbs, Trees, Oyles, Plants, [and] Stones . . .* (London, 1580); Ralph Bauer, "The Blood of the Dragon: Alchemy and Natural History in Nicolás Monardes's *Historia Medicinal,*" in John Slater, Maríluz López-Terrada, and José Pardo-Tomás, eds., *Medical Cultures of the Early Modern Spanish Empire* (Burlington, Vt., 2014), 81.

pounds were discussed alongside the sources cited by Monardes, including Aristotle, Avicenna, and Albertus Magnus.[37]

Gesner does what all translators do: he takes portions of the source and converts them into a slightly new text. Despite these changes in content, designed to appeal to an early-seventeenth-century, German-speaking audience, Gesner preserves the dialogue's most important formal and intellectual feature—the diverse scientific authorities and viewpoints that each interlocutor represents. Gesner's dialogue, like Monardes's original, provides a space in which ideas, evidence, and viewpoints are up for debate. The versions of Monardes that circulated in German literary markets thus resembled the Monardes of Spanish- and English-language circles, whereas the d'Orta who was known to Latin-, Spanish-, French-, and Italian-language readers bore little resemblance to the author who wrote in Portuguese. The reframing of d'Orta's dialogue marginalized from western European scientific discourse the Indian, Islamic, and South Asian informants whose ideas were voiced throughout the text.

Although they are collapsed into a single category of Iberian medical writers, García d'Orta and Nicolás Monardes held very different places in early modern lettered life. Where they wrote from (Goa and Seville) and what language they wrote in (Portuguese and Spanish) determined their histories of reception and circulation in a way that other factors, such as genre, form, and scientific content, did not. Because of the wider circulation of Spanish-language works relative to Portuguese texts, and almost certainly because Monardes was well known to readers by the time he published his dialogue, the aesthetic, medical, and scientific similarities of the *Colóquios dos simples* and *Diálogo del hierro* were lost in translation. Historians of science and literary scholars have argued—convincingly—that asymmetrical communication in Spanish and Portuguese persists today in academic conferences, citation rates, and graduate training within Latin American studies. As literary scholar Lisa Voigt has shown, critical scholarly works equate "Latin America" or "Iberia" with Hispanophone primary and secondary sources.[38]

37. [Jeremias Gesner], ed. and trans., *Ein nützlich und lustig Gespräche, Von Stahl und Eisen: Darinnen dieser Metallen Würdigkeit und Artzney Tugenden angezeiget werden* (Leipzig, 1615), 7–30, 39; Gesner, *De epilepsia theses . . .* (Basel, 1616).

38. Lisa Voigt, "'Por Andarmos Todos Casy Mesturados': The Politics of Intermingling in Caminha's *Carta* and Colonial American Anthologies," *Early American Literature,* XL (2005), 407–439, esp. 409, 430n. For examples of Iberian / Spanish conflation, see Jorge Cañizares-Esguerra, *Nature, Empire, and Nation: Explorations of the History of Science in the Iberian World* (Stanford, Calif., 2006), which concedes that the designation "Iberian World" is misleading because "the essays here are about the viceroyalties that made up the

These different histories of reception underscore the importance of reading Portuguese- and Spanish-language texts together to better understand what Iberian scientific writing looked like and how technical works circulated in various readership communities of early modern Europe, especially in Italy, England, and Germany. Attending to the print history of works like these dialogues provides a more nuanced interpretation of the nature of global Iberian empires as they influenced colonial knowledge production and daily life in newly interconnected world regions. For example, political scientist Cedric Robinson argues that the Portuguese empire ought to be called an "Italo-Portuguese empire" that stretched to northern Europe: "Italian capitalists situated themselves to play a critical role in determining the pace, the character, and the structure of the early trans-Atlantic slave trade of the next century," and without "the complicity of part of the English aristocracy and of the Portuguese and English merchant classes, and, of course, the clerical nobility of Rome, it is doubtful that a Portuguese Empire would ever have come into existence. Without that empire, nothing would be as it is." When we observe the Portuguese empire through the case studies of linguistic and generic translation presented in this chapter, we see, for instance, how Italian readers, unlike Lusophone audiences, learned nothing of d'Orta's engagement with Indian and South Asian medical and scientific traditions. The vision of the Portuguese colony that circulated in Italy did not include local actors, subaltern ways of knowing, or debates about the acquisition of knowledge. By attending to the nuances of dialogic exchanges and analyzing how they are modified in translations of content and genre, we can better appreciate how d'Orta's and Monardes's ideas spread among diverse literary publics in early modern Europe.[39]

An analysis of genre and print history allows us to study d'Orta's and Monardes's engagement with iron metals as well as seeds such as flax and spices

---

early modern Spanish empire and the new nineteenth-century national polities that succeeded them" (3). See also Henrique Leitão and Antonio Sánchez, "Zilsel's Thesis, Maritime Culture, and Iberian Science in Early Modern Europe," *Journal of the History of Ideas,* LXXVIII (2017), 191–210, which focuses on scholars who "have analyzed in detail the specificities of Spanish science" (199). For polemical scholarly responses to the marginalization of Portugal in the seventeenth century and our own time, see Boaventura de Sousa Santos, "Between Prospero and Caliban: Colonialism, Postcolonialism, and Inter-Identity," *Luso-Brazilian Review,* XXXIX, Special Issue: Portuguese Cultural Studies (2002), 9–43. I thank Ben Breen, Hugh Cagle, Edward Collins, and Hal Langfur for directing me toward these sources.

39. Cedric J. Robinson, *Black Marxism: The Making of the Black Radical Tradition,* 2d ed. (Chapel Hill, N.C., 2000), 105, 111.

such as cinnamon. To modern readers, these might seem to take us far away from ferrous metallurgy and iron minerals. But to the early modern healers who bought d'Orta's and Monardes's works and read them in their original languages or in substantially modified translations, goods like iron, flax, and cinnamon were part of a deeply interconnected web of colonial commodities and materia medica. These metals, seeds, and plants formed critical nodes in colonial scientific information gathering and the communication of local knowledges through imperial Iberian print networks. They become visible when we study the divergent fates of Spanish and Portuguese writers in European translations—even when the non-European ideas that informed these texts are rendered invisible.

In so doing, we see how iron circulated as matter that was used in diverse acts of medical healing in Spain and the Middle East, in histories of Ceylon as reported by Indian informants who classified their neighbors as "os negros," according to Portuguese sources, and, in pre-Columbian Mesoamerica, as a mode of communication with ancestral and otherworldly spaces (pyrite mirrors). We also see how a range of European actors read the presence or absence of iron as an index of human development, social sophistication, and colonial racial categories in different regions of the Atlantic and Pacific worlds. Tracing Iberian writers' treatments of South Asian and Amerindian beliefs about iron in the East and West Indies, as this section has done, reveals how subaltern spiritual traditions, medical practices, and material facts that could be perceived (or not) through the senses—including iron metals and skin color—were interpreted as meaning-making evidentiary nodes in larger debates about scientific knowledge, colonial life, and imperial letters. Although iron mining and refining played no practical role in sixteenth-century life in the Americas, the ideologies of iron that underwrote European attitudes about conquest and colonization throughout the Indies mattered deeply, and their consequences are felt today.

Copper

6 : NARRATIVE CIRCUITS OF NEW WORLD COPPER

In 1539, armed with his experience plundering Panama and Nicaragua and waging war against Inca ruler Atahualpa in the conquest of Peruvian land, tribute networks, and precious metals, Hernando de Soto—now christened as governor of Cuba—arrived in La Florida and marched northward in search of greater wealth. Instead of the gold and silver that Francisco Pizarro's men took from the Andes, Soto found Indigenous communities who depended upon the sea, with fish for nourishment and pearls for prestige, according to a Portuguese footsoldier whose account of the expedition was stamped with Inquisitorial approval. The author, known today only as o Fidalgo de Elvas (the Gentleman of Elvas), narrated how Soto's party passed quickly through Apalache lands in the northwest corner of La Florida, disappointed that rulers of Timucua-speaking towns like Ucita and Mocoço shared only agricultural goods with them, instead of metallic wealth. From there, the soldiers coursed through Mississippian societies in present-day Georgia and the Carolinas, where leaders like the cacica de Cutifachiqui directed them to regions rich in gold and copper—always uninhabited and well removed from their own lands. By the time the squadron arrived in Cutifachiqui, Indigenous sovereigns well knew of the Iberian men's destructive tendencies and traffic in women.[1]

1. Fidalgo d'Elvas, *Relaçam verdadeira dos trabalhos q[ue] ho governador dõ Fernãdo de Souto [e] certos fidalgos portugueses passarom no descobrimẽto da provincia da Frolida* [*sic*]: *Agora nuevamete feita per ho fidalgo Delvas* (Évora, 1557); Charles Hudson, "The Hernando de Soto Expedition, 1539–1543," in Hudson and Carmen Chaves Tesser, eds., *The Forgotten Centuries: Indians and Europeans in the American South, 1521–1704* (Athens, Ga., 1994), 74–103; see also the chapters by Randolph J. Widmer, "The Structure of Southeastern Chiefdoms," 125–155, Chester B. DePratter, "The Chiefdom of Cofitachequi," 197–226, and David J. Hally, "The Chiefdom of Coosa," 227–253. In this chapter, I follow Elvas's spelling for people and place-names. For a helpful correlation of dates, toponyms, and people mentioned in Rodrigo Ranjel (1546 / 1851), Elvas (1557), Fernández de Biedma (1544 / 1866), and El Inca Garcilaso de la Vega (1605), see John R. Swanton, "Parallel Itinerary of the Expedition," and "Indian Proper Names in the Four Narratives," in Lawrence A. Clayton, Vernon James Knight, Jr., and Edward C. Moore, eds., *The de Soto Chronicles: The Expedition of Hernando de Soto to North America in 1539–1543,* 2 vols. (Tuscaloosa, Ala., 1993), I, 311–354, 499–502. All translations from the Portuguese are my own. In this chapter, I cite place-

As stories of the party's violence circulated among and between Muscogee-, Catawban-, and Timucan-speaking communities—indeed, among such language variety that de Soto traveled with "diez y doze y catorze Interpretes para hablar a los Caciques, y Indios de aq̃ellas provincias" (ten and twelve and fourteen Interpreters to talk to the Caciques, and Indians of those regions), according to the secondhand synthesis of Andean chronicler El Inca Garcilaso de la Vega—another narrative emerged. This story, which included maps, reports, and one "true relation," focused on Soto's inability to locate metallic deposits: namely, the copper that was always just beyond his reach.[2]

In adapting a variety of printed forms to convey their faith in untried sources of imperial wealth, writers and reformers shaped the malleable possibilities of copper, "the most versatile metal known to man," as historian Eugenia Herbert writes, into creative narrative mediums. Artists and engravers used copper plates to convey images of New World people, places, and commodities, reinforcing colonial ideologies by binding printed and visual messages about "wild" Indigenous communities. Spanish and Portuguese authors in the Americas used stories about copper mines, refineries, and finished goods to convey narrative possibilities of new sources of colonial wealth. They took the form of the metal—wherein form served as a political framework that "affords repetition and portability across materials and contexts," as literary scholar Caroline Levine argues—and converted that potential into new modes of storytelling. As writers of firsthand accounts recycled patterns and motifs from earlier texts, and editors repackaged these works for new audiences, they created an archive of stories and narrative traditions that redefined the meaning of experience, eyewitness testimony, and knowledge of metals in the New World. Comparative analysis across Portuguese and Spanish linguistic and cultural lines allows us to read these texts with a healthy dose of skepticism. Owing to the ruptures of colonialism, scholars depend on documents like that produced by o Fidalgo de Elvas. By comparing the stories of copper that he casts in the *Relaçam verdadeira* with other forms of evidence from Soto's expedition, including secondhand accounts, geographic data, and material cultures, and by comparing these patterns of retelling with seventeenth-century promotional materials about the red metal, we gain a deeper understanding

---

names as they were written in Portuguese, followed by present-day equivalents (when possible) and Spanish terms (when helpful for comparative study).

2. El Inca Garcilaso de la Vega, *La Florida del Ynca: Historia del adelantado Hernando de Soto, governador y capitan general del Reyno de la Florida, y de otros heroicos cavalleros Españoles è Indios . . .* (Lisbon, 1605), 228v. The Gentleman from Elvas is identified by his home city, approximately fifteen kilometers west of Soto's native Badajoz.

of what copper meant to different groups of historical actors in contested colonial spaces.[3]

The two chapters in this part analyze iterative stories of copper in the interconnected regions of Iberia, Africa, and the Americas. This chapter attends to Hernando de Soto's search for copper works in La Florida, a region that included present-day Florida, Georgia, Alabama, Mississippi, and the Carolinas. The tale of Soto's march was narrated by Elvas, modeled on reports of Spanish agent Álvar Núñez Cabeza de Vaca, and refashioned by English polymath Richard Hakluyt.[4] The next chapter focuses on proposals for *asientos de minas* and *asientos de negros* (providers' contracts for copper mines and African slaves) in Cocorote, Venezuela. These texts were drafted by Andalusian council member Manuel Gaytán de Torres, partly following the model of royal slavery established in El Cobre, Cuba, and they were revised during debates with officials in Seville and Madrid. Part 3, building from Part 2, employs comparative literary analysis of Portuguese- and Spanish-language sources. But instead of marking divergent reception histories, as "Iron" did, the evidence in "Copper" shows where and how Iberian authors borrowed from each other and modified evidence to project particular visions of American wealth. Whereas Elvas transmuted absent evidence into fantastic stories of possibility and converted a failed search for gold into a new potential for copper, Gaytán de Torres used copper as his starting point. For him, the three stages of copper metallurgy

3. Eugenia W. Herbert, *Red Gold of Africa: Copper in Precolonial History and Culture* (Madison, Wis., 1984), 76; Michael Gaudio, *Engraving the Savage: The New World and Techniques of Civilization* (Minneapolis, 2008); Caroline Levine, *Forms: Whole, Rhythm, Hierarchy, Network* (Princeton, N.J., 2015), 3, 14.

4. Literary scholars Lisa Voigt and Anna Brickhouse have studied interimperial representations and, in Brickhouse's case, "the inter-indigenous translational web" of translator Juan Ortiz, a Spanish soldier who was captured in La Florida when he went looking for members of the Narváez expedition. By tracing the ways in which Cabeza de Vaca, El Inca Garcilaso de la Vega, and Hakluyt created their own versions of Ortiz, Voigt and Brickhouse show how a range of authors articulated their own ideas about Indigenous languages, message-shaping intermediaries, and cultural identities. My approach builds from theirs, focusing on the movement of copper goods and information about metals as they relate to the crafting of imperial images rather than the movement of ideas through speech in acts of self-fashioning. Our work suggests how diverse sixteenth- and seventeenth-century writers capitalized upon the story of the Soto expedition to project their own visions of imperial coherence and self-justification. See Voigt, *Writing Captivity in the Early Modern Atlantic: Circulations of Knowledge and Authority in the Iberian and English Imperial Worlds* (Williamsburg, Va., and Chapel Hill, N.C., 2009), 102–138; and Brickhouse, *The Unsettlement of America: Translation, Interpretation, and the Story of Don Luis de Velasco, 1560–1945* (New York, 2015), 34, 133–141.

served as a metaphorical model for the founding of a community of African copper miners and a new way of planning enslaved communities. This comparative framework reveals instances of imperial rivalry and borrowing as they developed in Portuguese and Spanish colonial projects across the Americas.[5]

The imaginative archive of colonial copper reveals a vibrant proliferation of literary forms: relations, true relations, translations, paintings, and charts whose features correspond to numbered guides in the body and margins of lettered reports; three-column notes that imperial secretaries created to organize projectors' ideas, council members' objections to them; and negotiated plans for settlement. Meanwhile, the sources of copper never materialized for Elvas or Soto. Gaytán de Torres's plan for Cocorote only become profitable in the eighteenth century as part of the estate of South American liberator Simón Bolívar. What these texts lacked in real-world impact, they made up for in imaginative scope. Rather than teaching us about the practices of empire as they unfolded on the ground, the works of o Fidalgo de Elvas and don Manuel, as well as the official responses to their projections, reveal what colonial actors and imperial agents believed possible in the sixteenth- and seventeenth-century Americas.[6]

The Atlantic World of Copper

Although copper is often called a "local" currency in early modern Europe because it was used for domestic transactions rather than international payments, it was a truly global mode of exchange. Copper was imported into France from Germany and Spain, into Germany from Sweden, and into the united crowns of Spain and Portugal from Japan, Sweden, and Austria (which primarily shipped to Spain) as well as from Flanders, Italy, and Morocco (the prime sources for Portugal, which traded most of its copper in Africa and India). When they could not find gold or silver, sixteenth-century agents like Soto settled on copper metals. In early-sixteenth-century Spain, *ducados* and *escudos* (gold coins) were worth 375 and 350 *maravedís,* respectively, and reales (silver currency) commanded 34 maravedís. *Vellóns* (copper coins), on the other hand, were only worth one-half maravedí.[7]

5. On comparative methodologies, see J. H. Elliott, *Empires of the Atlantic World: Britain and Spain in America, 1492–1830* (New Haven, Conn., 2006), xvi–xviii. For examples of works that employ frames of similarity and difference, see Ralph Bauer, *The Cultural Geography of Colonial American Literature: Empire, Travel, Modernity* (Cambridge, 2003); Voigt, *Writing Captivity,* 255–319.

6. Paúl Verna, *Las minas del libertador: Tres siglos y medio de historia venezolana, 1605–1972* (Caracas, 1977).

7. Frank C. Spooner, *The International Economy and Monetary Movements in France,*

Yet copper was highly valuable in other exchange contexts. Most notably, it was a critical material through which Iberian traders forged relationships with west African merchants who controlled access to the transatlantic slave trade. Copper was in high demand in Africa, and European traders competed to provide it. In the medieval era, the trade between gold-producing Africa and copper-producing Europe met in North and West Africa and solidified the economic power of the Malian empire *(mansa),* where traders from southern Europe—primarily Catalonia and Italy—bought gold in cities like Ceuta, and North African merchants purchased Mediterranean textiles, books, and copper metals in sub-Saharan African markets, according to Moroccan travel writer Ibn Battuta. Technology transfers seem to have accompanied these economic exchanges. Archaeological evidence of copper refining at Akjoujt, in the mineral-rich interior of present-day Mauritania, suggests that refiners followed North African and Spanish traditions more than the methods used in Central African metallurgical sites like Agadez (present-day western Niger).[8]

Although medieval sources document northward flows of gold and southern-bound shipments of copper, it is hard to fix rates of exchange until the early modern era, when competition among European factions drove up metallic prices in the Gold Coast. During the early seventeenth century, the Dutch West India Company (WIC) held a monopoly that set the parameters of trade at two ounces of gold for thirty-five pounds of copper. By the end of the century, English and French traders, eager to access these markets and break up the monopoly, paid forty pounds of copper for the same amount of gold. These copper goods took a variety of forms and uses, and they conveyed a range of meanings in West African port cities, southern trading regions, and Central West African markets. Some of the copper stayed on the Gold Coast, particularly basins, bowls, and manillas (bracelets that served as currency), but much of it was melted down, cast into new forms, and used to exchange goods with communities of the interior. Thus European copperwares, in addition to materials that were worked from native ores, reinforced political, economic, and social ties between and among African communities.[9]

In seventeenth-century West Africa, copper was in "almost universal demand" along the coastal region stretching from Senegambia to Angola, but

1493–1725 (Cambridge, Mass., 1972), 44–46; Michael Thomas D'Emic, *Justice in the Marketplace in Early Modern Spain: Saravia, Villalón and the Religious Origins of Economic Analysis* (Lanham, Md., 2014), 64.

8. Ross E. Dunn, *The Adventures of Ibn Battuta: A Muslim Traveler of the 14th Century* (Berkeley, Calif., 2012), 292–293; Herbert, *Red Gold of Africa,* 19, 127.

9. Herbert, *Red Gold of Africa,* 135.

consumers in local markets preferred different styles, and merchants expected that Portuguese, Spanish, Dutch, English, and French traders would adapt. Fugger agents in Antwerp delivered thick brass manillas to Elmina and slightly thinner varieties to Guinea. Buyers on the Senegalese coast sought brass objects for cooking, music, and dress, such as kettles, bells, trumpets, chains, and bracelets, but riparian communities of the interior insisted upon cookware and basins of different sizes than those used in coastal regions. In Gambia, mixed metallic objects, especially rings of copper, brass, and tin, dominated local trade, whereas merchants in Côte d'Ivoire preferred brass manillas and beads that could be exchanged throughout West Africa. Traders on the Gold Coast insisted on the greatest variety of objects, including brass bracelets, copper barber's basins, pots, pans, kettles, and rods, each of which commanded different exchange values. During the first half of the seventeenth century, traders in Benin and Cameroon demanded 25 pounds of copper pots to purchase one enslaved man (23.5 gulden), or 23 pounds (21.5 gulden) for a woman. In Bight, enslaved men were purchased for 23 copper rods (11.5 gulden), and enslaved women were sold for 18 rods (9 gulden).[10]

Copper—in all of its material forms and local variations—was linked to the transatlantic slave trade, from the fifteenth-century Portuguese empire to the beginning of the Industrial Revolution in England. Upon the discovery of deep-level copper ores in Cornish tin mines, refiners used local coal sources to smelt copper. With these copper metals, they built larger and more precise reverberatory furnaces for the manufacture of ironwares. This local access to coal, copper, and iron enabled large-scale mechanized production that transformed the British economy. As historian Candice L. Goucher argues, the "lasting links" between the institution of slavery, the slave trade, and emerging world capitalist systems "were partially constructed of African metals."[11]

Goods made of copper, iron, and bronze (copper and tin) that were manufactured in Africa crossed the Atlantic alongside enslaved women and men. "Oriki Oshún," a song sung in offering to the deity Oshún (Ochún)—associated in Cuba with the worship of the Virgin de la Caridad del Cobre ("la dueña del cobre," analyzed in the next chapter)—celebrates the Yoruba (present-day

10. Ibid., 127–128 (citing a contract in Jakob Strieder, *Aus Antwerpener Notariatsarchiven: Quellen zur deutschen Wirtschaftsgeschichte des 16. Jahrhunderts* [1930; rpt. Wiesbaden, 1962], 451–453), 136, 139.

11. Herbert, *Red Gold of Africa,* 146–148; Candice L. Goucher, "African Metallurgy in the Atlantic World," in Akinwumi Ogundiran and Toyin Falola, eds., *Archaeology of Atlantic Africa and the African Diaspora* (Bloomington, Ind., 2007), 277–291, esp. 277.

Nigeria) deity of motherhood as "Dueña del bronce" (ruler of bronze), whose "ojos brillan como el bronce, / tu piel es suave y tersa, / negra como el terciopelo" (eyes shine like bronze, / your skin is soft and smooth, / black as velvet). Archaeological excavations of enslaved people's living quarters in sugar and coffee plantations located in the Brazilian states of Matto Grosso, Goiás, Rio de Janeiro, and Minas Gerais reveal important evidence of copper material cultures among enslaved families. Among earthenwares, ceramic goods, and glass beads, archaeologists Luís Cláudio P. Symanski and Flávio dos Santos Gomes found numerous copper ornaments and a copper crucifix in sugar plantations, compared with "a sparse material culture" from coffee plantations, including a copper thimble, a copper button, and a few copper rings. Even in the most restricted circumstances, copper goods, worked into a variety of forms, played a role in the material cultures of African and Afro-descendant communities in the Americas.[12]

For European empires, the value of copper was clear: it was a mode of exchange that could initiate trade with West African merchants who controlled markets for ivory, gold, and enslaved people. For African purchasers, the value of copper was notably different. In some cases, transportable copper bracelets, rods, crosses, and ingots circulated as currency. In a broader sense, the metal's red, sonic, reflective properties connected the material plane of this world with that of the spirits. Red, white, and black form a color scheme that repeats itself throughout sub-Saharan Africa, with localized meanings in different communities. According to anthropologist Jan Vansina, for the Anziku (Tyo) of Kongo, red objects symbolize life and power as analogies to blood and fire, whereas white goods balance them by connoting "sacredness and peace." In Ndembu communities (present-day Zambia, Angola, and the Democratic Republic of the Congo), white objects signify ancestors, black goods convey the present human world, and red mediates the relationship between the two. Bambara communities in Mali connect copper with the placenta, whereas Tyo people ascribe it to "a male counterpart of the placenta, or at least the umbilical cord." Among African diasporic communities in Cuba, Oddúa, the orisha deity of creation and the enforcer of justice, is depicted with white, red, and black clothing and jewelry, as a sign of the complementary male (white) and

12. Ángel B. Alfaro Echevarría, *Memoria ritual* (Bogotá, 2007), 19, 121; Luís Cláudio P. Symanski and Flávios dos Santos Gomes, "Iron Cosmology, Slavery, and Social Control: The Materiality of Rebellion in the Coffee Plantations of the Paraíba Valley, Southeastern Brazil," *Journal of African Diaspora Archaeology and Heritage,* V (2016), 174–197, esp. 176, 177, 180, 182–183.

female (red) energies that are at work in childbirth and fertility. As these examples suggest, copper goods in precolonial Africa and African diasporic contexts enjoyed a wide signifying range.[13]

Yet, for as much as their meanings varied by region and over time, copper wares were consistently associated with ideas of power and permanence, perhaps explaining why so many kings in West and Central West Africa were keen to express their sovereignty and control of resources through copper objects. The kingdom of Benin—a powerful culture that was founded between the thirteenth and fourteenth centuries in present-day Nigeria and ruled until the end of the nineteenth century, when the British colonized the region—traces its origins to a refiner who arrived from the city of Ife and taught the men of the kingdom how to work with bronze metals. A creation story from the Dogon people of present-day Mali and Niger relates that metallurgists are born from the placenta of Nommo, the blood-red creator god and god of earth, creating a powerful connection between refiners, rulers, and the spirit world. Meanwhile, the soundscapes of copper objects, especially bells, drums, and trumpets, enable communication with ancestors and the divine, connecting human communities with the animating life forces of past and future. Given this range of spiritual, medical, and political meanings, it is perhaps unsurprising that copper became a key site of expression in the objects that Jesuit and Capuchin priests and their African converts employed in what art historian Cécile Fromont calls "the art of conversion."[14]

Copper meant different things to African communities at various historical moments; ore deposits likewise varied widely, and they were processed using slightly different technologies from one region to the next. One point of consistency was the demand for copper goods in West and Central West Africa and the eagerness with which sixteenth- and seventeenth-century European traders provided it. European projectors, in turn, contributed to imperial fantasies of a lucrative trade in copper and enslaved people by imprinting upon their readers the idea that copper mining, refining, and minting in the Ameri-

13. Alfaro Echevarría, *Memoria ritual,* 97; Jan Vansina, *The Tio Kingdom of the Middle Congo, 1880–1892* (London, 1973), 219, 235–236, 318, 386–387, and John Janzen, introduction to A. Fu-Kiau kia Bunseki, *N'kongo ye nza yakun'zungidila: Le mukongo et le monde qui l'entourait* (Kinshasa, 1969), 6–7, 120, 123, both cited in Herbert, *Red Gold of Africa,* 278–279, 281.

14. Alfaro Echevarría, *Memoria ritual,* 40; Germaine Dieterlen, "Contribution à l'etude des forgerons en Afrique occidentale," *Annuaire,* LXXIII (1965–1966), 10, cited in Herbert, *Red Gold of Africa,* 33–34; Cécile Fromont, *The Art of Conversion: Christian Visual Culture in the Kingdom of Kongo* (Williamsburg, Va., and Chapel Hill, N.C., 2014). See also Alisa LaGamma, *Kongo: Power and Majesty* (New York, 2015), 73–75.

cas was both possible and profitable. These writers imagined, by following a material good from Africa to the Americas, that colonial copper, like plantation monocultures, precious metals, and enslaved laborers, could become an engine of New World wealth.

Copper Fictions: Iberian Exploits in La Florida

Álvar Núñez Cabeza de Vaca opens and closes the report of o Fidalgo de Elvas, bookending the Portuguese account with Spanish precedents. In 1542, Cabeza de Vaca reduced his eleven years of shipwreck and wandering into thirty-nine slim sections that composed the *Relacion que dio Aluar Nuñez Cabeça de Vaca de lo acaescido en las Indias.* Thirteen years later, he standardized the text into thirty-eight formal chapters with names and numbers, and he appended it to eighty-four chapters of commentary as well as the relation of Hernando de Ribera on the province of Argentina. This work was published as *La relación y comentarios del Governador Alvar Nuñez Cabeça de Vaca, de lo acaescido en las dos jornadas que hizo a las Indias.*[15]

According to Fidalgo de Elvas's *Relaçam verdadeira,* Cabeza de Vaca was called to speak before a royal audience. There, he affirmed the veracity of what he had written, which more or less relayed what Elvas called "the misery of the land" ("miseria da terra"); at the same time, Cabeza de Vaca insisted that his men wanted to return to La Florida, where they had seen signs of wealth in the "rich land" ("terra rica"). Elvas added that the explorer wanted to say more, but he had promised his companion, Andrés Dorantes, who stayed in Mexico awaiting permission for a second expedition, that he would not share too many details of their plan.[16]

In exploiting the gap between written report and spoken intimation—and conveying the sense of what he could not say—Cabeza de Vaca encouraged his audience, including writer-soldiers like Fidalgo de Elvas, to imagine rich possibilities in the Americas, even amid excruciating tales of death and despair. Elvas writes that, after Cabeza de Vaca recounted his story to Holy Roman Emperor Carlos V, Pedro Álvarez Osorio, marques of Astorga, sent several of his relatives to march with Soto, including Antonio, Francisco, and García Osorio. Deep into their failed mission, the men tried to square their experiences with Cabeza de Vaca's report of finding cotton clothing ("roupa dalgodã"), a sign of civilization, alongside deposits of gold, silver, and precious stones where

15. *La relacion que dio Alvar Nuñez Cabeça de Vaca . . .* (Zamora, 1542); *La relación y comentarios del governador Alvar Nuñez Cabeça de Vaca, de lo acaescido en las dos jornadas que hizo a las Indias: Con privilegio . . .* (Valladolid, 1555).

16. Fidalgo d'Elvas, *Relaçam verdadeira,* vii(v).

"ainda nam avia chegado" (no one had yet arrived). When the expectation of wealth did not cohere with the reality of struggle, Elvas looked to his source to account for the difference between literary fashioning and lived experience. Curiously, even as Fidalgo de Elvas omitted evidence from his own relation, he took Cabeza de Vaca at his word.[17]

In truth, what Soto's men experienced was not all that different from what Cabeza de Vaca described; it was different from what they said he wrote. There are notable similarities between Cabeza de Vaca's *Relación y comentarios* (1555), which describes events from 1527 to 1537 in San Lúcar, Cuba, La Florida, Lisbon, and Castile, and Elvas's *Relaçam verdadeira* (1557), which describes events from 1539 to 1543 in Seville, Cuba, La Florida, and Mexico. These similarities, such as their insistence on the possibility of finding copper wealth, even, and especially, as Iberian soldiers died along the way, suggest that Cabeza de Vaca's literary precedent weighed heavily on the Portuguese footsoldier's firsthand report.[18]

The principal members of Cabeza de Vaca's group were Andrés Dorantes de Carranza, Alonso del Castillo Maldonado, and Estebanico, identified as a "negro Alarabe" (black Moor) from the coastal city of Azemmour, some eighty kilometers south of Casablanca. Although little is known about Estebanico, his movements throughout the text reveal how he skillfully accommodated to new cultural geographies. He traveled alternately with Dorantes, with Cabeza de Vaca and Dorantes, with Cabeza de Vaca alone, with del Castillo, and with Indigenous messengers, sometimes guiding as many as fifty Indians at once. In different ways and combinations, these men gathered information on the people, plants, foods, and medicines of the land, although Cabeza de Vaca remained the hero of the story.[19]

The group's first yield of any meaningful amount of metals, other than small samples of gold that they spied near Tampa Bay, or a few silver tailings ("taleguillas de plata") in the Mexican highlands, was the copper they received for curing the sick in the valleys east of Zacatecas. Outside of present-day Tamaulipas, Cabeza de Vaca was as impressed by the whiteness of the people ("mas blancos que otros ningunos de quãtos hasta alli aviamos visto") as by their

17. Ibid., vi, vi(v), cxlvii(v).

18. Ibid., vi(v).

19. Ibid., xxiiii, xxvi(v), xxix, xxxi, xxxii(v), xliii, xlviii, liiii(v). On Estebanico's movements as a cultural go-between, see Cassander L. Smith, "Beyond the Mediation: Esteban, Cabeza de Vaca's *Relación,* and Narrative Negotiation," *Early American Literature,* XLVII (2012), 267–291. See also Laila Lalami's imaginative reinterpretation of his story, *The Moor's Account: A Novel* (New York, 2014).

copper gift economy, on display when Dorantes received a large, round copper bell engraved in the form of a face, and squashes ("calabaças") from local healers ("fisicos") to convey the men's prestige and authority on their travels northward. There, it was said, they would find the foundries where the copper originated ("avia fundicion y se labraua de vaziado"). As much as Cabeza de Vaca insisted on his value in Native communities, and as much as critics have traditionally lauded his transculturated stance, his physical movements tell a different story: in the foothills of the Sierra Madre, a few hundred kilometers from Zacatecas and San Luis Potosí, skilled Indigenous informants sent his men away from the richest mines of Mexico.[20]

As they trekked through the Sierra de la Gloria in present-day Coahuila, the men found stones laced with iron slag and people who employed semiminerals in spiritual rituals, such as tailings of marcasite ("margaxita," FeS_2) and ground kohl. But they did not locate any metals until Cabeza de Vaca traded medical service ("mi officio de medicina") for information on copper wares. After he performed a public act of healing, working with a knife in one hand and a deer bone in another to remove an arrowhead embedded in a man's heart, Cabeza de Vaca displayed Dorantes's bell to the town's spiritual leader, who sent them southward, toward "muchas planchas de aquello enterradas: y que aquello era cosa que ellos tenian en mucho: y avia casas de assiento" (many copper sheets buried there, a thing that they regarded in great esteem, and there were houses seated there). As they would for Elvas, peopled places signaled good prospects on the path to unearthing fabled buried treasure.[21]

Now following the southern route ("el camino del maíz") rather than the northern course ("el camino de las vacas"), the men still ended up going northward. They crossed the Río Grande for the third time, near present-day Chihuahua, and marched another thirty-five days until arriving at the South Sea ("la mar del Sur"), where they found foodstuffs (maize, beans, deer) and promised signs of settlement: houses, blankets, beads, and a variety of stones that

20. Fidalgo d'Elvas, *Relaçam verdadeira,* xxxviii(v), xl, xxxxviii(v). On toponyms, see Rolena Adorno and Patrick Charles Pautz, *Álvar Núñez Cabeza de Vaca: His Account, His Life, and the Expedition of Pánfilo de Narváez* (Lincoln, Neb., 1999), I, 205–207. The largest copper mines in Mexico are concentrated in the western states of Guerrero, Michoacán and Jalisco, although gold, copper, and iron were often found mixed with silver deposits in and around Zacatecas and San Luis Potosí; see Luis Berrio de Montalvo, *En informe del nuevo beneficio que se ha dado a los metales . . .* (Mexico City, 1643), 44v–45, 51v. On Cabeza de Vaca's discourse of transculturation, see Carlos A. Jáuregui, "Going Native, Going Home: Ethnographic Empathy and the Artifice of Return in Cabeza de Vaca's *Relación," Colonial Latin American Review,* XXV (2016), 175–199.

21. Fidalgo d'Elvas, *Relaçam verdadeira,* xl–xl(v).

revealed the town's role as a trade center, including coral from the South Sea and turquoise from the north. After delivering all that they had, the people of Yaquí (Sonora) gave Cabeza de Vaca five high-quality emeralds worked into the shape of arrowheads, signifying ritual use in celebrations and dances. As he inquired about the origins of the stones, Cabeza de Vaca showed his ability to read different materials, including friendship arrows ("una flecha que es señal de amistad"), arrows exchanged for acts of healing, and healing stones ("las piedras y otras cosas que se crian por los campos tienen virtud") in Capoque and Han communities of Malhado and along the Río Grande. At first, he had mocked the stones' curative powers, to which a healer in Malhado (Galveston Island, Texas) promptly replied "que yo no sabialo que dezia, en decir que no aprouecharia nada aquella q̄ el sabia" (that I didn't know what I was saying by saying that nothing would be gained using what he knew).[22]

Indeed, it was Cabeza de Vaca who had nothing to show for his labor or knowledge, an inconvenience that he explained away. Many informants, he argued, intentionally led them away from mines; and despite rich samples ("muestras"), some communities, like the people of Río Petatlán (Sinaloa), showed little interest in gold, iron, copper, and "otros metales." His most damning explanation occurred when the group encountered Christians in the province of Nueva Galicia. There, Cabeza de Vaca's men were forced to trade what little wealth they had accumulated to save their Native guides from the Christians, who threatened to enslave them. The group forgot about the emeralds and handed them over amid a cache of weapons and leather pouches. With three different reasons to explain why he had no proof of wealth from America, Cabeza de Vaca converted printed words into evidence that he hoped might convince the crown to sponsor a second expedition.[23]

This transmutation was successful, at least in part, because it inspired Hernando de Soto. The Spanish adelantado-governor's search for new sources of wealth in La Florida was recorded by Elvas, who positioned his 1557 account within an imperial Iberian literary rivalry for fame and accomplishment. The title promised to truthfully tell of the many members of Portugal's petty nobility who served under Soto: *Relaçam verdadeira dos trabalhos q̄ ho governador dō fernādo de souto e certos fidalgos portugueses passarom no descobrimēto da provincia da Frolida* [sic]: *Agora nuevamēte feita per ho fidalgo Delvas* (True Relation of the Travails That the Governor Don Fernando de Soto and Certain Portuguese Gentlemen Experienced in the Discovery of the Province

22. Ibid., xvii(v), xxxviii, xliii–xlv(v). The 1542 edition indicates that Dorantes received the emeralds; see Adorno and Pautz, *Álvar Núñez Cabeza de Vaca,* I, 230.

23. Fidalgo d'Elvas, *Relaçam verdadeira,* xlvii(v), xlviii(v).

of Florida: Now Newly Made by the Gentleman of Elvas). This was not the first time that Iberian readers learned of Soto's exploits, as Spanish chronicler Francisco López de Gómara, discussed in Part 2, summarized "the discovery of La Florida" in his *Historia general de las Indias* (1553). However, the *Relaçam verdadeira* was one of the first eyewitness accounts to make its way into print. (See Map 3 for the expedition's route.)[24]

In preparing the manuscript for publication in Évora, some fifty-five kilometers west of Elvas, Spanish printer André de Burgos crafted an address to his intended audience, "o Prudente Leitor" (the Prudent Reader). Before moving to Évora, Burgos had practiced his craft in Seville. Under new sponsorship across the border, Burgos printed Portuguese feats of discovery. In his prefatory address to the *Relaçam verdadeira,* Burgos argued that Portugal's navigators excelled all European empires in the discovery of new worlds and new markets, a "natural" pursuit of novelty, per Aristotle. In service to his readers, he printed his book, "atrevēdome a ser escripta por homē portugues e ser escripta ho propio linguajem" (daring to be written by a Portuguese man in his own language).[25]

The language of publication contrasts with that of the expedition, for when the soldiers left behind five hundred "peças, índios e índias" (slaves, Indian men and women) in Aminoya (present-day Desha County, Arkansas), many of the children had learned to speak and understand Spanish ("entre os q̄es muitos moços e moças auia q̄ a lingoa espanhol falavam e ētēdiam"). The term *peça,* or *peça das Indias* (literally, "piece," or "piece of the Indies"), was used by Portuguese traders in West Africa to classify women and men of different ages as they were sold into slavery. The measurements were institutionalized, such that peças between the ages of eight and thirty-five were worth twice as much as those who were outside of the desired age range. As historian Stephanie Smallwood notes, this kind of commodification of black bodies—and its economic, epistemological, and social power—both stems from and "resides in language, in discursive forms (ledgers, bills of sale) carefully crafted to define and imagine things in terms that best facilitate their exchange and circulation." Elvas's text shows how the term *peça,* estranged from its origins as a term for an

24. Francisco López de Gómara, *Primera y segunda parte de la Historia general de las Indias: Con todo el descubrimiento y cosas notables que han acaecido dende que se ganaron ata el año de 1551* (Zaragoza, 1553), xxiii–xxiii(v).

25. "Andre de Burgos ao prudente lector," in Fidalgo d'Elvas, *Relaçam verdadeira,* ii–ii(v); Patricia Galloway, *The Hernando de Soto Expedition: History, Historiography, and "Discovery" in the Southeast* (Lincoln, Neb., 2006), 22–23. Burgos's patron, Henrique I, underwrote publications that converted Évora and its Jesuit controlled university into a vibrant political and intellectual center.

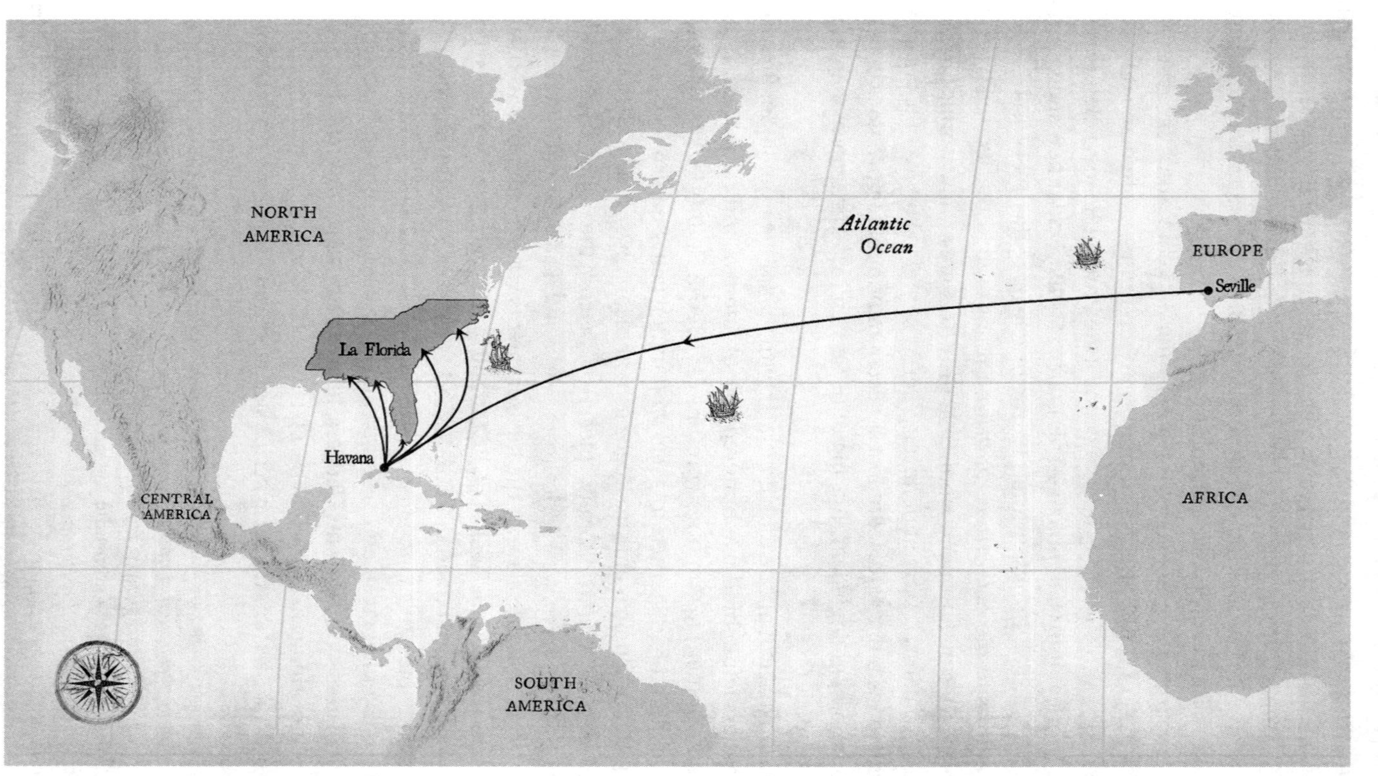

MAP 3. The Soto expedition's route from Seville to La Florida. Drawn by Lynn Carlson, GISP, Brown University

enslaved African bound for the New World, was repurposed to describe Amerindians who were enslaved in their own lands.[26]

The title and prefatory materials of Elvas's book foreshadowed Portuguese-Spanish tensions that unfolded in the narrative. Even before leaving Spain, the six hundred soldiers on the original mission were torn by faction; Elvas claimed that some Spaniards tried to pass as Portuguese so they could trade their inferior weaponry for better arms. By the time they departed from Cuba, the first stop on the voyage, Soto had five hundred soldiers and two Indigenous men whom he captured "assi por serem necessarias pera guia e lingoa, como por dizerem por acenos que auia muito ouro na Frolida" (because they were necessary as a guide and tongue and, as they told us through signs, there was a lot of gold in La Florida). In other words, after the first remove, Soto had already lost 17 percent of his soldiers and replaced them with Indigenous informants, who spun stories of New World gold. Soto would consistently ask about gold rather than copper, until he began conversing and compromising with Indigenous rulers well into the mission.[27]

Indigenous sovereigns, and the Iberian captives who served them, proved central to the movement of imperial knowledge, might, and defeat. The first meeting in the Timucua-speaking towns of Ucita and Mocoço (Mocoso) established a pattern that Soto's party would repeat for the next hundred miles. Soto spoke through the interpreter João (Juan) Ortiz, a Spaniard who had come to La Florida in search of the expedition of Cabeza de Vaca and Pánfilo de Narváez. He was taken captive and almost left for dead until Native women cured him with "zumos de yerbas" (herbal potions). Ortiz had lived in captivity for so long that he now pronounced his home city of Seville as "Xivilla," but one soldier, Álvaro Nieto, understood him and identified him as the missing Juan

26. Fidalgo d'Elvas, *Relaçam verdadeira,* clvii–clvii(v); James Alexander Robertson, ed. and trans., "The Account by a Gentleman from Elvas," in Clayton, Knight, and Moore, eds., *Soto Chronicles,* I, 214; C. R. Boxer, *The Golden Age of Brazil, 1695–1750: Growing Pains of a Colonial Society* (1962; rpt. Berkeley, Calif., 1969), 5, citing Luandan records from 1678; Stephanie Smallwood, "Commodified Freedom: Interrogating the Limits of Anti-Slavery Ideology in the Early Republic," in John Lauritz Larson and Michael A. Morrison, eds., *Whither the Early Republic: A Forum on the Future of the Field* (Philadelphia, 2005), 139–148, esp. 143.

27. Fidalgo d'Elvas, *Relaçam verdadeira,* ix, xviii. In Havana, Soto waited until his wife, doña Isabel de Bobadilla, could replace him as governor. On the Bobadilla family's relationship with the Colón brothers in Cuba, see Consuelo Varela, *La caída de Cristóbal Colón: El juicio de Bobadilla,* ed. Isabel Aguirre (Madrid, 2006), 237–257, especially the testimonies of Mateo Valenciano (208–209), Juan de Salaya (220–221), and Colón's *lugarteniente de justicia,* Rodrigo Pérez (227–235).

Ortiz. On Soto's behalf, he questioned the cacique Mocoço about whether he knew of any land with gold or silver. Mocoço replied that, although his lands were metal-less, he had heard that another cacique, Paracoxi, to whom he and Ucita paid tribute, had good land, "e q̄ a sua era ja milhor que a da costa e mais fertil e abondosa de mais" (and that it was better than that of the coast and the most fertile and abundant in maize). The soldiers considered this a promising step toward discovering a mine, but Mocoço effectively ensured that armed men would march thirty leagues from his town and arrive at his enemy's door to demand goods.[28]

The passage reveals a classic case of colonial misdirection: the soldiers asked about precious metals and received information on fertile soil. This formative first meeting suggested that the two groups defined wealth in different ways—one agricultural, one metallic. As we saw in Chapter 3, Taínos in La Española valued the deep continuities between animate plant and metallic matter. It is possible that Mocoço's reply gestures to a similar understanding. It is also possible that he is saying anything to send Soto's men elsewhere. The gap between Indigenous information on maize and Iberian pursuits of metals underscores the prism of difference through which Indigenous, Spanish, and Portuguese agents understood each other. The scene also reveals how Indigenous sovereigns, and the translators who gave voice to their responses, helped to foment disagreement within the Iberian squadron. On Mocoço's word, Baltasar de Gallegos, captain and *alcalde mayor* from Seville, arrived in Paracoxi with thirty Native messenger-guides at the same time Portuguese captain Vasco Porcalho de Figuerôa of Cáceres, just north of Soto's home city of Badajoz, abandoned the expedition.[29]

28. Fidalgo d'Elvas, *Relaçam verdadeira,* xxvii(v), xxviii; Hudson, "Soto Expedition," in Hudson and Chaves Tesser, eds., *Forgotten Centuries,* 96; Garcilaso de la Vega, *La Florida del Inca,* 48–49, 59. In Nondacao, near Cypress Creek (present-day Camp County, Texas), one cacique directed them through poor, unpeopled lands ("terra mal pouada e avia pouso mayz") by instructing his guides to turn east instead of west ("as guias q̄ aviā dir a ponēte guiavā para levante" [*Relaçam verdadeira,* cxliii–cxliii(v)]).

29. Elvas refers to Paracoxi as a person rather than a place. See Robertson's annotations in Clayton, Knight, and Moore, eds., *Soto Chronicles,* I, 186. For an excellent study of networks of translators, messengers, and go-betweens as meaningful shapers of information in the Native Southeast, see Alejandra Dubcovsky, *Informed Power: Communication in the Early American South* (Cambridge, Mass., 2016), esp. 30–56. Colonial sources tell different stories about Porcalho de Figuerôa. Compare the *Relaçam verdaderia* (xxix–xxx) with Adorno and Pautz, *Álvar Núñez Cabeza de Vaca,* I, 24, II, 48–51; Gonzalo Fernández de Oviedo y Valdés, "Natural y general hystoria de las Indias," ca. 1539–1548, MSS, HM177, 32v, Huntington Library, San Marino, Calif.; and Oviedo, *Historia general y natural de las*

To negotiate with Native Southeasterners, Soto's party relied heavily upon Indigenous intermediaries and Spanish subordinates. Baltasar de Gallegos gathered information about gold deposits in Superior Chief Paracoxi's land. There, Indigenous informants invoked the classical trope of an eternally golden landscape, directing the soldiers to the province of Cale, near present-day Ocala, Florida, "donde tudo ho mais do tēpo do anno era verão e avia muito ouro" (where for the greater part of the year it was summer and there was a lot of gold). Gallegos was suspicious of a report of Elysian Fields in La Florida, but Soto received the men and their message with great pleasure, believing "q̄ podia ser verdade ho q̄ os indios deziam" (that what the Indians said could be true). On this word-that-could-be-true, the party moved through the riverside settlement of Caliquem and the Yustaga town of Anapetaca (Napetaca) to arrive at Apalache, where the governor was told that inland regions were rich in gold. Native informants carefully guided the soldiers away from their own communities and toward a center of Indigenous control: Cutifachiqui.[30]

They learned about the community from a young boy ("moço") who was taken by two other captives ("Dos Indios que se tomaram em Napetuca") in Yupaha, a far-off place to the east ("muy longe pera dōde nacia ho sol"). The boy was brought before treasurer João Gaytán, to whom he relayed his story: in Yupaha, there was "hũa molher a ensenhoreava, e ho povo dōde resedia era đ admiravel grandeza: e que aquella señora tributauā muitos señores seus comarcãos: e hũs lhe davā roupa, e outros ouro em cantidade e đzia como se tirava das minas" (a woman who ruled the area, and the land where she ruled was of notable greatness. And that that woman collected tribute from many men of the neighboring lands. And they gave her clothing, and others gave gold in great quantity. And he said how they extracted it from mines). Elvas went on to explain that the boy told Gaytán how the people of those lands refined gold using technologies they had developed firsthand or received from the devil: "e su fundia e apurava como se ho vira fazer ou ho demonio lho ensinara" (and they smelted and purified it as they had seen done or how the

---

Indias, ed. Juan Pérez de Tudela Bueso (Madrid, 1959), 207 ("De las minas nuevamente halladas en la isla Fernandina," part 1, book 6, chap. 21).

30. Fidalgo d'Elvas, *Relaçam verdadeira,* xxx(v), xxxi, xxxviii. On Cale, see Robertson, "Account by a Gentleman from Elvas," in Clayton, Knight, and Moore, eds., *Soto Chronicles,* I, 188n64, and John Hann's note on the same (ibid.). Swanton locates Caliquem—called Aguacalecuen (Biedma) or Aguascaleyquen (Ranjel) and Napetaca (Napituca/Napetuca) near where the Santa Fe River branches off from the Suwannee River, in present-day Branford, Florida. See ibid., 189n80. On Napetaca, see Smithsonian Institution Bureau of American Ethnology, *Handbook of American Indians North of Mexico,* ed. Frederick Webb Hodge, 2d ed. (Washington, D.C., 1912), part 2, 28.

devil had taught them). In complementary pairs of smelting and refining, experienced artisanry and diabolical transmissions of knowledge, Elvas strips metallic purification of its Christian resonance and aligns Indigenous metallurgy with demonic arts. The young captive offered such detailed technical and economic information on refining, tribute labor, and trade that the soldiers, putting their faith in signs ("como se ho virã por os sinaes"), believed the story to be true. As the narrator put it in the final line of chapter 12, "Que quantos algũa coussa disso sabian deziam que era impossivel dar tam boa relação sem ho aver visto" (He knows so much of this thing that the soldiers said it would be impossible to give such a good account without having seen it).[31]

By relaying information on metals, news about the soldiers, and replies from sovereigns, Indigenous messengers connected different language and cultural communities. Archaeological, linguistic, and GIS data suggest that, during Soto's month-long march along the roads of Ꭓualla (Joara), near present-day Morganton, North Carolina, Iberian soldiers would have encountered at least three language communities: Muskogean and Catawaban in Cutifachiqui and Cherokee on the other side of the Appalachian Mountains. Despite belonging to different polities, the provinces were subject to the same female ruler, the cacica de Cutifachiqui, who used networks of captives and interpreters to command space and speech. When the soldiers captured three men outside

31. Fidalgo d'Elvas, *Relaçam verdadeira,* xlii(v), xliii. Rodrigo Rangel also details Native women's roles in community life. In an extended passage, he describes how people near Ichisi (Ocmulgee River, Georgia) use mulberry trees to fashion clothing:

> The white clothing in which those Indian women came clothed are some blankets of both coarse and fine linen. They make the thread of them from the bark of the mulberry trees; not from the outside but rather from the middle; and they know how to process and spin and prepare it so well and weave it, that they make very pretty blankets. And they put one on from the waist down, and another tied by one side and the top placed upon the shoulders, like those Bohemians or Egyptians who are in the habit of sometimes wandering through Spain. The thread is such that he who found himself there certified to me that he saw the women spin it from that bark of mulberry trees and make it as good as the most precious thread from Portugal that the women in Spain procure in order to sew, and some more thin and even, and stronger. The mulberry trees are exactly like those of Spain, and as large and larger; but the leaf is softer and better for silk, and the mulberries better for eating and even larger than those from Spain, and the Spainards also made good use of them many times, in order to sustain themselves.

Rangel, "Account of the Northern Conquest and Discovery of Hernando de Soto," ed. and trans. John E. Worth, in Clayton, Knight, and Moore, eds., *Soto Chronicles,* I, 247–306, esp. 271.

of Aymay (Himahi), at the confluence of the Congaree and Wateree Rivers—a space that they named Socorro (Relief)—the prisoners told them that the cacica awaited their arrival.[32]

In Cutifachiqui, located along the Wateree River in present-day South Carolina, the soldiers encountered a rich matrix of colonial possibility: mulberry trees that could underwrite a new silk industry, established networks of tribute collection, and a female ruler. She wasted no time in displaying her strength. Preceded by her sister, who arrived in a fleet of four canoes, the cacica was carried in on a dais, and from her heightened position she offered herself, lands, and subjects in "humble service." With this ceremonial exchange of speech, she placed a strand of pearls around Soto's neck and made the first in a series of calculations. Observing the soldiers' interest in the pearls and weighing it against their desire for women and metals, the cacica de Cutifachiqui presented her second offering: an abundance of turkeys; finely worked blankets dyed white, green, red, and yellow; richly colored animal hides; and pearls that had been buried in funerary rites. As Elvas chronicled the bounty of the land and the well-formed, civilized nature of the people ("a gēte era morena, bē đspuesta e proporcionada e mais polida q̄ nbūa da q̄ se vio em toda a terra"), his Indigenous informants related the history of a plague ("peste") that had caused them to relocate two years earlier. Perhaps balancing the threat of Christian presence against traditions of ancestor worship, the cacica directed the soldiers toward temples, where they disinterred fourteen *arrobas* of pearls, some of which had been worked into the shapes of birds and small children ("meninos") as a sign of their ritual nature.[33]

32. Fidalgo d'Elvas, *Relaçam verdadeira,* liii(v), lix. In his "Account," Rangel reported of Xualla, "There was better disposition to look for gold mines than in all that they had passed through and seen in that northern part" (Clayton, Knight, and Moore, eds., *Soto Chronicles,* I, 281). On geographic data, see Kathryn Sampeck, Jonathan Thayn, and Howard H. Earnest, Jr., "Geographic Information System Modeling of de Soto's Route from Joara to Chiaha: Archaeology and Anthropology of Southeastern Road Networks in the Sixteenth Century," *American Antiquity,* LXXX (2015), 46–66, esp. 52; Charles Hudson, *Knights of Spain, Warriors of the Sun: Hernando de Soto and the South's Ancient Chiefdoms* (Athens, Ga., 1997), 183.

33. Fidalgo d'Elvas, *Relaçam verdadeira,* liiii(v), lv–lv(v). On colonial designs for silk, see Allison Margaret Bigelow, "Gendered Language and the Science of Colonial Silk," *Early American Literature,* XLIX (2014), 271–325. Hann estimates two hundred pounds of pearls; Richard Hakluyt translates the line as "foureteene rooves of perles," glossed in the margins as "Three hundred ninetie two pounds of pearles found." See Hann, annotation to Robertson, "Account by a Gentleman from Elvas," in Clayton, Knight, and Moore, eds., *Soto Chronicles,* I, 196n121; [Fidalgo de Elvas], *Virginia Richly Valued, by the Description of the Maine Land of Florida, Her Next Neighbor . . . ,* trans. Hakluyt (London, 1609), 53.

In Cutifachiqui itself, they spied hatchets made of a copper-gold admixture, a detail that Elvas omits from the passage and instead inserts in the next chapter. They learned of similar metallic mixtures and technologies in Chiaha, about twelve days' journey ("doze jornadas") from the town. On May 30, 1540, the troop departed. To punish the Christians for their crimes against her people ("agravos q̄ os christãos aviā feito aos indios"), the Cacica de Cutifachiqui refused to provide guides ("guias") or porters ("tamenes pa cargas"). This Hispanized form of the Nahuatl term *tlamama* ("cargar" / to carry) suggests how Indigenous vocabularies in diverse regions of the Americas circulated through Spanish and Portuguese reports. When Soto forced her to escort them to Chiaha, she aligned with an enslaved man, identified only as the property of soldier André de Vasconcellos da Silva, and they used the journey as a pretense to escape from Iberian control.[34]

As the troops marched westward, becoming more violent and frustrated at the lack of gold, the soldiers began to articulate ideas about settlement rather than extraction. Once the land was settled ("povara"), they argued, it could provision ships to and from Mexico, Peru, Santa Marta, and Tierra Firme and thus be "aparelhada pera fazer proveito" (well appointed to be fruitful). According to Elvas, the only objector was Soto, who compromised the mission by allowing his experiences in Peru to shape his expectations and strategies of discovery, conquest, and governance in La Florida. Soto was so intent on finding Inca treasure in Mississippi ("outro tesouro como ho de Tabalipa señor do peru") that he could not see what the region truly had to offer. By looking only for what he already wanted to find rather than being open to new possibilities, Soto ensured that the expedition would fail. Colonial reports often emphasize the value of firsthand experiences and knowledge that cannot be acquired through textual transmission or study. But for Elvas, in this case, Soto's experience and eyewitness testimony was a stumbling block on the real road to wealth.[35]

After one month of marching, the party finally arrived in Chiaha, near present-day Dandridge, Tennessee, where Soto repeated the ceremonial speech acts that he had practiced earlier. There was one key difference: al-

34. Fidalgo d'Elvas, *Relaçam verdadeira,* lvii, lviii, lxiiii(v), lxviii; *Diccionario de la lengua española,* 23d ed., s.v. "tameme." Elvas concludes that the cacica conspired with her servants and enslaved men from the Iberian party: "Era muito certo que tinham cōversaçam de marido e molher e determinavā hirē se ābos pera Cutifachiqui" (*Relaçam verdadeira,* lx[v]).

35. Fidalgo d'Elvas, *Relaçam verdadeira,* lvi(v), lvii; and see Hann's annotations to Robertson, "Account by a Gentleman from Elvas," in Clayton, Moore, and Knight, eds., *Soto Chronicles,* I, 178n12.

though he still requested Indigenous porters, he promised that he would not take any more Indian women, for whom the price proved too dear. By giving his word, in recognition of the political and economic might of Indigenous sovereigns who thwarted his designs, Soto forged a new alliance and obtained his best information on another source of New World wealth—copper.[36]

When Soto's interpreters conveyed his customary inquiry about natural resources, the cacique of Chiaha offered precise details on the smelting of copper admixtures in Chisca, where "avia fundiçam de cobre e outro metal de aquella cor, senam quanto era mais acendrado, e de muyto mais perfecta cor e muyto milhor ao parecer e que nã se aproveitavã tanto delle por ser mais brando" (there was a foundry for copper and another metal of that color, if only a little purer, and of a much more perfect color and very better to behold, and that they did not make much use of it because it was softer). It is unclear whether this mixture was gold-copper or silver-copper, although, beginning in the nineteenth century, most historians and archaeologists believed it to be gold because of the location of goldfields and mines in present-day northern Georgia and southern North Carolina. They also point out that pre-Columbian copper artifacts were worked with cold-process techniques like hammering rather than the smelting technologies that Soto's informants relate.[37]

Other colonial sources described what seemed to be silver-copper admixtures, such as the "marveilous and most strange Minerall" refined by the Chawanook (Chowanoke) people of coastal Carolina, as relayed by colonial governor Ralph Lane, and reported as "whyte grayness of Mettall, which is to bee deemed *Silver*" by alchemist Thomas Harriot. Copper minerals were extracted from Chaunis Temoatan, a "Mineral Countrey" that was located some "twentie days journey overland" from Lane's post among the Mangoaks, according to his captive informant Skiko, the son of the Chawanook sovereign. These minerals, called *wassador* in Algonquian (a term also used for "every mettall whatsoever"), were, unlike English copper, "very soft, and pale," probably because of their mixed metallic content. Miners waded into shallow streams with large bowls whose openings were partly covered by animal hides, effectively serving

36. Fidalgo d'Elvas, *Relaçam verdadeira,* lxiiii; Sampeck, Thayn, and Earnest, "Geographic Information System Modeling," *American Antiquity,* LXXX (2015), 47.

37. Fidalgo d'Elvas, *Relaçam verdadeira,* lxiii–lxv; George F. Kunz, "On Gold and Silver Ornaments from Mounds of Florida," *American Antiquarian and Oriental Journal,* IX (1887), 219–227, esp. 225; Henry Lee Reynolds, "Algonkin Metal-Smiths," *American Anthropologist,* I (1888), 341–352. Such sources also distrust Indigenous technologies, so they should be taken with more than a grain of salt. As Reynolds writes in the often-racist modes of nineteenth-century scholarship, "The American Indian, in those days, was not the lazy, shiftless, and improvident being that the art of the European has made him" (344).

as placers (or *bateas,* discussed in Part 1). When they observed changes in the color of the current, as pieces of metal floated downstream, they submerged the bowls in order to "receive into the same as much oare as will come in." Then, having collected enough material to justify the trip, they "cast it into a fire, and forthwith it melteth, and doeth yeelde in five parts, at the first melting, two parts of metal for three parts of oare." This is an impressive yield, generating "so great store" that Lane reported seeing houses beautified "with great plates of the same." Lane went from Chawanook to the land of the Mangoaks, a distance that he placed at one day's journey traveling overland and a minimum of one week's journey traveling by river, for he was "very desirous by all meanes possible to recover the Mangoaks, and to get some of that their copper for an assay." He never made it, though, and the journey "fell out very contrary to all expectation, and likelyhood."[38]

Yet Lane believed that evidence of copper metallurgy testified to the region's economic potential: "Thus doeth M. Younghan affirme, that though it be but copper, seeing the Savages are able to melt it, it is one of the richest Minerals in the world." This Master Youngham was probably the metalsmith who appears in Lane's passenger list as Dougham Gannes (Joachim Ganz) and collaborated with George Nedham in copper assays at Keswick in 1581. English trials of copper and lead from 1579 to 1580, conducted by Nedham and refiners like Daniel Heghstetter on behalf of the Mines Royal Company, resulted in disappointing yields. Sometimes they lost up to half of the assay because of inferior equipment, such as "potts beinge oft broken and not tighte" or a "lacke of good blaste of the bellowes." A return of 40 percent ore from assays of copper from the Carolinas compared favorably with results in England.[39]

38. Ralph Lane, "An Account of the Particularities of the Imployments of the English Men Left in Virginia by Sir Richard Greenevill under the Charge of Master Ralph Lane Generall of the Same, from the 17. of August 1585 until the 18. of June 1586. at Which Time They Departed the Countrey: Sent and Directed to Sir Walter Raleigh," in Richard Hakluyt, *The Principal Navigations, Voyages, Traffiques, and Discoveries of the English Nation: Made by Sea or Overland to the Remote and Farthest Distant Quarters of the Earth at any Time within the Compasse of These 1600 Yeares,* 8 vols. (London, 1907), VI, 142–164, esp. 148–149.

39. Thomas Harriot, *A Briefe and True Report of the New Found Land of Virginia . . .* (Frankfurt, 1590), 10; Lane, "Account of the Particularities," in Hakluyt, *Principal Navigations,* VI, 151; Hakluyt, "The Names of Those, aswell Gentlemen as Others, That Remained One Whole Yeere in Virginia, under the Government of M. Ralph Lane," ibid., 138–140, esp. 139; David Beers Quinn, ed., *The Roanoke Voyages, 1584–1590: Documents to Illustrate the English Voyages to North America under the Patent Granted to Walter Raleigh in 1584,* Works Issued by the Hakluyt Society, 2d Ser., no. 104 (London, 1955), 196n; "Trial of Copper and

For Soto, reports of copper metallurgy in Chisca were decidedly appealing. This was not the first time Soto learned about foundries in the trade post located along the Nolichucky River in the stretch of the Appalachian Mountains that runs through present-day eastern Tennessee. However, it was the first time he received actionable information on how to reach a mining center. Other Indigenous sovereigns had encouraged the soldiers to depart for remote lands on dangerous routes ("a terra mal povooda e deziã q̄ avia serras q̄ os cavallos nã poderiã passer"). In contrast, the cacique of Chiaha, satisfied that his people would be safe, told Soto to travel by well-peopled places with guides who knew the geographic and linguistic way ("indios q̄ sabiã a terra de chisca, e a lingoa della").[40]

Geological and archaeological data from the Copper Basin of southeast Tennessee support the cacique's report. The region is home to three kinds of ore: top-level iron oxides (FeO_2); middle-level copper oxides (CuO), sometimes called "black copper"; and deep-level iron sulfides (FeS_2), often mixed with other minerals. Additionally, there are native copper (Cu) deposits mixed with lead (Pb) and other minerals along the western edge of the Appalachian Mountains in southwest Virginia. The saline marshes and salt mines of the valley near present-day Saltville, Virginia, allowed for an important salt trade between Mississippian communities and eastern groups with access to copper.[41]

Although the copper mines were probably too small to support anything more than local production, they were part of a long-range trade network that connected northern Iroquois copper-producing communities of the Great Lakes region with Algonquian communities that harvested seashells from the Chesapeake Bay as early as the Woodland period (600–1000 CE). This trade in animate red and white objects, which probably traveled along the Susquehanna River into present-day New York and from there to the Chesapeake,

---

Lead Sent by Daniel Heghstetter from Keswick," Queensborough, Mar. 21, 1579/1580, Elizabeth I, 164/36/iii, National Archives, Kew, U.K.

40. Fidalgo d'Elvas, *Relaçam verdadeira,* lxv.

41. M. L. Quinn, "Industry and Environment in the Appalachian Copper Basin, 1890–1930," *Technology and Culture,* XXXIV (1993), 575–612, esp. 577; Chester B. DePratter, Charles M. Hudson, and Marvin T. Smith, "The Route of Juan Pardo's Explorations in the Interior Southeast, 1566–1568," *Florida Historical Quarterly,* LXII (1983), 125–158, esp. 134–135; Maureen S. Meyers, "The Mississippian Frontier in Southwestern Virginia," *Southeastern Archaeology,* XXI (2002), 178–191, esp. 181, 186–188. It is worth pointing out that William Wallace Tooker interprets the toponym Chaunis Temoatan as "place of salt making." See Tooker, "Discovery of Chaunis Temoatan of 1586," *American Antiquarian,* XVII (1895), 3–15, esp. 8–9.

allowed diverse communities to acquire goods of spiritual significance and high social standing. As anthropologist George Hamell has shown for northern Iroquois communities, white shells symbolized light and social life, whereas red objects such as metallic copper (Cu), hematite (Fe_2O_3), and stones such as jasper and catlinite represented blood and antisocial balance. In their circulations aboveground and their burial in funerary rites, red and white objects symbolized the continuation of life. When situated alongside black goods, especially iron (Fe), obsidian, and charcoal, which were understood as asociality / absence, black metals and semimetals counterpointed the social circulations of white goods and the antisocial meanings of red wares. Taken together, the three colors formed complementary "semantically organizing principle[s] of ritual states-of-being and ritual material culture." Archaeological records suggest that copper objects were used in burial ceremonies throughout the Native Southeast before and after Afro-European contact, including sheet metal, jewelry, square fragments, and worked objects like bells, beads, and tools, in accordance with the deceased's age, gender, social status, and historical era. By overlaying archaeological and geographic data with textual interpretation of colonial sources, we see how, and perhaps why, Indigenous agents shaped Iberian movements in copper-networked lands like Chiaha.[42]

Predictably, Soto broke his promise and resumed taking Native women

42. April Lee Hatfield, "Spanish Colonization Literature, Powhatan Geographies, and English Perceptions of Tsenacommacah / Virginia," *Journal of Southern History,* LXIX (2003), 245–282, esp. 253; Charles Hudson, *The Juan Pardo Expeditions: Exploration of the Carolinas and Tennessee, 1566–1568* (Washington, D.C., 1990), 157–161; George R. Hamell, "The Iroquois and the World's Rim: Speculations on Color, Culture, and Contact," *American Indian Quarterly,* XVI (1992), 451–469, esp. 456–458. On copper, broadly, see Hudson et al., "On Interpreting Cofitachequi," *Ethnohistory,* LV (2008), 465–490, esp. 472. On precontact burial practices in southern Virginia, see Jane M. Eastman, "Life Courses and Gender among Late Prehistoric Sioan Communities," in Eastman and Christopher B. Rodning, eds., *Archaeological Studies of Gender in the Southeastern United States* (Gainesville, Fla., 2001), 57–76. For the Potomac River in the colonial era, see Stephen R. Potter, "Early English Effects on Virginia Algonquin Exchange and Tribute in the Tidewater Potomac," in Gregory A. Waselkov, Peter H. Wood, and Tom Hatley, eds., *Powhatan's Mantle: Indians in the Colonial Southeast,* 2d ed. (Lincoln, Neb., 2006), 215–241, esp. 218, 226–235. The archaeological record, particularly ceramic patterns that reflect multiple cultural influences of Pisgah, Qualla, Dallas, and Catawba traditions, provides further support for copper refining at Chisca. See Hudson et al., "Coosa: A Chiefdom in the Sixteenth-Century Southeastern United States," *American Antiquity,* L (1985), 723–737; Thomas McDowell, Nelson Lewis, and Madeline D. Kneberg Lewis, *The Prehistory of the Chickamauga Basin in Tennessee,* comp. and ed. Lynne P. Sullivan, 2 vols. (Knoxville, Tenn., 1995), I, 12–20. I thank Madeline Gunter Bassett for sharing archaeological sources on copper.

almost immediately after learning about copper metalwork. By June 9, four days after meeting the cacique of Chiaha, Soto took four women and two male porters in Tali, just across the Little Tennessee River, following the bend southward from Chiaha. Within one week, having arrived in Coça (Coosa), along the Coosawattee River of what is now northwest Georgia, he took Indian women and men and threw them in chains to signify their enslaved states ("q̄ tinha ē cadeas como escravos"). Just outside of Coça, near Ullibahali, he enslaved Indigenous porters and thirty women, an act he repeated in Toasi (Tawasa), five or six leagues away. His violent choices did not lead to new sources of wealth or information. Instead, Tuscaluscans set fire to everything the soldiers had, scorching their bodies, horses, clothing, sacraments, and pearls. Although the men bemoaned the loss of life and spiritual sustenance, stories of Native violence and attacks on Christians fitted easily into European expectations. Absence of New World wealth was more difficult to explain. Soto had planned to send pearls to Cuba to entice settlers, but now he had nothing to show for his time in La Florida.[43]

O Fidalgo de Elvas was forced to reveal how the men marshaled and concealed evidence as they constructed a literary narrative of conquest. Without gold, silver, or anything of value, he feared that the region would get such a reputation "que nam ouvesse home que a ella quisese hir quādo gente ouvisse mester" (that no man would want to go to the land that so greatly needs people). Soto thus withheld all news of the mission ("nam dar novas") so that no one would know what they had discovered and appropriated, and then taken and lost. By manufacturing reports of colonial encounter, Hernando de Soto curated a narrative of New World wealth. The Portuguese foot soldier who relayed his story pulled the curtain back on this process, perhaps comforted by the fact that Soto would never read his words.[44]

Armed with weapons, visions of metallic wealth, and Cabeza de Vaca's words, Soto's men reenacted formative scenes of colonial encounter in a new

43. Fidalgo d'Elvas, *Relaçam verdadeira,* lxii, lxvii(v), lxxi(v), lxxxi. John Swanton interprets Ullibahali as "Holiwahali," derived from the Muskogee morphemes "war" + "to divide"; see Robertson, "An Account by a Gentleman from Elvas," in Clayton, Knight, and Moore, eds., *Soto Chronicles,* I, 201. Indigenous place names reveal more than topographic features or geographic demarcations. As Dubcovsky argues, they "offer perhaps the most enduring clue to how Indians conceived their world" (*Informed Power,* 45). Dubcovsky and George Aaron Broadwell reconstructed Timucan grammar from extant records, suggesting how collaborative, transdisciplinary research can reveal new insights into fragmented Indigenous language data; see their "Writing Timucua: Recovering and Interrogating Indigenous Authorship," *Early American Studies,* XV (2017), 409–441.

44. Fidalgo d'Elvas, *Relaçam verdadeira,* lxxxi(v).

geography. In the Native Southeast, copper was the stuff of usable objects like hatchets, prestige goods like medallions, and spiritual symbols of the afterlife; its circulation brought diverse communities into economic, social, and sacred communion. As a literary trope in the hands of Cabeza de Vaca and Fidalgo de Elvas, the circulation of copper told a different story. As a narrative device and promotional tool, copper metals were central to the making and remaking of New World possibility through genealogies of Iberian letters. Cabeza de Vaca's tales inspired the expedition of Hernando de Soto, and Fidalgo de Elvas reframed the stories of both Spanish conquerors. This pattern did not end with a sixteenth-century Portuguese retelling of Spanish-led exploits. Instead, English, French, and German translations of the *Relaçam verdadeira,* published throughout the seventeenth and eighteenth centuries, show how diverse authors, editors, and printers in the early modern Atlantic world reiterated colonial accounts and reframed them once more for their own audiences.[45]

Telling in Translation: English Projections

One of the earliest and most influential translators was Richard Hakluyt, who translated the work more than fifty years after it had been published in Portuguese. Hakluyt's seventeenth-century translation revived some of Spain's earliest colonial voices: the Pizarros, Cabeza de Vaca, Soto. Using print to mediate the uneven chronologies of English and Spanish explorations, Hakluyt styled his edition in two different ways for two different audiences: *Virginia Richly Valued* (Figure 12) was directed toward the Virginia Company, whereas *The Worthye and Famous History* (Figure 13) was intended for a broader, yet equally interested, readership. Both translations shifted the center of colonial possibility from Spanish Florida to English Virginia, a move conveyed in a variety of print mechanisms, including font size, text placement, and titles.[46]

45. Garcilaso de la Vega, *Histoire de la Floride; ou, Relation de ce qui s'est passé au voyage de Ferdinand de Soto, pour la conqueste de ce pays,* ed. Pierre Richelet (Paris, 1670), rpt. as *Histoire de la conquête de la Floride; ou, Relation de ce qui s'est passe dans le decouverte de ce pays par Ferdinand de Soto* (Paris, 1711). The new title was perhaps inspired by Samuel de Broë's *Histoire de la conqueste de la Floride, par les Espagnols, sous Ferdinand de Soto* (Paris, 1685); compare with *De gedenkwaardige voyagie van Don Ferdinand de Soto, na Florida, en desselfs ontdekking van de Landen in dat gewest, met al wat aanmerkenswaardig op die vierjarige Reyse is vorgevallen* (Leyden, 1706).

46. David B. Quinn, "A List of Books Purchased for the Virginia Company," *Virginia Magazine of History and Biography,* LXXVII (1969), 347–369, esp. 349. In *Empires of the Atlantic World,* Elliott describes the dichronic approach required to tell the histories of imperial England and Spain as akin to "playing the accordion. The two societies under com-

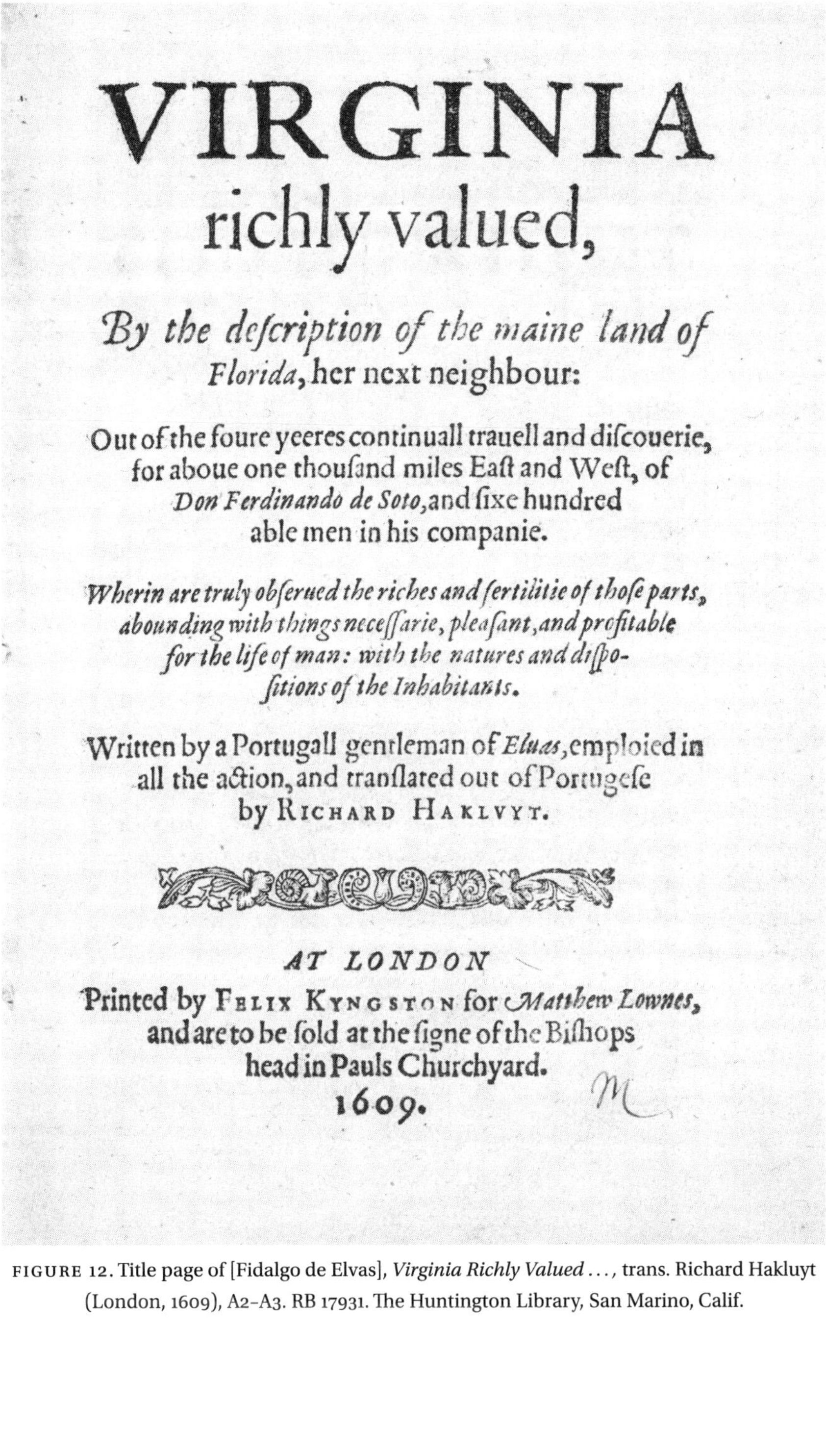

VIRGINIA
richly valued,

By the deſcription of the maine land of Florida, her next neighbour:

Out of the foure yeeres continuall trauell and diſcouerie, for aboue one thouſand miles Eaſt and Weſt, of *Don Ferdinando de Soto*, and ſixe hundred able men in his companie.

Wherin are truly obſerued the riches and fertilitie of thoſe parts, abounding with things neceſſarie, pleaſant, and profitable for the life of man: with the natures and diſpoſitions of the Inhabitants.

Written by a Portugall gentleman of *Eluas*, emploied in all the action, and tranſlated out of Portugeſe by RICHARD HAKLVYT.

AT LONDON

Printed by FELIX KYNGSTON for *Matthew Lownes*, and are to be ſold at the ſigne of the Biſhops head in Pauls Churchyard.

1609.

FIGURE 12. Title page of [Fidalgo de Elvas], *Virginia Richly Valued . . .*, trans. Richard Hakluyt (London, 1609), A2–A3. RB 17931. The Huntington Library, San Marino, Calif.

THE WORTHYE AND FAMOVS HIS-TORY, OF THE TRAVAILES,

Diſcouery, & Conqueſt, of that great Continent of *Terra Florida*, being liuely Paraleld, with that of our now Inhabited *VIRGINIA.*

As alſo

The Comodities of the ſaid Country, With diuers excellent and rich Mynes, of Golde, Siluer, and other Mettals, &c. which cannot but giue vs a great and exceeding hope of our *VIRGINIA*, being ſo neere of one Continent.

Accompliſhed and effected, by that worthy Generall and Captaine, **Don Ferdinando** *de Soto*, and ſix hundreth Spaniards his followers.

LONDON

Printed for Mathew Lownes, *dwelling* in Paules Church-yard, at the Signe of the Biſhops head. 1611.

FIGURE 13. Title page of [Fidalgo d'Elvas], *The Worthye and Famous History, of the Travailes, Discovery, and Conquest, of That Great Continent of Terra Florida . . .*, trans. Richard Hakluyt, Works Issued by the Hakluyt Society, no. 9 (London, 1611). British Library General Reference Collection C.33.c.19. Courtesy of the British Library

Hakluyt's choices reveal insight into his process of literary refashioning. To stories of "continuall travell and discoverie" and observations of the "riches and fertilitie of those parts," he added a precise account of "Divers excellent and rich Mynes, of Golde, Silver, and other Mettals, etc" in "our now Inhabited Virginia." Whereas Elvas stressed the work of discovery ("dos trabalhos q̄ . . . passarom no descobrimento da provincia da Frolida *[sic]*"), Hakluyt emphasized the ease of managing Indigenous "natures" and goods to provide "things necessarie, pleasant, and profitable for the life of man." The second edition, which moved the travails of Soto and his "able men" to the third line, further subordinated Iberian labor to English expectations: "a great and exceeding hope of our Virginia." By placing the original author in the final text block, Hakluyt created a narrative of "discovery and conquest" that was performed without discoverers or conquerors. He concluded by changing an uncertain number of Portuguese ("certos fidalgos portugueses") into "six hundreth Spaniards," effectively remaking colonial space and even the colonists themselves.

By changing the words of the title, Hakluyt also changed their presentation on the page. In the first edition, the largest single text element is the place: "VIRGINIA Richly Valued." In the second, however, the leading text block and the largest font are reserved for the promise of wealth: "THE WORTHYE AND FAMOUS HISTORY." Both editions employ the same basic style—a single-sheet, unframed title page that proclaims its contents in a series of increasingly smaller text blocks (four lines, four lines, and three in the first edition; seven lines to four in the second) before ending with a minimally decorative printer's device and publication information. Because the prefatory materials and body texts are identical, the rechristened title does not reflect any information learned between 1609 and 1611. It suggests how early modern print culture helped to produce stories of colonial wealth and shape them for different readers.

Hakluyt's text is a faithful-enough translation of Elvas's work, translating the spirit of a text rather than finding word-for-word equivalencies. As Saint Jerome quoted from a biography of St. Anthony of Egypt, "A literal translation from one language into another conceals, as with a coat, the original sense." Renaissance writers recuperated translation theories from antiquity, and they evaluated the merits of literary translations in similar terms. According to lexicographer John (Giovanni) Florio, a successful translation of Montaigne's *Essays* transported the text "from France to England; put it in English clothes;

---

parison are pushed together, but only to be pulled apart again," as motifs from the Spanish conquest are applied in English imperial ideologies, and Spanish American creoles adapt eighteenth-century British beliefs about political economy (xvii).

taught it to talk our tongue (though many times with a jerk of the French jargon)."[47]

Hakluyt's preface is another matter. Writing from Westminster Abbey on April 15, 1609, one year after Captain John Smith returned from Virginia and published his *True Relation of Such Occurrences and Accidents of Noate as Hath Hapned in Virginia since the First Planning of That Collony,* Hakluyt dedicated his first translation to "the Right Honourable, the Right Worshipfull Counsellors, and others the cheerefull adventurors for the advancement of that Christian and noble plantation in Virginia." As historian Peter C. Mancall suggests, "This was no mere supplication to a patron seeking support but a response to the efforts of Smith and his colleagues on that far shore." The dedicatory letter, reproduced verbatim in 1611, served the same purpose in both editions: to draw attention to the possibilities of metallic wealth in the virgin colony and to present a range of alternative industries, such as silks, wines, pearls, salt, and shipping routes to "Japan and China, which I finde here twice to be spoken of ("Chap. 31 & 32"). He noted both of these chapters in the margins, drawing readers' attention to various forms of colonial promise. Finally, Hakluyt placed his translation in dialogue with other works, including "the generall report of Cabeça de Vaca to Charles the Emperor," Cabeza de Vaca's "Italian relation," and the state-sponsored chronicle of Antonio de Herrera y Tordesillas, which he read in Spanish and cited almost word for word.[48]

Hakluyt's editorial practices throw into sharp relief the gap between what his sources say and what his prefaces say that they say. Although the *Relaçam*

47. Jerome, "Letter to Pammachius (395)," trans. Paul Carroll, and John Florio, "To the Courteous Reader: Preface to Translation of Montaigne's *Essayes* (1603)," both in Douglas Robinson, *Western Translation Theory from Herodotus to Nietzsche* (Manchester, U.K., 1997), 24, 133.

48. Richard Hakluyt, "To the Right Honourable, the Right Worshipfull Counsellors, and Others the Cheerefull Adventurors for the Advancement of That Christian and Noble Plantation in Virginia," Apr. 15, 1609, in [Elvas], *Virginia Richly Valued,* trans. Hakluyt, A2–A3; [Elvas], *The Worthye and Famous History, of the Travailes, Discovery, and Conquest, of That Great Continent of Terra Florida . . . ,* trans. Hakluyt, Works Issued by the Hakluyt Society, no. 9 (London, 1611); Peter C. Mancall, *Hakluyt's Promise: An Elizabethan's Obsession for English America* (New Haven, Conn., 2007), 270; "Relatione che fece Alvaro Nunez detto Capo di vacca: Di quello che intervenne nell'Indie all'armata, della qual ere governatore Pamphilo Narvaez, dell'anno 1527 fino al 1536 che ritornò in Sibilia con tre soli suoi compagni," in Giovanni Battista Ramusio, ed., *Terzio volume delle navigationi et viaggi* (Venice, 1565), 310. A new edition was reissued in 1606. See also Antonio de Herrera y Tordesillas, *Historia general de los hechos de los castellanos en las islas i terra firme del mar oceano,* 8 vols. (Madrid, 1601–1615), III, 309. Hakluyt introduced a comma and changed the capitalization of one word from the passage (década 3, libro 8, capítulo 8).

verdadeira tells of Indigenous leaders and interpreters who steered Soto's men away from metallic wealth, save for the moments when the soldiers' good behavior merited credible information, Hakluyt's introduction emphasizes "rich mines of gold reported to be in the province of *Yupaha*" and "copper hatchets found in *Cutifachiqui* . . . which were said to have a mixture of gold." Hakluyt effectively mapped the text on a cartographic imaginary of Yupaha, Cutifachiqui, and Chisca, lands "to come within our limits." The mines of Yupaha were "described in the twelfth Chapter of this Treatise," whereas "the famous golden province of *Chisca,*" which "I desire you likewise to take knowledge of," was plotted in the margins as "Chap. 15." Careful readers would see that Soto never found mines or refineries. They would also recall that the province of Chisca was where "avia fundiçam de cobre e outro metal de aquella cor" (there was a foundry for copper and another metal of that color). Hakluyt reduced this open-ended possibility to "a golden province," enabling his preface to tell a story that was not supported by narrative evidence. In a sense, this meant that he was true to the spirit of his sources, for Elvas had done much the same with Cabeza de Vaca.[49]

As imperial promoter, Hakluyt wanted to endorse all suggestion of colonial wealth; but as editor and translator, he had to acknowledge sources that he considered unreliable. Although he inveighed against Indigenous people—"great liars and dissemblers" who proved "as unconstant as the wethercock, and most readie to take all occasions of advantages to doe mischiefe"—he nevertheless spent three pages of his five-and-a-half-page "Epistle Dedicatorie" confirming what Elvas learned about mines and metals from informants in La Florida. He reproduced many of these exchanges in his letter, pointing readers to "a province called *Pacaha,* which hee was informed to be neere unto *Chisca,* where the Indians told him, that there was gold," and "*Chisca,* where the Indians said, there was a worke of gold and copper," glossed in the margins as "Chap. 24."[50]

Richard Hakluyt did not change the words of his source text, but by highlighting key passages in his preface and marking them in the margins, he changed the form of the *Relaçam verdadeira* for his Anglophone audience. He extracted discussions of mineral wealth and discovery from the larger body of the text and condensed them into a streamlined narrative, making his Iberian sources say what he wanted them to say. In translating Elvas and Elvas's reinterpretation of earlier texts, Hakluyt developed particular editorial and lit-

49. Hakluyt, "To the Right Honourable Counsellors," in [Elvas], *Virginia Richly Valued,* trans. Hakluyt, A2–A2v.

50. Ibid., A2–A3, A4.

erary practices that allowed him to communicate his theory of New World wealth, even—and especially when—that evidence was lacking.

Attending to the iterations of copper narratives allows us to distill, in however small a way, the facts and fictions of colonial encounter that are intimately entangled in the historical record. Although we can never really trust the language of our sources, especially regarding Indigenous histories, cultures, and technical knowledges, tracing the movement of ideas and experiences through networks of authors allows us to better understand who said what, in which region, and why. In this colonial variation on "telephone," in which Hakluyt retells Elvas's retelling of Cabeza de Vaca, we see how early modern European writers relay and conceal the pursuit of copper metals in La Florida to project visions of colonial possibility and to model imperial futures. These visions, founded upon Spanish, Portuguese, and English concepts of wealth, largely minimized or ignored the value that copper held in diverse communities of the Native Southeast. Documenting those omissions, as they moved between spoken acts and written words in multiple languages, provides insight into the multiple meanings of copper in economic exchanges, signifying material traditions, and as a source of imaginative potential in spaces of contested imperial power.

7 : LITERARY FORMS, IMPERIAL PROJECTIONS, AND THE LIMITS OF POSSIBILITY IN COPPER COLONIES

If precious metals were the knowledge sectors and currencies whose wealth drove imperial expansion and investment, copper was an unstable unit of exchange whose excessive minting glutted seventeenth-century Spanish markets. Between 1599 and 1606, Felipe III ordered some 22 million *ducados'* worth of *vellón* (copper alloy) to be minted, replacing what had been a silver-copper alloy with copper alone. When the crown found itself short on cash, largely because of seven decades of warfare against Protestant Habsburgs in the Dutch Republic, it minted more *maravedís de vellón* and levied higher taxes upon them. Manipulating internal currencies was more expedient than tinkering with seigniorage rates of silver *marcos* or gold ducados, both of which were central to global trade. This currency debasement strategy preserved Spain's place as a credible minter of global currencies, but it severely compromised domestic markets. The crown's monetary policy left Spain bankrupt by 1607 and thrust the interconnected economies of western Europe into crisis. The worst decade of these entangled economic and currency crises was the 1620s, consisting of a "commercial crisis" (England), a "trade crisis" (Holland), a "joint crisis in commerce and industry" (France), a "currency crisis" (Italy), and a "monetary crisis and panic" in the Habsburg empire (Germany and Austria).[1] Modern research in economics and psychology suggests that human beings respond differently to losses and gains. We are quite sad when someone offers us twenty dollars and pays us fifteen, and we are only moderately happy when someone offers us ten dollars and pays us fifteen. Once we consider something to be "ours," we do not like to lose it, and we take measures—even ones

1. Charles P. Kindleberger, "The Economic Crisis of 1619 to 1623," *Journal of Economic History,* LI (1991), 149–175, esp. 149–150, 152; Akira Motomura, "The Best and Worst of Currencies: Seigniorage and Currency Policy in Spain, 1597–1650," ibid., LIV (1994), 104–127; Earl J. Hamilton, "Spanish Banking Schemes before 1700," *Journal of Political Economy,* LVII (1949), 134–156. For larger discussions of the vellón crisis and concepts of value in early modern Spain, see Pierre Vilar, *A History of Gold and Money, 1450–1920,* trans. Judith White (London, 1976); *Disputase en Sevilla, entre el contador Antonio de Rojas, y Oracio Levanto, la introducion de la nueva moneda de plata y cobre, que se ha propuesto para consumo del vellon, y dase solucion a las dudas y dificultades que se an ofrecido* ([Seville], 1623).

that prevent us from benefiting in other areas—to protect against those losses. Economists and cognitive psychologists call these patterns "loss aversion" or "status quo bias." But once things are lost, we respond to crisis with creativity. New World projectors *(arbitristas)* figured that everything had already been lost, and imperial underwriters ought to entertain ideas they had once dismissed. These projectors, or writers who proposed to reform domestic and overseas governance and commerce—often with elaborate and largely untested ideas—imagined creative possibilities for the making of copper communities in the Americas.[2]

One projector, Andalusian council member don Manuel Gaytán de Torres, took some of those discarded ideas and repacked them into a new series of literary forms, including an eyewitness report, a painting, and three-column documents that allowed him to revise and resubmit ideas to Spanish imperial council members.[3] Whereas o Fidalgo de Elvas's *Relaçam verdadeira* (1557) recast elements of Álvar Núñez Cabeza de Vaca's *Relación* (1542) and *Relación y comentarios* (1555) to articulate Elvas's own version of New World possibility, don Manuel, as he calls himself in his *Relación y vista de ojos* (1621), drew from historical precedent in El Cobre, Cuba, and the three-stage processes of copper metallurgy to project a new kind of mining community. He imagined an enslaved, largely autonomous community of 710 African men and women who would raise their families in the Venezuelan town of Cocorote ("gold, reddish metal," derived from the Arawak term *korrokori*). As he envisioned it, Indigenous farmers from surrounding communities would provide fish and meat for African mining families, who would serve for the length of the *asiento* (providers' contract) that he sought from the crown. Although don Manuel did not specify what would happen to the families at the end of his asiento, he insisted

2. Amos Tversky and Daniel Kahneman, "Loss Aversion in Riskless Choice: A Reference-Dependent Model," in Tversky and Kahneman, eds., *Choices, Values, and Frames* (Cambridge, 2000), 143–158. The same cognitive patterns are observed in primates that are closely related to human beings. See Laurie R. Santos and Alexandra G. Rosati, "The Evolutionary Roots of Human Decision Making," *Annual Review of Psychology,* III (2015), 321–347. English and colonial authorities, like the officials at the Farthing Office in London, raged against "divers Projectors" whose schemes threated the economy: see "A Memorial from the Patentees for Copper Farthings," Mar. 4, 1697/8, Colonial Office, 324/6, 250–252, National Archives, Kew, U.K.

3. Although the painting is now lost, I collaborated with an undergraduate artist-researcher to recreate it. Rebecca Graham's painting of Cocorote, ca. 1621, appears on the cover of this book and in the preface. In the latter, we discuss our research at the Biblioteca Nacional and Archivo General de Indias, and Rebecca explains how her archival findings helped her to reproduce the missing image.

that Spaniards would play virtually no role in the community after it became operational, for many of the 110 Spanish officials required to open the mine would be replaced by African tradesmen.[4]

Recent work in the history of ideas, much of it focusing on England and Spain, provides a fuller and more informed overview of the diverse cultures of projecting and *arbitrismo* that circulated in the seventeenth-century Atlantic world. Some historians, most notably Arrigo Amadori, have attended, in particular, to Gaytán de Torres's proposed reforms within the Spanish monarchy. But no other study has examined how black artisan expertise and black community life informed don Manuel's vision for colonial copper mining. This chapter brings modern research on projecting and knowledge production, from scholars such as Amadori, Eric Ash, and Koji Yamamoto, into dialogue with the history of African knowledge and labor in colonial Cuba and Venezuela, as analyzed by historians such as María Elena Díaz and Miguel Acosta Saignes.[5]

4. Ramón Pané, *Relación de las antigüedades de los indios,* ed. and trans. José Juan Arrom (Mexico City, 2001), 35n114; Manuel Gaytán de Torres, *Relacion, y vista de ojos que don Manuel Gaytan de Torres ventiquatro de la ciudad de Xerez, haze a su Magestad en el Real consejo de las Indias, por comission que para ello tuvo de las minas de cobre que ay en las Serranias de Cocorote, provincia de Veneçuela* (n.p., 1621), 5, 8, General Reference Collection, C.62.i.19, no. 49, British Library, London. In this chapter, I use "African" and "black" (negro) interchangeably, because Gaytán de Torres intended to people the mines with women and men from Cape Verde. In other colonial contexts, however, the two terms are not necessarily synonymous. For a detailed analysis of archival records on racial classifications and vocabularies in colonial Mexico, see Ben Vinson III, *Before Mestizaje: The Frontiers of Race and Caste in Colonial Mexico* (New York, 2018). On Spanish imperial precedent in the marking of racial difference in British America, see Cassander L. Smith, *Black Africans in the British Imagination: English Narratives of the Early Atlantic World* (Baton Rouge, La., 2016).

5. Eric H. Ash, "Reclaiming a New World: Fen Drainage, Improvement, and Projectors in Seventeenth-Century England," *Early Science and Medicine,* XXI (2016), 445–469; Koji Yamamoto, "Reformation and the Distrust of the Projector in the Hartlib Circle," *Historical Journal,* LV (2012), 375–397; Arrigo Amadori, "Remedios para un cuerpo político que declina: El arbitrismo de Manuel Gaytán de Torres y el estrechamiento de los vínculos transatlánticos de la monarquía hispánica (siglo XVII)," *Anuario de Estudios Americanos,* LXXI (2014), 107–143; and Amadori, "Que se de diferente modo al govierno de las Indias, que se van perdiendo muy a prisa: Arbitrismo y administración a principios del siglo XVII," ibid., LXVI (2009), 147–179; María Elena Díaz, *The Virgin, the King, and the Royal Slaves of El Cobre: Negotiating Freedom in Colonial Cuba, 1670–1780* (Stanford, Calif., 2000); Miguel Acosta Saignes, *Vida de los esclavos negros en Venezuela* (Valencia, 1967). For comparative analysis of projecting in England and Spain, see Allison Margaret Bigelow, "Imperial Pro-

Although the crown declined to fund don Manuel's proposal, census records from the 1630s reveal that some of his ideas were put into practice—just on a much smaller scale than what he had articulated. In return, the projector was rewarded with a knighthood for his son, and don Manuel himself was invited to present other ideas on imperial reformation. In 1625, two years after the crown ruled against his plan for Cocorote, don Manuel offered an eight-point realignment of political and economic relations between Spain and Spanish America that would change silver shipping routes, reform copper currency (maravedís de vellón), eliminate certain administrative positions in the colonies, and replace selected Spanish officials with American-born subjects *(criollos)*. A comparison of the *relación* of 1621 and the revisions of 1625, triangulated through the modifications that don Manuel negotiated at council between 1621 and 1623 (now preserved in documents housed at the Archivo General de Indias in Seville), shows how Gaytán de Torres drew from Cuban precedent in El Cobre to design a new mining community in Venezuela and how he modified the designs over time. Most notably, this comparison documents how don Manuel reframed his second proposal around criollos, rather than his original vision of black family life, to cohere with imperial preferences for a whiter, more Spanish model of colonial society. In his mind, copper was a material good that held the key to Spain's economic and spiritual restoration and a narrative medium that could be molded into diverse models of colonial life. Spain's financial crisis enabled him to position colonial copper production as a solution to the problem and to convert the material stages of copper metallurgy into an imaginative blueprint for a new kind of mining community—one that centered, and then eliminated, African metallurgical knowledge.[6]

---

jecting in Virginia and Venezuela: Copper, Colonialism, and the Printing of Possibility," *Early American Studies*, XVI (2018), 91–123.

6. "Lo qe se podra hacer de presente acerca de las proposiçiones de don Manuel Gaytan de Torres," [ca. 1622 (because of references to papers held by council secretary Juan Ruíz de Contreras)], Archivo General de Indias (hereafter cited as AGI), Santo Domingo, 740, 8 fols., 8v. An eighteenth-century copy of the proposal ("Discursos que disponen medios para la restauracion de España con mayor Cantidad de Renta en la rl hacienda y menos Gabelas en estos Reynos, y aumento de su Poblacion y en las fuerzas de la Mar . . . ," Madrid, ca. 1747, MS, Biblioteca del Palacio Real, DIG/II/1452_B) thus begins with a family tree. See Amadori, "Que se de diferente modo al govierno de las Indias," *Anuario de Estudios Americanos*, LXXI (2014); minutes, Jan. 2, 1625, n.p., C.62.i.19.50, BL. Imperial officials seem to have read don Manuel's proposal with other ideas on navigational reform, including the work of fray Antonio Vázquez Espinosa. The first line of the minutes declares, "He Visto el

Copper Mining in El Cobre, Cuba

The history of copper mining in eastern Cuba figured heavily in the crown's interest in Venezuelan mines and its aversion to royal slavery. In the mid-sixteenth century, Portuguese explorer Fernando Núñez Lobo, then living in Santiago del Prado (Santiago de Cuba), discovered copper deposits twenty kilometers west of the city. He named the site El Cobre. In 1547, German miner Juan Tezel (Johann Tetzel) signed an asiento and was sent by Holy Roman Emperor Carlos V to supervise the site, though it never became operational. After Tezel's death, around 1578, Felipe II renegotiated the asiento with *sevillano* businessman Sancho de Medina Cerezo and his partner, Álvaro Clavijo de Loaisa. For the ten-year duration of the contract, the crown would collect one-twentieth of the copper produced in El Cobre, and Medina would people the mine with five hundred enslaved Africans, thirty unmarried artisan laborers, and one hundred married artisans who would travel with their families and receive land for their households. From the beginning, copper mining in the Americas was thus tied to biopolitical movements of women, men, and laborers from Africa and the Habsburg empire.[7]

Despite these royal concessions, El Cobre remained underproductive. When Medina Cerezo passed away, Clavijo de Loaisa took over the contract. He struggled to find enough workers and tools for the site, and when he arrived in La Española from Spain, the city of Santo Domingo had just been attacked. The workers refused to travel through enemy lands to reach Santiago de Cuba. By 1583, Clavijo de Loaisa requested an extension on his asiento. It seems that his request went unfulfilled because, in the late 1580s, Rodrigo Manuel Núñez Lobo (brother of the discoverer) acquired the rights to the mines. Under his direction, Hernán Manrique de Rojas, lieutenant governor and a wealthy landholder, brought twenty-two enslaved Africans to grow food for the complex. Little is known of El Cobre under Núñez Lobo's ownership, although one gov-

---

Memorial del Pe Maestro Fray Anto Vazquez acerca del armada que se a propuesto aya en el Mar del Sur que V. Magd se sirbio emitirme para decir lo que sintía" (I have seen the report of the Father Master fray Antonio Vázquez regarding the navy that he has proposed to station in the South Sea, which Your Majesty has requested sent to me to review).

7. Modesto Bargalló, *La minería y la metalurgía en la América española durante la época colonial: Con un apéndice sobre la industria del hierro en México desde la iniciación de la Independencia hasta el presente* (Mexico City, 1955), 213; David C. Goodman, *Power and Penury: Government, Technology, and Science in Philip II's Spain* (Cambridge, 2002), 110–113; "Emplazamiento y compulsoria a Gaspar de Manzanas," Madrid, Apr. 4, 1569, AGI, Patronato Real, 292, ramo 123, no. 3; "Real Provisión a los herederos de Sancho de Medina Cerezo," Aug. 12, 1578, Madrid, AGI, Indiferente, 426, legajo 26, fols. 138v–139.

ernor who reviewed the state of the mine up to 1587 determined that nothing had changed.[8]

What we do know is that, in the late sixteenth century, the crown appropriated the mines and refineries of El Cobre, and the shift from private hands to royal administration caused dramatic changes in labor and demographic conditions for enslaved and free miners. Soon after the establishment of the Artillería de la Habana, Capitán don Francisco Sánchez de Moya departed from Cádiz in 1597 to administer the newly constituted Real de Minas in El Cobre, designed as one of the armory's main sources of copper. According to records that were included in a late colonial dispute between the people of Santiago and the heirs of the mine owners, when Sánchez de Moya arrived in eastern Cuba in 1599, he brought twelve African smelters ("realengos fundidores") from Santiago to El Cobre. There, he received six or seven huts, one wooden smelting house, two refining wheels, and food to sustain the new community, including lands sown with yucca, squash, maize, and plantains, as well as a fishing boat. Four years later, Spanish subjects in Cuba were ordered to move from the northern and western regions to the copper mines of the southeast. From 1603 until 1607, local administrators and imperial officials reorganized the mining district under a new jurisdiction, the Departamento Oriental, and El Cobre reported to a new regional capital, Santiago de Cuba. Despite substantial changes in political, legal, and labor policies, the site remained underproductive. By 1616, the crown was so unhappy with the economic returns and the practice of royal slavery that it sought to transfer the mines back to private hands. Juan de Eguiluz, a wealthy accountant and local official *(alcalde mayor),* stepped forward to sign an asiento. By 1620, when Manuel Gaytán de Torres departed from Cádiz toward Venezuela on March 15, stopping in Cuba before and after arriving in the Venezuelan colony, El Cobre was firmly in Eguiluz's control.[9]

The crown became uncomfortable exercising direct control over enslaved miners in El Cobre, in part because they powerfully articulated their relationship to the land, its resources, and its spiritual community. In 1604, a Marian

8. I. A. Wright, *The Early History of Cuba, 1492–1586* (New York, 1916), 310–311.

9. Olga Portuondo Zúñiga, *La virgen de la caridad del Cobre: Símbolo de Cubanía* (Santiago de Cuba, 1995), 27, 36, 89; Isabelo Macías Domínguez, *Cuba en la primera mitad del siglo XVII* (Seville, 1978), 66–67; "Resolviendo el litigio entre los herederos de Juan de Eguiluz y Francisco de Salazar y los naturales del pueblo de Santiago del Prado sobre las minas de cobre," Apr. 7, 1800, Archivo Nacional de la República de Cuba (ANRC), Reales cédulas e ordenes, 4 fols., 1, 21.37; Díaz, *The Virgin, the King, and the Royal Slaves of El Cobre,* 333; Bargalló, *La minería y la metalurgía en la América española durante la época colonial,* 213; Mar. 15, 1620, AGI, Contratación, 5371, no. 27, fol. 1.

virgin appeared to three enslaved men—Juan Moreno, of African descent, and Rodrigo and Juan de Joyos, "hermanos y yndios naturales" (brothers and Indians of the land), as Moreno identified them. The material apparition of the virgin and the lettered confirmation of her identity formed a central part of African families' claims to belong to the copper-rich lands of eastern Cuba. By invoking a sense of historical place and continued lineage, at once combining past and future, miners of African and mixed-race descent used their relationship to the Virgin, a Marian saint associated with fertility, childbirth, and family, to argue against their relocation across the island. As Moreno declared in a petition of 1677, when he requested permission for cobreros not to be removed to Havana to rebuild the fortress that English forces had attacked in 1662, black miners were the pillars of Santiago's economic, legal, and spiritual community. Speaking as their captain, he affirmed, "Negros y mulatos criollos de dichas minas somos cassados y thenemos mas familias que siempre hemos sustentado quieta y pacificamente estando ocupados quando se a ofrecido en el trabajo de d[ic]has minas fabrica de la Santa Yglesia y leales vasallos de su mag[esta]d emos acudido con toda prontitud a n[ues]tra costa" (we the blacks and creole mulattos [mixed-race people born in the Americas] of the aforesaid mines are married with families for whom we have always provided quietly and peacefully with our work that we have offered in the labor of the aforementioned mines of the Holy Church and as loyal subjects of Your Maj[est]y we have attended with all promptness at our own cost). Moreno skillfully connected the generative potential of the Virgin with African families in El Cobre to ensure that the community would remain in place.[10]

This authoritative affirmation suggests how enslaved miners developed sophisticated rhetorical strategies to protect their communities, even as the crown denied their rights to their own labor, bodies, and families. Moreno's statement challenges our idea of the relationship between enslaved peoples and sovereign rulers. His assessment of miners' economic contributions also contradicted royal reports. One survey of El Cobre, conducted at the end of the seventeenth century, claimed that the mines were "totalmente perdidas, ciegas y arruinadas, sin fabricas para la fundicion ni instrumentos ni proporciones para ello" (completely lost, blind, and ruined, without factories to refine

10. Apr. 1, 1687, AGI, Santo Domingo, 363, fols. 12v–18v, in Díaz, *The Virgin, the King, and the Royal Slaves of El Cobre,* 99–100, 341–342, app. 4 (Díaz carefully analyzed and generously transcribed the 1687 deposition); Fernando Ortiz, *La virgen de la caridad del Cobre: Historia y etnografía,* ed. José Antonio Matos Arévalos (Havana, 2008), 236; July 13, 1677, AGI, Santo Domingo, 1631, fols. 454–455v, in Díaz, *The Virgin, The King, and the Royal Slaves of El Cobre,* 339–340, app. 3.

metals nor instruments or means to do so). By pitting the economic interests of the crown against its commitment to Catholic worship, Moreno leveraged the relation of the enslaved to the Virgin into rights for the community. The Virgin would go on to become the symbol of the Cuban nation, following the independence movements of the nineteenth century, and to index fraught relationships between the state, the church, and the people under U.S. imperialism, the Batista regime, and the revolutionary politics of the Communist Party from 1959 to our own time. When don Manuel drew from the precedent of El Cobre to project a new vision for Cocorote, he did so knowing that the mines had yet to produce any copper of note. And yet, the lack of material evidence did not dissuade projectors like him, or local officials, from insisting that wealth was within reach. Rather than tangible proof of metallic production, El Cobre provided a model of potential that offered don Manuel a range of ideas about royal slavery and private finance.[11]

The Legacy of El Cobre in Cocorote

Capitán Juan Moreno did not know his story would influence the politics of race and religion in Cuba after the turn to nation-statehood or that the legacy of El Cobre would inform seventeenth-century ideas about extractive industries and spiritual community in other regions of Latin America. As Gaytán de Torres authored his report from Havana on June 10, 1621, he considered the roles of African miners, *asentistas,* and various forms of slavery in his designs for Venezuela.

When Gaytán de Torres requested to relocate African men from the fortress of Havana to Venezuela, he sought the same concessions that Eguiluz had received: a shipping license for a 250-ton boat "con los pertrechos y cossas neçecsarias para el Beneficio de las dichas Minas ... como se conçedio a Juan de eguiluz Para Las Minas de cobre de cuba" (with the instruments and things necessary for refining in the aforesaid mines ... as was conceded to Juan de Eguiluz for the copper mines of Cuba). After surveying the mines of Cocorote (present-day state of Yaracuy, Venezuela), he communicated his results in three evidentiary forms: a prose report, published (presumably) in Spain; a painting (now lost) of Cocorote's mountains, navigable rivers, and mines and

11. "Resolviendo el litigio ...," Apr. 7, 1800, ANRC, Reales cédulas e ordenes, 21.37, 3v; Portuondo Zúñiga, *La virgen de la caridad del Cobre;* Ortiz, *La virgen de la caridad del Cobre;* Díaz, *The Virgin, the King, and the Royal Slaves of El Cobre,* 4–8, 17–20. On the twentieth and twenty-first centuries, see Lillian Guerra, *Visions of Power in Cuba: Revolution, Redemption, and Resistance, 1959–1971* (Chapel Hill, N.C., 2012); and Jalane D. Schmidt, *Cachita's Streets: The Virgin of Charity, Race, and Revolution in Cuba* (Durham, N.C., 2015).

refineries; and a *carta de marear* (navigational chart, also lost), which detailed the region's ports and suggested how transatlantic traffic in laborers and copper would enrich the Spanish empire.[12]

Gaytán de Torres imagined that readers would consult all three works. The *Relación,* or what he calls in third-person prose "este su parecer y vista de ojos" (this, his ruling and eyewitness report), frequently references the painting and the map. It also includes a numbering guide ("guarismo"), which allows readers to plot elements from the text onto the painting and chart, as don Manuel instructs: "Y donde se hallare numero de guarismo corresponde al de la pintura" (And where a number from the guide is found, it corresponds to that of the painting). He incorporates numbers into the body and marginalia, underscoring the multigeneric information conveyed in lines such as "toda la serrania que està entre las dos quebradas, de numero 1. y número 4." and "la primera casa [8.] donde se ha de moler, que es la que muestra la pintura" (the entire mountain chain that is between the two ravines, marked 1. and 4.; the first house [8.], where metals will be crushed, is what the painting shows).[13]

This combination of lettered and visual forms allowed don Manuel to argue for the productive potential of copper mining in Cocorote. Imperial officials had some sense of the site, which was "discovered" by Alonso Sánchez de Oviedo in 1612, but it had remained unworked. In an attempt to gain royal support, Venezuelan governor don García Girón sent samples from Cocorote to Seville for inspection and assay. Before setting sail for Cocorote, don Manuel met with officials from the Consejo de Indias. They asked two pointed questions: whether miners in Venezuela could excavate the one hundred *quintales* (one thousand pounds) of copper per day needed to support current rates of coinage, military demand for artillery, and general purposes ("gasto ordinario") in Spain, and whether the Aroa River valley could support the development of a large-scale mining complex in Cocorote. Don Manuel thus aimed to show, in words and images, that Cocorote was capable of providing all the copper required by the crown—and more, over time—and that the area's ample pastures, arable lands, navigable rivers, and sound ports would sustain the mining complex, for "son bastantes para lo que se pretende, y hay todo lo que

12. "En conformidad de lo que el sr secretario Juan Ruiz de Contreras ha dho a mi don Manuel Gaytan de Torres Beinte y Quatro de la çiudad de Jerez; de parte de la Junta de guerral del Consejo Real de Las Indias doi esta relaçion en cuya conformidad hare las capitulaçiones y dare las fianças que la Junta de guerra mandare lo qual ha de ser por tiempo de diez años" (copy of the Consejo de Indias, marked "Sobre el assiento"), 1622, AGI, Santo Domingo, 740, fols. 2–2v.

13. Gaytán de Torres, *Relacion, y vista de ojos,* 1–1v, 2, 3v, 22v.

la imaginación puede desear para el manejo y beneficio de tan gran riqueza" (they are sufficient for what is needed, with everything that the imagination could desire for the management and benefit of such great wealth). In a series of council meetings and metallurgical assays, Gaytán de Torres molded his report into the kind of story that would suit imperial interlocutors.[14]

His survey determined that, in one day's work, three enslaved miners could remove 36 *arrobas* of material (913 pounds) and that one-third of it ("al tercio") was copper, but assays in Seville proved even more favorable. They reflect how colonial matter was converted into imperial evidence as asentistas negotiated their contracts. In October 1621, Gaytán de Torres led don Antonio Manrique, treasurer of the Casa de la Contratación, to the Casa de la Fundición in Seville. They observed as artillery refiner Pedro González assayed one quintal of "tierra negra" (black earth) in a well-heated blast oven. He removed one bar's worth of metal, weighing 24.5 pounds. Ninety minutes later, González performed a second assay with another quintal, producing two bars that weighed a total of 31 pounds. At 9 p.m., secretary Bartolomé López de Salas certified the results. The next day, master refiner Francisco de Ballesteros confirmed that "le parece sera tan bueno como el de la havana y tan bueno y mexor que el de ungria" (it seemed to him to be as good as the copper from Havana and as good as and better than that of Hungary). Cauldron maker Juan Borque noted that the Venezuelan copper contained too much iron for his trade, but it could make hollow objects like artillery, bells, and mortars. When Manrique inspected the oven a final time, he found 19 pounds of metal caked to the bottom but able to be removed from the chamber, so he concluded that the Venezuelan sample produced 74 pounds of copper from 2 quintales of raw material. This impressive yield of 37.5 percent copper was approximately 13.6 percent higher than what don Manuel reported from his assay in Cocorote.[15]

By 1655, after years of evaluating proposals from Spanish, German, and English projectors, council members realized that they had been continually deceived by fraudulent presentations of evidence. With great exasperation, one official clarified how asentistas brought good samples of copper to establish the terms of the contract and then sent material from their mines, "de que se sigue traer la maleza que se ha reconocido" (which explains why we are

14. Ibid., 1, 2v, 12–12v; F. Urbani, "Las minas de Cobre de Aroa a la luz de la Relación de Manuel Gaytán de Torres, 1621," *Boletín geológico y minero,* CIII (1992), 156–185, esp. 156–158.

15. Gaytán de Torres, *Relacion, y vista de ojos,* 12; "La Casa de la Conttrazon 2 de noviembre sobre las diligas que hizieren con don Manuel Gaytan y en bian testimonio de la fundizion del Cobre, a su Mgd," 1621, AGI, Santo Domingo, 740, fols. 2v–4v.

faced with such iniquities). In don Manuel's case, however, Manrique had received the copper directly from officials in Havana ("los dhos offes Reales de la havana").[16]

For his part, don Manuel was more interested in the biopolitical possibilities of labor in Latin America than in the technical details of an assay in Spain. He concluded that the mines could support Spanish demand for copper by "regulado la cantidad de negros que aplica al trabajo de las minas" (regulating the number of blacks who are applied to mine work). In an elaborate, seven-page list of laborers, officials, and soldiers, along with a running count of what each post would cost, the projector explained how such biopolitical regulation would work. The list was arranged hierarchically, starting with Spanish officials and ending with African miners. On top would be a governor of refineries and foundries, followed by a lieutenant governor, master of the foundries, clerk, and "dos negros que den recado a todos los oficiales y negros" (two blacks who give account to all of the officials and blacks).[17]

The seven articles and four appendices of the *Relación,* as well as don Manuel's conversations with imperial officials in Seville, offer a blueprint for founding a new kind of place. In his plan, diverse Indigenous communities—including Guamanteyes (in Puerto Cabello), Caquetíos (along the Río Tocuyo), and Kalinas (relocated from the Lago de Tacarigua [Valencia] to the mouth of the Río Patanemo, on the Caribbean Sea)—would be reduced to Spanish governance. From Lisbon or Cape Verde, 710 African women and men would be brought to Venezuela at a cost of 71,000 ducados; 110 Spaniards would oversee the complex. African artisans would eventually replace Spanish laborers in trades like iron- and steelwork, "porque los negros estaran despiertos en los oficios, y ocuparan algunos, que [h]oy es fuerça los hagan Españoles" (because the blacks will be awakened to the trades, and they will occupy some that are necessarily filled by Spaniards today). When officials from the Consejo de Indias pressed him on this point, he insisted that, once the mine was operational ("puesto todo en exon"), master artisans could return to Spain, "por qe su pretension no es estar en las Yndias" (because their purpose is not to be in the Indies). When asked whether he really needed so many African miners or whether some could be replaced with people from America ("gente de las yn-

16. Letter of La Casa de la Contratación to the Consejo de Indias, Apr. 13, 1655, fol. 1, and "La Casa de la Conttrazon 2 de noviembre . . . ," 1621, AGI, Santo Domingo, 740, fol. 2v. English and German subjects included Henrique Habet and Nathaniel ("Natanual") Maston de Alencastro; see "Sobre las convenienias qe tiene dar por asiento las minas de Cocorote," May 1656, fol. 5, ibid.

17. Gaytán de Torres, *Relacion, y vista de ojos,* 5, 12.

dias"), don Manuel conceded that half of the Spaniards could be replaced with criollos to serve as officials and soldiers, but he could not have fewer Africans without decreasing copper production. Gaytán de Torres did not mention the sophisticated technologies used to process base metals in West and West Central Africa, where "the most important and deeply respected of artisans were the metallurgists who worked in either iron or copper," but his ideas about the capabilities of African refiners suggest some awareness of these traditions. Instead, he crafted his words to appeal to the logic that equated African miners with beasts of burden, insisting that costs would decline over time because Cocorote's two main "tools" would reproduce themselves "con el ayuda de Dios . . . que son los negros y ganados" (with the help of God . . . which are the blacks and cattle).[18]

To persuade the crown that his was a viable plan, he explained each part of the refining process in detail—from extraction to refining and shipping—and he specified how Indigenous, African, and Spanish men, as well as African women, would contribute to each step. First, eight Spaniards would monitor companies of twenty African men to mine copper; two miners, one a master of his trade, would oversee the operation, and they would be paid a base salary, plus wages for each day. Then, ten African men with twenty carts, also watched by a Spaniard, would transport metal from open-pit mines to six new ovens, one for each day of the workweek, placed slightly below the refineries that discoverer Sánchez de Oviedo had built in the ravine "que los Indios llaman de Guanariguaguo" (which the Indians call Guanariguaguo). There, twelve African men and one Spanish overseer would heat the material to release chemicals like sulfur.[19]

After this preparatory work, the metal would pass through four metallurgical "houses." The first house was for crushing, which would be performed by African women: "lo han de moler las negras, por ser oficio de poco trabajo" (black women must grind the metal, because it is a task of light labor). Gaytán de Torres meticulously counted black men in his list of laborers and signaled their presence in the painting, noting, "Ha de haber ocho mayordomos para andar cón los ciēto y sesenta negros de las minas, veinte negros a cargo de

18. Ibid., 5, 8–8v, 9, 11–11v; "Bisto el memorial de don Manuel Gaitan de Torres acordo el conso que se le preguntase que numero de xente es la que pretende que se acomote en la habana," [1622?], AGI, Santo Domingo, 740, fol. 2; Frederick C. Knight, *Working the Diaspora: The Impact of African Labor on the Anglo-American World, 1650–1850* (New York, 2010), 30.

19. Gaytán de Torres, *Relacion, y vista de ojos,* 2v, 5v, 7. Today, the site is the State Park of Quebrada Las Minas: http://www.yaracuy.net/parques/parque-bolivariano-minas-de-aroa.

cada uno," "Para quemar el metal en los seys hornos, cargarlos, y descargarlos, ha de aber doze negros," "Para llevar el metal de los seys hornos a la primera casa [8.], dōde se ha de moler, quatro negros para las canoas" (There must be 8 overseers to accompany the 160 blacks in the mines, 20 blacks in the charge of each one; to heat the metal in the six ovens, load them, and empty them, there must be 12 blacks; to bring the metal from the six ovens to the first house [8], where it must be ground, 4 blacks for the canoes).[20]

In contrast, he consistently left black women as an undistinguished group: "lo han de moler las negras," "y las negras han de hacer la empleita" (black women must grind the metal . . . and black women must do the weaving). He assumed that, because all the male artisans would be married to African women, the community would grow over time ("los negros han de multiplicar, como se ve en todas las Indias"), and there was no need to count the bodies of black women because they would equal the number of men. These marriages were designed for the protection of the men, the encouragement of their work, and the avoidance of sin ("que para tenerlos seguros, y que assistan con gusto al trabajo, y no vayan a menos, y se escusen pecados"). He added that women would be necessary for certain aspects of minework, as well as "otros oficios livianos, y hazer de comer a los negros, y hilar algodon para vestuario de sus maridos y hijos" (other light trades, and to make food for black men, and thread cotton for the clothing of their husbands and children). Gaytán de Torres offered precise ideas about black women's labor—preparing food to nourish and sustain their families, making clothing to protect their husbands and children, and giving birth to those children within a Christian framework of marriage—while remaining imprecise on the number of black women themselves. Instead of counting them, his list often glosses "otras tantas negras" (so many other black women).[21]

Manuel Gaytán de Torres believed unequivocally in the economic productivity of slave labor, and he never mentioned moral or ethical problems with the slave trade. But his vision of mining community, grounded in Catholic institutions and culinary traditions that African miners could introduce to a Venezuelan climate "acomodado a su naturaleza" (accommodated to their nature), outlines a model of colonial design that went beyond the production of imperial wealth.[22]

To that end, Gaytán de Torres argued that African copper miners needed to share with Spanish subjects a linguistic homeland—one that was mediated

20. Gaytán de Torres, *Relacion, y vista de ojos,* 5v, 7.

21. Ibid., 5v, 8, 8v.

22. Ibid., 8v.

by the kinds of Portuguese slave traders who monopolized the asiento during the period of the Iberian union. He explained in cruelly straightforward terms the advantages of buying enslaved "negros de ley" in Lisbon: "por valer alli baratos, y tener tomada la tierra, y hallarse algo ladinos, y algunos oficiales, y si no se pudiere acomodar toda la cãtidad, se comprara el resto en Santiago de Caboverde, que son negros de ley" (because they do not cost a lot in those parts, and having taken to the land, they are found to know the language, and some are officials. And if the entire lot cannot be accommodated, the rest will be bought in Santiago de Cape Verde, because they are blacks of *ley*). In contrast, miners who were brought directly from Angola "no son negros de tanto trabajo, ni tan buena ley, como los de Caboverde, y tan bozales que cuando llegan, en un año no son de provecho" (do not work so hard, or follow such good laws, as those of Cape Verde, and they are so unseasoned that when they arrive, after one year they are of no use). In alliterative pairs of *ladinos* (Spanish-speaking Africans) and *ley,* don Manuel explained why exposure to the Portuguese language would facilitate the building of community life in Venezuela. His use of the term *ley* demands further attention.[23]

The concept that united these linguistic and economic benefits for the mining community of Cocorote was *ley.* According to sixteenth-century lexicographer Sebastián de Covarrubias, the word primarily denoted law (human, natural, religious), although its secondary and tertiary definitions included fidelity to a master ("Ley si[g]nifica alguna vez fidelidad como el criado que tiene ley con su amo") and standardized qualities of taxable commodities ("Ser de ley una mercaderia, estar conforme a las leyes y aranzeles"). In metallurgical contexts, *ley* referred to metallic content or mineral grade, as in "plata de alta ley" (high-grade silver) or "plata de baja ley" (low-grade silver). When don Manuel referred to "negros de ley," he capitalized upon the legal, religious, and technological connotations embedded in the term, extending the metallurgical properties of copper to symbolic domains of community life.[24]

23. Ibid., 8v, 9; "Asientos de negros con diferentes compañías y particulares," 1595–1727, AGI, Contaduría, 261; "Visitas gobernación de Cartagena," 1619, AGI, Escribanía, 632A; Linda A. Newson and Susie Minchin, *From Capture to Sale: The Portuguese Slave Trade to Spanish South America in the Early Seventeenth Century* (Leiden, 2007), esp. 101–135; Acosta Saignes, *Vida de los esclavos negros en Venezuela;* Filipa Ribeiro da Silva, "Crossing Empires: Portuguese, Sephardic, and Dutch Business Networks in the Atlantic Slave Trade, 1580–1674," *Americas,* LXVIII (2011), 7–32.

24. *Tesoro de la lengua castellana, o española: Compuesto por el licenciado don Sebastian de Cobarruvias Orozco, capellan de su Magestad . . .* (Madrid, 1611), s.v. "ley." See also Frédérique Langue and Carmen Salazar-Soler, eds., *Diccionario de términos mineros para la América española, siglos XVI–XIX* (Paris, 1993), 318–319; and Stuart B. Schwartz, *All Can Be*

Just as he counted African women and men in different ways, he also described the physical spaces of women's and men's labor in different terms. After women ground, crushed, and reduced metals in their house, copper would pass through male metallurgical spaces. These were marked 9, 10, and 11 on the painting, and they were measured in precise terms. As Gaytán de Torres mapped the refineries in prose and pictographic prose, he explained,

> Sucessivo a esta casa [9.] ha de estar otra de ciento y diez pies de largo cō un ingenio que ha de mover y veynte y dos pares de barquinos, onze por cada lado.
>
> Y fundido el metal de primera fundicion, se ha de llevar a otra casa [10.] de sesenta pies de largo dōde se ha de afinar, y adulçar con otro ingenio de la misma forma que ha de mover doze pares de barquinos, seys por cada lado.
>
> Despues de afinado, y adulçado el cobre, se ha de llevar a otra casa [11.] de cinquenta pies de largo, donde ha de aver cinco ingenios diferentes, donde se ha de hazer tableros el cobre, y pesar, y quadrar de la forma que el que viene de Ungria.
>
> Next to this house [9.] there must be another of 110 feet long with a movable refinery and twenty-two pairs of bellows, eleven on each side. And once the metal is smelted in the first refining, it must be brought to another house [10.], seventy feet long, where it must be made fine and sweet with another refinery of the same movable kind with twelve pairs of bellows, six on each side. After the copper is made fine and sweet, it must be brought to another house [11.], fifty feet long, where there must be five different refineries, where the copper must be cut into grids, and weighed, and squared into the form of the copper that comes from Hungary.[25]

In contrast to the women's refining house, male workshops were measured, and men's work was described metonymically in "pairs of bellows." The technological stages of copper metallurgy led to increasingly smaller and more specialized facilities—from 110 feet to 70 feet to 50 feet—in three main stages:

Saved: Religious Tolerance and Salvation in the Iberian Atlantic World (New Haven, Conn., 2008). On *ley* in books of mining, see Juan de Cárdenas, *Problemas y secretos maravillosos de las Indias* (1591; rpt. Valladolid, 2003); Alvaro Alonso Barba, *Arte de los metales en que se enseña el verdadero beneficio de los de oro, y plata por açogue . . .* (Madrid, 1640); and Juan Ordóñez Montalvo, *Arte o nuevo modo de beneficiar los metales de oro y plata y de plata con ley de oro, por azoguc . . .* (Mexico City, 1758).

25. Gaytán de Torres, *Relacion, y vista de ojos,* 3.

reduction, purification, and casting into uniform molds, such as the squares and sheets of Hungarian copper that circulated throughout the Habsburg empire. When council members interrogated these technical aspects, don Manuel explained that, at present, material was extracted from the mines, crushed into small pieces by black manpower ("a fuerça de golpes de braços de negros"), and melted into mounds that were shipped to Seville. His model was more specialized and mechanized. Water-powered refineries would reduce operational and labor costs, and updated tools would produce purer (and more expensive) copper by allowing refiners to remove the sulfurous elements that made copper turn brassy.[26]

This emphasis on purification was not just an economic argument; it marked a decisive shift in don Manuel's representation of black and Indigenous community participation in the life of Cocorote. The rhetoric of metallic purity, the spatial organization of the site, and the procedural stages of copper refining provided the intellectual framework for Gaytán de Torres's modeling of a productive and reproductive mining community, which he explained as an extension of evangelizing campaigns in Indigenous communities. As he put it, once more referring to himself in the third person, "Porque sabe es el principal intento de V.M. y del Real Consejo, reduzir a nuestra santa Fe Catolica los Indios que ay en todo lo descubierto, y que se descubriere de las Indias, y poblarlas de Christianos, y ser forçoso para poner en perfeccíon las minas y fundiciones del cobre, poblar, y fundar de nuevo tres lugares, con que se consiguen ambos intentos" (Because he knows that it is the principal intent of Your Majesty and the Royal Council to reduce to our Holy Catholic Faith the Indians who are in all of the discovered lands, and those that will be discovered in the Indies, and to people them with Christians, and that to put the copper mines and refineries into practice it is necessary to people, and found once more three places, with which both aims will be achieved). This line establishes his three-part plan to reduce Indigenous people to Christianity, purify their souls, and cast them into the mold of the Church Universal. The three stages of copper metallurgy—reduction, purification, and casting—suggest how don Manuel transmuted material practices from the technical arts into broader colonial designs.[27]

Like the other stages, *reducción* was more than a technical procedure; it was an established jurisprudential framework through which Roman imperial ad-

26. Mark Häberlein, *The Fuggers of Augsburg: Pursuing Wealth and Honor in Renaissance Germany* (Charlottesville, Va., 2012); "Bisto el memorial de don Manuel Gaitan de Torres . . . ," [1622?], AGI, Santo Domingo, 740, 1–1v.

27. Gaytán de Torres, *Relacion, y vista de ojos*, 9.

ministrators had incorporated diverse linguistic and ethnic communities from Sicily to Asia into the standard form of a province. This legal process required a coeval remaking of political landscapes and physical spaces. For example, through the legal work of reducción, subjects in Sicily retained local identities and laws and participated in the larger, legally constituted fabric of Roman imperial citizenship, or *civitas*—what historian Clifford Ando calls "a metonym for both city and political community." Here we observe clear implications for don Manuel's localized model of mining community as well as the broader legal policies of the Spanish empire in Venezuela (Little Venice) and the New World, where the Spanish empire imagined itself a New Rome. Throughout Latin America, reducciones acted as what historical geographer Heidi Scott, studying the Andes, calls "entangled spatiality of power struggles," in which nuanced, competing, and local interests defied binary divisions like "Indigenous" or "European" and what literary scholar Daniel Nemser identifies as the racial infrastructure that critically shaped colonial Mexico. Don Manuel incorporated Indigenous people and Africans into his vision of mining community, but one group was made of spiritual matter, and the other was purely physical.[28]

The second step, purification, plays on the minimal pair *fundición* (refining, smelting) and *fundación* (founding). For early moderns, the latter term connoted the founding of a church, convent, or city, following the Latin *funditio*. As such, Gaytán de Torres promised the crown of "el gran servicio que se harà a Dios nuestro Señor, reduziendo a su Yglesia los Indios de la provincia de Nir[g]ua, y otros muchos que estan en la Venéçuela sin conocer a Dios, que sera el mayor fruto de esta obra; dirà aqui donde se han de hazer sus fundaciones cōforme lo que ha visto en la dicha provincia" (the great service that will be made to God our Father, reducing to the Church the Indians of the province of Nirgua, and many others who are in Venezuela without knowledge of God, which will be the best fruit of this work: so he will say here where the foundations must be made, according to what he has seen in the aforesaid province). By infusing the technical stages of metallurgical labor with political and spiritual registers, don Manuel molded his plan for the mining community into a spiritual vision that cohered with imperial sensibilities. In these sections, un-

28. Clifford Ando, *Law, Language, and Empire in the Roman Tradition* (Philadelphia, 2011), 3–4; Heidi V. Scott, "A Mirage of Colonial Consensus: Resettlement Schemes in Early Spanish Peru," *Environment and Planning D: Society and Space*, XXII (2004), 885–899, esp. 895; Daniel Nemser, *Infrastructures of Race: Concentration and Biopolitics in Colonial Mexico* (Austin, Tex., 2017); Sabine MacCormack, *On the Wings of Time: Rome, the Incas, Spain, and Peru* (Princeton, N.J., 2009).

like in the lists and catalogs found elsewhere in the *Relación,* he underscores the role of Indigenous people in the refounded Cocorote.[29]

The final step, casting, involved the conversion of these reduced, purified souls into usable goods. In don Manuel's operational model of copper refining, the copper moved from the first reduction houses (women's spaces) to the second purifying plants (men's spaces) before entering the third space: a fifty-foot-long refining house with five different refining ovens *(ingenios).* There, the refined and "sweetened" copper ("afinar, y adulçar") was converted into cathodes ("tableros") that were weighed and cut into uniform squares, "de la forma que el que viene de Ungria" (like the form in which it comes from Hungary). This final stage of copper metallurgy served as blueprint for the conquest and colonization of the region. Indigenous souls would become part of the Church Universal, and their acceptance of the doctrine of transubstantiation would convert Kalinas, Guamanteyes, and Caquetíos into Catholic souls that resembled their brethren in other regions of the Spanish empire, such as the Hungarian lands that formed part of the Habsburg empire.[30]

Don Manuel's proposal differed notably from other ideas about the spiritual conquest of Venezuela. Consider the words of fray Matías Ruíz Blanco, for whom the conquest of the Cumanagoto and Palenque peoples of coastal Venezuela left Spaniards "con obligacion de poblar, y sugetar à los Indios, y ponerlos en forma, y con Ministros que los educassen" (with an obligation to people, and subject the Indians, and put them in form, and to do so with ministers who will educate them). In contrast, Gaytán de Torres converted the material stages of copper metallurgy into a metaphor for colonization—and a new idea of peopling, in which Indigenous souls, not Christian bodies, were key.[31]

In don Manuel's plan, the soldiers in this spiritual conquest would come from African, Spanish, and creole communities, joined by two hundred *indios encomendados,* two hundred enslaved African porters, and mixed-race men "of competent age," all rewarded differently for serving. Indigenous people would be released from *encomienda* service and made, with their heirs and descendants, into *vecinos* ("queden abeçindados") of Nirgua, whereas the families of black and mixed-race soldiers would receive goods during the war and be relieved of their taxes thereafter (4 *pesos de a ocho*). The families of Spanish

29. Gaytán de Torres, *Relacion, y vista de ojos,* 9–9v. Covarrubias traces them to the same Latin root: "FUNDAR, Latine fundo" and "FUNDIR, del verbo Latino fundo . . . pero vulgarmente llamamos fundir": *Tesoro de la lengua castellana o española,* s.v. "fundar," "fundir."

30. Gaytán de Torres, *Relacion, y vista de ojos,* 3.

31. Matías Ruiz Blanco, *Conversion de Piritiv de Indios Cumanagotos, Palenques, y otros . . .* (Madrid, 1690), 42.

and creole soldiers would receive honors fit for *hidalgos* and knights in Spain, with privileges passed to their heirs "en todos los reynos y señoríos de su Mgd" (in all of the kingdoms and lordships of Your Majesty). This war, waged once and for all in Nirgua, would root out the bad seeds of the region ("Con lo qual se hare de una vez la guerra y la Provinçia quede Limpia de tan mala similla"), and it would establish the conditions under which diverse populations would live.[32]

Unlike the case of the soldiers, don Manuel never specified how many Indigenous people would contribute to the copper complex. In one part of the text, he noted that Cocorote would need eight Indians in the port of La Concepción to load and unload goods (usually men's work) and help prepare corn (usually women's work), but he did not specify how the eight would be divided by gender. An uncertain number of Native people from Paraguachoa (Parabachoa), held in the encomienda of Francisco de Artiaga, would fish. To help with ranching, he would enlist however many people remained from the encomienda of Francisco de Vera in Maracay. At one time, Vera held one hundred Indians in encomienda, but by 1621, it was greatly reduced. In 1609, it had been vacated as punishment for a lack of proper titles and "malos tratamientos a los indios y rescates" (bad treatment of the Indians and goods). Don Manuel argued that the remaining population could learn to ranch if the crown sent "algunos Indios diestros que les enseñen" (some skilled Indians to teach them). In his plan to found a town of Guamanteyes who had been tricked ("por engaño") into relocating from the plains *(llanos),* he explained that this community of "poco mas de mil" (a little more than a thousand) could contribute "cosa de ciẽ personas" (about a hundred people) to transport copper by canoe from the Aroa River to Puerto de Cabello. These diverse Andean communities spoke a variety of languages and lived in different places, but don Manuel counted them all in equally fuzzy ways: "los que quedan" (those who remain), "poco mas de mil" (a little more than one thousand), "cosa de cien personas" (about one hundred people).[33]

Don Manuel's rhetoric of spiritual peopling is undercut by his attempt to provide concrete details about Indigenous participation in the founding of Cocorote. Just as he praises the technical competencies of African miners and equated black bodies with beasts of burden, so, too, does don Manuel deal paradoxically with the place of Indigenous people in his vision of the mining community. In most of the document, Indigenous people are absent. They

32. "En conformidad," 1622, AGI, Santo Domingo, 740, fols. 3v–4, 4v.

33. Gaytán de Torres, *Relación, y vista de ojos,* 6v, 7–7v, 11; Ismael Silva Montañes, *Hombres y mujeres del siglo XVI venezolano,* 4 vols. (Caracas, 1983), IV, 366.

appear most extensively in his plan for spiritual conquest as one of the most conventional justifications for Catholic military activity. Then, Indigenous farmers and fishers—all men—appear infrequently and in inconsistent numbers to provide food for African miners. Even the foods that are most associated with Indigenous women, such as maize, are equated with African lifeways: "de maiz, yuca, platanos, aviamas y otras legumbres, todas comidas que usan los negros" (of corn, yucca, plantains, squash, *aviamas* [derived from the Kalina *auyamá],* and other legumes, all foods that blacks use).[34]

What don Manuel envisioned, essentially, was a community of African artisan families who would coordinate with Indigenous and Spanish agents to ship copper from Cocorote to Puerto Cabello and Borburata, where it would be refined into artillery for sale in Latin America. This was not a mercantilist mode of political economy wherein enslaved Africans and indios encomendados extracted materials that were manufactured in Spain. This was a mode of production centered on African women and men perfecting their technical knowledge of copper mining and refining to raise their children, cook foods they preferred, and live largely free of Spanish oversight—provided they produced enough copper.

Officials in Seville, Madrid, and Aranjuez reviewed the technical and economic merits of don Manuel's proposal between the fall of 1621 and the spring of 1623, calling on him to explain his model of colonial development in face-to-face meetings. Some of these meetings produced novel forms of record keeping, such as the three-column notes that Juan Ruíz de Contreras organized for the minutes of the Junta de Guerra. In the left-hand column, council members noted their objections to the *Relación.* In the middle column, Ruíz de Contreras glossed don Manuel's response to the objections. In the right-hand column, left blank, he would have (presumably) listed the council's assessment of each revised point (Figure 14). By analyzing these debates and comparing elements of the *Relación* (1621) with the projector's second work, *Que se de diferente modo al govierno de las Indias* (1625), we see how don Manuel once more molded the material potential of copper metals into a narrative of New World possibility and a vision of colonial life. This time, he did so by focusing on shipping routes of silver galleons rather than colonial copper production and by replacing largely autonomous African artisans with American-born officials of Spanish descent.[35]

34. *Diccionario de la lengua española,* 23d ed., s.v. "auyama," https://dle.rae.es; Gaytán de Torres, *Relacion, y vista de ojos,* 8v.

35. "Las dudas que por parte del consejo sean puesto a don Manuel Gaitan que an resultado de la vista de su Relacion y respuesta que a ellas se da," ca. Aug. 18, 1622 (when don

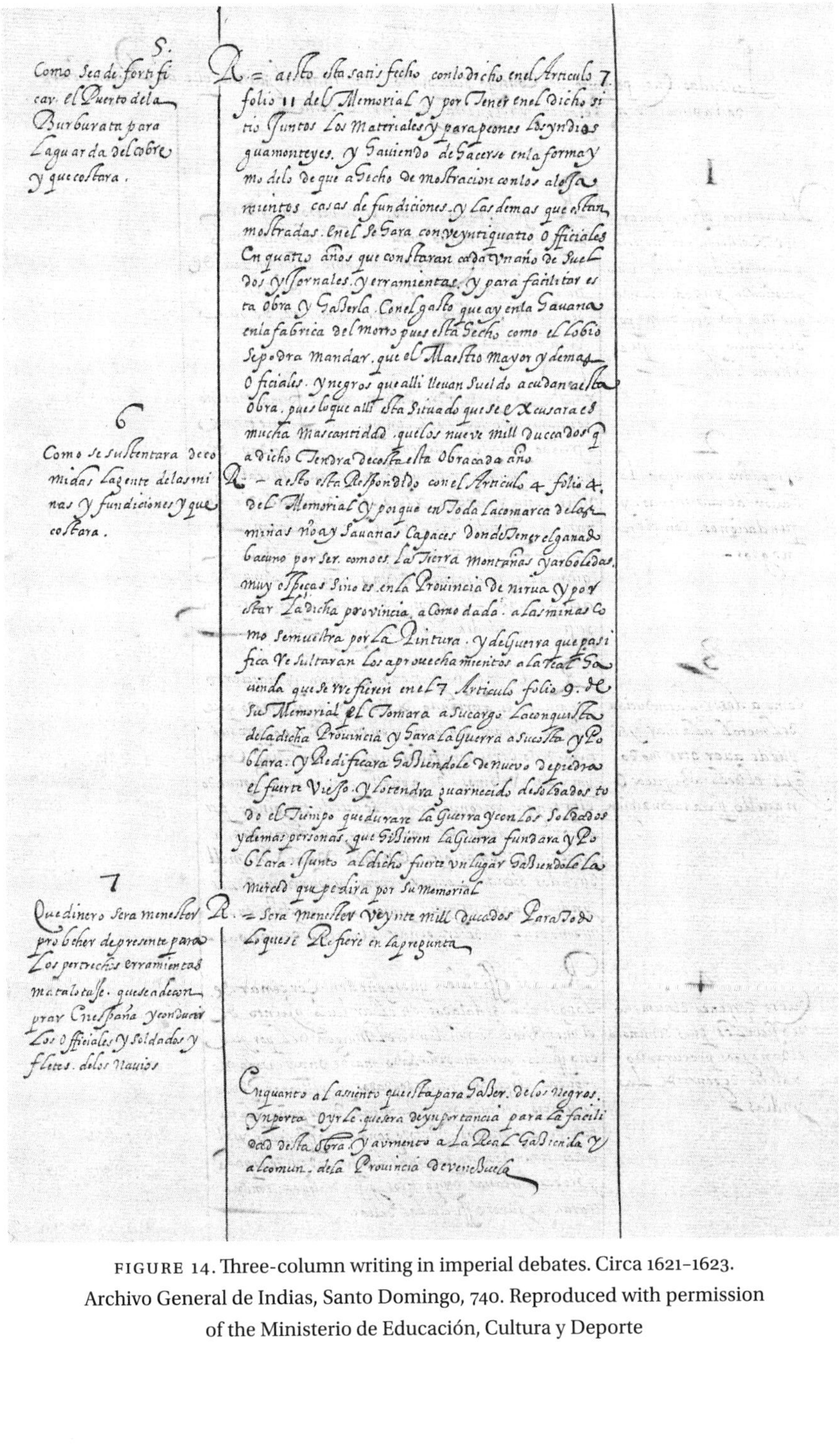

5\. Como se a de fortificar el Puerto de la Burburata para la guarda del cobre y que costara.

R = a esto esta satisfecho con lo dicho en el Articulo 7 folio 11 del Memorial y por tener en el dicho sitio juntos los materiales y para peones los yndios guamonteyes. y sauiendo de hacerse en la forma y modelo de que a hecho demostracion con los alojamientos casas de fundiciones y las demas que estan mostradas en el se hara con veynte y quatro officiales en quatro años que constaran cada vn año de sueldos y jornales y erramientas. y para facilitar esta obra y hacerla con el gasto que ay en la hauana en la fabrica del morro pues esta hecho como el lobio se podra mandar que el Maestro mayor y demas officiales y negros que alli lleuan sueldo acudan a esta obra. pues lo que alli esta situado que se escusara es mucha mas cantidad que los nueve mill ducados que a dicho tendra de costa esta obra cada año

6\. Como se sustentara de comidas la gente de las minas y fundiciones y que costara.

R = a esto esta respondido con el Articulo 4 folio 4 del Memorial y porque en toda la comarca de las minas no ay sauanas capaces donde tener el ganado bacuno por ser como es la tierra montañas y arboledas muy espesas sino es en la Prouincia de nirua y por estar la dicha provincia a comodado a las minas como se muestra por la pintura. y de guerra que pasifica resultaran los aprouechamientos a la Real hacienda que se refieren en el 7 Articulo folio 9 de su Memorial el tomara a su cargo la conquista de la dicha Prouincia y hara la guerra a su costa y poblara y redificara hauiendole de nuevo de piedra el fuerte viejo y lo tendra guarnecido de soldados todo el tiempo que durare la guerra y con los soldados y demas personas que hizieren la guerra fundara y poblara junto al dicho fuerte vn lugar hauiendole la merced que pedira por su memorial

7\. Que dinero sera menester prebeher de presente para los pertrechos erramientas materiales que se a de comprar en españa y conducir los officiales y soldados y fletes de los nauios

R = sera menester veynte mill ducados para todo lo que se refiere en la pregunta

En quanto al asiento que esta para hazer de los negros ynporta oyrle que sera de ynportancia para la facilidad desta obra y aumento a la Real hacienda y al comun de la Prouincia de venezuela

FIGURE 14. Three-column writing in imperial debates. Circa 1621–1623. Archivo General de Indias, Santo Domingo, 740. Reproduced with permission of the Ministerio de Educación, Cultura y Deporte

The Legacies of Don Manuel's Designs

In 1622, one year into the official review of don Manuel's proposal, he discussed the biopolitics of his plan with Rodrigo de Aguilar y Acuña, who was working on an assemblage of colonial law that was ultimately completed by Juan de Solórzano y Pereira. In these conversations, don Manuel proposed that all of the Africans who were no longer needed at the fortress of Havana could be relocated to Venezuela. He also recommended purchasing eight hundred or one thousand enslaved people over the next two years from Portuguese slave traders Antonio Fernández de Elvas and Diego López, capitalizing on the crown that Spain and Portugal shared.[36]

After pressing don Manuel about the number of African miners and the production of currency and weapons in Venezuela, don Juan de Billela, former *visitador general* (general inspector) of New Spain, made a back-of-the-envelope calculation in two parts. First, he listed the major economic, social, and biopolitical costs of the plan: minting coins, relocating African slaves from Havana "donde son Nezessos" (where they are needed), providing another 200 hundred enslaved Africans, relocating a town of 1,200 Indians to a new settlement in Borburata, and building a fortress. He determined, "Todo es de tan ymposible execuçion como se deja entender y que No puede tener efeto" (All of it is of such impossible execution that it must be understood that it cannot take effect), leaving no room for doubt: "Aunque las minas fueran de plata O de oro No se pudiera sacar de ellas La Recompensa del gasto" (Even if the mines were of silver or gold, the costs would never be recovered from them).[37]

Rodrigo de Aguiar sent the documents to the Junta de Guerra), AGI, Santo Domingo, 740, fol. 2.

36. "En conformidad," 1622, ibid., fol. 2. On Fernández de Elvas, see "Asientos de negros con diferentes compañías y particulares," 1595–1727, AGI, Contaduría, 261; "Visitas gobernación de Cartagena," 1619, AGI, Escribanía, 632A; Linda A. Newson and Susie Minchin, *From Capture to Sale: The Portuguese Slave Trade to Spanish South America in the Early Seventeenth Century* (Leiden, 2007), esp. 101–135. This Diego López is presumably Diego López de la Nava, captain of a slave ship bound for Cartagena; see "Registros de esclavos," 1621, AGI, Contratación, 2883. On Solórzano Pereira, see his *Política Indiana,* ed. Miguel Angel Ochoa Brun (1629; rpt. Madrid, 1972), 6 vols. Gaytán de Torres also identified Simón and Lorenzo Pereira, brothers from Oporto, Portugal, as other slave traders. See "Bienes de difuntos: Diego de Pereira y Felipa Núñez," 1621, AGI, Contratación, 950, no. 29. See also Acosta Saignes, *Vida de los esclavos negros en Venezuela,* 4–5; and Filipa Ribeiro da Silva, "Crossing Empires: Portuguese, Sephardic, and Dutch Business Networks in the Atlantic Slave Trade, 1580–1674," *Americas,* LXVIII (2011), 7–32.

37. "Consulta de el Sr don Juo de Billela," [ca. May 1623] (following the dates of adjacent documents), AGI, Santo Domingo, 740, fol. 1.

Faced with this decisive ruling, in 1625 don Manuel revised his visions of colonial community and the relationship between colony and metropole. Switching from third-person to first, he argued for reforms both top-down and bottom-up, blaming Spain's wretched state on colonial officials: "Me haze dificultoso, pues son de los ministros que en las Indias las goviernan que con el poder, y mano de sus oficios se llevan lo mas, y mejor de las Indias" (It is difficult for me, because the ministers in the Indies who govern with power and right rule of their offices take the most and the best from the Indies). As in his first survey, Gaytán de Torres invoked his firsthand experience as an authorizing source ("y lo afirmo como testigo de vista"). To complement this perspective, he addressed the king in embodied terms: "V. Excelencia, que es para abrir los ojos, y para poner el remedio" (Y[our] Excellency must open his eyes and apply the remedy), "Y pues oy tiene V. Excelencia noticia de lo que voy tratando, serà justo ponerle el ombro al remedio" (and since Y[our] Excellency now has notice of what I say, it would be just to put some muscle [shoulder] into the remedy). The *Relación, y vista de ojos* (1621) enumerated the bodies of enslaved African women and men, whereas *Que se de diferente modo al govierno de las Indias* (1625) foregrounded the king's two bodies: his political office (the source of authority) and his physical body (eyes that understand, muscled shoulders capable of effecting change).[38]

In this second proposal, the key to ensuring Spain's health and wealth was, not to produce gold or silver in America, but to transport it safely across the Atlantic Ocean. Gaytán de Torres argued that warships should guard Caribbean ports from pirates like "el Draque" (Francis Drake) and "Guaterral cosario" (Ralegh the corsair), much as Portuguese forces in Brazil and Angola responded to "el poder de Argel, y Olanda en el modo q̄ an tomado los Moros en andar en navios de alto bordo" (the power of Algiers and Holland in the way in which the Moors have taken to storming ships). By relocating six galleons and two brigs to Puerto Rico from Santo Domingo and Portobelo—essentially half the infantry—and paying soldiers well, in good coin ("buena moneda, y el sueldo considerable"), Gaytán de Torres argued that the united crown of Spain and Portugal could enjoy economic growth without exploring for mines or developing new metallurgical technologies.[39]

Some ideas, such as navigational timetables that reduced time in Caribbean

38. *Que se de diferente modo al govierno de las Indias, q̄ se van perdiendo muy apriessa con el que oi tienen, y modo para su pratica* (n.p., n.d.), 1, 1v, 4, 4v, Ayer 652.G28 A, Newberry Library, Chicago. See also Ernst H. Kantorowicz, *The King's Two Bodies: A Study in Mediaeval Political Theology* (Princeton, N.J., 1957).

39. *Que se de diferente modo al govierno de las Indias,* 3–4, 10v.

ports, were designed to restrict colonial commerce, control access to goods, and squeeze a second silver galleon into the calendar year. This additional passage would allow for greater circulation in Mediterranean ports like Genoa, where consumers might purchase commodities like "la maquina de corambre, cochinilla, y otros generos de supremo valor" (the machine of hides, cochineal, and other things of supreme value).[40]

Other policies extended agency to criollos, such as don Manuel's call for capable creole soldiers ("aquellos que estan aptos para serlo") to defend Caribbean ports and to replace administrative positions once reserved for Spaniards with criollos of "buen talento, letras, y pluma" (good talent, letters, and pen). In the early years of conquest, it was necessary to import lettered men from Spain because only the poorest sorts ("pobres soldados, hombres desacreditados, y tales") went to the Americas. But now, men of good reason could be found in even the most remote colonies. As he put it, "Aunque no tenga un lugar sino veinte Españoles tienen forma de govierno de Alcaldes, y Regidores, y todos a una mano hombres practicos en negocios, y libros de quenta y razon, porque el que en las Indias no es tratanta no junta dineros" (Even though a place has not even twenty Spaniards, they have a form of government with mayors, judges, and at one's beck and call experienced businessmen, books of account and reason, because he who does not traffic will not make money in the Indies). As a cost-saving measure, he argued that some of these posts could be eliminated in some towns, such as accountants, treasurers, and factors. Whereas don Manuel's first prose report revolved around black family life, his second vision of colonial life shifts considerably. The only reference to Africans is a scant line asking that the crown, under cover of the royal treasury, "ymbie Negros a algunas partes de las Indias, y que se den fiados a los vecinos" (send blacks to some parts of the Indies, guaranteed to property holders).[41]

This change should not be taken to mean that fewer Africans were enslaved in Venezuela by 1625. Throughout the seventeenth century, Dutch-Portuguese rivalry in Brazil and West Africa led to sharp spikes in the forced arrivals of

40. Ibid., 5–12v, esp. 9v.

41. Ibid., 4, 14–14v, 15–15v; Gregorio López Madera, "Por derecho de V Mgd nos hemos Juntado diversas Vezes a ver y Berificar el libro de mano que don Manuel Gaytan de Torres veinte y quatro de la Ciudad de Xerez . . . ," Jan. 2, 1625, fol. 6v, BL. The title is crossed out, so it looks like "~~Por derecho de V Mgd ^ nos los lis-dos greg-o lopez madera D. Seb-an de -alobos p-l m-s fro dom-o cano nos hemos Juntado diuersas Vezes a ver y Berificar el libro de mano que Don Manuel Gaytan de Torres veinte y quatro de la Ciudad de Xerez a dado a varios discursos para la restauracion desta Monarquia y vistos y exsaminados quanto hauemos podido todos sus Capitulos respendiendo a cada vno de por si nos aparecido lo siguiente~~."

African women and men in the Americas. Eager to tell imperial officials what they wanted to hear, Gaytán de Torres founded his revised vision of colonial life on creole scribes, not African miners.[42]

The development of new forms of writing and recording was arguably the most tangible result of Gaytán de Torres's career as a projector. In response to his work of 1625, jurist Gregorio López Madera proposed the creation of a new imperial post in which two men would request three-year reports from council chambers, relating "las personas que tiene por mas benemeritas para Prelacias, Plazas mayores y menores y demas officios" (the people who received awards for prelates, major and minor positions, and other offices). The holders of such offices, like writers of relaciónes before them, would organize knowledges, ideas, and projections from the Americas into reports for official Spanish consumption.[43]

An inventory reported in Caracas on June 25, 1638, indicates that some of don Manuel's ideas were put into practice, but on a dramatically smaller scale than what he imagined. One month earlier, treasurers Francisco de Sojo and Hernando García de Rivas went to survey the mines, conduct a census of Cocorote, and determine the value of chattel property ("Ynstrumentos y pertrechos"). They arrived in Cocorote with a list of fourteen questions that they asked of all witnesses: questions 1–4 and 11–14 dealt with refining equipment and infrastructure (charcoal- and water-powered refining ovens, mules, molds, transportation routes, a reverberatory oven, the refinery, and cattle); questions 5–10 asked about the thirty-four enslaved African miners—six women and twenty-eight men—that refiner *(fundidor)* Gerónimo Martínez Pincón had brought from Havana in 1632 with permission from former Venezuelan governor Francisco Núñez Melián. Only one question addressed the women: witnesses were asked to confirm whether they were worth three hundred pesos each "y no mas porque no tienen ofiçio ninguno" (and no more because they did not have any trade whatsoever). Notably, whereas Martínez Pincón identified the miners in terms of gender and civil status ("entre Ellos seis henbras y algunos casados"), other officials classified them by language,

42. David Eltis and David Richardson, eds., *Extending the Frontiers: Essays on the New Transatlantic Slave Trade Database* (New Haven, Conn., 2008); Seymour Drescher, "The Long Goodbye: Dutch Capitalism and Antislavery in Comparative Perspective," *American Historical Review,* XCIX (1994), 44–69; Robin Law, "The Slave Trade in Seventeenth-Century Allada: A Revision," *African Economic History,* XXII (1994), 59–92, esp. 62.

43. López Madera, "Por derecho de V Mgd," Jan. 2, 1625, 3v. On New World genres, see Walter Mignolo, "Cartas, crónicas y relaciones del descubrimiento y la conquista," Luis Íñigo Madrigal, ed., *Época colonial,* vol. I of *Historia de la literatura hispanoamericana* (Madrid, 1982), 57–116, esp. 59–98.

noting that there were thirty-one *bozales* (speakers of African languages) and three ladinos.[44]

By 1638, the twenty-eight men from Cuba had become seventeen in Cocorote, including three refiners (Gabriel, Antón Caraballo, Joan Mulato), six assistants, two carpenters (Gonzalo, Sebastián), four welders (Bartolomé, Domingo, Gonzalo, Mazanga), and two tanners (Simón, Gaspar), as well as Blas, an elder ("negro biexo") who had once been an overseer ("mandador"). The six women became eleven, all unnamed ("las onza negras q̄ ay en estas minas"). Given that only one man survived to old age, we may conclude from the inventory's silence that some of the missing nine men ran away or died from harsh labor, food shortages, or unfamiliar conditions. The additional women might have arrived on the *Nuestra Señora de la Concepción del Rosario,* a 130-ton slave ship that was licensed in Seville, departed from Angola for Mexico in 1635, and wound up in the Venezuelan port of La Guaira in 1637, where treasurers Sojo and García de Rivas taxed the 109 Africans who disembarked.[45]

The census of 1638 does not explain the increase in the female population or the decline in the male population. Instead, witnesses focused on the technical skills of African miners and the relationships between miners, Spanish artisans, and local officials. Royal notary Gerónimo Fernández, resident in Cocorote since its founding, testified that he knew two of the refiners, "Alejandro" and "El Mulato." Other witnesses identified them as Antón Caraballo and Joan Mulato. But Fernández's favorable assessment of their knowledge ("el estado q̄ esta la ynteligenzia dellos en el saver fundir") aligned with other statements. According to Fernández, mine administrator Capitán Andrés Román had estimated their combined worth at eight hundred pesos de a ocho, even though they were not master refiners. Fernández did not know any of the other African

44. "Pidenlos ofre- q- se les advierta lo que deben hazer en las minas tración de la mina," Santiago de León de Caracas, June 14, 1638, AGI, Santo Domingo, 740; "Los oficiales de Beneçuela remiten los testimonios inclusos sobre la tasacion de la mina del cobre," Caracas, June 25, 1638, ibid., fols. 10–13v; "Auto en que se mda comprar esclavos pa la mina," La Guaira–Santiago de León de Caracas, Feb. 26–May 19, 1631, ibid., fols. 2–2v. Núñez Melián tried to purchase thirty more enslaved Angolans from Pedro Fernandes Pinero, but the crown did not allow it.

45. "Autos e ynformacion sobre las labores y sustento que avian en las minas de cobre que para ello sacado qdo entro en su ministon el capitán don brme de mesa," May 21, 1638, ibid., fol. 1v. One official noted, "No se le entrego ni avia mas sementa que en el un tablon de que a pequeño de yucca nueva . . . que en dos meses no esta para sacar." On the *Nuestra Señora de la Concepción,* see Acosta Saignes, *Vida de los esclavos negros en Venezuela,* 79; "Voyage 29684, NS del Rosario (1635)," *Trans-Atlantic Slave Trade Database,* http://www.slavevoyages.org/voyage/29684/variables.

men, save for Blas, but he suggested the carpenters and welders were worth five hundred pesos each, more than the crown's estimate of four hundred, because "saviendo qualquiera cosa en que puedan aprender y descuydar al maestro" (knowing anything of the sort they could learn and ease the work of the master tradesman).[46]

A religious official interviewed in Cocorote offered a different view of the relationship between miners, the crown, and the church. For the previous five years, fray Joan Bautista, president of the Franciscan Convent in Nueva Segovia de Barquisimeto, had lived in Cocorote. He named the three enslaved refiners—Gabriel, Antón Caraballo, and Joan Mulato—specifying that they, like the other Africans, were property of the crown ("dixo este testigo conoze tres negros fundidores de su magestad," "dixo que save y conoze los otros seis negros q̄ de su Magd," "dixo q̄ conoze a los dos negros curtidores de su magestad destas minas y que saven a cuydar a curtir y coser fuelles," "dixo que conoze las onze negras que estan en estas minas de su magestad" [this witness said he knows the three refiners owned by Your Majesty; he said that he knows of and knows the other six black men owned by Your Majesty; he said that he knows two of the black tanners owned by Your Majesty in these mines and that they know how to care for leather and make bellows; he said that he knows the eleven black women in these mines owned by Your Majesty]). The only two groups for whom he did not indicate royal ownership were Blas and the carpenters. The person suited to assess the carpenters' knowledge was master carpenter Simón de Arce, who made refining ovens. He affirmed the skills of two black carpenters, Gonzalo and Sebastián. Although they were not master carpenters ("no son maestros"), Arce insisted that Gonzalo was a skilled craftsman who could repair anything in the refineries ("todo lo que fuere nezesario"). If asked to repair a broken wagon, he could do that, too ("y si le ofrezere rreparar una carreta si se quebrare Lo sabe hazer"). These testimonies offer a small glimpse into community formation in Cocorote. Even though African refiners were considered royal property ("los tres negros que ay de su Magd"), the testimonies suggest the limits of the crown's authority in Cocorote. Witnesses mentioned technical skills that were proved by experience and known publicly, but they were not certified.[47]

46. "Los oficiales de Beneçuela remiten los testimonios . . . ," Caracas, June 25, 1638, AGI, Santo Domingo, 740, fols. 17v, 19, 20, 21v.

47. Ibid., 19–19v, 21v–24, 30v–31. Fernández mentioned the crown's connection to Indigenous laborers and their abuse by the previous governor, but not to African miners or refiners. The *interrogatorio* asked whether "treinta peones Yndios" had repaired the large canals that conducted water to the refining ovens. Fernández affirmed that sixty peons had

From August 1639 through September 1648, only thirteen children were born to black women in the mining community; twelve children to six couples, while one single mother refused to name the father of her child. There were twenty-five black women in the mines at this time, but only these six mothers were married to African men; other women would have remained single, and others still would have found partners—willingly and unwillingly—in Indigenous, Spanish, or creole men. There was not a midwife in Cocorote, so these children were probably delivered by someone like María de la Mota, who was brought from the Aroa River valley to assist enslaved women in childbirth. She received a salary of thirty pesos for midwifery and curing blacks "de las enfermedades que ella entendiese" (of the illnesses that she understands), suggesting that she might also have been of African descent. By 1649, María de la Mota was replaced with a physician, Diego Jiménez Lozano. Before his arrival, miners were treated with herbs and potions that reflect combinations of African, Indigenous, and European practices and beliefs about health, such as brass *(azófar),* yellow ointment *(ungüento amarillo),* saffron *(azofrán),* chamomile, pepper, cloves, honey, sugar, tobacco, chickens, and firewater *(aguardiente).* Harsher treatments involved sublimated mercury *(solimán),* which was used on "negros bubosos" (blacks with sores).[48]

Although the population did not increase in the way that don Manuel projected, other elements of his proposal did take root in Cocorote. Records from 1657 show that African ironworkers produced a range of goods for the mining complex, including hammers, pickaxes, forceps for the smith's forge, nails to repair mine carts and seal bellows, and screws for refining ovens, as well as general goods like hatchets, mortars, bells, hooks, pots, saucepans, saws, and hinges for the church doors. Some goods were designed for African artisans, such as "un cuchillo para un negro" (a knife for a black man). The mining complex never reached the scale that Gaytán de Torres thought was possible in the 1620s. But by the eighteenth century, the mines were part of the estate of the family of revolutionary hero Simón Bolívar. Proceeds from the enslaved laborers of Cocorote thus helped to finance the independence of Venezuela.[49]

---

worked for fifty days "Por cuenta de su magestad" and that they were only paid for some of the work, with two reales each and six bottles of wine (18–18v).

48. Acosta Saignes, *Vida de los esclavos negros en Venezuela,* 161–165, 170. See also Pablo F. Gómez, *The Experiential Caribbean: Creating Knowledge and Healing in the Early Modern Atlantic* (Chapel Hill, N.C., 2017).

49. Paúl Verna, *Las minas del libertador* (Caracas, 1977); Acosta Saignes, *Vida de los esclavos negros en Venezuela,* 154, 166–167, 170.

By comparing don Manuel's colonial projections over time in printed forms (1621, 1625) and conversation with imperial officials (1621–1623), we learn little about the realities of copper mining in Venezuela. Instead, we see what New World writers and imperial underwriters thought about their place in the world and what kinds of political, social, and economic transformations they thought were possible in a moment of imperial reimagining. We also see what kinds of discursive strategies these projectors used to convince the crown to share their visions. For Gaytán de Torres, the material potential of copper that could be crushed, refined, and cast into globally recognized modes of exchange was the imaginative blueprint for the making of colonial community. Attention to these forms of copper projecting, as they were designed and remade for imperial consumption, allows us to better understand the history of Iberian ideas about American colonization as they changed over time. From localized models of black community life that were grounded in African knowledge of copper metals and metallurgy, don Manuel revised and resubmitted his vision for Venezuela, instead centering the silver galleons and American-born criollos who could replace Spanish peninsular administrators. Don Manuel incorporated African artisan experience into his model of community foundation in 1621 and erased those ways of knowing from his conversations with imperial officials and revised proposal. By charting this erasure in a short period of time, this chapter offers a glimpse of how African metallurgical knowledge informed Spanish ideas about New World possibilities at a critical moment in imperial reimagining and how those possibilities were quickly flattened into traditional ideologies of embodied labor rather than novel ideas of subaltern technical knowledge.

In showing how Manuel Gaytán de Torres drew from the precedent of El Cobre and how o Fidalgo de Elvas framed Hernando de Soto's failed search for copper as a response to Álvar Núñez Cabeza de Vaca, Part 3 of this book suggests how ideas about copper mining and colonization moved between and among linguistic and regional traditions. To understand how don Manuel projected his vision of Cocorote, we must know the history of slavery in El Cobre. And to appreciate how Richard Hakluyt, like Elvas before him, fashioned a narrative of potential from absent evidence, we must consult the work of writers like Cabeza de Vaca. These authors and their ideas about European colonization—waged under the auspices of Spain, Portugal, or England—did not live in isolated, self-contained worlds. They drew from each other's stories to spin tales of their own, converting written words into material that was as malleable and protean as the copper metals upon which they founded their ideas.

Silver

8 : AMALGAMATING KNOWLEDGE, TRANSLATING EMPIRE

Álvaro Alonso Barba was a priest from Andalusia who lived most of his life in the Andes. Arriving in Tarabuco (present-day Chuquisaca, Bolivia) around the turn of the seventeenth century, Barba spent the next forty-odd years ministering to miners in the "partes mas grabes de aquel Arcobispado" (most severe regions of that archdiocese), such as the provinces of Pacajes, Lípez, and Oruro, before being moved to Potosí. With the support of Juan de Lizarazu, president of the Audiencia de Charcas, the highest administrative body in the region, Barba's *Arte de los metales* was published in Madrid, by the crown, in 1640.[1]

Barba's book, like his metallurgical expertise, blended concepts and expressions from Andean and Spanish technical arts. These sophisticated hybrid knowledges were promoted by the same imperial apparatus that underwrote the book's publication, supported the author's travel, and meticulously restricted the movements of Indigenous and African miners whose humanity and intellect it denied. The technologies that Barba describes, especially new methods of amalgamating silver with mercury, depended upon the labor and ideas of miners from diverse racial, ethnic, and linguistic communities. As scholars like Ananda Cohen-Aponte, Carolyn Dean, and Dana Leibsohn have shown in the visual arts, hybridity in technical and mechanical arts like mining

1. Josep M. Barnadas, *Álvaro Alonso Barba (1569–1662): Investigaciones sobre su vida y obra* (La Paz, 1986), 26–31; "Informaciones: Álvaro Alonso Barba y Garfias," Feb. 4, 1658, Archivo General de Indias (hereafter cited as AGI), Charcas, 96, no. 9, fol. 3. On February 15, 1637, Barba dedicated the work to Lizarazu while in Potosí. On March 1, Lizarazu wrote a letter of support for the work, which was endorsed on March 15 by officials from the Villa Imperial and representatives of the city's mercury smith guild *(gremio de azogueros)*. From there, publication slowed. On September 28, 1639, don Paulo de Barondelet (Carondelet, baron de Villers) approved Barba's book for publication in Madrid. Finally, on February 3, 1640, Dr. don Francisco Murcia de la Llana certified, in his capacity as general book corrector, that the book was fit for publication; see Barba, *Arte de los metales en que se enseña el verdadero beneficio de los de oro, y plata por açogue . . .* (Madrid, 1640), paras. 2–4v. On the office of the book corrector in Spain and its colonies, as well as the Murcia de la Llana family's place within networks of writers, printers, and royal censors, see Félix Díaz Moreno, "El control de La Verdad: Los Murcia de La Llana, una familia de correctores de libros," *Arbor*, CLXXXV, no. 740 (2009), 1301–1311.

and metallurgy was equally grounded in the epistemic violence and asymmetries of colonial power.[2]

To correct some of those asymmetries, the chapters in this section identify linguistic signatures of Indigenous miners whose voices have not often been heard within the colonial scientific historiography. This chapter outlines the development of the silver industry in Mexico and the Andes, contextualizing the political, economic, technological, and linguistic changes that I then study in the following two chapters. There, by analyzing blends of Spanish, Quechua, and Aimara as they appear in works like Barba's *Arte de los metales,* mine owner Luis Capoche's *Relación de la villa imperial* (ca. 1585), and overseer García de Llanos's *Diccionario y maneras de hablar que se usan en las minas* (1609), as well as manuscripts, council records, and colonial letters, I identify when speakers of Indigenous languages coined technical terms and contributed key ideas to the Andean silver industry. Pinpointing the moments when these terms were written out of scientific literatures in Europe, as Barba's *Arte de los metales* was translated into English (1670–1740), German (1676–1763), and French (1730–1750), then creates a documentary record of Indigenous knowledge production and its omission in print. Although I do not have enough evidence to create the same kind of record for African miners, it is my hope that scholars will borrow methods from this and the following chapters on color, *casta* (caste), and the erasure of subaltern knowledges, in conjunction with new research by historians and literary scholars like Christina Mobley, James H. Sweet, and Sara E. Johnson, to develop language-centered approaches that can shed light on African diasporic knowledges in diverse colonial contexts.[3]

Rethinking the Translation of Empire

Before the publication of the *Arte de los metales,* word had spread in the Andes of Barba's scientific collaborations with Indigenous mining communities. For

2. Ananda Cohen-Aponte, "Decolonizing the Global Renaissance: A View from the Andes," in Daniel Savoy, ed., *The Globalization of Renaissance Art: A Critical Review* (Boston, 2017), 67–94, esp. 70–75; Carolyn Dean and Dana Leibsohn, "Hybridity and Its Discontents: Considering Visual Culture in Colonial Spanish America," *Colonial Latin American Review,* XII (2003), 5–35.

3. Christina Frances Mobley, "The Kongolese Atlantic: Central African Slavery and Culture from Mayombe to Haiti" (Ph.D. diss., 2015); James Sweet, "Research Note: New Perspectives on Kongo in Revolutionary Haiti," *Americas,* LXXIV (2017), 83–97; Sara A. Johnson, "'Your Mother Gave Birth to a Pig': Power, Abuse, and Planter Linguistics in Baudry des Lozière's *Vocabulaire Congo,*" *Early American Studies,* XVI (2018), 7–40.

example, upon hearing about a mysterious metallic vein located in a small hill adjacent to the church of an Indigenous settlement *(ranchería)* that surrounded the town of Oruro, the priest tried its dense, white soil (*tierra blanca,* or *kontai* in Quechua) and found it good for making crucibles. He published his results ("publiqu[é] su uso") and declared the soil—used by Andean artisans to polish metals—to be "as good as the finest of China." In turn, officials of the Real Audiencia praised Barba for communicating his thoughts in speech and writing ("de palabra y por escrito") in the Villa Imperial, "como a cabeça de todos los mineros y minerales" (as the head of all mine[r]s and minerals).[4]

In his technical descriptions of amalgamation methods, heat-based refining treatments, and specialized instruments, Barba reveals a form of metallurgical expertise that combines Andean and Spanish knowledge systems. Around 1609, he developed a method of amalgamating silver ores with heat-based treatments *(cazo y cozimiento)* that allowed refiners in Potosí to adapt the Mexican method of amalgamation to the colder temperatures of the Andes. With his awareness of the many mixed metals of the Andes, Barba recommended that refiner *(el beneficiador)* "Sepa conocer los metales" (know how to know about metals), including which ores to amalgamate and which ones to smelt. In examples that were as cautionary as they were unbelievable, Barba describes how this inclusive metallurgical approach led to incredible wealth in the New World—wealth that others had ignored. In one passage, he explains how he revived a mine that had been abandoned by Spaniards because the ore could not be amalgamated. One day, an Andean miner from Jaquegua, province of Los Lípez, brought a sample from a slag heap outside of the abandoned mine. Barba, "eminent" in Quechua and Aimara, cultivated relationships with miners like this unnamed collaborator. After determining that it was not possible to amalgamate the ore, Barba smelted it ("por fuego") and increased the site's profitability by an astounding (albeit self-reported) 200 percent. Once valued at 4 or 5 pesos per quintal (100 pounds), silver metals from Xaqueagua now earned 900 pesos per quintal. As he related his service to the crown, Barba reminded imperial officials of this "más que ordinaria noticia" (extraordinary notice). With his mastery of new amalgamation technologies and time-honored practices of smelting, and his ability to match mixed ores to different metallurgical treatments, the priest became one of the most prominent voices in the colonial Andean mining industry.[5]

4. Barba, *Arte de los metales,* 56; "Informaciones," Feb. 4, 1658, AGI, Charcas, 96, no. 9, fol. 3v. On early modern translations of *minero* as "mine" and "miner," see the Introduction.

5. Barba, *Arte de los metales,* 38v, 39; "Informaciones: Alvaro Alonso Barba Toscano,"

Following the first print run of the *Arte de los metales,* the crown requested that Barba return to Spain to reform its mines and refineries. In his first petition for a license to complete this requested trip—submitted in 1649 and resubmitted in 1654—Barba noted that mixed metallic deposits of silver (Ag) and lead (Pb) in Niebla, an imperial Roman mining outpost along the banks of the Río Tinto in southwestern Andalusia, resembled those of the Andean provinces of Oruro, Cochinoca, and Iroco, where colonial miners extracted silver from abandoned Inca imperial slag piles. They used amalgamation methods that were unknown to even the most revered European metallurgists, such as German mineralogical writer Georgius Agricola, whom Barba calls "el mayor maestro de estas materias" (the greatest master of these matters). The larger, if more subtle, point was that, just as Spain had been a mining colony of imperial Rome and just as the Inca empire had mined Potosí, imperial Spain now mined the Andes and could benefit from its natural and human resources. But unlike traditional invocations of the *translatio studii* or *translatio imperii,* in which the path of empire and civilization follow the westward course of the sun, Barba envisions Andean knowledge as a site of epistemological exchanges, with science and technology moving both East and West.[6]

Barba eventually made his way to Spain in 1658, via a Dutch ship out of Buenos Aires. As he traveled through the iron-rich regions of the Basque Country to Andalusia, he interviewed local miners while his companion, Agustín Núñez de Zamora, "persona de los mas inteligentes de las Indias, en las materias de beneficos de metales" (among the most intelligent people in the Indies on matters of metalwork), studied mountain colors and landscapes ("terruños") for signs of mineral deposits. After spending all of 1659 investigating Spain's metallic wealth, Barba asked to return to Alto Perú, but the crown insisted that he conduct additional experiments. In 1662, he repeated his request, having performed and documented his work in several relations, testimonies, and accounts ("memoriales"). With a touch of bitterness, Barba noted that he had offered to do these things in 1649 and had now fulfilled his duties to the crown. Sensing that his appeal might be rejected, he began to suggest skilled miners who could replace him. He identified two equally qualified groups of experts: "personas de Alemania, u de las Indias" (people from Ger-

---

1650, AGI, Charcas, 93, no. 19, fol. 90v; "Memorial de A. Alonso Barba al Lic. Juan Gonzáles," Madrid, Feb. 10, 1659, AGI, Indiferente General, 774, quoted in Barnadas, *Álvaro Alonso Barba,* 179–184, esp. 182; ibid., 55–59.

6. "Memorial de Alvaro Alonso Barba al rey," La Plata, 1649, AGI, Indiferente General, 771, quoted in Barnadas, *Álvaro Alonso Barba,* 150–155, esp. 152.

many or the Indies), especially miners who were skilled in prospecting, or "[lo] que llaman catear" (what they call *catear*).[7]

The Real Academia Española traces the roots of the verb *catear* to the Spanish noun *cata* (a test), derived from the Latin verb *captāre* (to capture, seek, or take). But, according to the RAE's *Corpus diacrónico del español* (CORDE), *catear* first appears in the Spanish lexicon in 1571, when new laws *(ordenanzas)* were declared regarding the treatment of Indigenous miners and laborers in the Peruvian province of Huamanga. Barba's explanation of the material practices of mineral prospecting suggest why *catear* may stem from Andean roots rather than Latin etymologies. Writing for a royal audience unfamiliar with Andean mining practices and expertise, and perhaps unlikely to acknowledge them, Barba defined the skills that were embedded in the term: "buscar por los cerros las betas de metales encubiertas, por los indicios, y muestras dellas, que conocen por experiencia los que por exte exercicio llaman cateadores" (to look in mountains for veins of hidden metals, using the indexes and signs of the veins, which they who are called *cateadores* know from experience in this exercise). The Hispanized verb *catear* seems to fuse two Quechua terms that were grounded in experiential knowledge under- and aboveground, as recorded by Jesuit linguist Diego González Holguín: *çatticcayani* ("estar caydo atollado, o dentro en cosa honda y en peccados, o en grande ocupacion" [to have fallen in a problem, or inside of a deep thing and in danger, or in a grand charge]) and *çatita* ("hombre sabio entendido esperimentado, y machucho en todo versado" [a wise man who understands through experience, and (is) sensibly versed in all things]). Colonial dictionaries from other regions of Peru, such as that prepared by Dominican missionary Domingo de Santo Tomás, suggest related but slightly different connections, situated by activity and geography: *qatiy* ("continuar alguna cosa" [to continue something]) and *qata* ("recuesto de monte" [the cliff of a mountain]).[8]

Although Spain had no shortage of mineral wealth, with some thirteen thou-

7. "Memorial de Alonso al Rey," 1659, ibid., 185–195, esp. 186; "Memorial de Álvaro Alonso Barba al Rey," 1662, ibid., 218–226, esp. 222.

8. Barba, *Arte de los metales,* 222; *Diccionario de la lengua española,* 23d ed., s.v. "catear," "cata," "catar," http://dle.rae.es; Real Academia Española, Banco de datos, *Corpus diacrónico del español* (CORDE), ibid.; Diego González Holguín, *Vocabulario de la lengua general de todo el Perú llamada lengua qquichua o del Inca* (1608), 3d ed. (Lima, 1989), s.v. "çatticcayani" and "çatita o çattiscaruna, o çattisca soncoyoc"; Domingo de Santo Thomas, *Lexicón o vocabulario de la lengua general del Perú* (1560), ed. Julio Calvo Pérez and Henrique Urbano (Lima, 2013), s.v. "qatiy," "qata." I thank Nicholas Q. Emlen for helping me with these terms.

sand registered veins, Barba argued that his homeland lacked "cateadores" who knew how to search for and find hidden mines ("las que no se muestran manifiestas"). In the interest of monarchial prosperity and the common good, he suggested that the crown introduce American metallurgical technologies to gold-rich Galicia and bring skilled cateadores from the Andes, including Spanish-born subjects like Zamora or Capitán Juan de Figueroa, "para que huviesse en España maestros del Arte de los metales, y enseñassen el modo de su beneficio a los que tratassen dello" (so that there might be in Spain some masters of the art of metals, and they could teach the method of amalgamation to those who could use it here). In addition to modeling Andean arts as they had been mastered by Spanish colonists, Barba recommended that Spain adapt mining laws from the Andes, where decrees that rewarded mine discoverers were publicly announced. In Spain, even the most knowledgeable writers who had published on the topic ("aun de personas entendidas que lo han publicado en sus escritos, y libros inpressos") thought that miners were prohibited from discovering new sites.[9]

Mining, like other extractive industries in the Americas, has often been studied as part of transatlantic mercantilism, wherein raw goods from the colonies became finished products in Europe. In some cases, these goods were sold back to colonial subjects at rates that were difficult to afford. New approaches to mercantilism and recent research by historians and historians of science on the cultural meanings and knowledges embedded in colonial goods—from chocolate and tobacco to mahogany, pearls, and quinine—provide richer, more nuanced understandings of merchantable commodities and transatlantic traffic.[10]

Likewise, as Barba's case suggests, the extraction, processing, minting, and trading of silver was, not a straightforward, mercantilist exchange, but rather a complex, negotiated translation of knowledge and goods within the Spanish empire. This chapter examines the silver industry's progress within such imperial parameters, zooming in and out to show how Spanish and non-Spanish

9. "Memorial de A. Alonso al Rey (1662)," quoted in Barnadas, *Álvaro Alonso Barba,* 223–224.

10. See, for instance, Marcy Norton, *Sacred Gifts, Profane Pleasures: A History of Tobacco and Chocolate in the Atlantic World* (Ithaca, N.Y., 2008); Jennifer L. Anderson, *Mahogany: The Costs of Luxury in Early America* (Cambridge, Mass., 2012); Matthew James Crawford, *The Andean Wonder Drug: Cinchona Bark and Imperial Science in the Spanish Atlantic, 1630–1800* (Pittsburgh, 2016); and Molly A. Warsh, *American Baroque: Pearls and the Nature of Empire, 1492–1700* (Williamsburg, Va., and Chapel Hill, N.C., 2018). On mercantilism, see Philip J. Stern and Carl Wennerlind, eds., *Mercantilism Reimagined: Political Economy in Early Modern Britain and Its Empire* (New York, 2014).

actors, including African, Asian, and, especially, Amerindian communities, influenced and were influenced by political, economic, technological, and linguistic changes. These changes were so dramatic that historian Peter J. Bakewell, one of the foremost experts on mining in colonial Latin America, called the consequences of the industry "almost beyond measure."[11]

A Brief History of Colonial Silver: Land, Law, and Labor

Following the earliest years of the Spanish conquest (1492–1537), Holy Roman Emperor Carlos V established the viceroyalties of New Spain (1535) and Peru (1542) to administer Spain's expansive territories in the Americas and organize the extraction of colonial wealth. As had been the case with European viceroyalties like Aragón and Naples, the crown appointed Spanish nobles to serve as viceroys. A few years after their arrival, Antonio de Mendoza and Luis de Velasco, holding office in Mexico, and Francisco de Toledo, governing in Peru, instituted policies that regulated mine labor, encouraged "discovery," and promoted silver production in the newly minted administrative regions of Potosí (1545) and Zacatecas (1546).[12]

This elaborate viceregal redistricting was justified in large part by East Asian demand for silver. In the markets of early modern Japan and, especially, China, silver commanded a favorable exchange rate of nearly 2:1, relative to the price of gold in Europe. After establishing a post in Manila in 1571 and introducing amalgamation to Potosí in 1572, Habsburg agents used profits from their exchanges of New World silver for East Asian gold to buy and sell people and goods in Africa and Europe, inaugurating what some economists identify as the origins of global economy.[13]

Soon after the "discovery" of Potosí's wealth, the silver metropolis was rechristened as the Villa Imperial de Potosí in honor of its economic importance to Spain's transatlantic and transpacific empire. Home, at the turn of

11. Peter Bakewell, "Mining in Colonial Spanish America," in Leslie Bethell, ed., *Colonial Spanish America,* vol. II of *The Cambridge History of Latin America* (Cambridge, 1997), 202–249, esp. 249.

12. Joaquín Pérez Melero, "From Alchemy to Science: The Scientific Revolution in Spanish American Mining and Metallurgy," in Gary D. Rosenberg, ed., *The Revolution in Geology from the Renaissance to the Enlightenment* (Boulder, Colo., 2009), 51–61, esp. 54–56.

13. Dennis O. Flynn and Arturo Giráldez, eds., *Metals and Monies in an Emerging Global Economy* (Aldershot, U.K., 1997), xix–xxii; Flynn and Giráldez, "Born with a 'Silver Spoon': The Origin of World Trade in 1571," *Journal of World History,* VI (1995), 201–221. Gold traded in Canton between 1:5.5–1:7, whereas Spanish exchange rates fluctuated from 1:12.5–1:14. At times, gold was worth twice as much as silver, and at other times, it was worth slightly less; see ibid., 206–207.

the seventeenth century, to some 160,000 people of Andean, Spanish, African, Portuguese, Flemish, and Italian descent, Potosí was one of the world's largest cities. Its vibrant markets sold silks and spices from China and the Middle East, while playhouses staged Indigenous and Spanish classics and cathedrals elevated the preparation of the sacrament with stunning displays of earthly wealth, including chalices, baptismal fonts, and urns made of silver and gold. Many of these wares were crafted by Indigenous metalsmiths, including teams of husbands and wives. Under the Inca empire, women and men mined silver and gold as couples; the joint practice of silverwork in the colonial era may be one of the many strategies that Andean miners used to negotiate the technological, economic, and cultural shifts from Incaic to Hispanic empire.[14]

Just as imperial officials dramatically remapped colonial territories and remade their populations, so, too, did things shift in economic terms. In the heart of this exploitative industry, Indigenous, African, and Spanish women and men in Mexico and Peru developed technical skills that allowed them to discover mines, operate their own companies, contract themselves as wage laborers in mines and refineries, and provide goods and services to mine owners and managers.[15]

14. Peter Bakewell, *Silver and Entrepreneurship in Seventeenth-Century Potosí: The Life and Times of Anthony López de Quiroga* (Albuquerque, N.M., 1988), 191. On Flemish miners, see the mining companies and powers of attorney of Adrián Enríquez, Juan de Bruselas, Pedro Panus, Guillermo de Dyste, Andrés de Lovaina, and Dionysio de Holanda, recorded by notary Lázaro del Águila, in Archivos y Bibliotecas Nacionales de Bolivia (hereafter cited as ABNB), Escribanía Pública 3, Potosí, Lázaro del Águila: Jul. 12, 1559, 673v–674; June 21, 1559, 564–565; Sept. 18, 1559, 948–949; Sept. 18, 1559, 941v–943. On Potosí, see Luis Capoche, *Relación general de la villa imperial de Potosí: Un capítulo inedito en la historia del nuevo mundo* (1585), ed. Lewis Hanke, vol. CXXII of Biblioteca de autores españoles desde la formación del lenguaje hasta nuestros días: Relaciones histórico-literarias de la América meridional (Madrid, 1959), 102, 106; and Bartolomé Arzáns de Orsúa y Vela, *Historia de la villa imperial de Potosí* (1737), ed. Hanke and Gunnar Mendoza, 3 vols. (Providence, R.I., 1965); Lolita Gutiérrez Brockington, *Blacks, Indians, and Spaniards in the Eastern Andes: Reclaiming the Forgotten in Colonial Mizque, 1550–1782* (Lincoln, Neb., 2006); Alberto Crespo R., *Esclavos negros en Bolivia* (La Paz, 1977); Carlos Sempat Assadourian, *El tráfico de esclavos en Córdoba de Angola a Potosí, siglos XVI–XVII* (Córdoba, 1966). On silversmiths, such as Domingo Pacocaua, Agustín Carlos Atacuri, and married couples like Ventura Pérez and María Magdalena Pérez Chumacero, see Mario Chacón Torres, *Arte virreinal en Potosí: Fuentes para su historia* (Seville, 1973), 9–12, 24, 143, 150–151. On pairs of Incaic miners, see Pascale Absi, *Los ministros del diablo: El trabajo y sus representaciones en las minas de Potosí* (La Paz, 2005), 294.

15. Dana Velasco Murillo, *Urban Indians in a Silver City: Zacatecas, Mexico, 1546–1810*

In Potosí, by the turn of the seventeenth century, the balance of wage and draft labor tipped among Indigenous communities, as wage earners *(mingados)* outnumbered tribute laborers *(mitayos).* Andean miners accustomed to Incaic imperial systems of draft labor, called *mit'a* in Quechua and adapted to the *mita* imposed by Viceroy Toledo, began leasing their labor to owners of mines and refineries. Whether they worked directly in the silver industry or in ancillary professions created by Potosí's concentration of wealth and mining activities, many *indios mingados* used their wages to hire replacement mitayo workers. Relative to the weekly wages of other hired hands, substitutes earned 4 reales more than indios mitayos; combined with their weekly mita wages, which ranged between 13.75 and 17.5 reales, these skilled miners drew approximately 40 reales a week, not including what they took home in *kajcheo,* or silver mined for personal use. Within the coercive structure of the silver industry, many Andean miners negotiated the terms of their own labor.[16]

In New Spain, the system of allowing miners to prospect for silver on their own time and reserve collections for personal use was called *pepena,* derived from the Nahuatl *ni-tlapepena* ("Escoger lo mejor" [to choose the best]). In both regions, these arrangements generated important sources of income for miners, who often selected high-grade ore that they sold to other Native refiners. Andean refiners who received kajcheo metals treated them with a combination of reduction ovens *(guairachinas),* muffle furnaces *(tocochimbos),* and, as new archaeological research by Pablo Cruz and Florian Téreygeol suggests, reverberatory furnaces. In Mexico, Indigenous miners often sold pepena ore to African metallurgists who operated small-scale refineries on the outskirts of Zacatecas. There, they worked with stone furnaces and hand bellows *(parada de fuelles)* that were well suited to traditional methods of smelting rather than low-grade ores that were more profitably amalgamated with mercury and controlled by Spanish hands. Pepena and kajcheo systems were small in scale

(Stanford, Calif., 2016); Jane E. Mangan, *Trading Roles: Gender, Ethnicity, and the Urban Economy in Colonial Potosí* (Durham, N.C., 2005).

16. Peter Bakewell, *Miners of the Red Mountain: Indian Labor in Potosí, 1545–1650* (Albuquerque, N.M., 1984), 112, 123–125, 181 (mitayos and wages); Nicholas A. Robbins, *Mercury, Mining, and Empire: The Human and Ecological Cost of Silver Mining in the Andes* (Bloomington, Ind., 2011), 33–36 (mita). González Holguín suggests Quechua etymologies from *kacca* (rock or stone: *peña*), borrowed from agricultural tribute systems, called *kakacuni* ("contribuir cosas de comer, todos, para la provision del tambo por paga"); see González Holguín, *Vocabulario de la lengua general de todo el Perú,* s.v. "kacca," "kakacuni." On coercion, see Enrique Tandeter, *Coacción y mercado: La minería de la plata en el Potosí colonial, 1692–1826* (Buenos Aires, 1992).

compared with operations in Zacatecas and Potosí, but they made a large difference to miners and their families, who now added an extra day's work to their earnings and transmitted specialized metallurgical knowledge through networks that were outside of Spanish oversight.[17]

Potosí formed the heart of the Black Legend with "almost unremitted bleakness," a reputation ensconced as what one governor called "un pueblo levantado tumultariamente por la codicia al pie de la riqueza que descurbrió una casualidad" (a town raised in tumult by greed at the foot of wealth discovered by accident). In fact, the silver industry developed because of technical skills, Indigenous knowledges, and imperial organization, as well as chance, luck, and greed. The pursuit of imperial wealth severed Indigenous communities from harvest cycles that nourished their social and spiritual lives. It forcibly separated families and kinship networks on a shockingly large scale in which violence, exploitation, and a disregard for life underwrote the global expansion of the Spanish empire. Potosí was then, and remains, a devastatingly clear example of violent imperial processes that were enacted across the interconnected continents of Asia, Africa, Europe, and the Americas. At the same time, many Andean women and men migrated voluntarily with their families to Potosí in search of economic opportunities, and they were compensated well enough to justify the move. To understand this paradox, we must know the

17. Alonso de Molina, *Vocabulario en lengua castellana y mexicana y mexicana y castellana* (1571), ed. Miguel León-Portilla (Mexico City, 1970), 57v; Alonso Urbano, *Arte breve de la lengua otomí y vocabulario trilingüe: Español-náhuatl-otomí* (1605), ed. René Acuña (Mexico City, 1990), s.v. "Escoger lo mejor"; and Frances Karttunen, *An Analytical Dictionary of Nahuatl* (Norman, Okla., 1992), 190; Julio Sánchez Gómez, "La primera mitad del siglo XVII," in Sánchez Gómez, Guillermo Mira Delli-Zotti, and Rafael Dobado, eds., *La savia del imperio: Tres estudios de economía colonial* (Salamanca, 1997), 143–144, 214; Bakewell, *Miners of the Red Mountain,* 67, 76–77; El Ynca Garcilaso de la Vega, *Primera parte de los Comentarios reales: Que tratan del origen de los Yncas, reyes que fueron del Peru, de su idolatria, leyes, y govierno en paz y en guerra: De sus vidas y conquistas, y de todo lo que fue aquel imperio y su republica, antes que los españoles passaran a el* (Lisbon, 1609), 223v–225v (pepena and kajcheo); Pablo Cruz and Florian Téreygeol, "Los hornos de reverbero andinos: Dinámicas de transferencias e innovaciones de tecnologías metalúrgicas indígenas y europeas," *Estudios atacameños* (forthcoming); Mary Van Buren and Claire R. Cohen, "Cambios tecnológicos en la producción de plata después de la conquista española en Porco, Bolivia," *Boletín del Museo Chileno de Arte Precolombino,* XV (2010), 29–46; Van Buren and Barbara H. Mills, "Huayrachinas and Tocochimbos: Traditional Smelting Technology of the Southern Andes," *Latin American Antiquity,* XVI (2005), 3–25 (refining ovens); P. J. Bakewell, *Silver Mining and Society in Colonial Mexico: Zacatecas, 1546–1700* (Cambridge, 1971), 126, 144 (African miners in Mexico).

history of silver metallurgy in colonial Latin America and the ways in which diverse women and men shaped new methods of amalgamation.[18]

In the ten-year period between 1545 and 1555, two events, one in the Andes and one in Mexico, would dramatically reshape the history of colonial silver. First, in 1545, Diego Huallpa, a Chumbivilca herder from the Jauja valley, "discovered" the Cerro Rico de Potosí (Rich Mountain of Potosí)—or, more accurately, he revealed the presence of silver ores to an Indigenous metalsmith, who conveyed the information to Spaniards. Second, some ten years later, Indigenous miners, colonial agents, and Fugger officials stationed in Pachuca, Mexico (approximately eighty-five kilometers outside of Tenochtitlán), perfected a large-scale method of amalgamation. With the discovery of new sources of silver and the development of new techniques to process every variety of silver ore, the silver industry became the prime mover of increasingly interconnected market and knowledge economies in Spanish America. By the 1560s, the value of ores mined in the Cerro Rico had declined substantially—from one hundred marks per quintal to two marks, according to some estimates. Because refiners spent more on fuel and labor than they reaped in silver from these low-grade ores, silver production dropped. But the new method of amalgamation used mercury as a reagent to extract silver particles, rather than relying on heat alone. When the method was introduced to Potosí from Pachuca in 1572, refiners in the Andes learned, as had metalworkers in Mexico, that they could profitably extract silver with minimal costs from even the most refractory ores. If a quintal yielded even an ounce and a half of silver, refiners could still turn a profit. That American silver played such an important role in the early modern global economy was due, in part, to the continent's abundant mineral deposits. But it was mostly due to new technologies that allowed refiners to profitably process a wider variety of ore than traditional methods permitted, and to Indigenous imperial precedents and European systems that promoted silver production by managing flows of people, goods, and ideas.[19]

Amalgamation was the most important of those new technologies, and it came about in a surprising way. In the 1550s, Bartolomé de Medina left his wife, children, and business in Seville and departed for New Spain. Upon ar-

18. Bakewell, *Miners of the Red Mountain,* 110–128, 142; Manrique de Lara, quoted in Arzáns de Orsúa y Vela, *Historia de la villa imperial de Potosí,* I.cxxxi.

19. Gwendolin Ballantine Cobb, *Potosi and Huancavelica: Economic Bases of Peru, 1545–1640* (Ph.D. diss., University of California, Berkeley, 1947), 124, cited in Jason W. Moore, "The Modern World-System as Environmental History? Ecology and the Rise of Capitalism," *Theory and Society,* XXXII (2003), 307–377, esp. 335; Bakewell, "Mining," in Bethell, ed., *Colonial Spanish America,* 239; Bakewell, *Silver Mining and Society in Colonial Mexico,* 138.

riving in Pachuca around 1553, he began to experiment with a new method of metallurgical processing that he had learned of in conversation with a German man, who told him that it was possible to extract silver cheaply "without smelting, or refining." In Pachuca, Medina built an elaborate refining complex *(hacienda de minas)* around the silver mine of Purísima Grande, changing the course of colonial history. With Medina's method of amalgamation, silver was profitably extracted from ores whose complex combinations of chemical elements, especially sulfur (S) and copper (Cu), had made such refractory metals difficult to process. This mid-sixteenth-century technology allowed for the expansion of the colonial silver industry, and the Spanish empire, for the next hundred-odd years.[20]

Medina's reported speech and fuzzy conflation of metallurgical methods like smelting and refining reveal his background as a merchant, not a miner, and suggest why he might have selected Pachuca as the seat of his new experiments. According to a Spanish-language *relación* of 1580, and its accompanying hybrid pictorial map of Zempoala (about twenty-two kilometers south of Pachuca), the region was home to three main Indigenous communities: Nahuas, who controlled most of the land and extracted tribute payments; Otomís, who formed the bulk of the population; and Chichimecas, who were displaced by Nahuas but still had some uncultivated lands. Map 4 suggests how these ethnolinguistic groups would have arranged themselves geographically in the pre-Columbian period; for context, the map overlays some of the major mineral deposits worked in and around Pachuca during the colonial era. Evidence from neighboring towns suggests that non-Mexica people from towns like Tepeapulco had been drafted into mine labor in Pachuca since the 1540s, within the first ten years of Franciscan missionary planting. These tribute miners were probably drawn from Otomí communities, who represented approximately 65 percent of the population and had been drafted into Mexica tribute systems throughout the pre-Columbian period.[21]

20. Modesto Bargalló, *La amalgamación de los minerales de plata en hispanoamérica colonial* (Mexico City, 1969), 54, citing Medina's *merced* from Jilotepeque, Dec. 29, 1555. Various identities have been suggested for the "German [man]," including Hans Christoph Pronner, a Fugger agent in Spain, Gaspar Loman, a German who lived in Sultepec, about 100 kilometers southwest of Mexico City, and Juan Enchel, one of the German metallurgists who were sent to Sultepec by Seville-based Fugger agents as early as 1536. See Bargalló, *La amalgamación,* 61–63; Bargalló, *La minería y la metalurgía en la América española durante la época colonial: Con un apéndice sobre la industria del hierro en México desde la iniciación de la Independencia hasta el presente* (Mexico City, 1955), 94–95.

21. Karl W. Butzer and Barbara J. Williams, "Addendum: Three Indigenous Maps from New Spain Dated ca. 1580," *Annals of the Association of American Geographers,* LXXXII

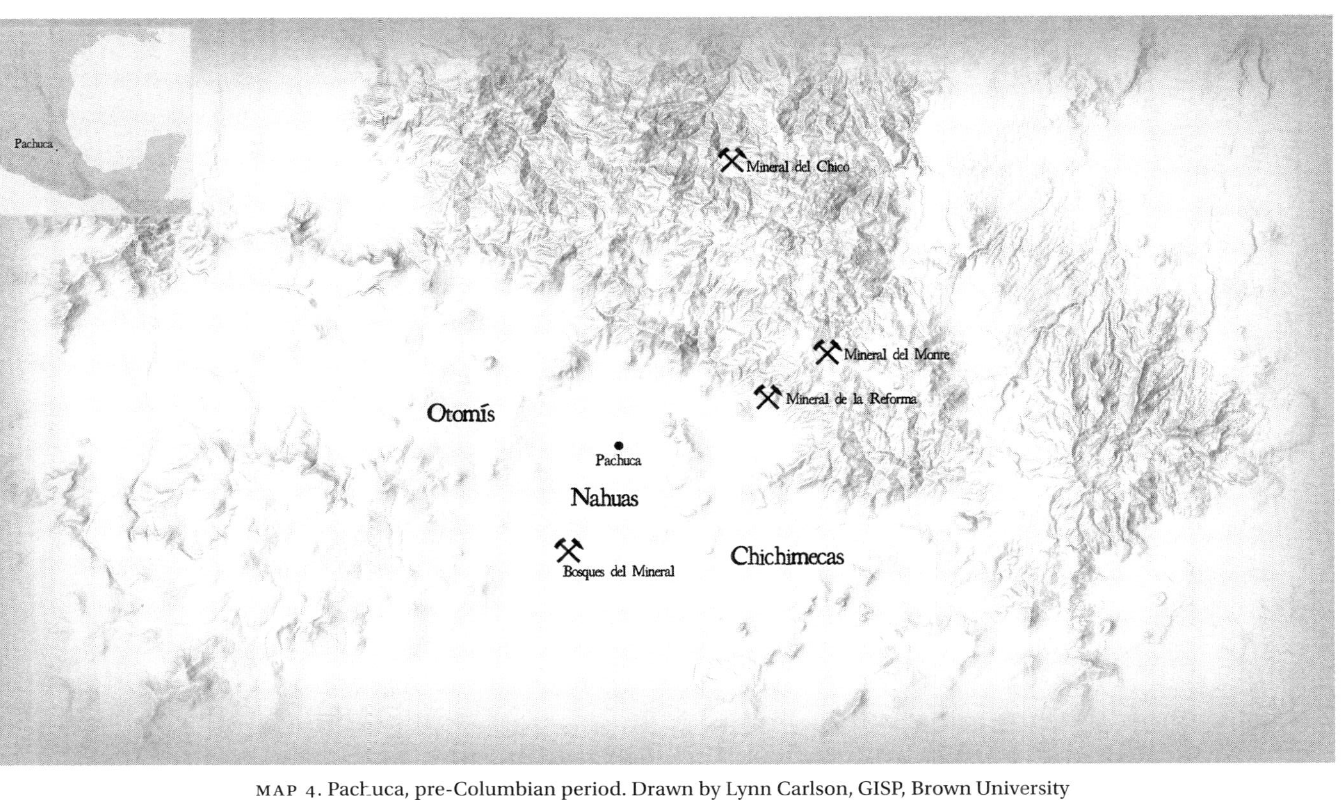

MAP 4. Pachuca, pre-Columbian period. Drawn by Lynn Carlson, GISP, Brown University

By settling on Pachuca, Medina capitalized on imperial Mexica networks of silver miners, refiners, and trade routes. Archaeological data on Postclassic Mesoamerica (1200–1530 CE) shows that between 90 and 98 percent of obsidian traded in Mexica markets originated in Pachuca. Because obsidian was both a utilitarian good and a medium used in ceremonial worship, obsidian trade routes were part of commercial traffic and spiritual pathways. Pachuca's role in the obsidian trade suggests the long range and deep roots of Mexica networks in which stones, jewels, and precious metals figured prominently.[22]

Other rulerships, such as the expansive Tarascan state in west Mexico, specialized in extracting, refining, and producing copper rather than silver. In the seventy years that preceded the arrival of the Spanish in Mexico, Tarascan rulers solidified their control of gold and copper routes; copper goods came primarily from territories in west Mexico, whereas gold objects, most of which were employed in ritual use, came largely from central and south Mexico. Although the Tarascan state had some access to silver, much of what Tarascans delivered to Spaniards in the 1530s was silver-plated copper. In the early sixteenth century, the most reliable silver networks in Mexico were controlled by the Mexicas, whose management of tribute laborers, knowledgeable artisans, raw materials, and finished goods allowed colonists like Medina to operationalize large-scale mines and refineries around new metallurgical processes.[23]

The technological success of colonial amalgamation thus reflects the contributions of several entities: German financial networks that organized Spanish mines; a Spanish merchant in Mexico; and Mexica imperial systems that organized natural resources and specialized knowledges into efficient networks for the production and distribution of metals, minerals, and stones. The conversations that Medina held with the German man before leaving Spain were, not the product of chance, but the result of Habsburg imperial structures that placed prominent German banking families in control of Spanish assets once mined by the Roman empire. Nor was Medina's choice of Pachuca coincidental. It, too, was a site whose production of imperial wealth had been

(1992), 536–542, esp. 540–541; Jesús Ruvalcaba Mercado, "Agricultura colonial temprana y transformación social en Tepeapulco y Tulancingo (1521–1610)," *Historia mexicana,* XXXIII (1984), 424–444, esp. 426, 433.

22. Geoffrey E. Braswell, "Obsidian Exchange Spheres," in Michael E. Smith and Frances F. Berdan, eds., *The Postclassic Mesoamerican World* (Salt Lake City, 2003), 131–158, esp. 157, cited in Michael E. Smith et al., "Sources of Imported Obsidian at Postclassic Sites in the Yautepec Valley, Morelos: A Characterization Study Using XRF and INAA," *Latin American Antiquity,* XVIII (2007), 429–450, esp. 445–446.

23. Helen Perlstein Pollard, "The Political Economy of Prehispanic Tarascan Metallurgy," *American Antiquity,* LII (1987), 741–752, esp. 741–745.

carefully incorporated into Mexica political economy throughout the pre-Columbian era.

As it became more established within Latin America, the colonial amalgamation method continued to knit together diverse body politics and ways of knowing. In the 1560s and 1570s, Iberian miners and metallurgists like Portuguese subject Enrique Garcés (who became a printer upon securing his fortune in silver) traveled from Lima to central Mexico. In turn, Mexican miners like Pedro Fernández de Velasco accompanied them to adapt the technologies to South American conditions and mineralogies. When Fernández de Velasco arrived in Peru from New Spain in 1572 and revealed the method to local officials, Viceroy Toledo was said to have pronounced the union of silver and mercury, analogized to the mountains of Potosí and Huancavelica, "the most important marriage in the world."[24]

In Mexico, Medina's "patio" method, so named because refiners mixed metals on sun-drenched patios to reduce heating costs, was a ten-step process. It began with mineral crushing (1), after which ground metals were arranged (2) on patios into piles that held two to four thousand pounds of material. Then, using sunlight as the only catalyst, refiners treated the piles in several stages of incorporation, mixing reagents like salt and iron sulfide or copper sulfate *(magistral)* into the silver mounds *(tortas),* at which time the mixture would harden (3–4). After carefully adding mercury to the mass (5), refiners then stomped the mixture with their feet to allow for greater incorporation (6). (In the Andes, such workers were called *repasaris,* a neologism that combines the Spanish verb *repasar,* "to mix," and *-is,* the Set A pronoun for first-person plural, "we" inclusive, in the Quechua of Potosí.) Next, they washed the solution (7) and removed (8) partially formed amalgams of silver and mercury *(pella).* At this point, pella amalgams were approximately 20 percent silver and 80 percent mercury. To separate the incorporated metals (9), refiners fired them in pineapple-shaped molds *(piñas).* Finally, those hundred-pound piñas of silver were melted into ingots or bars and sent to the mint and tax house for processing (10). Refiners in the Andes added a round of roasting and suspended mixing vats over open flames to account for the region's different silver compositions and colder temperatures, relative to central Mexico.[25]

24. Bargalló, *La minería y la metalurgía,* 79; Fernando de Montesinos, *Anales del Perú* (ca. 1639), ed. Víctor M. Maurtua, 2 vols. (Madrid, 1906), II, 51.

25. Bargalló, *La minería y la metalurgía,* 127–129; Bargalló, *La amalgamación,* 105–106, 346; Bakewell, *Silver Mining and Society in Colonial Mexico,* 140–142; Bakewell, *Miners of the Red Mountain,* 20–21; "Memorial de don Gonçalo Gomez de Cervantes del modo de vivir que tienen los indos, y del beneficio de las minas de la plata, y de la cochinella," Am2006,

In both regions, women joined men in silver refining, particularly in sorting and washing metals. In the Andes, sorters were called *palliris,* a Hispanized form of the Quechua and Aimara terms *pallani* (to gather something by hand) and *pallatha* (to collect little by little, as if choosing the best), and a close cousin of the Incaic imperial expression for a noble woman, *palla* ("Muger noble adamada galana"). In Mexico, the connection between women and mineral washing was cultural, not linguistic. Physician Juan de Cárdenas, born in Spain and educated at La Universidad de México, foregrounded the roles of African women and Indigenous men in separating fine silver particles from partially formed amalgams, writing, "Y esto es lo q̄ se desliza al tiempo del lavar, y esto es lo q̄ hallan las negras, ò indios en el rio quando van a buscar polvillo, y pella" (And this is what slides off during mineral washing, and this is what the black women or Indians find in the river when they search for mineral dust *[polvillo]* and partial amalgams *[pella]*). For his part, Cárdenas's contemporary, Alonso de la Mota y Escobar, bishop of Tlaxcala, insisted that only Indigenous miners understood proper washing techniques and that their knowledge surpassed that of Africans and Spaniards. As writers debated the technical merits of mining women and men, their explanations translated specialized vocabularies into everyday speech, at once clarifying what Cárdenas calls "terminos o vocablos de repassar, encorporar, jūtar, y otros semejantes" (terms or words like "mix," "incorporate," "join," and other similar expressions), and signaling the industry's gender-, ethnic-, and racially inclusive nature.[26]

Such patterns continued in the eighteenth century. Mexican projector Juan Ordoñez Montalvo argued that refiners could increase production

---

Drg.210, 173v–176v, British Museum, London; Juan de Cárdenas, *Problemas y secretos maravillosos de las Indias*... (1591) (Valladolid, 2003), 86v. There are many varieties of Quechua, so I interpret the *-is* marker within Quechua *potosino,* following Celestino Choque's study of regional pluralizers used in present-day Bolivia. The first-person plural marker *-nchik* is heard in the northern region (La Paz and north of Potosí) as "purinchik," whereas in Potosí it is usually "purinchis." Speakers in Chuquisaca and Cochabamba use similar forms: "purinchij" and "purinchiq." See Choque, *La EIB entre los quechuas: Testimonio de parte (1990–1994)* (La Paz, 2005), 41. On local Quechua pluralizers and written morphologies, see Pedro Plaza Martínez, "Normalización de la escritura del Quechua en Bolivia," *Pueblos indígenas y educación,* no. 54 (Quito, 2004), 31–50, esp. 43–44.

26. González Holguín, *Vocabulario de la lengua general de todo el Perú,* s.v. "palla" and "pallani"; Ludovico Bertonio, *Vocabulario de la lengua aymara* (1612) (Cochabamba, 1984), s.v. "pallatha"; Cárdenas, *Problemas y secretos maravillosos de las Indias,* 89, 90, 91v; Alonso de la Mota y Escobar, *Descripción geográfica de los reinos de Nueva Galicia, Nueva Vizcaya y Nuevo León* (1602), ed. Joaquín Ramírez Cabañas, 2d ed. (Mexico City, 1940), 150–151.

from 550,000 to 719,000 *marcos,* an astonishing increase of 24 percent, if they treated richly concentrated silver particles *(polvillos)* that remained in mixing bins (called *xicaras,* after Mesoamerican drinking gourds) following the first round of processing. It was hard, tedious work to remove and wash these powdery fragments, and Ordoñez Montalvo insisted that only women *(planilleras)* had patience for such a task. When twentieth-century writers explained the method, *planilleras* became *planilleros* (gender-inclusive / masculine), erasing their presence.[27]

The methods of amalgamation described in colonial sources were both new and not new (as I discuss in Chapter 10, below). Refiners in Europe had long used mercury to extract precious metals from partially processed slag heaps, a time-intensive process whose costs were justified only on the highest grades of gold and silver. But most of the world's silver is mixed with other substances, such as lead (Pb), tin (Sn), iron (Fe), copper (Cu), and sulfur (S), presenting great technical difficulties and offering little incentive to treat composites like *negrillos* (silver sulfides), one of the most common varieties of silver found in the deepest levels of Andean mines. In 1596, Viceroy don Luis de Velasco y Castillo, son of the eighth viceroy of New Spain, arrived in Peru and concluded that many mines were unworked because the costs exceeded the benefits. This changed in the early 1570s. By reducing processing costs, the patio method transformed the possibilities of American silver and allowed refiners in Mexico and the Andes to treat a wider variety of silver on a commercially viable, industrial scale.[28]

Such a notable economic shift required remapping distribution networks within mining communities (Map 5). In the Andes, ancestral Inca pathways

27. Juan Ordóñez Montalvo, *Arte o nuevo modo de beneficiar los metales de oro y plata y de plata con ley de oro, por azogue . . .* (Mexico City, 1758), 24. Edward Halse defined a *planillero* as "Mex. operator on the planilla (1), always paid by weight or measure of concentrates produced; usually old men (ancianos), who use a horn spoon [*see u.* cuchara (1)] and smoke cigarettes while they work." See C. B. Dahlgren, *Minas históricas de la República mexicana* (Mexico City, 1887), 241, being "a translation of the American work, *Historic Mines of Mexico*" (Halse, vii), cited in Halse, *A Dictionary of Spanish, Spanish-American, Portuguese, and Portuguese-American Mining, Metallurgical, and Allied Terms,* 3d ed. (London, 1926), s.v. "planillero." Halse's *Dictionary* was popular enough to support multiple print runs in London (1908, 1914) and Philadelphia (1926), and its author was equally transatlantic. Halse held memberships in two prestigious scientific societies, the Sociedad Científica Antonio Alzate, based in Mexico, and the Institute of Mining and Metallurgy, based in London. I thank Philip Gura for pointing me to this interesting volume.

28. ABNB, Cabildo de Potosí Libros de Acuerdos 8, 1596, fols. 3v–12, 5; Bakewell, *Silver Mining and Society in Colonial Mexico,* 138.

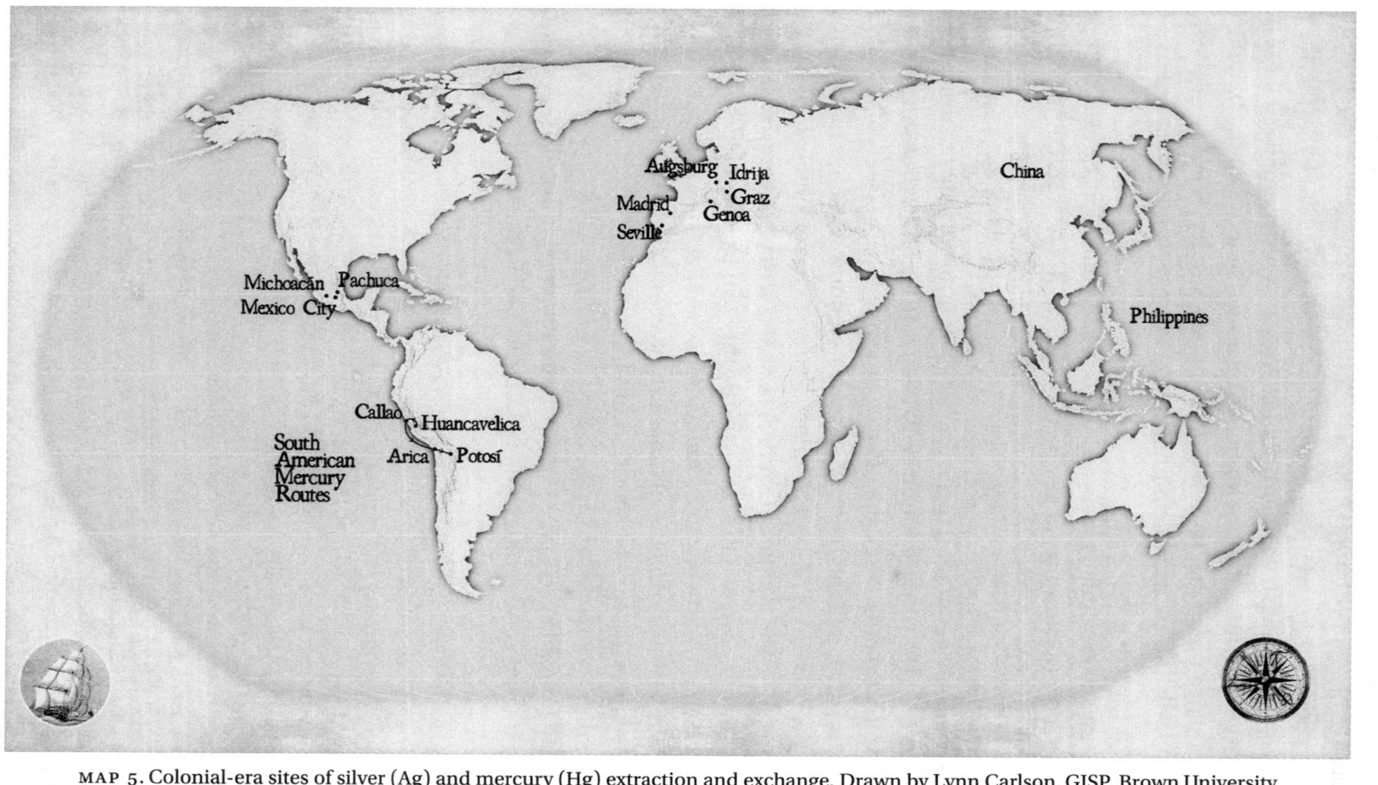

MAP 5. Colonial-era sites of silver (Ag) and mercury (Hg) extraction and exchange. Drawn by Lynn Carlson, GISP, Brown University

built for spiritual and economic tribute were repurposed into transportation networks through which miners brought mercury from Huancavelica to the port of Callao, outside of Lima, some 240 kilometers from the mine. After transporting the highly unstable reagent from an altitude of 3,675 meters above sea level down to the coast, shippers packaged it for transport by sea to Arica, some 1,000 kilometers from Callao, and then overland to Potosí, a city that sits at 4,100 meters above sea level. Prices were marked up accordingly along the way, as mercury that sold for forty *pesos ensayados* per quintal in Huancavelica commanded more than sixty pesos in Arica and up to eighty-five pesos in Potosí, according to official prices set by the crown.[29]

In New Spain, where there was no local source of mercury, the connections were both transoceanic and terrestrial, showing how new amalgamation technologies incorporated Mexico, the Philippines, and rival sides of the House of Austria into Spain's global empire. The challenging topography of the central Mexican highlands led to a constellation of innovative transportation networks to supply the silver-rich regions of the interior with Spanish mercury. Under the auspices of the Habsburg empire and the powerful Fugger family—Augsburg-based bankers and merchants who held the *asiento (appalt)* to extract mercury from Spain's largest mine—the reagent was shipped from Almadén, two hundred kilometers southwest of Madrid, to the Mexican port of Veracruz. Between 1571 and 1574, Fugger agents exported 3,000 quintales of mercury to New Spain. Production increased steadily through the early years of the seventeenth century, peaking at 24,531 quintales between 1616 and 1619.[30]

Transatlantic shipments of people and goods were key to New Spain's production of silver and to colonial ideas about Spain's place in world history. Mercury from Almadén had been extracted since the first century CE, when Spain was a Roman imperial mining colony. For writers like José de Acosta, Spain's experience as a site of extractive colonial wealth prefigured its relationship to Indigenous empires in the New World. After an extensive discussion of Pliny's *Natural History*—including a section on the Roman prohibition against mercury refining in Spain, for fear that the material would be lost to contraband—

29. "Memoria y Relación de las minas de açogue del Piru," Apr. 20, 1607, fols. 1–16, Biblioteca Nacional, Madrid, MS 3041, 2v–3; "Açogue de Guancavelica y sus tragines, asta potossi," 1612–1615, fols. 127–150, in "Memorias y gobierno de las minas de azogue del Perú, su descubrimiento y beneficio en diversos tiempos," ibid. See also Clara López Beltrán, *Estructura económica de una sociedad colonial: Charcas en el siglo XVII* (La Paz, 1988); López Beltrán, *La ruta de la plata: De Potosí al Pacífico; Caminos, comercio, y caravanas en los siglos XVI y XVII* (La Paz, 2016).

30. Bakewell, *Silver Mining and Society in Colonial Mexico*, 18–21, 151–156.

Acosta explained why the example of antiquity was relevant to his readers. As he saw it, Incaic royalty and Indian laborers who worked in Huancavelica failed to distinguish between the use values of mercury (*azogue,* Hg) and mercury sulfide (*cinabrio,* HgS). They carefully extracted sulfides and vermillion (lead oxide, PbO), what Quechua speakers called "llimpi," because it served them well in painting their bodies, faces, and idols, just as Pliny described pagan practices "of the Romans and Ethiopians," but Andean miners left mercury intact. For Acosta, the past was precedent. Inca and Roman imperial models offered practices to emulate and avoid in natural resource management, labor systems, and the collection and dissemination of natural knowledge.[31]

Colonial writers did not just look to imperial histories of the West; the East Asian demand for American silver forced Iberian agents to contend with Asian

31. Pliny the Elder, *Natural History: A Selection,* trans. John F. Healy (London, 1991), 304; Joseph de Acosta, *Historia natural y moral de las Indias, en que se tratan las cosas notables del cielo, y elementos, metales, plantas, y animales dellas: Y los ritos, y ceremonias, leyes, y govierno, y guerras de los Indios* (Seville, 1590), 223. El Inca Garcilaso de la Vega (1539–1616) disagreed with Acosta's version, arguing that the absence of mercury processing reflected Incaic imperial governance, not a lack of knowledge: after witnessing the debilitating effects of mercury, Inca kings prohibited their subjects from mining it. In deference to the wisdom of Incaic law, Indigenous people promptly forgot what mercury was or what they called it. What the Inca kings did allow, according to Garcilaso, was *ichma* (cinnabar powder), though it was reserved for women of royal linage; he states that Father Acosta conflated noble women's use of the scarlet-crimson powder ("carmesí") with purple-hued *llimpi.* Garcilaso's response is part of his effort to distinguish Inca and non-Inca peoples; cinnabar cosmetics included a pore-cleansing facial bath, but face painting was a non-Incaic practice (*Comentarios reales,* 224). Colonial sources suggest more overlap between Andean cultures than Garcilaso does. See González Holguín, s.v. *llimppicuni,* "pintarse con bermellon la cara y embijarse" (paint one's face with vermillion and one's body with annatto), and *llimppicuna,* "Todas maneras de colores del lacre con que pintan vasos de madera" (all the colors one paints with) *(Vocabulario de la lengua general de todo el Peru);* and see Bertonio, who separates Aimara and Christian definitions of *llimphitha* with the sign of the cross: "Iluminar, o matiçar con varias colores † Y tambien adornar los vasos, derretiendo estaño enlos huecos que hazen para ello" (Illuminate, or tinge with various colors † And also to adorn vessels, melting tin in the holes that they make for that) *(Vocabulario de la lengua aymara,* 204). Jorge de Fonseca concluded that military and cosmetic applications were fundamentally human activities, and even the most barbarous communities would share them: "qe no ay gente tan barbara qe con varios modos no aya acudido a estas Dos cosas" ("Relacion sumaria de las minas de azogue q̄ ay en estas provincias del Peru . . . escrita por Jorge de Fonseca Minero al exmo señor marques de Guadalcacar Virrey de estos reynos," Lima, Nov. 22, 1622, "Memorias y gobierno de las minas de azogue del Perú, su descubrimiento y beneficio en diversos tiempos," MS 3041, 268–280v, esp. 268, Biblioteca Nacional).

cultures, technologies, and political economies, as well. In 1606, Viceroy Juan de Mendoza y Luna, marqués de Montesclaros, reported hearing that Japanese metallurgists who amalgamated silver with Chinese mercury found "the mercury in China is of a very good kind for metals." Gold refiners in the Philippines also confirmed the merits of mercury from China. Colonial officials thus encouraged subjects to find providers in East Asia and to resolve the logistical and economic difficulties of multiple exchange values, units of measure, and shipping an unstable reagent in lead containers soldered with brass across the Pacific Ocean.[32]

Throughout the seventeenth century, officials in Mexico and Madrid weighed the costs and benefits of transpacific and transatlantic commercial partnerships. Even though he was two years late on his promise to deliver mercury from Manila to Mexico and Peru, merchant Pedro de Baeza appeared before the viceregal court in 1608 to ask for additional credit. Viceroy Velasco approved the extension, arguing that "'what's his name' *(fulano)* de Baeza" was the only merchant in the colony who understood Asian markets well enough to meet Mexican demands.[33]

Things were no better by midcentury, when the Austrian Habsburgs and Spanish crown fought on opposite sides of the Thirty Years' War (1618–1648). To subsidize its military, Austria sold mercury to Spain. In turn, Spanish agents sent the reagent to refiners in the New World, who sold silver in Asia to underwrite Spain's military operations against Austria. This trade was mediated through the same kind of providers' contracts that Fugger factors negotiated at Almadén and Baeza secured in Manila. This time, it was for Friedrich Ober-

32. "Carta del virrey Juan de Mendoza y Luna, marqués de Montesclaros," Mexico City, Oct. 28, 1605, AGI, Mexico, 26, no. 69, 17 fols., 4. Japanese refiners paid 25 silver taels for each quintal of Chinese mercury, but a quintal in the East was 130 pounds; in Mexico, it weighed 100 pounds. After converting taels into Spanish currency, a 130-pound quintal would cost 275 *reales de plata,* plus 47 reales for shipping (40 reales by sea and 7 by land). At these rates, the crown could deliver mercury at 45 pesos, 5 reales per 100-pound quintal, fewer than half of the 96 pesos, 4 *tomines* that it was charging refiners at the time. Mendoza did not want refiners to become dependent on an unreliable supply or become aware of radically different prices circulating in the same markets, so he advised against the trade. See "Carta del virrey marqués de Montesclaros," Mexico City, Oct. 28, 1605, AGI, Mexico, 26, no. 69, 17 fols, 4v–5.

33. "Carta del virrey Luis de Velasco y Castilla," June 23, 1608, AGI, Mexico, 27.52, fols. 54v–55v. On October 2, 1607, Pedro de Baeza presented his proposal to the conde de Lemos, president of the Consejo de Indias, who published the account as Jesús María, *Este memorial, es traslado de otro que di a Su Magestad en mano propia quando le hable y le di cuenta deste negocio y asiento del azoque, en dos de Octubre de 1607 . . .* ([Madrid?], [1607?]).

holtz (Overholz) of Graz. When he went bankrupt in 1629, his trading partners, Genovese bankers Bartolomeo, Stefano, and Antonio Balbi, then stationed in Madrid, inherited the contract and managed it until 1646. By using familial networks and interimperial connections, the Balbi brothers negotiated fixed-term commercial arrangements to ship mercury from Idrija to Venice and, from there, to Spain and Mexico. Because of the competing lines of the House of Austria, an incredibly disruptive war spreading across central Europe, and demands of refiners in Peru who also imported mercury from Idrija, refiners in Mexico remained consistently undersupplied and officials continued to court relationships with potential suppliers in Asia and Europe.[34]

In the final quarter of the century, officials in Madrid and Mexico engaged in another series of debates over central European and East Asian mercury, this time enlisting religious missionaries in Guangdong (Kuangtung) and Fujian (Fokien) to investigate the quality of Chinese mercury. According to Luis Cerdeño Monzón, lawyer for the Consejo de Indias and advocate for the poor, mercury could be purchased cheaply in Guangdong, shipped to Manila through Macao and on to Mexico as part of the Acapulco galleon, all for less than what the crown paid in Germany. When Viceroy Gaspar de la Cerda y Mendoza reported that Chinese quicksilver had been favorably assayed in Mexico, the Consejo de Indias ruled on June 23, 1694, that Spain should discontinue trade with Germany and investigate once more its connections in Asian markets.[35]

At the beginning of the century-long search for mercury, Portugal and Spain were one crown, and Spain claimed the Dutch republics in Europe and Jamaica

34. The dates refer to the years when mercury was delivered, not the time frame specified in the contracts. See Eberhard Crailsheim and Eva-Maria Wiedenbauer, "Central Europe and the Atlantic World: The Mines of Idria and the American Demand for Mercury (1556–1646)," in Renate Pieper and Peer Schmidt, eds., *Latin America and the Atlantic World: Essays in Honor of Horst Pietschmann* (Cologne, 2005), 297–317, esp. 308–314.

35. "Petición sobre enviar azogue de China a Nueva España," ca. Mar. 28, 1689, AGI, Filipinas, 28.153, fols. 1424–1432; "Minuta de consulta del Consejo de Indias dando parecer contrario a que se continué el tratado de azogue con Alemania," June 23, 1694, in "Expediente sobre remisión de azogue a Nueva España," 1692–1694, ibid. See also "Copia de lo que Juan Luis de Wafemberg, superintendente de las minas de azogues, dio por escrito al conde de Mansfelt," n.d., "Memoria de los papeles que se envían a Luis Cerdeño y Monzón sobre remisión de azogues de Filipinas a Nueva España," Madrid, Mar. 12, 1693, and "Carta del conde de Galve, virrey de Nueva España, dando cuenta del ensaye del azogue de la China remitido por el gobernador de Filipinas, la bondad de su ley y el fomento que está haciendo para traer más qy quedar entendiendo en el ensaye de azogues de Alemania," Mexico City, Jan. 19, 1692, ibid. On Cerdeño y Mondón, see Madrid, July 25, 1675, AGI, Indiferente General, 441, libro 27, fols. 308v–309v.

in the New World. Spanish imperial geographies looked very different by the second half of the century, but colonial refiners faced the same logistical problems. Questions about public and private contracts that could link Mexico, Manila, and Germany punctuated the seventeenth century. Between 1606 and 1694, official debates about mercury supplies were entertained at multiple councils and articulated in a variety of spoken and written forms: *cartas* (letters), *expedientes* (proceedings), *relaciones* (relations), *minutas* (minutes), *memorias* (accounts). The political and economic networks that were forged in nearly one hundred years' worth of debate suggest how colonial wealth influenced relationships throughout the ends of the Spanish empire.

The extent to which officials in New Spain invested in mercury suppliers and distribution networks in Europe and Asia underscores an important part of the history of American silver. This was not just a story about finding lodes in Latin America and making money in China with enslaved and coerced laborers from African and Amerindian communities. It was about new metallurgical methods that made it practical to refine silver and position it in global markets, and about building economic and information networks that were credible enough to sustain global trade.

If it is impossible to separate colonial silver from global economic history, it is equally impossible to understand this history without knowing how metallurgical technologies developed in the early Americas. At every step in the mining, refining, and minting of colonial silver, Indigenous knowledges and empires played larger roles than the historiography has typically acknowledged, from Bartolomé de Medina's selection of Pachuca for his assays into amalgamation to the "discovery" of Potosí.

Along these lines, the revelation of the Cerro Rico to Spanish officials looks quite different when viewed from the perspectives of its key Andean agents. According to padre Acosta, in 1542, Diego Huallpa chased a llama that had gone astray from his pack, and he found himself stumbling over the Cerro Rico de Potosí. As he grasped for a plant to brace his fall, he noticed that its extirpated roots were caked in clumps of silver. Because Huallpa did not recognize its color, he presented it to an expert refiner, Guanca, in the mining community of Porco, a multiethnic community that had been ruled by the Siwaruyu-Arakapi diarchy and produced silver for the Incas. The skilled metallurgist, now working as an independent wage laborer *(yanacona)* in the *encomienda* of Gonzalo Pizarro, recognized the value of the high-grade ore. In 1545, Guanca revealed it to his boss, Spanish miner Juan de Villareal.[36]

36. Acosta, *Historia natural y moral de las Indias*, 208–209. On the Quilloca *ayllu* (kinship group), see Thomas A. Abercrombie, *Pathways and Memory of Power: Ethnography*

The story of the "discovery" of Potosí to Spanish miners turned as much upon divisions within Indigenous communities as it did upon new structures of colonial power. Huallpa was Chumbivilca, a non-Inca community that had been incorporated into the southwestern end of Incaic empire, the Kuntisuyu, by Inca Pachacuti in his final campaign against them. At the time of Huallpa's "discovery," Chumbivilcas would have been joined to a broad network of Inca tribute communities for more than seventy years, a substantial amount of time that nevertheless remained within living memory. The material conditions of high-grade silver—namely, the position of ores relative to the surface and their suitability for smelting—meant that traditional sites of metallurgical processing, such as Porco, remained vibrant centers of technical expertise and economic power after the Spanish conquest, and that skilled metallurgists like Guanca could take advantage of non-Inca laborers like Huallpa.[37]

The development of amalgamation technologies, in making it profitable to treat low-grade ores that were found at greater profundities, expanded the scale and scope of the silver industry and remapped relationships between Andean herders like Hualpa and metallurgists like Guanca. These different modes of silver processing also shifted the sites of dominance from Incaic to Hispanic empires, providing both opportunities and disadvantages for women and men from diverse Indigenous communities. Some of their stories made their way into books like Acosta's, whereas most miners from the sixteenth- and seventeenth-century Andes remain anonymous. Although Álvaro Alonso Barba does not name any of his Indigenous collaborators, reminding us of the always-unequal nature of colonial collaboration, his technical treatise sheds light on aspects of Andean metallurgy ignored by histories like Acosta's.

Documenting Indigenous Knowledges: Barba's Arte de los Metales

Barba's book, in its transatlantic circulations, bore testimony to the incorporation of Indigenous knowledges in the Andes and to their omission from

---

and History among an Andean People (Madison, Wis., 1998), 238. For an analysis of *yanaconaje* in Incaic and Hispanic empires, see Frédérique Langue and Carmen Salazar-Soler, eds., *Diccionario de términos mineros para la América española (siglos XVI–XIX)* (Paris, 1993), 633–634; Rodolfo Cerrón-Palomino, *Voces del Ande: Ensayos sobre onomástica andina* (Lima, 2008), 75–88. Cerrón-Palomino suggests that *yanacona* is derived from the composite **yana(yaku)-kuna,* or *yana* (person who serves) + *ya* (continually) + *ku* (dative; for me), against earlier scholarship that suggested a plurarlization *(kuna)* of the color term "black" *(yana).*

37. John H. Rowe, "Inka Culture at the Time of the Spanish Conquest," in Julian H. Steward, ed., *Handbook of South American Indians,* 7 vols. (Washington, D.C., 1946), II, 183–330, esp. 206–207.

works translated into other European vernaculars. In the century that followed the first print run in Madrid, multiple editions of the *Arte de los metales* were printed in English, French, German, and Spanish. Each edition translated localized particulars of colonial Latin American mining technologies into their own cultural contexts, for their own readership communities. These works, ranging from complete translations of books 1 and 2 to selections from books 1 through 5, included three editions in Spanish (Madrid, 1640, 1680, 1729), six in German (Hamburg, 1676, 1739; Leipzig, 1678, Frankfurt, 1726; Vienna, 1749, 1767), four in French (Paris, 1730, 1733, 1751; the Hague, 1752), and four in English (London, 1670, 1674, 1738, 1740). There were also four editions known to early modern readers but not found today: one in German (n.p., 1696), one in Latin (Nuremberg, 1687), and two in Spanish (Córdoba, 1674; Madrid, 1680).[38]

In addition to differences in the language of publication, each book entered literary markets through different kinds of publishers, all of whom had different relationships with larger issues of empire, governance, and commerce. The Spanish and Stuart crowns published Barba's work and its translation for readers in Spain and England, whereas private, family-run print shops disseminated materials in France and Germany. Such printers included Guillaume Saugrain, who published the first Francophone translation of Barba in the same year that his press commemorated French imperial expansion into Africa with Jean Baptiste Labat's *Voyage du Chevalier des Marchais en Guinée, Isles Voisines, et a Cayénne* (1730). German readers learned of Barba through Gottfried Schultzens Kosten, a printer who specialized in translations of herbals and household remedies, such as Hannah Woolley's cosmetic delights for ladies, Nicholas Culpeper's botanical compendium, and a book of curiosities, including chocolate and tobacco.[39]

The range of editions published in Spanish, English, German, and French reveal when and how colonial scientific concepts were transmitted and lost in translation. Translators handled natural philosophical terms with ease, be-

38. Barnadas, *Álvaro Alonso Barba,* 254–257. Although no copies of the *Tratado del arte metálico* (Córdoba, 1674) remain extant, it was reviewed in the *Journal des sçavants* on February 11, 1675. The German volume is cited in John Ferguson, *Bibliotheca Chemica: A Catalogue of the Alchemical, Chemical, and Pharmaceutical Books in the Collection of the Late James Young of Kelly and Durris,* I (Glasgow, 1906), 70.

39. Hannah Woolley, *Frauen-Zimmers Zeit-Vertreib . . .* (Hamburg, 1674); Nicolaum Culpepern, *Culpepers Testament Oder Letzter Wille* (Hamburg, 1675); ["John Chamberlayne" and Philippe Sylvestre Dufour], *Schatzkammer Rarer und neuer Curiositäten / In den allerwunderbahresten Würckungen der Natur und Kunst / Darinnen allerhand seltzame und ungemeine Geheimnüsse / bewehrte Artzneyen / Wissenschafften und Kunst-Stücke zu finden . . .* (Hamburg, 1689).

cause Aristotelian texts were taught, glossed, paraphrased, commented on, and disputed throughout Renaissance Europe. The common curricula of universities ensured that most students had some exposure to the scientific literatures of antiquity—or, rather, classical natural philosophy as it had been recuperated in the medieval and early modern eras. But the same translators stumbled over hybrid technical terms that blended classical traditions and Amerindian vocabularies, and they adopted a range of strategies to handle complex and unfamiliar phrases. Sometimes, translators elected to leave curious new words in the source language; at other times, they tried to find near equivalents in their target languages or coined new expressions altogether. In the double translation of colonial scientific literatures—first, from Indigenous knowledges into Spanish and then from Spanish into European vernaculars—mistranslation was all but inevitable.[40]

Although the translated language of colonial science can be imprecise, this seemingly fuzzy language is important. Colonial scientific terms are linguistic artifacts that preserve the traces of skilled miners and refiners who "wr[ote] *without* letters," as Walter D. Mignolo puts it, and left their mark on the silver industry through Hispanicized forms of Native American languages. These nouns and verbs resist easy translation into other languages because they represent linguistic and conceptual blends of local scientific knowledges.[41]

Tracing mistranslated terms can help to resolve a methodological problem that has long plagued histories of mining in the colonial period. We know that Indigenous and mixed-race miners formed the majority of the workforce; because they did not leave many written records of their work, their ideas have been difficult to recover. To read around and beyond archival silences, historians, linguistics, and archaeologists have developed multidisciplinary modes of inquiry, including archaeometallurgy, ethnohistory, and oral history. My methods of combining comparative literary analysis, translation studies, and historical linguistics join those efforts to reveal where and how Andean vocabularies and knowledges shaped the science of colonial silver.[42]

40. "Natural Philosophy after the Translations: Its Role and Place in the Late Middle Ages," in Edward Grant, *A History of Natural Philosophy: From the Ancient World to the Nineteenth Century* (New York, 2007), 143–169.

41. Bargalló, *La amalgamación*, 221; Walter D. Mignolo, *The Darker Side of the Renaissance: Literacy, Territoriality, Colonization*, 2d ed. (Ann Arbor, Mich., 2003), 319. See also Elizabeth Hill Boone and Mignolo, eds., *Writing without Words: Alternative Literacies in Mesoamerica and the Andes* (Durham, N.C., 1994).

42. Julio Sánchez Gómez, *De minería, metalúrgica y comercio de metales: La minería no férrica en el Reino de Castilla, 1450–1610*, 3 vols. (Salamanca, 1989), I, 321. On methods,

For example, instead of using a traditional Castilian term for "sediment," such as *hez,* derived from the Latin *fez,* or *asientos* (sediment), related to *pos* (sediment), derived from the late Latin *pausāre,* Barba uses a Hispanized form of Quechua to instruct his readers to add mercury in two rounds. With this critical technique, the reagent absorbs more of the silver and forms less sediment along the bottom of the mixing bin, or, as Barba puts it, "mientras mas fuere menos conchos se causaràn" (the more you do this, fewer sediments will be produced). By approximating the Quechua word, "qqunchu," into its closest Spanish sound, "conchos," Barba records a moment in which Indigenous refiners left a linguistic footprint upon amalgamation technologies as they were practiced in the Andes. Instead of using one of their many words for "sediment," Spanish-speaking miners instead employed a term derived from Quechua. This suggests that the idea to add mercury in two rounds originated with Quechua-speaking miners. Had it been their idea, Spaniards would have named and claimed it in their own language.[43]

European translators did not know what to make of a word like "conchos," and they revealed great methodological flexibility in their attempts to translate it. Edward Montagu, first earl of Sandwich, interpreted the unfamiliar term "conchos" as something he recognized, "conchas," such that Anglophone readers learned that the more mercury they added, "the fewer inequalities like Oyster shells will be produced." Johann Lange rendered the line in exactly the same way, translating Montagu's "Oyster shells" into "Auster-Schalen." The earliest French edition, completed by Charles Hautin de Villars in 1730, skipped the passage. In 1750, Nicolas Lenglet du Fresnoy expressed the idea without translating "conchos": "se mêle avec le nouveau Mercure qu'on y met, et celui-ci aide à l'autre à se former en corps" (it is mixed with the new mercury placed there, and it helps the other to form as a body). Multilingual, syncretic forms of colonial knowledge were thus translated out of European scientific literatures in different ways; mineral sediments became seashells in England

---

see Pablo José Cruz and Jean-Joinville Vacher, eds., *Mina y metalurgia en los Andes del sur: Desde la época prehispánica hasta el siglo XVII* (La Paz, 2008), esp. Florian Téreygeol and Celia Castro, "La metalurgia prehispánica de la plata en Potosí" (11–28); C. Cohen, T. Rehren, and M[ary] van Buren, "La *huayrachina* por dentro y por fuera: Un estudio arqueometalúrgico de la tecnología de fundación de plomo en Porco-Potosí, Bolivia" (29–56); Pablo Cruz and Pascale Absi, "Cerros ardientes y *huayras* calladas: Potosí antes y durante el contacto" (91–120); and Tristan Platt and Pablo Quisbert, "Tras las huellas del silencio: Potosí, los Inkas y el virrey Toledo" (231–278).

43. Barba, *Arte de los metales,* 53v, 54v; González Holguín, *Vocabulario de la lengua general de todo el Peru,* s.v. "qqunchu."

and Germany, and evidence of Andean languages was omitted or rephrased in France.[44]

Montagu's misreading occurred precisely at the time when early modern English was shifting away from the grammatical gender that it inherited through language contact with German and French during the medieval era. In turn, his book was reprinted throughout the eighteenth century. In 1674, two years after Montagu lost his life commanding a fleet in the Third Anglo-Dutch War, a new edition of his work was issued in London, consolidating his two-book translation into a single volume. Nearly fifty years later, London bookseller Olive Payne, perhaps most famous for selling Daniel Defoe's library—which included the work of Bartolomé de Las Casas, Sir Walter Ralegh, and Alexandre Exquemelin—bound Montagu's translations to two other works on mining: Gabriel Plattes's *Discovery of Subterraneall Treasure* (London, 1639), which Payne renamed "A Discovery of All Sorts of Mines from Gold to Coal," and Thomas Houghton's *Compleat Miner* (London, 1688). In 1740, printer James Hodges edited and reissued Payne's *Collection of Scarce and Valuable Treatises upon Metals, Mines and Minerals* (1738), using the same title. Aside from minor punctuation changes, Montagu's translation appeared verbatim in all four editions, including the Englishing of "conchos" as "Oyster Shells."[45]

44. [Edward Montagu], trans., *The Second Book of the Art of Mettals, Wherein Is Taught the Common Way of Refining Silver by Quicksilver: With Some New Rules Added for the Better Performance of the Same*... (London, 1670), 72; [Johann Lange], trans., *Albaro Alonso Barba, Eines Spanischen Briesers und hocherfahrnen Naturkündigers Berg-Büchlein: Darinnen Von der Metallen und Mineralien Generalia und Ursprung* . . . (Hamburg, 1676), 184; Charles Hautin de Villars, *Traité de l'art métalique: Extrait des oeuvres d'Alvare-Alfonse Barba, célébre artiste dans les mines du Potozi* . . . (Paris, 1730); [Lenglet du Fresnoy], trans., *Métallurgie; ou, L'art de tirer et de purifier les métaux* . . . , I (Paris, 1751), 191. I translate technical terms from the German with T. E. R. Singer, *German-English Dictionary of Metallurgy: With Related Material on Ores, Mining and Minerals, Chrystallography, Welding, Metalworking, Tools, Metal Products, and Metal Chemistry* (New York, 1945). I thank Claudia Engelmann and Patrick Erben for their help in transcribing and translating German-language texts. In this section, I cite from the two-volume edition of Montagu's work, published as Albaro Alonso Barba, *The Art of Metals, in Which Is Declared the Manner of Their Generation and the Concomitants of Them: In Two Books* . . . , trans. Edward [Montagu] (London, 1674), indicated with Roman numerals (I and II). The 1676 edition of Lange's work shares the same pagination as the 1726 edition, digitized by the Sächsische Landesbibliotek–Staats-und Universitätsbibliothek Dresden, Technische Universität Dresden, for interested readers.

45. Anne Curzan, *Gender Shifts in the History of English* (New York, 2003); Olive Payne, trans., *A Collection of Scarce and Valuable Treatises upon Metals, Mines, and Minerals, in Four Parts* (London, 1738); J[ames] Hodges, *A Collection of Scarce and Valuable Treatises*

Lange's translation was also reprinted in several editions, almost immediately and throughout the eighteenth century. Two years after its publication, printer Johannes Größe included it in an anthology of other mineralogical writers, published in Frankfurt and Leipzig in 1678. Nearly one hundred years later, the first New World edition of Barba's book was published in Ephrata, Pennsylvania, in 1763. Although the community of German Pietists published several works on religion and natural science, few were written by Catholic priests in Latin America. Lange's translation did not stay in German-speaking Pennsylvania, though. Having circulated in multiple linguistic, scientific, and political contexts in the colonial and early national Americas, it became, fittingly, part of George Washington's library.[46]

From the late seventeenth through the mid-eighteenth century, the Indigenous roots of colonial amalgamation were translated out of literary history in western Europe and German-speaking British North America. The time, place, and languages of publication are important, because this is the moment in which scholars have located changing attitudes about science, modernity, and the knowledge-making power of language in the West. As Mignolo argues, early moderns considered Spanish, Italian, and Portuguese as the preeminent languages of Renaissance arts and sciences, while French, English, and German became "the languages of modernity" whose "knowledge-generating" grammars were better suited for Enlightenment-era definitions of "reason

---

upon Metals, Mines, and Minerals ... (London, 1740); Tim Severin, *In Search of Robinson Crusoe* (New York, 2002), 181–183.

46. Albaro Alonso Barba, *Gründlicher Unterricht Von den Metallen, Darinnen beschrieben wird, wie sie werden in der Erden generirt; und was man insgemein dabey findet,* trans. G. R. (Ephrata, Pa., 1763); Lawrence Washington, Bushrod Corbin Washington, and Thomas Blackburn Washington, *The Final Sale of the Relics of General Washington* ..., comp. Stan V. Henkels ([Philadelphia, 1891?]), 133. A note underneath the auction item declares, "The sale of BARBA's was prohibited in Spain, under the penalty of the Inquisition," an idea that traces to eighteenth-century reprints. Payne and Hodges write, "I am informed by a Gentleman of undoubted Credit, that the Sale of *Barba's* Book is prohibited in *Spain,* under the Penalty of the Inquisition, and is so scarce in *England,* that I am informed there is but one Copy of the *Spanish* Edition, which is in Sir *Hans Sloan's* Library" ("Advertisement concerning the Present Edition," in Payne, *Collection of Scarce and Valuable Treatises,* n.p.; "Advertisement concerning the Present Edition," in Hodges, *Collection of Scarce and Valuable Treatises,* A4–A4v). Works published in Ephrata around the same time as J. Georg Zeisiger's translation include reissues of Nicodemus's *Die Beschreibung Des Evangeliums Nicodemi* ... (Ephrata, Pa., 1748); *Von der Historia Des Apostolischen Kampffs* ... (Amsterdam, 1764); and ample Franklinia, including as *Der Americanische Calender Auf das 1772ste Jahr Christi* ... (Ephrata, Pa., 1771), as well as Franklin's autobiography, *Der Weg zum Glück, Oder: Das Leben von Dr. Benj. Franklin* ... (Ephrata, Pa., 1796).

in philosophical ideas and scientific arguments." These languages did not change at phonetic, semantic, or morphosyntactic levels; what changed was how they were perceived to produce and convey knowledge. If seventeenth- and eighteenth-century Atlantic translations obscured the epistemological and material contributions of Indigenous miners, transmuting "qqunchu" and "conchos" into "shells" and "Schalen," then a new attention to the language of colonial science—as it was organized into treatises, instruction manuals, and relaciones in sixteenth- and seventeenth-century Latin America—allows for their recovery and reappreciation. Such work is the subject of the next two chapters.[47]

47. Mignolo, *Darker Side of the Renaissance,* viii–ix.

9 : COLOR AND *CASTA* IN THE ANDEAN SILVER INDUSTRY

The ability to amalgamate silver with mercury, using the methods developed by *sevillano* merchant Bartolomé de Medina in the 1550s, allowed refiners to profitably extract ores from a wider variety of silver metals, ranging from native or unmixed metals to the most complex combinations of ferrous, cupric, and sulfuric elements. In the shift from smelting to amalgamation, mineral classification, sorting, and naming became more difficult, intricate, and important. In response, miners in the Andes developed extensive color vocabularies that they recorded in new ways, incorporating terms derived from Spanish (with Latin and Arabic roots), Quechua, and Aimara. Analysis of these color terms and the forms in which they were written and published shows how the silver industry drew from and gave greater authority to existing discourses of race, color, and *casta.*

Andean definitions of mineral sorting incorporated technical arts and lettered life. The act of sorting itself was called *pallar,* a Hispanized form of the Quechua term *pallarcarini* ("Coxer muchas cosas juntas" [To gather many things together])—and, as we saw in the previous chapter, the Aimara term *pallatha* ("Recoger poco a poco como escogiendo lo mejor" [To collect little by little, as if choosing the best]). According to the mining lexicon written by Potosí mine overseer García de Llanos in 1609, *Diccionario y maneras de hablar,* there were three main forms of mineral sorting, each associated with specific people, places, and material practices. The first form of sorting, "en la haz de la tierra" (on the surface of the earth), was typically practiced on ore found outside of the mine, called "quitamama." This term is composed of the Quechua roots *qquita*—what Diego González Holguín translates as "cimarron huydor" (runaway fleerer)—and *mama,* or "Veta, o caxa de todo metal como curimama veta de oro etc." (vein, or wall of a vein of all metal, such as curimama, a vein of ore, etc.). Spanish speakers translated *quitamama* into racialized terms, calling it "metal cimarrón" (runaway metal) or "metal cimarrón o huido" (runaway, or escaped, metal). As we will see throughout this chapter, the racializing of Andean concepts and classifications was common in the mining industry. Within this general form of surface-level sorting, Garcia de Llanos included three other subgroups. The first subgroup consisted of selling sorted ore, called *pallaco,* for refining with other metals. This was often performed by Aimara-speaking *palladores* (sorters) from the Uruquilla *ayllu.* The second subgroup sold pallaco to Indigenous refiners. The final subgroup involved sorting metals in slag piles, called *repallar,* formed by the Spanish prefix *re-* (repeat) and the Hispanized verb *pallar.*[1]

Next among the major categories of sorting was cleaning metals on patios and in front of homes—primarily the work of young boys and some old men ("muchachos y algunos indios viejos"), called *palliris*—and taking count of miners and their hauls. Lastly, in amalgamation refineries of Potosí, "pallar" referred to the separation and washing of partially formed amalgams *(pella).* As in Mexico, this work was usually performed by women: "se ocupan más mujeres que indios" (more women are employed in it than Indian men). To call an Indigenous woman "mujer" rather than "india" was not unprecedented; it is yet another example of how our knowledge of Indigenous women's contributions to the silver industry have been shaped by colonial categories and expressions.[2]

As García de Llanos's definition suggests, "pallar" signified technical practice above- and belowground, commercial activity in silver markets, and the writing and recording of such work. To convey the intersection of lettered writing systems and technical literacies in Andean mining communities, the overseer referred his readers to the entry for "quilcar." González Holguín translated the Hispanized form of the Quechua verb *quellccani* as "Escrivir debuxar pintar" (write, draw, paint). Jesuit missionary Ludovico Bertonio in 1612 similarly defined the Aimara verb *quellcatha* as "Asseytar, Pintar or Rascuñar o dibuxar al modo de indios, que pintan los cãtaros y otros vasos" (to oil, paint, or scratch, or to draw in the mode of the Indians, who paint pitchers and other vessels). These definitions suggest how the need to count miners and yields required specific forms of colonial scientific-administrative writing. "Pallar" in Potosí was not just an act of mineral sorting or selling—it was an act of writing. At the end of their shifts, miners emptied their hauls onto the floor of a hut ("bohío," imported into Andean Spanish from Taíno languages of the Caribbean) and sorted their metals, as García de Llanos glossed in parentheses ("[que es pallar]"). Spaniards who observed the process borrowed Andean

1. García de Llanos, *Diccionario y maneras de hablar que se usan en las minas y sus labores en los ingenios y beneficios de los metales* (1609), ed. Rose Mary Buchler, Gunnar Mendoza, and J. V. Murra (La Paz, 1983), 97–98; Diego González Holguín, *Vocabulario de la lengua general de todo el Perú llamada lengua Qquichua, o del Inca* (1608), 3d ed. (Lima, 1989), s.v. "pallarcarini," "qquita," and "mama"; P. Ludovico Bertonio, *Vocabulario de la lengua aymara* (1612) (Cochabamba, 1984), s.v. "pallar."

2. Llanos, *Diccionario y maneras,* ed. Bulcher, Mendoza, and Murra, s.v. "pallar." On women miners, see Allison Margaret Bigelow, "Women, Men, and the Legal Languages of Mining in the Colonial Andes," *Ethnohistory,* LXIII (2016), 351–380.

definitions of sorting and applied them to new forms of record keeping made necessary by the lucrative silver industry. A new expression was thus coined in Potosí: "y así se dice pallar los indios al tomarles cuenta y asentarles lo que han trabajado, lo cual asimismo se dice quilcar" (and so they say that *pallar* the Indians means to take account of what they have worked, which is the same as to say *quilcar*). The Hispanized verb was so commonly used among Spanish speakers that "jamás se dice en nuestro vulgar" (it is never said in our own tongue).[3]

Once readers turned from the "p" section ("pallar") to the "q" pages ("quilcar") of García de Llanos's dictionary, they found overlaps and divergences in Hispanized forms of sorting, writing, and painting. There were two primary ways to "escribir o quilcar los indios" (write or write-paint the Indians): one, when miners presented themselves on Monday morning before their masters *(dueños)* or overseers *(mayordomos),* who recorded their names, ayllus (lineages), and *pueblos* (towns / people); the other, when miners finished their shifts at the end of each day to "pallar o dar cuenta de su trabajo" (*pallar,* or give account of, their work). On these days, the owners or overseers would note in their books *(libros de memoria)* the days and hours that a miner had worked, signaled with dashes and half-dashes for a full or half-day of work. For this reason, García de Llanos writes, "Se dice en el Cerro haber quilcado al haber tomado cuenta de esta suerte a los indios y de aquí es lo mismo quilcar o haber quilcado que haber pallado, y así se usa de lo uno y de lo otro sin diferencia, aunque por diferentes razones" (It is said in the Cerro that to have *quilcado* is the same as to have taken account in this way of the Indians, and thus it is the same to say *quilcar* or having *quilcado* as to say having *pallado.* And so they are used indifferently, although for different reasons). As technologies like amalgamation enabled refiners to profit from a wider variety of metallic mixtures, sorting became an especially important skill. And, as a response to the new emphasis on the classification of silver ores, miners and refiners coined new literary expressions to organize labor forms, incorporating Andean ideas of nonalphabetic script into Spanish letters.[4]

At the same time, miners developed diverse expressions and technologies to classify mixed metals and describe their suitability for amalgamation. Silver mixed with base metals like copper (Cu) and iron (Fe) responded better to

3. Llanos, *Diccionario y maneras,* ed. Bulcher, Mendoza, and Murra, 97–98, 109; González Holguín, *Vocabulario de la lengua general de todo el Perú,* s.v. "quellcani, qquellccacuni"; P. Ludovico Bertonio, *Vocabulario de la lengua aymara* (1612) (Cochabamba, 1984), s.v. "quellcatha 3 quc."

4. Llanos, *Diccionario y maneras,* ed. Bulcher, Mendoza, and Murra, 109–110.

heat-based processing, whereas other kinds were more profitably amalgamated. Refiners had to know the difference if they wanted to earn a living. Silver mineralogies are now known by chemical signatures, like those of high-grade metals found in the Andes, such as acanthite (Ag_2S), andorite ($PbAgSb_3S_6$), chlorargyrite ($AgCl$), matildite ($AgBiS_2$), miargyrite ($AgSbS_2$), pyrargyrite (Ag_3SbS_3), and tetrahedrite ($(Ag,Cu,Fe,Zn)_{12}Sb_4S_{13}$). But before the advent of modern chemistry and spectrometer technologies, miners sorted and named metals using data they gathered from their senses. In the Andes, these names often reflected color, smell, taste, and visual cues as they were perceived by speakers of Quechua, Aimara, and Spanish.[5]

Touch and smell provided some clues into silver classes, but padre Álvaro Alonso Barba argued in his foundational book of mining, *Arte de los metales* (1640), that sight was the most important mode of category-making because it mapped onto color. Barba believed that sight was the most reliable sense ("el mas cierto desengaño") and that color terms were familiar to nonspecialists, so the easiest way to acquaint new miners with different silver metals was to explain them through color. At the same time, Barba insisted that readers defer to experience; nature resisted generalization, and it was impossible to explain specialized knowledge through print alone. For example, gold normally grew in soil that was red ("colorado") or dark-chestnut ("amarillo retinto, como el ladrillo muy cozido"), but it was also found among white caliche rocks. Barba concluded that, in provinces like Oruro and Chayanta, there were no hard-and-fast rules about the relationship between color perception and metallic content.[6]

Writers in Spain also used color to classify metallic matter, although there are important differences between peninsular and colonial discourse. Bernardo Pérez de Vargas, writing from Madrid in 1569, used a three-part, color-based system of metallic classification, much as Barba argued that miners in the Andes grouped metals into three categories: "que llaman Pacos, Mulatos, y Negrillos" (which they call *pacos, mulatos,* and *negrillos*). In Spain, the "colors" were "shiny" ("un resplandor que paresce incorporado con el color a manera de luz"); "white" ("lo blanco"), which included silver (Ag), tin (Sn), lead (Pb), and iron (Fe); and "reddish-blonde" ("Rubio"), which included gold

5. Mark B. Abbott and Alexander P. Wolfe, "Intensive Pre-Incan Metallurgy Recorded by Lake Sediments from the Bolivian Andes," *Science,* CCCI (2003), 1893–1895, esp. 1893.

6. Alvaro Alonso Barba, *Arte de los metales en que se enseña el verdadero beneficio de los de oro, y plata por açogue* ... (Madrid, 1640), 23v. On first-person observations and scientific writing, see Beth Tobin, *Colonizing Nature: The Tropics in British Arts and Letters, 1760–1820* (Philadelphia, 2005), esp. 158–167.

(Au) and copper (Cu), the latter of which he deemed "tirante a prieto requemado" (turning towards burnt black). Pérez de Vargas and Barba use some of the same color terms, including "pardos cenizosos o negros" (ashen, gray or black), "color Pardillo" (a little gray), and "prieto" (black), but designations like "mulato," "negrillo" and "castas" belong exclusively to the colonies. In grouping pacos, mulatos, and negrillos of different hues, shines, and etymologies into metallic "castas," Barba's treatise sheds light on the relationship between silver, the *sistema de castas,* and New World knowledges.[7]

Research on the sistema de castas has expanded considerably across diverse academic disciplines within the past twenty years. Anthropologists, art historians, historians, and literary scholars like Magali Carrera, Laura Lewis, Ilona Katzew, Jane Landers, Ruth Hill, María Elena Martínez, Matthew Restall, Bianca Premo, James H. Sweet, Larissa Brewer-García, Daniel Nemser, and Miguel Valerio have investigated the development of racial classification and racist ideologies in painted and printed texts from colonial Latin America.[8]

7. Barba, *Arte de los metales,* 39v; Bernardo Perez de Vargas, *De re metalica: En el qual se tratan muchos y diversos secretos del conocimiento de toda suerte de minerales, de como se deven buscar ensayar y beneficiar, con otros secretos e industrias notables . . .* (Madrid, 1569), 23.

8. Magali M. Carrera, *Imagining Identity in New Spain: Race, Lineage, and the Colonial Body in Portraiture and Casta Paintings* (Austin, Tex., 2003); Laura A. Lewis, *Hall of Mirrors: Power, Witchcraft, and Caste in Colonial Mexico* (Durham, N.C., 2003); Ilona Katzew, *Casta Painting: Images of Race in Eighteenth-Century Mexico* (New Haven, Conn., 2004); Katzew, *Contested Visions in the Spanish Colonial World* (Los Angeles, 2011); Jane Landers, "Africans and Native Americans on the Spanish Florida Frontier," in Matthew Restall, ed., *Beyond Black and Red: African-Native Relations in Colonial Latin America* (Albuquerque, N.M., 2005), 53–80; Landers and Barry M. Robinson, eds., *Slaves, Subjects, and Subversives: Blacks in Colonial Latin America* (Albuquerque, N.M., 2006); Ruth Hill, "Between Black and White: A Critical Race Theory Approach to Caste Poetry in the Spanish New World," *Comparative Literature,* LIX (2007), 269–293; María Elena Martínez, *Genealogical Fictions: Limpieza de Sangre, Religion, and Gender in Colonial Mexico* (Stanford, Calif., 2008); Restall, *The Black Middle: Africans, Mayas, and Spaniards in Colonial Yucatan* (Stanford, Calif., 2009); Bianca Premo, "Familiar: Thinking beyond Lineage and across Race in Spanish Atlantic Family History," *William and Mary Quarterly,* 3d ed., LXX (2013), 295–316; James H. Sweet, *Domingos Álvares, African Healing, and the Intellectual History of the Atlantic World* (Chapel Hill, N.C., 2011); Larissa Brewer-García, "Imagined Transformations: Color, Beauty, and Black Christian Conversion in Seventeenth-Century Spanish America," in Pamela A. Patton, ed., *Envisioning Others: Race, Color, and the Visual in Iberia and Latin America* (Leiden, 2015), 111–141; Raquel Albarrán, "Colonial Assemblages: Objects, Territories, and Racialized Subjects in Pre-Independence Latin America (1492–1810)" (Ph.D. diss., University of Pennsylvania, 2016); Daniel Nemser, *Infrastructures of Race: Concentration and Biopolitics in Colonial Mexico* (Austin, Tex., 2017); Miguel Alejandro Valerio,

Collectively, this work shows that, in sixteenth- and seventeenth-century Latin America, the sistema de castas organized people into socially constructed racial and ethnic hierarchies, including the most common categories of "Spanish," "black," and "Indian," as well as mixed-race categories like *castizo, morisco, mestizo, mulato,* and *zambo.* Despite colonial and imperial attention to difference, there was never "a coherent ideology of race" in the early Americas because classifications were "changeable," "blurred," "personal," and "relativist." According to Laura A. Lewis, "casta" represented an "ambiguous and flexible set of qualities," whereas "race" involved "taxonomies developed to exclude from power individuals western science construed as essentially different"; thus, the sistema de castas worked legally and socially as "something of a capacity, elaborated through the genealogical, moral, and operational aspects of a person's place in relation to other persons," with "distinct but interlocking kinds of power" that individuals negotiated in different forms and places over time. As much as imperial and colonial systems pretended to color-based order, individual experiences, family histories, religious affiliations, language communities, and class hierarchies competed to inform colonial racial and casta classifications. Whereas Ilona Katzew suggests that *casta* was "a metaphor used to categorize people," Matthew Restall argues, "We might see the entire casta 'system' as . . . a metaphor, one that featured a highly plastic terminology of socioracial categories." This chapter builds from other scholarly treatments of race and casta by examining the discursive development of those categories within the Andean silver industry, one of many colonial scientific domains. By analyzing the linguistic registers of racial classifications in multilingual spaces like the Andes and studying how such lexicons were applied in vernacular scientific writing and practice, we obtain a new perspective on the history of racial thinking in the early Americas.[9]

During the sixteenth and seventeenth centuries, scientific writers in Spain and the Americas classified human, animal, plant, and metallic bodies using the same terms. Miners of Indigenous and Spanish ancestry believed that metals grew like plants underneath the surface of the earth. Whether plant, metal, or human, all were considered animate elements in a world whose genesis and daily workings were explained by micro- and macrocosmic

---

"The Queen of Sheba's Manifold Body: Creole Black Women Performing Sexuality, Cultural Identity, and Power in Seventeenth-Century Mexico City," *Afro-Hispanic Review,* XXXV (2016), 79–98.

9. Restall, *Black Middle,* 84, 92, 95–96, 100, 108; Lewis, *Hall of Mirrors,* 4–5; R. Douglas Cope, *The Limits of Racial Domination: Plebeian Society in Colonial Mexico City, 1660–1720* (Madison, Wis., 1994), 7, 21–26; Katzew, *Casta Painting,* 202.

analogy. Some of the same factors in casta classification influenced the making of metallic categories, including color, labor, and place, although they did so in different ways.[10]

Tracing the etymologies of terms like *metal cimarrón* sheds light on the relationship of color and casta in the colonial Andean silver industry. *Cimarrón* was derived from the Latin *cyma* (concavity) and the Greek *κῦμα* (swollen; pregnant woman). In the New World, the word's gendered roots were applied to humans, animals, and plants who were found out of place. Specifically, Spanish speakers repurposed the feminized etymologies of antiquity into the peaks and valleys of mountains that dotted Caribbean islands, equating the full bellies of pregnant women with the mountain geographies where Indigenous and African women and men escaped from colonial rule. The earliest references are traced to a "grande novedad" (great novelty) from San Juan de la Maguana, a site of Indigenous resistance to Spanish rule on La Española. There, nature writer and gold refiner Gonzálo Fernández de Oviedo y Valdés described how, in 1543, a Spanish platoon sent in search of "negros Alçados q̄ se han Rebelado del serviçio delos xpaños" (escaped Africans who have rebelled against the service of the Spaniards) stumbled upon "un Indio çimarrō (o bravo) q̄ Andaua En Cueros e conçiertas varcas tostadas a pelear / o matar Algunos ~~(~~puercos çimarrones (o saluajes đlos quales Ay innumerables Enesta ysla)" (a runaway [or brave] Indian wearing hides and with certain burnt sticks to fight with or kill some ~~(~~[crossed out] runaway pigs [also called wild, of which there are many in this island]). "Tā varia leçion e tan Apretado Caso" (Such a diverse lesson and such a charged case) was omitted from Oviedo's comprehensive natural history, *Historia general delas Indias* (1535), but included in manuscript revisions that he made in Santo Domingo and Spain between 1539 and 1548.[11]

The story went like this. The Spanish party wasted no time in killing the pigs, for it had been some days since they had eaten meat. Soon, the platoon understood its error, "sin saber su popriedad / o Exerçiçio delos đhos puercos e

10. Barba, *Arte de los metales*, 39v; Carmen Salazar-Soler, "Álvaro Alonso Barba: Teorías de la antigüedad, alquimia y creencias prehispánicas en las ciencias de la tierra en el nuevo mundo," in Berta Ares Queija and Serge Gruzinski, eds., *Entre dos mundos: Fronteras culturales y agentes mediadores* (Seville, 1997), 269–296; Allison Margaret Bigelow, "La dote natural: Género y el lenguaje de la vida cotidiana en la minería andina," *Anuario de estudios bolivianos*, XXII (2016), 145–168.

11. Gregory R. Crane, ed., *Perseus Digital Library*, http://www.perseus.tufts.edu/hopper/morph; Real Academia Española, Banco de datos, *Corpus diacrónico del español* (CORDE), http://www.rae.es; Fernández de Oviedo y Valdés, "Natural y general hystoria de las Indias," ca. 1539–1548," MSS, HM177, 67v–68v, Huntington Library, San Marino, Calif.

puerca" (without knowing the ownership or exercise of the aforesaid pigs, male and female). As the Indigenous man explained in Spanish—a language he had learned well enough to know that he wanted to escape from Iberian rule—he had gone in the company of the pigs, "mansos (Ael) e Con Aq̄lla Compañia hazia su vida e Comia e dormia Entreellos" (obedient [to him] and with that company he made his life and ate and slept among them). For twelve years, the man had cared for the pigs, and they, in turn, had cared for him. Each pig had a name and a role within the group. The daring pig ("muy gran ventor") blazed trails, the reticent pig ("mas Rezio e mas pessado") hunted for meat, generally a "puerco çimarrō" (runaway pig), and the female pig provided comfort to both ("consorte e Coadjutor de los dos"). When the party could not find meat, or when certain fruits were out of season, such as "hobos" (jobos, from the *Spondius mombin* tree mentioned in Chapter 3), the man "sabia hallar çiertas Rayzes Con q̄daua de Comer A aq̄lla su Compañía e A el no le faltava" (knew how to find certain roots with which he fed that company and he did not want for anything).[12]

Taken with the news of a man who forsook human society to live among the company of pigs, Oviedo concluded the chapter with a sonnet about the loss of virtue. After quoting Francesco Petrarca's Italian-language original, Oviedo prosified the stanza in Spanish and explained its meaning. The faculty of reason distinguished human and animal, but in this case, "El Indio siendo Animal Raçional e humano ombre, se Convertia En puerco / o hazia su vida bestial dela forma q̄s dho" (the Indian being a rational animal and human man, was converted into a pig / or he made his bestial life as has been said above). Historian Marcy Norton reads this passage as part of a tradition of "Amerindian ontologies," in which human-animal relationships express forms of agency and subjectivity that were unfamiliar to Europeans. Within this context of the human and the nonhuman, it is no coincidence that Oviedo goes on to explain what, exactly, constitutes a cimarrón: "y el indio Apartandose đla exçelençia dela Razō y sin tener Cuēta ni Respeto ni temor Asu dios / huyendo delos ombres se Consētava de beuir Conbestias y ser bestial" (and the Indian separating himself from the excellence of reason and without account nor respect nor fear of his god / fleeing from men he consented to live with beasts and to be bestial).[13]

12. Oviedo, "Natural y general hystoria de las Indias," 67v–68.

13. Ibid., 67v–68v; Marcy Norton, "The Chicken or the *Iegue:* Human-Animal Relationships and the Columbian Exchange," *American Historical Review,* CXX (2015), 28–60. See also José Juan Arrom, "Cimarrón: Apuntes sobre sus primeras documentaciones y su probable origen," *Revista española de antropología americana,* XIII (1983), 47–57.

A half-century later, the term *cimarrón* had made its way from La Española to the Andes as a scientific and social descriptor. The term *metal cimarrón* was so frequently used in Potosí that García de Llanos defines it multiple times in his dictionary—once under the general category of metals and once as a synonym for *quitamama* ("runaway metal"). Whereas his work generally shows how Spanish speakers borrowed Andean classifications, including, as I discuss below, what Spanish-speaking miners came to call *metales mulatos,* other books show how Andean writers used the term. For Felipe Guaman Poma de Ayala, Indigenous cimarrones indexed cultural decline from Inca times. Remarking on Spanish imperial practices of surveying Native communities and assessing their tribute obligations, Guaman Poma argued that the census should not include any "yndio ladron ni cimarron, guagamundo ni que tenga yn[dia] delos p[adres] ni de espanol" (Indian thief or runaway, vagabond nor any who has an Indian woman who belongs to a priest or Spaniard). In his view, a cimarrón had no biological, spiritual, or economic community. Although they came from a range of racial and ethnic groups, including "harrieros, mulatos y negros, *yanaconas* del *tanbo y* meson" (harriers, mulatos, and blacks, [and] *yanaconas* from the inns and lodging houses [located along the *Qhapaq Ñan*]), cimarrones delighted in corrupting young women, especially by taking them to mines and plazas to meet men who labored underground. As Indian girls mixed with miners and overseers, they left their towns and became "bad women" ("putas y malas"), as Guaman Poma explained in prose and pictures (Figure 15); this new practice represented the worst combination of Incaic and Catholic empires. Guaman Poma's hybrid alphabetic-visual text suggests how terms like *cimarrón* circulated in different regions of colonial Latin America, and how diverse writers reinterpreted these racial and ethnic classifications to suit their own arguments and convictions.[14]

Like García de Llano's dictionary and Guaman Poma's lettered-pictographic work, Álvaro Alonso Barba's *Arte de los metales* incorporates Andean and Spanish ways of knowing into his technical writing. Specialized Andean mining knowledges are transmuted into a racialized colonial scientific vocabulary, such as the one that Barba uses to classify stones and metals within different "suertes" (sorts), "géneros" (genres / genera), and "castas" (castes). To understand the relation of color and caste and the extent to which color classifica-

14. Llanos, *Diccionario y maneras,* ed. Bulcher, Mendoza, and Murra, 89, 90, 110. Felipe Guaman Poma declared, "Que los dhos ynos destos rreynos ā uzado lo q̄ no uzavan los cristianos ni en tienpo de los yngas no hazia tal insenansa," in Poma, "El primer nueva corónica y buen gobierno," MS, [1615], Royal Library of Denmark, GKS 2232, 4° 866–868, http://www.kb.dk/permalink/2006/poma/880/en/text/?open=id2977584.

FIGURE 15. "Ansi defiende del español a su hija y su pe y su madre los pobres ynos," in Felipe Guaman Poma de Ayala, "El primer nueva corónica y buen gobierno . . . ," MS, [1615]. Gl. kgl. S. 2232, 4°. Courtesy of Det Kongelige Bibliotek

tions of silver metals influenced ideas about race and hierarchy in the human kingdom, we need to study Barba's metallic categories and their translations, attending to the moments when they do or do not align with larger racial taxonomies and color classifications.

Barba describes castas, géneros, and suertes of metals and stones of various hues. Some were racialized, such as red-, white-, and black-hued materials; others, including green- and orange-toned samples, were not. Samples of conchite shells that he found between Potosí and the province of Los Lípez are "un genero de piedras cristalinas, puras, y transparentes" (a genre / *genera* of pure, transparent crystal stones) and "Desta casta" (of this caste). The ancients once called them conchites because they resembled seashells, but "oy no tiene lugar este modo de pensar, sirviendo de desengaño la maravillosa veta, o suerte de piedra parda aherrumbrada, y en partes amarilla, que esta en el camino que desta Villa va al valle de Oronesta" (today that mode of thought has no place, having been undeceived by the marvelous vein, or kind of gray *[parda]* iron-colored stone, and yellow in parts, that is on the way from this villa to the Valley of Oronesta [Oroncota]). Elsewhere, in the province of Omasuyo, Barba inspects a heavy, dense, dark, shiny ore with high concentrations of iron. He reports, "Dan color de finissima sangre sus piedras, se se refriegan unas con otras, como la hematites, de cuya casta son sin duda, y abundantissimas de hierro, de que me desengañè con muchas experiencias" (Its stones give off a most fine blood color, if you use some to cool the others, like hematite, of whose caste they certainly are, and most abundant in iron, of which I freed myself from illusion with many experiences). In other words, both clear, white stones and crimson-colored rocks could be called *castas.*[15]

As he groups these "pure, transparent, crystal stones," found adjacent to yellow-gray specimens, and "blood-red rocks" into "castas," Barba's taxonomy of red-hued metals reveals a gap between the color properties of metallic matter and their metallic categories. In book 2, Barba groups blood-red *rosicler* and dull-red *cochizo* as negrillos. The first, a shiny, high-grade ore that became a perfect red when pulverized ("dà color de finissima sangre su polvo desmenuçado"), was always classified as negrillo. But the second, a silver-bearing ore mixed with copper, iron, zinc, and sulfur, now known as tetrahe-

15. Barba, *Arte de los metales,* 14, 31. We now call this iron oxide (Fe_2O_3); see Georg Petersen G., *Mining and Metallurgy in Ancient Perú,* trans. William E. Brooks (Boulder, Colo., 2010), 7. Barba speculated that it might have played a role in pre-Columbian metallurgy: "Quiza seguian los Indios algunos ramos de metal precioso que entre ellas iban de que hasta agora no tenemos noticia" (31). For suggesting the toponymic correction of Oroncota, I thank Kris Lane and Clara López Beltrán.

drite ($[Ag,Cu,Fe,Zn]_{12}Sb_4S_{13}$), was less shiny, less red, and lower grade. It was "casi desta casta" (almost of this caste) because it was not as easy to crush, contained more lead, and "no dà tan facil, y perfeto color de sangre como el" (does not as easily give such a perfect color of blood as the other metal). In other words, blood-red ores were negrillos, but naturally darker lead-silver mixtures were not. Barba's uneasy classification of red-hued metals and their values within the black-named category points to a gap between the name of the category and the properties of metallic matter within it. (For a correlation of metallic names across Spanish colonial sources and their European translations, see Appendix 2, below.)[16]

Throughout the *Arte de los metales,* Barba's classifications of mixed metals suggest that the language of racial classification (negrillo, mulato) does not align with the color properties or content of ores, and that the same words hold different values in social and metallic categories. He uses *casta* to classify black, red, and white minerals, metals, and stones, and he treats it as a synonym for *suerte* (sort) and *género,* which was translated in the seventeenth century as "genre," "gender," "kind," "type," "sort," "manner," "race," "lineage," "parentage," and "offspring."[17]

Edward Montagu and, following him, Johann Lange used many of these terms in their English- and German-language translations, but they avoided the cognate *cast[e] (kaste),* a term that had existed in English since 1555 and had been explicitly tied to the New World since the publication of Sir Walter Ralegh's *Discoverie of Guiana* (1591). When Barba discusses the "casta" of white crystalline stones, Montagu and Lange translate it as "sort" or "kind," rendering the phrase as "Of this sort, although much smaller" and "Deregleichen Arth, wiewol viel kleiner" (the same kind, although much smaller). On the casta of stones extracted from the Inca mine in Omasuyo, they write "to whose

16. Barba, *Arte de los metales,* 39v; Abbott and Wolfe, "Intensive Pre-Incan Metallurgy," *Science,* CCCI (2003), 1839.

17. Cesar Oudin, *Tesoro de las dos lenguas francesa y española: Thresor des deux langues françoise et espagnolle . . .* (Paris, 1607), 283; Sebastián de Covarrubias Orozco, *Tesoro de la lengua castellana, o española* (Madrid, 1611), 866; John Minsheu, *Hēgemōn Eis Tas Glōssas Id Est, Ductor in Linguas: The Guide into Tongues . . . with Their Agreement and Consent One with Another, as Also Their Etymologies, That Is, the Reasons and Derivations of All or the Most Part of Wordes, in These Eleven Languages, Viz. . . .* (London, 1617), 102. Modern geologists associate *caparrosas* (copperas) with chemically similar varieties of *piedra lipes* (Lipes stone), *misi, sori,* and chalcanthite ($CuSO_4 \cdot 5H_2O$), and iron metals like magnetite (variously FeO, Fe_2O_3, or Fe_3O_4) that grew interlaced with gold (Au) and silver (Ag) (ibid., 41, 45v). Chemical formulas for Andean stones and rocks come from Petersen, *Mining and Metallurgy in Ancient Perú,* trans. Brooks, 3–12, esp. 3, 7, 12.

species undoubtedly it belongs." Metallic castas from Latin America thus became "kinds," "sorts," or "species" in their European translations.[18]

Montagu's avoidance of the cognate is especially interesting because he often hewed so close to the Spanish that he coined clunky neologisms in English, including "caxon" (mixing bin, from the Spanish *cajón*) and "repass" (to mix thoroughly, from the Spanish *repasar*). Montagu also repurposed existing words in English, as when Barba's "pella" (partially formed amalgam) became "pellet," the medieval term for "cannonball." For Barba, *casta* was one of many modes of classification, but for Montagu, *casta* meant something else—something that resisted translation and caused him to avoid it.[19]

Barba's classifications—*castas, suertes,* and *géneros* for black, red, and white metals and stones—point to fluid color terms and categories, with tensions and discrepancies that suggest why translators might have preferred to avoid the term *casta* altogether. Although this language evokes the sistema de castas that figured so largely in colonial science and society, the logic does not. When human bodies were arranged by color and caste, Africans and their American-

18. *Oxford English Dictionary,* s.v. "caste," n., 1a, citing William Waterman's translation of Johannes Boemus, *Omnium gentium mores, leges, et ritus* . . . (Augsburg, 1538); and W[alter] Ralegh, *Discoverie of the Large, Rich, and Bewtiful Guiana* . . . (London, 1596); Albaro Alonso Barba, *The Art of Metals, in Which Is Declared the Manner of Their Generation and the Concomitants of Them: In Two Books,* trans. Edward [Montagu] (London, 1674), I, 57, 130; J[ohann] L[ange], trans., *Albaro Alonso Barba, Eines Spanischen Briesters und hocherfahrnen Naturkündigers Berg-Büchlein: Darinnen Von der Metallen und Mineralien Generalia und Ursprung* . . . (Hamburg, 1676), 47, 108–109. Compare also Barba, *Arte de los metales,* 41, 45v, with Barba, *Art of Metals,* trans. [Montagu], II, 15, 35, and [Lange], trans., *Albaro Alonso Barba,* 140, 155. Because Lange works from Montagu, rather than Barba, I cite his work in full only when it departs from the English translation.

19. "Caxon" was defined as *"a Chest full of Ore ground to be refined"* in Royal Society of London, *Philosophical Transactions: Giving Some Accompt of the Present Undertakings and Labours of the Ingenious in Many Considerable Parts of The World,* IX, *Beginning the Second Century: For the Year MDCLXXIV* . . . (212). Compare Barba, "Es remedio muy a proposito pella de plata no muy exprimida, para recogerla, si se repassa el caxon con ella; abraça tambien la mayor parte de la lis que huviere" (*Arte de los metales,* 53) with Montagu's almost incomprehensible phrase: "The proper remedy for this is to repass the Caxon with Pellet of Silver, not over small, so shall the dry Plate be collected together, and the greatest part of the *Lis* also, if there were any there" (*Art of Metals,* II, 68). The sentence makes even less sense in Lange: "Silber-Kugeln nicht gar zu klein wieder durchgehen lasse, so wird das trockene Metall, und der gröste Theil der Lis, so einige verhanden, zusammen gebracht werden" (Let pass again the silver-masses, not too small, so the metal became dry, so too the greater part of the *lis,* if some is present, may be brought together) (*Albaro Alonso Barba,* 181–182).

born descendants were placed in the lowest categories and subjected to the worst kinds of treatment; their humanity was denied consistently, over time, for generation upon generation. But in metallic castes, negrillos were among the most valuable in metallic weight *(ley),* explaining why Barba called cochizos "metal riquisissimo" (a most rich metal).[20]

By looking closely at when and how translators deal with *castas de metales* like pacos, mulatos, and negrillos, we can understand when readers outside of colonial Latin America saw that the language of mineral sorting aligned with color and caste and when racialized colonial discourse diverged from the terms of color classification. We can identify the divergence in part because Montagu translates the same words in different ways at different points in the text. Sometimes he translates *negrillo* as a color, such as "black Oar" and "black Silver Oar" in book 1, and other times he leaves it in the source language. For example, Barba begins his chapter "On the Knowledge of Metals" ("Del conocimiento de los metals, y diferencias que dellos ay") by describing how miners sorted them into "tres suertes, o diferencias generales los reduzen los mineros; que llaman Pacos; Mulatos, y Negrillos" (three kinds, or general differences to which the miners reduce them: which they call pacos, mulatos, and negrillos). Montagu changes the line to read, in English, "The Miners reduce these differences unto three general heads, which the *Spaniards* call, 1. *Pacos,* 2. *Mulatos,* and 3. *Negrillos.*" The text's multiple translations—first, from Quechua and Aimara into Spanish, and then from Hispanized Andean expressions into English (and German, based on the English)—reveals complex interactions of color and casta in colonial scientific literatures, making visible the otherwise invisible contributions of Indigenous miners' classifications and knowledge systems.[21]

The divide between the logic of sorting and the language of classification reflects the contributions of those who sorted and those who published, even as the language of sorting conflated the two (pallar / quilcar). Mineral sorting was primarily performed by Andean women and men, whose knowledges and vocabularies Barba translated for his readers. Sometimes, Barba converted nouns in Aimara and Quechua, such as *suruxchi* and *suruchiq,* both meaning

20. Barba, *Arte de los metales,* 39v.

21. Ibid.; Barba, *Art of Metals,* trans. [Montagu], I, 39–41, II, 8; [Lange], trans., *Albaro Alonso Barba,* 33, 134. The English-language editions of 1738 (Payne, trans., *Collection of Scarce and Valuable Treatises,* 113) and 1740 (Hodges, *Collection of Scarce and Valuable Treatises,* 129) both adopt the numbering system that Lange used in the German translation of 1676: "1. *Pacos,* 2. *Mulatos.* and, 3. *Negrillos.*" Barba's pun encompasses the alchemical sense of metallic reduction and grammatical meaning.

"to drip," into Hispanized terms like *soroches*. This approximation preserves the labor practices that were embedded in the word's Andean roots, because the silver-lead alloy quickly melted into a liquid. However, its sulfur content, as a sign of its great wealth ("señal de su mayor riqueza"), was the defining feature of *soroches*—not the low melting point. Distancing himself from the naming of these ores, Barba explained, "Todos los que llamā soroches, mulatos, y negrillos ... abundan de açufre conocidamente" (All those that they call *soroches, mulatos,* and *negrillos* ... are known to abound in sulfur).[22]

Throughout books 1 and 2 of the *Arte de los metales,* Barba uses the phrase "que llaman" (which they call), or variant expressions like "se llama" (which is called), "llamado/a/s" (called), or "llaman" (they call), 122 times. He does not use them equally, though. Twenty cases (16 percent) appear in singular, adverbial, adjectival, or infinitive forms ("llama," "se llama," "que llama," "llamóse," "llamado," "llamarse"). Five cases (4 percent) appear in first-person plural ("llamamos" [we call]). Twenty-two cases (18 percent) are in third-person plural, past or present ("llaman," "llamavan," "llamaron," "se llaman," "le llaman"). The majority of Barba's definitions—75 terms (61 percent)—use the expression "que llaman" (what they call); 44 of those cases (59 percent) are derived from Andean names for metals, instruments, topographic features, or places. Similarly, in the 13 cases (11 percent) in which Barba uses a form of "llaman" rather than "que llaman" ("llaman," "llaman comunmente," "llaman comunmente los beneficiadores," "así llaman los mineros"), 9 terms (69 percent) are of Andean origin. In contrast, of the twenty cases (16 percent) in which Barba uses third-person singular, an infinitive, a gerund, or a modifier (llamado / a), fourteen terms (70 percent) stem from European alchemical traditions, natural philosophy, or place-names from the Old World. In other words, Barba describes a variety of concepts, practices, and tools employed in alchemical and Andean technical arts. But he uses different discursive forms to explain them, as "que llaman" and its variants more often refer to Andean mining technologies, and "se llama" and its variants are more frequently traced to European roots. These semantic patterns provide clues that identify where Indigenous terms appear in colonial mining practices and vocabularies.[23]

22. Barba, *Arte de los metales,* 19; Cerrón-Palomino, *Voces del Ande,* 111–119; Langue and Salazar-Soler, *Diccionario de términos mineros,* 557. González Holguín defined *sorochi* as "Margagita" in *Vocabulario de la lengua general de todo el Peru.*

23. These figures are based on a thorough count, but even with OCR scans, Google Books, and combing through records by hand, I am sure to have missed some cases. I classified terms with bilingual dictionaries by Santo Tomás, González Holguín, García de Llanos, and Bertonio. When Barba's words originated in Spanish but their meanings devel-

Within each of the three categories of silver metals—reddish (paco), black (negrillo), and in-between (mulato)—there was wide color variation, some of which stemmed from the physical properties of the metals, such as their exposure to oxygen, elemental composition, and the depth of the deposit from which it was extracted. Miners in Mexico and the Andes confronted the challenges of classifying dynamic, mixed-metallic matter. In one recent study of silver in Zacatecas, concentrations of silver (Ag) in galena (PbS) ranged from .11 to .69 percent weight in one mine and .04 to .36 percent in a second site. During the colonial era, these varieties of argentiferous galena were called *tescatete,* a Hispanized term whose Nahuatl roots may reflect the color perceptions of Indigenous miners. *Tezcatl* indicates metallic shine or reflection ("espejo para mirarse en el"), whereas *tezcatlauitl* refers to fine red ochre, often bearing iron oxides ("almagre fino"), and *tezcauauhtli* signifies small bits of black ashes ("bledos o cenizos negros"). In the Andes, a change in shine indicated that silver metals had converted from negrillos to pacos, as sulfuric elements were released during heating. Barba explains, "El mudar color el metal, perdiendo el brillar que antes tenia, bolviendose de negrillo en paco, es la señal mas cierta de que està bien dispuesto para el açogue, aunque ay en esto latitude grandissima" (The clearest sign that a metal is well disposed to mercury is when it changes color, losing the brilliance that it once had and returning from a negrillo to a paco, although there is great latitude in this).[24]

Much of the variation in silver classification stems from the ways in which speakers of different language groups perceive color. *Paco* was a Hispanized

---

oped in the Andes, such as "caja," I classified them as Spanish, following definitions from the sources. As García de Llanos explains for "caja," "Parece vocabulo castellano y por tal se debe tener, aunque pudiera haberse derivado de *cascasca,* que en la general significa cosa pegada" (It seems to be a Castilian word and that is how it should be understood, although it could be derived from *cascasca,* which in the general language [Quechua] means "thing that is stuck") (*Diccionario y maneras de hablar*). I drew additional insight from patterns in the translations, as when Montagu translates Barba's phrase "que llaman" in different ways with Andean and European terms. For example, Barba's phrase "bitumen, que llaman grassa" (*Arte de los metales,* 41) becomes "Brimstone" (*Art of Metals,* II, 15), whereas Barba's reference to Andean materials, "las que llaman copaquiras" (41v) becomes "of which sort are those they call *Copaquiras"* (II, 15).

24. Barba, *Arte de los metales,* 47v; Thomas G. Sharp and Peter R. Buseck, "The Distribution of Ag and Sb in Galena: Inclusions versus Solid Solutions," *American Mineralogist,* LXXVIII (1993), 85–95; Alonso de Molina, *Vocabulario en lengua castellana y mexicana: Y mexicana y castellana* (1571), ed. Miguel León Portilla (Mexico, 1970), 112v. Depending on mixtures of lead, sulfur, copper, and silver, argentiferous galena could appear black, gray, green, white, or orange: see Langue and Salazar-Soler, *Diccionario de términos mineros,* 557; Barba, *Arte de los metales,* 39v.

form of the Quechua term *ppaqu* (reddish); as Barba puts it, "En la lengua general de aquesta tierra quiere dezir bermejo" (In the general tongue of this land it means a red color). Bilingual Quechua-Spanish dictionaries and specialized mining dictionaries from Potosí confirm this definition. González Holguín defines the Quechua terms *ppaccu, ancha paccu, pacco,* and *ppaccuyani* as "cosa bermeja rubia roxa" (a thing reddish-blonde red), "el bermejo" (the red color), "el rubio" (the blonde), and "pararse roxo o ruvio" (to become red or blonde). García de Llanos glosses *paco* simply as "quiere decir bermejo" (it means reddish), pointing readers to the more comprehensive definition listed under "metal." And yet, *pacos* included argentiferous galena (PbS), called "plata blanca" (white silver), *tacanas,* "de aquel color negro amasado, sin resplandor ninguno" (of that mixed black color, without any shine), and *soroches,* "de ordinario negro" (usually black). Silver forms varied from one mine to the next. Tacanas were generally black ("de ordinario negro"), but they could also appear "parda, y cenicienta, que llaman llipta" (gray and ashen, which they call *llipta* [Quechua: ash]). The color possibilities of *plata bruta* (cuppelated silver), which was rich in lead (Pb), varied even more. Forms of *plata bruta* could be "negro, pardo, ceniciento, verde, blanco, y naranjado, que llaman suco" (black, gray, ashen, green, white, and orange, which they call *suco*).[25]

Unlike the etymology of *paco,* which is clearly traced to Andean roots, the name *negrillo* drew from a conceptually available Spanish discourse on color. The proliferation of color terms expressing forms of metallic blackness in books like Barba's *Arte de los metales* may also reflect Indigenous and Spanish miners' contact with Africans in Potosí. Notarial records indicate that Afri-

25. Barba, *Arte de los metales,* 39v; González Holguín, *Vocabulario de la lengua general de todo el Peru,* 271, 334; García de Llanos, *Diccionario y maneras de hablar,* ed. Bulcher, Mendoza, and Murra, 40, 62, 96. González Holguín defines *lliptta* as balls of ash that Andean people chewed with coca to make the leaves more appetizing ("Panecitos de ceniza quero en por apetite para comer coca"), suggesting how Indigenous miners adapted color terms from food production and mine labor, in which the consumption of coca played an important role in keeping hunger and altitude sickness at bay during long shifts (214). Bertonio emphasizes brilliance rather than grayness: *lliphiphitha* (equivalent to "ppallchacatha"), "Reverberar las cosas lisas, las armas acicaladas, el agua, las estrellas quando centellean etc" (to reflect smooth things, [such as] clean weapons, water, the stars when they sparkle, etc.), and *lliphilliphi,* "Y esso espejuelo" (And this means mirror-like) (*Vocabulario de la lengua aimara*). The foundational study of color perception in Latin America is Brent Berlin and Paul Kay, *Basic Color Terms: Their Universality and Evolution* (Berkeley, Calif., 1969). See also Berlin, Dennis E. Breedlove, and Peter H. Raven, *Principles of Tzeltal Plant Classification* (New York, 1974); Kay, *The World Color Survey* (Stanford, Calif., 2009); Kay and Chad McDaniel, "The Linguistic Significance of the Meanings of Basic Color Terms," *Language,* LIV (1978), 610–646.

can miners appeared soon after the first Spanish strikes of 1545. By the end of the century, Potosí's approximately five thousand black laborers had shifted to aboveground work in refineries, the mint, or supporting industries, where they worked as artisans (bakers, carpenters, *chicheras, pulperos*), vendors, and household servants.[26]

Despite the different etymologies of *pacos* and *negrillos,* both categories contained a dizzying degree of internal variation. Just as the color properties of *pacos* could range from red, white, gray, and black to green or orange, so did the category *negrillo* fail to account for the hues of negrillo metals. For this reason, Barba insists, "No todos los metales negros se comprehenden debaxo de nombre de negrillos" (Not all black metals are understood by the name *negrillos*), because some black metals could be "pacos" or "mulatos." As these examples show, the metallic categories of "pacos" and "negrillos" were named for colors, but those colors did not align with the metals contained within the categories, or "castas de metales."[27]

Montagu and Lange kept the names of these metallic categories in the source language, suggesting that they understood the difference between the color of a metal and the name of its category. Montagu wrote (and Lange followed), *"Paco* in the general language of this Country, is as much as to say of a Red colour, and such more or less are the Stones, which they call *Metal Paco,* although in *Berengula de Pacages,* they call the Green Mettals of Copper by the same name," and "The *Negrillos* have been discovered by, and take their name from their colour, although all Black Mettals are not comprehended under that name."[28]

Alongside color, miners used sensory perceptions like texture, smell, taste, and sound, as well as physical location, to describe and classify material samples. These diverse ways of organizing metallic matter resulted in fluid systems of classification, even—and especially—as such classifications pretended to order. Aboveground, refiners classified pacos by color, but under-

26. Peter Bakewell, *Miners of the Red Mountain: Indian Labor in Potosí, 1545–1650* (Albuquerque, N.M., 1984), 192–193; Kris Lane, "Africans and Natives in the Mines of Spanish America," in Matthew Restall, ed., *Beyond Black and Red: African-Native Relations in Colonial Latin America* (Albuquerque, N.M., 2005), 159–184; Lane, "Slavery and the Casa de la Moneda in Seventeenth-Century Potosí," in Mónica Ghirardi, ed., *Territorios de lo cotidiano, siglos XVII–XX: Del antiguo virreinato del Perú a la Argentina contemporánea* (Rosario, 2014), 101–114.

27. Barba, *Arte de los metales,* 39v.

28. Barba, *Art of Metals,* trans. [Montagu], II, 8–9; [Lange], trans., *Albaro Alonso Barba,* 135.

ground miners identified them by what Barba calls their "sweet, peaceable" odor.[29]

There were also regional variations. In the province of Berenguela de Pacajes, "paco" meant "metales verdes cobriços" (green, copper-bearing metals), or any metal that was steel-like ("acerado"), glassy ("espejado"), or negrillo ("otros que llaman negrillos"). In this way, some miners classified silver metals by negation—a reddish paco was defined by not being a black negrillo. In Mexico, "The basic distinction was between black and red (*negros* and *colorados*), a distinction which later observers have explained in chemical terms." There, colorados were surface-level deposits that took their names from the iron oxides that tinted them red, whereas negros, as in the Andes, were deep-level metals rich in sulfur and sometimes lead.[30]

To modern readers, these may sound like racial binaries, but to colonial miners, the distinction between red and black signaled the need for different metallurgical methods. As Barba explains, each kind of metal took its own form of refining: "Los metales pacos, que no tienen cosa que resplandezca, o brille son los propios para açogue.... El beneficio propio del machacado es el tintin. De los soroches el fuego. El rosicler, y cochiço se deve fundir como la tacana: los negrillos son tambien mas para fundicion que para açogue" (Pacos that have no resplendence or shine are appropriate for mercury.... The appropriate treatment for *machacado* is *tintín.* For soroches it is fire. Rosicler and cochizo should be smelted like tacana: negrillos are also more for smelting than for mercury). These names were derived from labor practices, such as heavy hitting (tacana) and the sounds made during mineral crushing (tintín), and languages like Quechua and Aimara (paco, soroches), Latin (machacado,

29. Barba, *Arte de los metales,* 2. Smell indexed promising mineral deposits and life-threatening conditions; as Barba reports, two Galician miners discovered a high-grade vein of tacanas in the mine of San Cristóbal, province of Los Lipes, but they were forced to abandon their contract because Indigenous miners perished in the mine. After a few years, the smell dissipated, but miners continued to die when they entered the site (*Arte de los metales,* 2v). For taste-based classification, see "Del conocimiento de las tierras por el sabor" (ibid., 4), and for sound, see Barba's explanation of *tintín* processing (72–73).

30. Barba, *Arte de los metales,* 39v; P. J. Bakewell, *Silver Mining and Society in Colonial Mexico: Zacatecas, 1546–1700* (Cambridge, 1971), 130. Modesto Bargalló adds, "Mineros y personas poco doctas en las cosas de minería, reducían los minerales de plata a dos clases ... No necesitamos advertir que en el Cerro de Potosí exstían más de dos especies de minerales le plata" (Miners and people with little knowledge of mining affairs would reduce silver minerals to two classes.... We do not need to point out that in Potosí there were more than two kinds of silver minerals) (*La amalgamación de los minerales de plata en Hispanoamérica colonial* [Mexico City, 1969], 101–102).

derived from "macho"), and French (rosicler, or "rose-colored"). If a metal was shiny, because of its sulfides, it had to be smelted; a dull metal, like a paco, "soroche," or "muerto," suggested that it responded well to mercury.[31]

The names of mixed-metallic categories did not convey ideas about mineral weight, grade, or value; metals named after European languages were not more valuable than those whose names drew from racial or ethnic inequalities in the Americas. Each metal required different metallurgical methods and materials to become useful for human society and valuable in markets. The key was to match each kind of silver to its most profitable mode of refining. In developing new ways of classifying and naming metals based on physical properties and refining techniques, colonial miners incorporated a variety of linguistic and conceptual influences. Although they used the language of the sistema de castas, the values and colors that miners assigned to mixed metals like mulatos and negrillos did not align with casta categories of the same names. In the mining industry, color was part of a broader matrix of category-making modes. It provided the names of categories, but not the logic of categorization.

The metallic casta that best reveals the gap between color and category is, without doubt, *metales mulatos.* According to García de Llanos, Andean miners classified metals by space, or underground location, using observable physical properties to understand the inner essences of mixed metals. Pacos were found closest to the surface, negrillos were extracted at the deepest levels, and ash-colored mulatos ("cenicientos") marked the transition between the two, occupying an intermediary space for the length of two or three human bodies ("estados"). To describe something that was "in between" ("medio entre dos extremos que es mediano"), Quechua speakers called it "pactascak," "pactas mitta," or "chaupi mitta." Speakers of Aimara said "taypirana," meaning "lugar del medio, o lo que esta en medio de alguna llanada, o cerro, o pueblo" (middle place, or that which is in the middle of a plain, or mountain, or town). Spanish speakers seem to have translated Andean concepts of spatial intermediaries into a classification that to them meant "in between": "mulato." This explains why writers in Spain, such as Pérez de Vargas, used some of the same color terms as Barba and García de Llanos ("negro," "pardo") but did not describe metals as "mulatos." In the translation from spoken classifications underground to written distinctions aboveground, Andean spatial concepts *(chaupi mitta, taypirana, quitamama)* became part of a colonial discourse of mixture, race, and color: *metales mulatos, negrillos, cimarrones.* When traced to their etymological and conceptual origins, explicitly racialized terms like "mulato" and "cimarrón" prove that Indigenous miners contributed to the conceptual

31. Barba, *Arte de los metales,* 32, 39v, 40v.

foundations and daily practices of the colonial Andean silver industry. Their lexical footprints also document how Indigenous contributions were translated out of the printed records that reached scientific reading communities in Europe.[32]

Just as Spanish-speaking miners converted Andean spatial classifications into racialized terms, so did European writers translate color properties of silver metals and metallic categories in ways that cohered with their own ideas of color and race. When Barba explained that *plata bruta* (cupellated silver) could be "naranjado, que llaman suco" (orange, which they call *suko*), Montagu translated the phrase as "Orange Tawny, which they call *Suco.*" Notably, he retained the source language for nouns in the rest of the passage, writing *"La Tacana," "Lipta,"* and *"Pacos."* Montagu recognized their naming functions, as distinct from their color signifiers, and preserved Barba's two terms for "orange"—"naranjado," derived from the Arabic *nāranǧ,* and "suco," derived from Aimara or Quechua.[33]

However, "Orange Tawny" is nowhere to be found in Barba's color vocabulary. Translators John Minsheu (1617) and César Oudin (1607) equated "naranjado" with "orange," variously tracing "naranjado" to Latin roots, "Citreus color," and translating the term accordingly, "Of an Orenge colour," or reaching the same conclusion without the etymology: "de couleur d'Orange, orãgé." Montagu used the broader context of racialized colonial scientific discourse, with its "castas" of metales mulatos and negrillos, to transmute a neutral "naranjado" into his own racialized vocabulary of "Orange Tawny." Where did he get the idea that such metals were tawny? Most likely, from color properties associated with the adjective "mulato," which, according to the *Oxford English Dictionary,* had signified "tawny" since 1622.[34]

32. Llanos, *Diccionario y maneras de hablar,* ed. Bulcher, Mendoza, and Murra, s.v. "Quemazones"; González Holguín, *Vocabulario de la lengua de todo el Peru,* s.v. "Medio entre dos extremos que es mediano"; Bertonio, *Vocabulario de la lengua aymara,* s.v. "taypirana."

33. Barba, *Arte de los metales,* 39v; Barba, *Art of Metals,* trans. [Montagu], II, 9–10; [Lange], trans., *Albaro Alonso Barba,* 135. Bertonio defines *suko suko ccahua* as "striped" ("bareteada, o listada"), perhaps related to *suca,* canals to irrigate the dry fields of the *altiplano* (322). Jesús Lara points to the Quechua *suk'a* (salitre); see *Diccionario qhëshwa-castellano / castellano-qhëshwa* (Cochabamba, 1971), cited in Horacio Magliola Mundet, *Venero lingüístico altiperuano en la minería de la plata* (Córdoba, 1992), s.v. "suco."

34. Minsheu, *Hēgemōn Eis Tas Glōssas,* s.v. "an Orenge, or Orange"; Oudin, *Tesoro de las dos lenguas francesa y española,* s.v. "naranjado." The term "mulatto" arrived through James Mabbe's English-language translation of Mateo Alemán's *Guzmán de Alfarache* (1600) (*OED,* s.v. "mulatto"). The work was published as Matheo Aleman, *The Rogue; or,*

But in the mining industry, mulatos were not brown; they were gray-colored. According to Potosí-based historian Bartolomé Arzáns de Orsúa y Vela, reflecting on the early colonial period from his eighteenth-century perch, there were two kinds of metales mulatos. The first was "de color de cáscaras de nueces verdes, y algunos son muy ricos y arman sobre espejuelos blancos que tocan algo en Amarillo, y tienen mucha plata blanca (algunos reducen este género de metales a los mulatos, otros a pacos)" (the color of green walnut shells, and some are so rich and grow upon slightly yellowish mica and they have a lot of galena *[plata blanca]* [some reduce this genre of metals to mulatos, others to pacos]). The second was an ash-hued ore ("ceniciento") laced with silver lines ("plata hilada"). According to García de Llanos, this kind of mulato was "de un color ceniciento, a lo cual dicen mulato" (an ash color, which they call mulato); gray metales mulatos were different from gray cenicientos.[35]

Underground, "metales mulatos" grew between pacos and negrillos; above-

---

The Life of Guzman de Alfarache, trans. James Mabbe (London, 1622). Between 1600 and 1604, several editions of Alemán's work were published across Europe, including Brussels (Juan Mommarté y Rutgerio Velpio, 1600; Roger Velpius, 1604), Lisbon (Jorge Rodrígues a costa de Luys Perez, 1600; Pedro Craasbeck, 1604), Paris (N. Bonfond, 1600), Madrid (Yñiguez de Lequerica, 1600), Milan (Bordon, 1603), Tarragona (Felipe Roberto a coste de Hieronymo Martin, 1603), and Zaragoza (Angelo Tauanno, 1603). On "tawny": only in the context of heraldry did the adjective "orange" overlap with "tawny," though this quinary definition was far from the standard interpretation (*OED:* "A tawny-coloured roundel; a roundel tenné"). French translators did not equate "naranjado" or "suco" with "tawny" *(fauve).* Hautin de Villars condensed the passage on tacanas into a single sentence and collapsed the Spanish and Andean terms "naranjado" and "suco" into a single word, "orangé" (Charles Hautin de Villars, *Traité de l'art métalique, extrait des oeuvres d'Alvare Alfonse Barba, célébre artiste dans les mines du Potozi . . .* [Paris, 1730], 31–32). Lenglet du Fresnoy footnoted the explanation of pacos and their Quechua roots: "Cependant les mineurs les réduisent à trois espéces générales qu'ils nomment Pacos, Mulatos, et Negrillos. Ils appellent *Mulato,* ce qui tient le milieu entre le *Paco* (1) et le *Negrillo.* Le Minerai *Mulato,* est presque toujours accompagné de Marcassite. Il y a moins de cette espéce, que des deux autres. La couleur noire donne le nom au *Negrillo,* et sert à le faire reconnoître, quoiqu'on ne comprenne pas tous les Minerais noirs sous le nom de *Negrillos.* La *Tacana,* Minerai riche et ordinairement noir, quoique sa couleur soit aussi quelquesois grise et cendrée, se réduit sous l'espéce des Pacos, ainsi que le Plomo, qui est de l'Argent brut, dont la couleur a coutume d'être noire, grise, verte, cendrée, blanche, et orangée, et qu'on nomme quelquefois *Suco.*" See [Lenglet du Fresnoy], trans., *Métallurgie ou l'art de tirer et de purifier les métaux: Traduite de l'espagnol d'Alphonse Barba avec les dissertations les plus rares sur les mines et les opérations métalliques,* I (Paris, 1751), 137–138. I thank Amanda Herbert for references on early modern English color theory.

35. Bartolomé Arzáns de Orsúa y Vela, *Historia de la villa imperial de Potosí* (1737), ed. Lewis Hanke and Gunnar Mendoza, 3 vols. (Providence, R.I., 1965), I, 143.

ground, metallurgists treated them in a similarly intermediary fashion. As silver refiner Juan de Alcalá y Amurrio explained in a volume that he wrote to his son and dedicated to his wife, doña Maria Montero de Barrios, some mulatos formed in the warring opposition of cold exhalations and hot soils and were thus "inclinadas al metal negrillo, y así participó aquel congelo dos contrarias naturalezas; la del negrillo quedando con los mismos humores es llenos de su revelde frialdad, y crudesa" (inclined toward the negrillo metal, and so it participated in the congealing of those two contrary natures, and its negrillo part has the same humors, full of its rebellious coldness and rawness). Others behaved more like pacos and could be amalgamated with mercury, because they "heredaron con la secreta influencia de los astros la naturaleza del paco, y sus humores dociles" (inherited from the secret influence of the stars the nature of the paco and its docile humors). In addition to natural philosophical ideas about humors and the relation of the heavens and the underworld, Alcalá y Amurrio invoked earthly metaphors that reflected his experiences as a father. In the fifteenth of his nineteen rules for silver refining, he analogized the origins of mulatos to parental influences, explaining that metal was like a child who inherited some characteristics ("el natural") from the father and some from the mother.[36]

Unlike other writers, Alcalá y Amurrio avoided color descriptions when he explained the properties of cenicientos in his fourteenth rule: "no son pacos, ni negrillos, ni mulatos, sinó de un genero mostrenco, que ni hace etremo como el paco, ciuo antipoda es el negrillo, ni hace medio como el mulato, que se cria al fin del paco, y al principio del negrillo, formandose la materia de su congelacion de una y otra causa, porloque le pusieron nombre de mulato" (they are not pacos, nor negrillos, nor mulatos, but rather a rootless kind that neither forms a pair of opposites, as the paco does with its antipodal negrillo; nor do they form a middle way, like the mulato that grows after the paco and before the negrillo, instead coming into being through another cause, for which it is called mulato). This explanation of minerogenesis and composition expands upon Barba's version, which argued, "Metal mulato es un medio entre pacos, y negrillos, y assi lo criò la naturaleza entre los dos, tiene el color baço" (The mulato metal is a middle way between pacos and negrillos, and so it was reared by nature between the two, and it has the color of spleen). Barba's geohumoral theory aligned metales mulatos with the traditional humoral color schemes of early modern science, in which cold, dry, black, earthy elements conveyed melancholic properties of black bile, as distinguished from blood-

36. Juan de Alcalá y Hamurrio, *Directorio del beneficio del Azogue en los metales de Plata: Y documentos que dá un Padre aun Hijo, en sus reglas, y adbertencias* (Lima, 1737), 93–93v.

red cosmological bodies that were analogized to the warm, wet roots of air. Alcalá y Amurrio offers another explanation: because cenicientos did not fit into any of the existing categories of metallic antipodes—paco and negrillo—they were grouped discursively with the general category of "other" metals, mulatos, even though they were found near top-level pacos ("en el ház de la tierra") and in veins that led to soroches, which explained why they were generally smelted ("en vetas q̄ luego dan en soroches de fundicion, como tambien es el benefo delos senicientos").[37]

Even as they disagree on the science of metallic classification, Barba and Alcalá y Amurrio concur that metales mulatos were somewhere between splenetic black and shiny gray. And yet, European translators assigned a completely different color term to metales mulatos: brown *(braunen)*. According to Montagu and echoed by Lange, *"Mulatos* is a colour between the *Pacos* and *Negrillos;* and in the Mines, Mettal of that colour is produced in the same order; it is of a Brown colour." As with the Andean translation of "chaupi mitta" and "taypirana" into "metales mulatos," and the transatlantic translation of "suco" into "Orange Tawny," translators once again interpret metallic color properties through the lens of their own ideas of race and color, derived from the human kingdom. In Europe, "mulatos" were "brown."[38]

Notably, Montagu here erased correspondences that he had elsewhere preserved. For example, in chapters 35 and 36 of book 1, Barba invoked the color logic of humoral theory to describe the medical "faculties, or virtues" of purgative stones, poisons that corrupted the bowels, and semiminerals that were used to treat melancholic patients, such as white-hued silver and mercury; jet black "açabache" (agate stone, SiO_2), "sori" (sory, or vitriol-bearing, today equated with chalcanthite, or $CuSO_4 \cdot 5H_2O$), and "melanteria" (iron sulfide, $FeSO_4 \cdot 7H_2O$); and ash-gray ("ceniciento") "melia" and "eretria" soils (called by the same names in Agricola). Although Montagu skipped some of the materials in Barba's list, such as "piedra Arabica" (Arabus lapus, or Arabic stone, which appears in Montagu but not in Lange) and "[piedra] Judaica" (Lapis judaicus, or Jews' stone, absent from both translations), he faithfully translated most of the descriptions: "Silver, Quicksilver . . . are white of colour; *la tierra Pingiti, Jeat, Sori, Melanteria* are black; of an ash-colour are the *Eritrian,* and the *Melian* earth." These passages throw into sharp relief Montagu's different handlings of the humoral terms of metales mulatos from the Andes in book 2 and semimetals of the Old World in book 1. By interpreting mulatos as brown rather than spleen-colored, Montagu's translation suggests how readers out-

37. Ibid., 92v–93; Barba, *Arte de los metales,* 37v.

38. Barba, *Art of Metals,* trans. [Montagu], II, 9; [Lange], trans., *Albaro Alonso Barba,* 135.

side of Latin America might have understood Barba's racialized discourse of mineral sorting—and how they reinterpreted mining lexicons in their own ways.[39]

As we have seen, in the tripartite system used by "los mineros; que llaman Pacos; Mulatos, y Negrillos," color terms and racial groups did not neatly align. Not all pacos were red, not all black metals were negrillos, and mulatos were "splenetically" and spatially in between. In its translation into European scientific writing, "brown" became fixed to "metales mulatos," and Spaniards, not miners, did the naming: recall Montagu's translation, "The Miners reduce these differences unto three general heads, which the *Spaniards* call, I. *Pacos,* 2. *Mulatos,* and 3. *Negrillos.*" Montagu distinguished miners from Spaniards in a way that Barba had not—probably because most of the miners whose words and ideas appeared in Barba's book were not of Spanish origin.[40]

Unlike the English and German translators, French translator Hautin de Villars credited miners, not Spaniards, with these naming conventions ("cependant les Mineurs les réduisent à trois Sortes, ou Diférences générales, qu'ils nomment PACOS, MULATOS, et NEGRILLOS"). He also departed from other translators by leaving mulatos without a color signature, noting, "PACO veut dire *Rouge,* NEGRILLO veut dire *Noire,* et MULATO veut dire, *Minéral,* qui tient le milieu entre le Paco et le Negrillo" (*Paco* means red, *negrillo* means black, and *mulato* means metal, whose hue is between that of the *paco* and the *negrillo*). When *mulato* meant "a Brown colour," whether in English or German, it was the work of Spaniards; when miners did the naming, as in Spanish and French texts, mulatos were ambiguously in the middle.[41]

39. Barba, *Arte de los metales,* 35v–37; Barba, *Art of Metals,* trans. [Montagu], I, 150–156; [Lange], trans., *Albaro Alonso Barba,* 124–128v; Petersen, *Mining and Metallurgy in Ancient Perú,* trans. Brooks, 3, 7. The stones are described by classical and early modern authors like Pliny (*Natural History,* X, *Books 36–37,* trans. D. E. Eichholz [Cambridge, Mass., 1962], book 36, 153, for *Arabus lapus*) and Agricola (*De Natura Fossilum [Textbook of Mineralogy]* [1546], trans. Mark Chance Bandy and Jean A. Bandy [New York, 2004], book 1 [*eretria* and *melia* soils], book 3 [*sori* and *melanteria*]). On Jews' stone, see Christopher J. Duffin, "Lapis Judaicus or the Jews' Stone: The Folklore of Fossil Echinoid Spines," Geologists' Association, *Proceedings,* CXVII (2006), 265–275; Pouya Faridi et al., "Randomized and Double-Blinded Clinical Trial of the Safety and Calcium Kidney Stone Dissolving Efficacy of Lapis Judaicus," *Journal of Ethnopharmacology,* CLVI (2014), 82–87.

40. Barba, *Art of Metals,* trans. [Montagu], II, 8; [Lange], trans., *Albaro Alonso Barba,* 134–136.

41. Villars, *Traité de l'art métalique,* 30, 31. Fresnoy ascribes the system of sorting and labeling to miners, not Spaniards; see [Fresnoy], trans., "Cependant les mineurs," *Métallurgie,* I, 137.

Even as they deal differently with color signifiers, all three translators leave the main terms of mineral classification—*paco, mulato,* and *negrillo*—in the source language, declining to relegate the Spanish *mulato* into well-established cognates like the English "mulatto" (1591) or the French "mulat." In both cases, the term arrived through contact with Iberian languages. The *Corpus diacrónico del español* (CORDE) suggests that the word *mulato* entered Spanish as early as 1543, tying the word to the Americas with Alonso Borregán's *Crónica de la conquista del Perú* (ca. 1565). Much later, in 1702, but before the French translation of Barba's book, lexicographer Abel Boyer defined "Mulat" or "Mulátre" as a noun: "celui *ou* celle qui est né d'une Indienne et d'un Negre, *ou* d'une Negre et d'un Indien, *ou* qui est né de Pere et de Mere de differente Religion parmi les Espagnols" (he or she who is born of an Indian women and a black man, or of a black women and an Indian, or of a black woman and an Indian man, or, among the Spaniards, someone who is born of a father and mother of a different religion). Despite the conceptual availability of terms like *mulatto* and *mulat* in English and French, Montagu and Hautin de Villars avoided these cognates. Unlike the case of negrillos ("black Oar," "black Silver Oar"), no one translated the word *mulato,* perhaps recognizing in it something that they could not convey in their respective language.[42]

42. *OED,* s.v. "mulatto" (n. and adj.), citing Job Hortop's *Travailes of an English Man Containing His Sundrie Calalmities Indured by the Space of Twentie and Odd Yeres in His Absence from His Native Countrie*... (London, 1591); [Abel] Boyer, *Dictionnaire royal, françois et anglois*... (La Haye, 1702), s.v. "Mulat, te ou Mulâtre S." Jean-François Féraud traced "mulat" and "mulâtre" as adjectives (1) and nouns (2) acquired with language contact from Portuguese rather than Spanish, and white parents replaced Indigenous mothers and fathers: "Qui est né ou née d'un nègre et d'une blanche (ce qui est assez râre) ou d'un blanc et d'une négresse; ce qui est très-comun. Il ou elle est *mulâtre;* un valet *mulâtre,* une fille *mulâtre.* C'est *un mulâtre, une mulâtre.* Plusieurs au *fém.* disent *mulatresse"* (Jean-François Féraud, *Dictionaire critique de la langue française,* 3 vols. [1787–1788], s.v. "Mulat, ou Mulâtre, adj. et subst.," *Dictionnaires d'autrefois,* ARTFL Project, University of Chicago, http://artfl-project.uchicago.edu/node/17). CORDE (http://www.rae.es) cites the manuscript as an anonymous report, whereas Teofilo Ruíz attributes it to Master Vargas's *Recibimiento que se hizo en Salamanca a la princesa doña María de Portugal, viniendo casarse con el príncipe don Felipe, colegido por el maestro Vargas* (1543), ed. Jacobo Sáns Hermida (Salamanca, 2001), 7–8, 79–80, cited in Teofilo F. Ruiz, *A King Travels: Festive Traditions in Late Medieval and Early Modern Spain* (Princeton, N.J., 2012), 293–294. The literary record places "mulatto" in English slightly before that, with an account of the conquest of the Azores that was annexed to a printing of Abraham Fleming's celebration of the life of the Protestant martyr William Lambe; see Fleming, *A Memoriall of the Famous Monuments and Charitable Almesdeedes of the Right Worshipfull Maister William Lambe*... (London,

When metallic categories appear together, translators tend to keep them in the source language; when a term appears independently, the same translators interpret it as a color rather than a category. In book 1, Barba notes that pacos were often found in proximity to white alabaster rocks ($CaSO_4 \cdot 2H_2O$), called "cachi," after the Quechua term for salt (NaCl), and that the "chumpi" stone, named for its gray color ("pardo") and iron-ish casta affiliation ("es piedra de casta de Esmeril, con participacion de hierro"), was often found alongside "metales negrillos, y rosicleres, en Potosi, Chocaya, y otras partes" (negrillo metals and rosiclers, in Potosi, Chocaya, and other regions). Even though the terms *paco* and *negrillo* are separated by only one sentence, Montagu treats them differently, keeping *pacos* in the source language and translating *negrillos* as a color ("black Mettals"): *"Cachi,* another sort of Stone white like Alabaster, soft and easie to break in pieces, is all this Country called Salt. Much Lead is engendered in this kind of Stone, in the veins of *(Metales pacos)* which is the name the Miners here give unto their Silver Oar. *Chumpi* (which is so called, because it is of a grey colour) is a Stone of the kind of Esmeril mixed with Iron; it shines a little, and is very hard to work, because it resists the fire much. It is found in *Potosi* and *Chocaya,* and *Otras partes,* with the black Mettals and *Rosicleres."* As he studiously avoids the English term "caste," Montagu retains the source language for all of the terms that he believes to be proper nouns, such as names of stones, places, and *"(Metales pacos)."* He employs the same technique with a term that he mistakenly interprets as a toponym: unlike Potosí or Chocaya, "Otras partes" is not a place. It just means "other places."[43]

Montagu's reading of "negrillos" as "black Mettals" and deference to "pacos" suggest that he interprets Barba's color terms and classification system as Spanish, even though Barba explained that these were New World knowledges. Consider book 1's elaborate explanation of Andean corrections to the learned medieval mineralogist and Dominican friar Albertus Magnus:

> Criase en todo genero de minas, y especialmēte en las de cobre, y negrillos de plata, por lo mucho que del participan; y por esto quiza

---

1580). The edition, held at the Bodleian Library and digitized on Early English Books Online, lists a print date of 1580, though the appendix records events from June 23, 1583.

43. Barba, *Arte de los metales,* 12–12v; Barba, *Art of Metals,* trans. [Montagu], I, 48–49; [Lange], trans., *Albaro Alonso Barba,* 134–136. Elsewhere, terms that are italicized and glossed parenthetically, such as "(the piece of Silver being about the bigness of *Botijuela*)," are then defined in the margins: *"Botijuela* is a Spanish vessel, which contains about a Gallon" (Barba, *Art of Metals,* trans. [Montagu], I, 95). For an untranslated term, perhaps left unfinished, see *"[farellon]"* (ibid., 96).

> dixo Dioscorides, que era la margarita un genero de mineral de cobre. Y aunque Alberto, y otros la juzgaron por totalmente esteril, y que no contenia en si metal ninguno, la esperiencia ha enseñado lo contrario, y en el asiento de minas de Monserrate, en los Chichas, quando se començarō a trabajar sus vetas, tanto tenian de plata sus metales, quanto se via en ellos de margarita; y en este cerro de Potosi, y otros, una especie que ay della muy menuda, entre los negrillos, es muy cierta señal de su riqueza. Ay tantas suertes de margaritas, quantas las ay de metales, a quienes en sus colores representan, es la mas ordinaria la dorada.
>
> It grows in all kinds of mines, especially in those of copper and silver *negrillos*, because copper participates greatly in them; perhaps that is the reason why Dioscorides said that the marcasite is a kind of copper mineral. And although Albert and others judged it completely sterile, and that it contained no metal at all, experience has shown the contrary, and in the contract mine of Monserrat, in Chichas, when they began to work its veins they found so much silver in its metals, as much as they saw in marcasites. And in this mountain of Potosi and others there is a kind that is very small, and among the *negrillos* it is a sure sign of wealth. There are so many sorts of marcasite, as many as there are of metals that represent themselves in their colors, but the most common is the golden one.

By using *negrillo* two times in quick succession and once specifically in the context of Potosí, Barba makes clear the origins of the word, classificatory logic, and theory of minerogenesis that it reflects. *Negrillo* was rooted in Andean knowledges and lexicons, not the received wisdom or vocabulary of the Old World. Nevertheless, Montagu translated both phrases—"negrillos de plata" and "entre los negrillos"—as color terms rather than metallic categories: "the black Silver Oar." Even when Barba indicated that the term referenced a specialized mining lexicon, "los que llaman negrillos en todo aqueste Reyno" (what they call *negrillos* in this entire Kingdom), Montagu translated it as "that which in *Peru* is called the black Oar."[44]

In passages where Barba distinguished between negrillos and black-hued metals, Montagu preserved distinctions that he had elsewhere collapsed. Soroches, tacanas, *polvorillas,* rosicleres, cochizos, and negrillos have different characteristics. According to Barba, polvorilla is a kind of tacana, "no quaxada, ni empedernida, muy rica en metales pacos, en negrillos no tanto, por la mezcla que tiene de cobre" (not leaden, nor hard, very rich in paco metals, in ne-

44. Barba, *Arte de los metales,* 10v; Barba, *Art of Metals,* trans. [Montagu], I, 40–41; [Lange], trans., *Albaro Alonso Barba,* 33.

grillos not so much because of its mixture of copper). Montagu left both *paco* and *negrillo* in the source language: *"Polvorilla* is *Tacana;* not congealed, nor stony, but is rich in that Oar they call Pacos, but in the *Negrillos* not so much." As Barba explained, the difference between negrillos and black-colored metals was not a question of observable, external content (matter) but rather of reactions to chemical treatments that revealed a mineral's inner essence (spirit). Negrillos were defined by their high copper content ("lo que en el negrillo principalmente prevalece es el cobre, o actual, o virtual"), whereas black metals were high in lead or antimony ("que llaman en algunas partes maçacote"). Depending on its degree of elemental mixtures, "el metal negro" could be smooth ("liso") or textured, taking on the appearance of a page leaf or feather ("que haze unas como hojas, o plumas"). Montagu marked the differences between these chemical compositions, noting, "That which predominates in the *Negrillos,* is Copper," as distinct from "The Black Mettal which feels like Lead" and "Those *Negrillos,* which have lustre."[45]

Barba explained several times that *negrillo* did not mean "black ore" and that it was occasionally used to describe mixtures of copper, which were called "negrillo" because they looked black ("por el color se llama[n] negrillo[s]"). Montagu translated these lines with fidelity: "which for the colour-sake they call *Negrillo.*" He was also faithful in his translation of Barba's explanation that negrillos were named for their color, but not all black metals were negrillos ("al negrillo dà el nombre, y conocimiento su color, aunque no todos los metales negros se comprehenden debaxo de nombre de negrillos"). Anglophone readers learned, "The *Negrillos* have been discovered by, and take their name from their colour, although all Black Mettals are not comprehended under that name." Montagu understood that *negrillo* did not mean "black metal," but he still translated it as such at certain moments in his texts—all of which occurred when "negrillo" appeared alone or with "paco," but never with "mulato." When "negrillo" and "mulato" appear together, Montagu chose not to translate either term. In using different strategies to translate the same racialized color terms, sometimes rendering "mulato" as "brown" and sometimes leaving it in the source language, Montagu seems to understand that their definitions depend on context and connotation rather than words alone, and that cognates like *metales mulatos* resist easy interpretation.[46]

45. Barba, *Arte de los metales,* 40; Barba, *Art of Metals,* trans. [Montagu], II, 11–12; [Lange], trans., *Albaro Alonso Barba,* 136–137.

46. Barba, *Arte de los metales,* 30, 39v; Barba, *Art of Metals,* trans. [Montagu], I, 124, II, 9; [Lange], trans., *Albaro Alonso Barba,* 104, 135. Lange writes *"Negrilla,"* probably reflecting an imperfect copy rather than linguistic gender (*Albaro Alonso Barba,* 104). On

Analyzing case studies of translation within books 1 and 2 of Barba's *Arte de los metales* and tracing those translations through their various iterations in English and German provides new insight into the complex language of race, casta, and metallic classification. As we have seen, mining vocabularies were explicitly racial, but the social or economic values ascribed to mixed metals did not align with Spanish colonial assessments. For example, within the mining industry, metales mulatos and negrillos were not less valuable than pacos. These valuations depart notably from the ways in which colonial casta systems and imperial law evaluated the worth of black and mixed-race people, denying their value as human beings and insisting on specific prices for women, men, and children of various ages, origins, and skin tones. The gap between the language of color and the logic of value reveals the influences of those who wrote (primarily Spanish speakers) and those who mined (primarily Quechua and Aimara speakers). As they translated the specialized knowledges and vocabularies of Andean miners into written Spanish, authors like Barba and García de Llanos drew from a lexicon of racial and color classification that had been developed on the Iberian peninsula in response to deep traditions of intellectual, economic, and biological exchanges with people from Africa and the Middle East. In the Andes, Spanish speakers applied old terms in new ways, faced with a range of material samples that were as difficult to classify through the senses and explain in words as they were important to imperial economics. By analyzing the language of racial classification in the Andean silver industry, we gain a deeper understanding of the complex relationship of race to color as it developed in colonial Latin America—and as race (mulato) became bound to color (brown, *braunen*) in translation.[47]

A renewed attention to the language of color also reveals how specific Indigenous communities participated in the silver industry. Because most miners left no written evidence of their work, or only fragmentary writings at best, we know little about Andean women and men who mined and refined metals. By tracing color signatures through texts like Barba's and connecting them to different-hued knots and cords of Andean *khipus,* we may begin to

---

translation, see Douglas Robinson, *Western Translation Theory from Herodotus to Nietzsche* (Manchester, U.K., 1997); and Carmen Codoñer and Juan Antonio González Iglesias, eds., *Antonio de Nebrija: Edad media y renacimiento* (Salamanca, 1994), esp. 235–438.

47. Jerome C. Branche, *Colonialism and Race in Luso-Hispanic Literature* (Columbia, Mo., 2006), 32–113; Martínez, *Genealogical Fictions,* 25–87; Albert A. Sicroff, *Los estatutos de limpieza de sangre: Controversias entre los siglox XV y XVII,* trans. Mauro Armiño (Madrid, 1985).

identify communities whose technical literacies have gone unacknowledged in the historiography of colonial silver.

Language, Color, and Indigenous Literacies

As Barba and Alcalá y Amurrio showed, some gray metals were categorized as pacos, like cenicientos (ashen), called *llipta* in Quechua. Other gray metals were neither pacos nor mulatos but were called *oques,* from the Quechua *oqque*—what González Holguín calls "color de sayal, o ceniziento, o rucio" (the color of a cassock, or ashen, or dapple gray horse). Barba offered a synonym, "frailesco" (friar-ish), arguing that miners developed the term *oque* for gray ores because of the gray-robed Franciscan friars who ministered to the region. Bertonio offers a similar taxonomy of priests by their orders, in Aimara: Franciscans were "cchahkcchi padre"; Dominicans, "Hanko P[adre]."; Augustinians, "Chaara padre." Other orders were listed under the names of their founders rather than the entry for "frayle." Montagu kept the term *oque* in the source language: "others they call *Oques,* which in the language of this Country is as much as to say *Fraylescos,* because it is of the colour of a Friers coat." He preserves the meaning of *oque*—that it is derived from the color of a friar's robe—but once again confuses Quechua, Hispanized Quechua, and Spanish.[48]

Oque is not catalogued in García de Llanos's mining dictionary; nor does it appear in Luis Capoche's *Relación de la villa imperial.* Barba's aside on Andean miners' analogizing Franciscan friars to mineral bodies is the only record that I have found in colonial sources. To understand Barba's color terminology, we must look outside of Potosí and to Andean writing systems like the khipus that Indigenous communities used to convey information on agricultural production, silver tribute payments, and calendar dates.

Much as books are made up of words that are made up of letters, khipus use cotton strings of different lengths and colors, arranged into vertical columns that descend from a central thread, knots that are tied in different directions (left-right or right-left), and various forms (single / simple, triple / long, and figure eight) to tell the stories of their communities. Although we understand very little about these writing systems, scholars have made important advances in their studies of khipus over the last twenty years. Based on their

48. Barba, *Arte de los metales,* 32; Barba, *Art of Metals,* trans. [Montagu], I, 133; [Lange], trans., *Albaro Alonso Barba,* 111; González Holguín, *Vocabulario de la lengua general de todo el Peru,* s.v. "oqque"; Bertonio, *Vocabulario de la lengua aymara,* s.v. "Frayle de S. Francisco." Bertonio grouped Mercedenians with Dominicans, writing "vel Hanko padre" (ibid., s.v. "Frayle dela merced").

correlations of khipu and manuscript records from Limatambo, eighty kilometers due west of Cusco, archaeologist Martti Pärssinen and linguist Jukka Kiviharju offer a tentative interpretation of colonial-era categories of cultivated plants, birds, and precious metals that were grown, collected, and accounted for by the town and its cacique. Anthropologist Sabine Hyland's research in the town of Mangas, in the Peruvian province of Ancash, suggests how the multidimensional aspects of khipu writing, such as knots that are tied from top-right to bottom-left, in the form of a Z, or from the top-left to the bottom-right, in the form of an S, reflect the social status of the individuals whose stories they record; S knots relay the tales of people from the "upper" part of the world *(hanan),* whereas Z knots are reserved for those from the "lower" part *(hurin).* As literary scholar Rolena Adorno argues, the complementary balance of hanan / hurin is a common way of marking space and making meaning throughout the Andean world, and it was used to order and understand political dynasties, administrative functions, kinship networks, gender relations, and sacred spatialities in the pre-Columbian and colonial eras. Spanish imperial officials capitalized on ancestral Incaic hanan / hurin division in some regions, such as Huamachuco and Cajamarca, which had been organized as a single entity under the Inca empire. In 1565, when colonial jurisdictions and *corregimientos* were established, Spanish administrators followed the spatial logic of Inca systems.[49]

Given the guarded traditions of khipu literacies, *oque* probably reflects a local color vocabulary rather than one that circulated widely. Colonial writers like Capoche noted that communities defined color meanings on their own terms, such that "la inteligencia de estos hilos no es general" (the knowledge of these threads is not general). In one region, yellow threads signified silver production, but in another, such cords were black. According to Frank Solomon's study of khipus in present-day Tupicocha, Huarochirí province (some 185 kilometers northwest of Huancavelica), blue-gray threads called "oques" were restricted to one ayllu. The specific color signature of an extended kinship network, united by blood, language, and trade over a large geographic area of

49. Martti Pärssinen and Jukka Kiviharju, *Textos andinos: Corpus de textos "khipu" incaicos y coloniales,* I (Madrid, 2004), 52; Sabine Hyland, "Cómo los quipus indican 'el hanan y el urin': Un estudio en la tridimensionalidad de textos hechos en cuerdas," *Willka Nina* (Cusco, 2015), 34–38; Rolena Adorno, *Guaman Poma: Writing and Resistance in Colonial Peru,* 2d ed. (1986; rpt. Austin, Tex., 2000), 89–120; John E. Staller and Brian Stross, *Lightning in the Andes and Mesoamerica: Pre-Columbian, Colonial, and Contemporary Perspectives* (New York, 2013), 45–46. On the spatial influence of hanan / hurin arrangements in contemporary urban spaces, see Christien Klaufus, *Urban Residence: Housing and Social Transformations in Globalizing Ecuador,* trans. Lee Mitzman (New York, 2012), 91, 100–101.

"vertical archipelagos" may explain its infrequent use by colonial writers. Because ayllu kinship networks controlled the production and movement of goods throughout the *altiplano*, not unlike the ways in which artisan guilds regulated the production of different colors of mineral- and plant-based pigments in the colonial era, it is possible that Barba recorded the color term spoken by miners from the ayllu that used oque-colored cords in its khipus.[50]

We know that, like alphabetic literacies elsewhere in the early modern world, khipus were closely guarded ways of knowing, not widely shared literary cultures. Colonial writers praised the amount of information that master khipu readers *(quipocamayos)* managed within Andean communities. Describing the role of these respected teachers on *mita* reckoning days in Potosí, García de Llanos noted, "Hay mucho que entender con estos quipocamayos o contadores de nudos" (There is much that these *quipocamayos* or counters of knots understand). Jesuit writer José de Acosta wondered more generally at strings of reds ("colorados"), greens ("verdes"), blues ("azules"), and whites ("blācos") that marked things and made them known, as much about civil and sacred life as printed books can relate. In a remarkable equation of alphabetic and knotted literacy, the Jesuit priest wrote, "Porq̄ quāto los libros puedē dezir de historias, y leyes, y ceremonias, y cuētas de negocios, todo esso suplē los Quipos tan puntualmente" (Because as much as books can tell of histories, and laws, and ceremonies, and commercial accounts, the khipus provide all this most directly).[51]

The term's rarity might thus allow us to identify Barba's unnamed collaborators, albeit with caution. We cannot use contemporary evidence alone to read the colonial past, because Andean communities—like all human societies—negotiate change and continuity over time. There is potential to correlate localized color symbolisms of khipus and specific color terms from mining and metallurgical books, though such a project would require a better under-

50. Luis Capoche, *Relación general de la villa imperial de Potosí, un capítulo inédito en la historia del nuevo mundo* (1585), ed. Lewis Hanke (Madrid, 1959), 138–139; Frank Salomon, *The Cord Keepers: Khipus and Cultural Life in a Peruvian Village* (Durham, N.C., 2004), 187; Gabriela Siracusano, *El poder de los colores: De lo material a lo simbólico en las prácticas culturales andinas, siglos XVI–XVIII* (Buenos Aires, 2005), 57, 138–139. For a discussion of John Murra's formative theory of "vertical archipelagos," see Mary Van Buren, "Rethinking the Vertical Archipelago: Ethnicity, Exchange, and History in the South Central Andes," *American Anthropologist*, XCVIII (1996), 338–351.

51. Llanos, *Diccionario y maneras de hablar*, ed. Bulcher, Mendoza, and Murra, s.v. "quipocamayos"; Joseph de Acosta, *Historia natural y moral de las Indias, en que se tratan las cosas notables del cielo, y elementos, metales, plantas, y animales dellas: Y los ritos, y ceremonias, leyes, y govierno, y guerras de los Indios* (Seville, 1590), 410.

standing of the visual-material forms of khipu writing and the relationship between color classification and writing systems in the colonial era. In other words, such a project would require that scholars of the past—in multiple academic disciplines—collaborate with the living members of the communities we study. This would not be easy work, but it could provide new insights into the knowledges and experiences of the women and men who shaped the colonial Andean silver industry in ways the colonial historiography has not always appreciated.[52]

By tracing mistranslated terms through Spanish colonial texts and their European iterations, this chapter has created a documentary record of Indigenous knowledge production and its silencing. As spatial concepts like quitamama, chaupi mitta, and taypirana were transmuted into racial categories like cimarrón and mulato, these Indigenous knowledges were replaced with an emerging discourse of color, casta, and race. Instead of analyzing racial ideologies as a series of ideas that arrived from Spain and were transformed by the realities of colonial life, as important scholars in colonial studies have done, this chapter has taken a different approach to the history of the sistema de casta. It examined how culturally specific concepts of color were enlisted in a critical colonial scientific domain, and it analyzed the accommodation of Indigenous classification methods into racialized Spanish expressions.

This chapter's use of linguistic analysis and comparative literary study offers two ways of advancing our grasp of the relationship between Indigenous knowledges, colonial science, and racial thinking, but as the example of *oque* in Andean khipus suggests, there is more work to be done across the disciplines. The evidence presented here complements the methodological approaches used in earlier chapters: Part 1's combination of linguistic data, visual analysis, and study of folklore documents the influence and erasure of Taíno and African agencies in the gold industry of the Caribbean; Part 2's analysis of genre and print history reveals how medical writers like García d'Orta and Nicolás Monardes voiced diverse knowledge systems in their works—only for Orta's citations of subaltern ways of knowing to become lost in the linguistic and generic shift from a Portuguese-language dialogue to a Latin-language natural history; Part 3's attention to form and translation in colonial projections and their European revisions. The final chapter traces the long arc of colonial translations and mistranslations of amalgamation technologies. It begins by showing how colonial agents incorporated Indigenous ideas of ma-

52. The grafting of an essential timelessness onto Andean histories is a deeply troubling historiographic trend. See Ross W. Jamieson, "Colonialism, Social Archaeology and *Lo Andino:* Historical Archaeology in the Andes," *World Archaeology,* XXXVII (2005), 352–372.

terial similarity and difference into the new method of amalgamation, and it ends by analyzing eighteenth-century European representations of those methods. Scientific writers in Enlightenment Europe denied the epistemological sophistication of metallurgical techniques from Latin America, even as they admitted the practical efficacies of such methods. As they waxed poetic on the importance of experience, prestigious writers like Ignaz von Born defined "true" scientific knowledge in theoretical terms rather than observed applications. In this paradoxical process, their Enlightenment projects marginalized the contributions of non-European agents.

10 : THE COLONIAL SCIENCE OF LIKE AND UNLIKE

Colonial scientific writers like padre Álvaro Alonso Barba, mine overseer García de Llanos, and merchant Bartolomé de Medina did not just combine Indigenous ways of knowing with their own. They also synthesized received traditions of antiquity, often in ways that revealed the limits of classical knowledge and medieval Scholasticism in explaining sixteenth- and seventeenth-century technologies. In the Americas, as in Europe, refiners described the generation of metals and their (al)chemical reactions in the humoral language of Empedoclean root theory and Aristotelian natural philosophy, which classified matter as hot, dry, cold, and wet, corresponding in various degrees to the four roots of fire, air, earth, and water. According to the logic of antiquity, only "unlike" forces such as hot and cold, or male and female, could cause matter to change shape and come into being. Although natural philosophers like Empedocles, Plato, and Aristotle disagreed on many details about generation, they agreed that the union of similar bodies could lead to growth, but such unions were never generative. As Aristotle explains, "Everything that naturally comes to be is either an opposite or consists of opposites," and "everything changes from opposite to opposite." For example, a log set on fire was "coming into being" as fire took hold of something not on fire (wood) and caused it to change shape. In contrast, a log added to a fire enabled growth, because "like" matter increased that which was already in process (a fire).[1]

Scientific concepts of similarity, difference, and the causative spark of change circulated widely throughout early modern Europe, but writers working in different regions and language communities created their own expressive metaphors and analogies. Even when refiners in Germany, Italy, Spain, and Latin America used similar vocabularies and worked with technologies that were transferred throughout the Habsburg, Holy Roman, and Hispanic

1. Edward Grant, *A History of Natural Philosophy: From the Ancient World to the Nineteenth Century* (Cambridge, 2007), 27–51, 153–156; Ann Blair, "Natural Philosophy," in Katharine Park and Lorraine Daston, eds., *The Cambridge History of Science,* III (Cambridge, 2003), 365–406; M. R. Wright, *Empedocles: The Extant Fragments* (Indianapolis, 1995); Aristotle, *Physics,* trans. Robin Waterfield (New York, 1996), 1.5.188b21, 3.5.204b35; Aristotle, *On Generation and Corruption,* trans. H. H. Joachim, in William David Ross, ed., *The Works of Aristotle,* 12 vols. (Oxford, 1908), II, 1.5.322a15–16.

empires, the words that they used did not mean the same things. This chapter analyzes some of those terms—namely, concerning similarity ("friendship," "sympathy," "likeness," "love") and difference ("enmity," "antipathy," "unlikeness," "hatred")—to show how the combination of New World and Old World knowledges allowed for the development of colonial amalgamation technologies in the sixteenth and seventeenth centuries and how eighteenth-century writers reframed the definition of scientific knowledge to argue that amalgamation was a European invention. Studying those variations on a theme, and comparing them with models of the attraction of like to like and like to unlike as they were put into practice in the early Americas, reveals how Indigenous knowledges and hybrid colonial epistemologies shaped critical new metalworking technologies. I thus begin with European theories of likeness and attraction, then juxtapose them with evidence from colonial sources. I conclude by showing how Enlightenment-era writers in Europe, echoed by eighteenth-century authors in the Americas, used the language of colonial treatises to argue in word and image for the European origins of the technology. Like the rest of the book, this chapter charts a critical genealogy of the incorporation and erasure of Indigenous scientific knowledge in the colonial mining industry.

Like to Like

Refiners on both sides of the Atlantic Ocean recognized certain metals as friendly bodies, but they defined friendship in different terms, even when they cited the same authorities. Italian refiner Vannoccio Biringuccio, who had studied in central Germany and practiced his craft for many years as a munitions smelter for Pope Paul III, noted that cold, dry, silver (Ag) and hot, humid, lead (Pb) shared a naturally "friendly union" ("d'unione amichevole"). Contrary to writers who framed likeness as the source of friendship (like attracts like), Biringuccio posits opposition as the source of metallic sympathy ("simpasta con laltra") and equates it with the sort of complementary properties that could be applied in "secret" methods like amalgamation ("Et q̄sto tal secreto"). Biringuccio's recipe for amalgamation involved rubbing mercury with steel to activate its humid properties ("in humidendola cō aceto") before incorporating it with soliman ($HgCl_2$), green copper (Cu), and common salt (NaCl) in vats of partially processed gold (Au), silver (Ag), iron (Fe), or any other metallic substance recovered from a slag heap. The idea was to activate the oppositional energies that made silver and mercury different—dryness and moistness—rather than to play on their similarly cold roots. Biringuccio explained this small-scale, time-intensive process in emotionally neutral language: "Il mercurio pigli di sustātia cħ cōtēgano le materie, e al fine el mercurio cosi disposto cō staccio o lavādo si sepera dalla terrestrita, e cosi recuparae el uſo mercurio" (The mercury takes from the substance that the material contains, and in the end the mercury is so disposed that with a sieve or by washing it is separated from the earth, and so you recover your mercury).[2]

This nonaffective vocabulary was shared by miners in Germany who subscribed to similar alchemical principles. In 1574, Saxon metallurgist Lazarus Ercker described gold amalgamation in these terms: grind mercury finely until it had completely "taken" the precious metal "into itself" ("Reibkeuln so lang bis das Quecksilber alles Goldt an sich genommen hat") before drawing out mercury from the pressed gold. Nine years later, English translator John Pettus faithfully preserved this nonaffective lexicon: "Grind it well and so long, till the *Quick Silver* hath taken up all the *Gold*." Ercker and Pettus relied upon alchemical terms and materials like alembics, into which they added water to "draw the Quicksilver from the prest *Gold* in it" ("distilirn das Quecksilber darein"), rather than on Biringuccio's discourse of friendship and complementarity.[3]

Mineralogical writers throughout early modern Europe drew from alchemical discourse and analogical thinking. Authoritative tomes like German physician Georgius Agricola's Latin-language *De re metallica* (1556)—and translations of Agricola that were modified for different audiences, such as the Spanish-language work of alchemist Bernardo Pérez de Vargas, *De re metalica* (1569)—described refining methods in terms that resembled Biringuccio, Ercker, and Pettus. For example, Pérez de Vargas invoked the language of friendship and familiarity to explain how to separate mixtures of gold and silver using a variety of alchemical methods. Because of their "hermandad y parentesco" (brotherhood and parentage), most metals were mixed. Pérez de Vargas, translating Agricola's book 7 faithfully enough, unlike other passages of the text, explained that silver was naturally accompanied ("trae consigo") by gold and copper and that gold was naturally accompanied by silver, copper, and black lead. Even iron contained elements of silver, gold, black lead, and copper. To separate base and precious metals, readers were instructed to wash and grind them before mixing with reagents ("cosas que le ayuden"),

2. Vannoccio Biringuccio, *De la pirotechnia: Libri. X., dove ampiamente si tratta non solo di ogni sorte et díversita di Miníere, ma anchora quanto si rícerca intorno à la prattica dí quelle cose di quel che si appartiene a l'arte de la fusione over gitto de metalli come d'ogni altra cosa simile à questa* . . . (Venice, 1540), 14v, 22v, 142.

3. Lazarus Ercker, *Beschreibung: Aller Fürnemisten Mineralischen Ertzt unnd Berckwercks* . . . (Prague, 1574), 44v, 49v, 52; John Pettus, trans., *Fleta Minor; or, The Laws of Art and Nature in Knowing, Judging, Assaying, Fining, Refining, and Inlarging the Bodies of Confin'd Metals* . . . (London, 1683), 115, 122.

such as *almartaga* (lead oxide or litharge), *molibdeno* (molybdenum), and well-prepared iron tailings ("escoria de hierro bien preparado"). Finally, they were to heat the mixture in a refining oven, which would purify it of the lead and litharge and allow for gold and silver to be separated with *aqua fortis.* All of these mid-sixteenth-century texts, published after Bartolomé de Medina's amalgamation method was fully operational in Mexico, emphasized labor-intensive techniques that fomented the contrary energies of precious metals and reagents.[4]

In the mid-seventeenth century, nearly one hundred years after the American silver industry had transformed the global economy—in large part, thanks to scalable amalgamation methods—refiners in England continued to suggest that amalgamation was not worth the trouble, because natural philosophy taught that like could not change like. In his *Discovery of Subterraneall Treasure* (1639), Hartlib Circle correspondent Gabriel Plattes followed conventional European metallurgy, arguing that silver mixed with mercury would "forsake the Earthy and stony substance, and joyne it selfe with the Lead and Quick-silver by an attractive vertue," but "the quantity would not pay for halfe the charges and labour." In an elaborate enactment of the process, Plattes narrated the initial coming-into-being and final separation of silver and mercury in emotionally neutral verbs like "rise up" and "fall down": "Yellow silver I *amalgamed* againe with new quick-silver, and set it in gentle heat about a week, then in very strong heat for 6. houres; so that the *quick-silver* rose up, and fell downe again upon the silver; till such time as that it had carryed up all the silver from the bottome of the glasse into branches like trees." At least one reader agreed and marked the copy, now held at the British Library, "Probatum est." According to this logic, colonial amalgamation technologies were impossible, because, as Plattes put it, mercury was "the most friendly *mineral* to the *royall mettalls,"* and "by no meanes or Artifice whatsoever" could it "be fixed and coagulated into either of the Royal Mettalls." Like attracted like but left it unchanged.[5]

4. Bernardo Pérez de Vargas, *De remetalica: En el qual se tratan muchos y diversos secretos del conocimiento de toda suerte deminerales, de como se deven buscar ensayar y beneficiar, con otros secretos e industrias notables*... (Madrid, 1569), 95, 108v. Elsewhere, Pérez de Vargas intervenes with details about Iberian mining. Agricola's assertion that "wretched travelers are struck down by rapacious and cruel men born to theft, sacrilege, invasion, and robbery" here becomes "Otros desterramos con gran regozijo a las Indias, o alomenos con grandes esperanças" (52v). Compare with Georgius Agricola, *De re metallica* (1556), trans. Herbert Clark Hoover and Lou Henry Hoover (New York, 1950), 10.

5. Gabriel Plattes, *A Discovery of Subterraneall Treasure* . . . (London, 1639), 32, 37, 39,

By reconsidering the science of similarity, colonial refiners proved that generative sameness was not only possible but also profitable. European treatises, written in Italian, German, English, Latin, and Spanish, reveal important technical and discursive divergences in Atlantic world metallurgy. Pressing metals and mercury through cheesecloth-like fabrics and reducing the mixture on a stovetop involved different procedures and operational scales than colonial technologies that amalgamated silver with mercury in massive piles or thousand-pound vats suspended over open flames. In the Andes, novel linguistic expressions accompanied these new modes of metallurgical mixture. Like Biringuccio, Agricola, Pérez de Vargas (translating Agricola), Ercker, Pettus (translating Ercker), and Plattes, colonial writers drew from alchemical discourse, often invoking the language of friendship to explain metallic affinity and incorporation. Crucially, though, they described this "friendly union" in very different terms.

Instead of a precious metal that "takes up" mercury, metallurgists in Mexico and Peru explained amalgamation technologies with a discourse of love, embrace, and penetration. Physician Juan de Cárdenas argued in 1591 that sympathy and sameness were the enabling conditions of erotic desire: "Se aman, y apetecen la plata y el azogue, procurandose mediáte la dicha amistad abraçar, y unir el uno con el otro, esta amistad podemos conjeterar que procede de la grã similitud que estos dos minerales tienen, pues son tan semejantes que en color, en complession en pesso, y aparencia exterior, casi no se differencian" (Silver and mercury love and long for each other, procuring through the aforementioned friendship to embrace and unite, the one with the other; we can conjecture that this friendship proceeds from the great similitude that those two metals have, for they are so similar that in color, in complexion of weight, and exterior appearance they are hardly distinguished). Refiners added heat so that the mass of silver, metal, and mercury would "recozerse, abraçarse, y encorporarse" (unite, embrace, and incorporate): "para aver de abraçarse con la plata, y assi es que aquel metal, toma mas presto la ley, o se encorpora mas presto que le meten en estufas calientes, o esta en tierras calientes, o por alguna via goza de mas calor" (to embrace silver, and so it is that that metal

---

41. Compare this with Biringuccio's discussion of silver and lead mixtures and the amalgamation of gold and silver in *Pirotechnia,* 9–10v, 142; and Agricola, *De re metallica,* trans. Hoover and Hoover, 297–300, which includes a three-page footnote by the Hoovers on the history of amalgamation (note 12). They cite A. Dick's translation of book 11 of Biringuccio's *Pirotechnia,* rpt. in John Percy, *Metallurgy: The Art of Extracting Metals from Their Ores,* part 1 (London, 1880), 559–563. They conclude, as does Percy, that the technology was invented in Europe and imported to the New World by Spain.

more quickly comes to grade, or incorporates more quickly if it is put in a hot stove, or in a hot land, or if in some way it enjoys greater heat). This push and pull of likeness and unlikeness, or "grandissima amistad, y analogia" (great friendship and analogy) pitted against "terrible enemistad y odio" (terrible enmity and hatred), animated all of the cosmos, from the workings of planets in the heavens to the embrace of silver and mercury in Mexican refineries.[6]

Cárdenas then distinguished between the welcoming flame of mercury (Hg) and silver (Ag) and the spark of oppositional heat provided by other reagents, especially salt (NaCl). Mercury was the "friendly, familiar" agent ("es tan amigo, y familiar ala plata") whose analogical friendship enabled the act of metallic incorporation: "Mediante la tal amistad, y analogia le abraçe, y atrayga, para que abraçado lo uno con lo otro" (Through the aforesaid friendship and analogy it embraces it, and attracts it, so that the one will be embraced with the other). In contrast, salt was added, "no para q̄ se abraçe con nadie, sino para que como material caliēte sirva de dar calor, y actuar el azogue, y otrosi ayudar a recozer, fermētar, y esponjar todo aq̄l metal, porq̄ mejor le pueda penetrar el azogue, y abraçarse cō la plata" (not to embrace with anyone, but rather so that, as a hot material, it serves to give heat and actuate the mercury, and similarly help to collect, ferment, and spunge all of that metal, so that mercury can better penetrate and embrace silver). Unlike Biringuccio, Cárdenas does not downplay the attractive properties of friendship or familiarity that silver and mercury shared. His theory of mixture depends precisely on the attraction and loving embrace of like to like (silver and mercury), as well as a penetrative embrace of like to unlike (amalgams and salt).[7]

These scientific theories of similarity and difference also informed ideas on human social relationships. As Aristotle argued in *Politics,* the text used by Juan Ginés de Sepúlveda to justify the subordination of Indigenous people to the *encomienda* system, only "those which are incapable of existing without each other must unite as a pair." Opposites, such as male and female, or master and slave, form unions based on necessity, lack, and privation. Women and men join "for breeding (and this is not from choice; rather, as in the other animals too and in plants, the urge to leave behind another such as one is oneself

6. Juan de Cárdenas, *Problemas y secretos maravillosos de las Indias* (1591) (Valladolid, 2003), 87, 88–88v, 89–89v. I thank Fred Anderson for suggesting "love and long for" as an alliterative translation of "se aman y apetecen." See Psalms 107:9 and Philippians 1:8, KJV. Biringuccio admired mercury's penetrative qualities ("per virtu dela sua sottigliezza potente a penetrare in tutte le cose"), but he avoided these kinds of erotic explanations (Biringuccio, *De la pirotechnia,* [22v]).

7. Cárdenas, *Problemas y secretos maravillosos,* 88v.

is natural)," whereas master and slave are bound "for preservation." Despite differences between "that which naturally rules and that which is ruled," Aristotle affirms, "master and slave benefit from the same thing."[8]

Although Aristotle does not use the term "friendship" to describe this bond in the *Politics,* he returns to the topic of master, slave, and friendship in book 8 of the *Ethics,* where he argues that master and slave can be friends, depending on context and definition. When a slave is understood as a thing that benefits the master's estate, akin to the relationship "between craftsman and tool, soul and body," master and slave share no friendship, for "there is nothing common to the two parties: the slave is a living tool and the tool a lifeless slave. Qua slave then, one cannot be friends with him." However, friendly relations were possible when servitude and similarity were redefined in friendships of pleasure ("convenience") or commerce, which involved exchanges of commodities (quid pro quo) or gifts ("moral exchange"). As unlikes were drawn into "justice," revised definitions of friendship allowed for a reconsideration of the rule of sameness. When both parties agree to the terms of their union, they find a kind of justice and, thus, a kind of friendship. An enslaved man can befriend his master "in so far as he is a man, for there seems to be some justice between any man and any other who can share in a system of law or be party to an agreement." That second part is crucial. Friendship is possible only inasmuch as the enslaved man agrees to the master's codes; if he agrees to be a slave, then the master agrees to treat him as a friend.[9]

If master and slave could not be one soul shared in two bodies, they did still have bodily closeness, for "the slave is a sort of part of his master like a sort of living but detached part of his body." The slave's unsuitability for freedom was written on his body—"strong enough to be used for essentials," unlike the master who was "useless for that kind of work, but fit for the life of a citizen"—and yet the flexible doctrine of friendship allowed for the most embodied of differences to become shared points of affiliation. In other words, analogical thinking enabled that which was different to also be considered as similar. The same doctrinal flexibility categorized natural philosophical explanations of material change, such as the generation of tissue with proper nourishment. Aristotle saw two ways of categorizing human development: on the one hand, food was

8. Aristotle, *Politics: Books I and II,* ed. Trevor J. Saunders (Oxford, 1995), 1252a26–31, 1252a34.

9. Aristotle, *Ethica Nicomachea,* ed. W[illiam] D[avid] Ross (London, 1931), 1161a–1161b. On the role of artisan labor in shaping ideas of matter and material transformation in master-slave relationships, see Orlando Bentancor, *The Matter of Empire: Metaphysics and Mining in Colonial Peru* (Pittsburgh, 2017).

unlike tissue and thus could be understood as like-to-unlike; on the other, the food was transformed into flesh and thus could be understood as like to like. Such was the conceptual flexibility of analogical thinking: one process could be understood in entirely different ways.[10]

Colonial writers who analogized metals to humans and created "castas de metales" used the flexibility of analogical thinking to define similarity and difference. Writing in the mid-1630s, Álvaro Alonso Barba insisted that the "friendship" of silver and mercury allowed them to generate new amalgams *(pella)*. For Barba, metallic closeness ("vezindad") and convenience ("conveniencia") were revealed "por la facilidad cō que con ellos se une, los penetra, y embeve, convietiendolos en la que llamamos pella" (by the facility with which mercury unites, penetrates, and drinks in the silver metals, converting them into what we call *pella*). If friendship and similarity were the catalytic conditions of conversion, the amalgam's coming into body was made possible by the nature of mercury itself: "Estando el açogue en su naturaleza siempre, quanto es de su parte està dispuesto para abraçar la plata, y unirse con ella" (When the time comes, mercury, always being true to its nature, will be disposed to embrace the silver and unite with it). The mutual appeal and natural appetite of two agreeable bodies allowed for the productive extraction and purification of silver metals.[11]

Affective enactments of cosmological change and metallic conversion were conventional terms of early modern natural philosophy, and they allowed writers in Latin America to situate themselves within a learned audience of global scientific thinkers. In contrast to their peers in Europe, Barba and Cárdenas transmuted the love of likeness into that of generative embrace and desire. In making sameness a source of material change, colonial writers and refiners distinguished their methods of amalgamation from the theories and practices of the Old World.

Like to Unlike

The logic of antiquity, as it was recuperated in medieval and Renaissance science, emphasized the productive yoking together of opposites. Agricultural writers from Saʿd ibn Aḥmad Ibn Luyūn al-Tujībī in Andalusia to Walter Blith in England depended upon the "warring strife" of contrary soils and seeds

10. Aristotle, *Politics,* 1254b27–30, 1255b10–13; Aristotle, *De generatione et corruptione,* trans. Harold H. Joachim, in W. D. Ross, *The Works of Aristotle Translated into English,* II (Oxford, 1922), 321b32–322a4.

11. Alvaro Alonso Barba, *Arte de los metales en que se enseña el verdadero beneficio de los de oro, y plata por açogue . . .* (Madrid, 1640), 65–65v.

to sustain life on earth. As Ibn Luyūn explained, "Los contrarios remedian el daño de los contrarios: el calor destruye los trastornos del frío y el frío destruye los trastornos del calor. Hay que ingeniárselas y aprender a corregir cada caso: la tierra con el riego se enfría y se calienta con el laboreo y el estercuelo. Hágase así" (Contraries remedy the damages of contraries: heat destroys the imbalances of cold and cold destroys the imbalances of heat. You must engineer them and learn to correct each case: irrigated soil becomes cold and must be revived with labor and dunging. Do it like so). Blith outlined a similar remedy "for whatever causeth Barrennesse," instructing farmers "to provide a Soyle that will stand in constant opposition to it, and so though one waste another, and both are weakned, yet the Earth is thereby bettered."[12]

In classical natural philosophy and alchemical traditions of the medieval Middle East and Latin West, plant, human, and metallic matter is animated by the interplay of likeness and unlikeness. When Empedocles observed that the forces of Love and Strife motivated human actions, he formulated micro- and macrocosmic analogies to suggest that these forces governed the world. The animate plants, animals, minerals, and oceans of the sublunar realm, and the stars, planets, and constellations of the heavens, were composed of the same four primary elements, albeit in different proportions of water, earth, air, and fire. They followed the same rules of push and pull of like and unlike bodies. Aristotle, for his part, argued that there were only two or three roots, because fire, air, and water were already made of composite elements. The philosopher considered these elements in successive, rather than oppositional, terms, consistent with his idea "that every place admits of the distinction between above and below": earth, the first layer of our planet, was cold and dry. It was surrounded by a sphere of cold, humid water, which was encased within a world of humid, hot air. A ring of fire, which was hot and dry, surrounded the world.[13]

Natural philosophers generally agreed that like attracted like and unlike repelled unlike. According to Empedocles, under the auspices of Love, contrary elements were drawn together in a generative union that would be ultimately undone by Strife, a divisive force that tore opposites apart and sent each element to take comfort in its own likeness. These cyclical flows created a delicate cosmic equilibrium: the contrariety of Love and Strife balanced each other to

12. [Sa'd ibn Aḥmad Ibn Luyūn al-Tujībī], *Ibn Luyūn: Tratado de agricultura,* ed. Joaquina Eguaras Ibáñez (Granada, 1988), 200; Walter Blith, *The English Improver; or, A New Survey of Husbandry: Discovering to the Kingdome . . .* (London, 1649), 110.

13. Wright, *Empedocles;* Peter Kingsley, *Ancient Philosophy, Mystery, and Magic: Empedocles and Pythagorean Tradition* (Oxford, 1995); Aristotle, *Physics,* trans. Waterfield, 1.6,189b1–8; 4.4.211a4–5.

ensure the continuation of life, a process of generation and coming together that was complemented and completed by an ensuing separation, or tearing asunder. Aristotle thought it was silly to ascribe these changes to emotions, because "Love does not combine hatred and make something from it, and hatred does not act on love in an equivalent fashion either." Rather, "Both of them act on some third thing." Aristotle believed that this underlying thing was matter itself: *"Something* underlying substances, something for them to come from." As a statue was sculpted from gold or a person became educated, they were, in a sense, activated by oppositional forces, because such forces drove them to change from one form or condition into another. For Aristotle, unlike Empedocles, "opposite" meant "what is uneducated" or suffered "shapelessness, formlessness, and disorder." The things underlying these material transformations were, respectively, gold metals and a human being, "one in number, but two in form."[14]

In this way, Aristotle responds to the ideas of his teacher, Plato, regarding matter, form and generation. In the Platonic tradition, matter without form was a feminine, maternal *chora*—a shapeless receptacle that was not air, fire, nor water—which necessarily sought something to fill its eternally empty space. The union of matter to form was made possible by desire and difference, the moment when some men, "their next incarnation," became women and the gods begat "sexual desire" by animating male and female bodies, from the lungs, kidneys, and bladder to marrow and "seed," in different ways. In the seventeenth century, neoplatonic accounts of women, men, and desire born of difference were staged by playwrights like Lope de Vega, for whom only "la diferencia causa novedad y despierta el deseo" (difference causes novelty and awakens desire). As these examples suggest, early modern authors did not inherit a singular or stable tradition from antiquity, as natural philosophical writers offered different explanations of generation and decay in sub- and supralunar realms.[15]

Sameness bound bodies into being; difference made them productive. In

14. Wright, *Empedocles;* Kingsley, *Ancient Philosophy;* Harold J. Cook, "Medicine," in Park and Daston, eds., *Early Modern Science,* 407–434; Aristotle, *Physics,* trans. Waterfield, 1.6.189a5, 1.6a20–27, 1.7.b10–16, 1.7.b23–24.

15. Plato, *Timaeus and Critias,* trans. Robin Waterfield (Oxford, 2008), 50d–51a, 91a–91b; Lope de Vega, *La Dorotea,* ed. and trans. Alan S. Trueblood and Edwin Honig (Cambridge, Mass., 1985), 1.3. On early modern translations of this passage, see Prudence Allen, *The Concept of Woman: The Early Humanist Reformation, 1250-1500,* part 2 (Grand Rapids, Mich., 2002), 868–869. For Aristotle's gloss of Plato's concepts, see *Physics,* ed. Waterfield, 1.6.189b1 15.

this way, classical natural philosophers distinguished friendly, homosocial love from generative, heterosexual love. In the formative terms of Cicero's *De amicitia* (44 BCE), perhaps the preeminent friendship treatise in antiquity to find its way into movable type, "Ther is nothyng that draweth ony thyng unto it / ne that holdeth it faster / than lyklynes draweth friendship," for "ther is nothyng more desyrous of his lyke and semblable." The pronoun "his" is decisive, as Cicero famously defined "Sely Wymmen" and "they that were wretchid" as not "apte to friendship," because their great want forced them to seek friendship from a position of need, not of will. Early moderns like Michel de Montaigne made this definition more explicit, defining the flame of heterosexual love as "more active, more scorching, and more intense" than its homosocial equivalent. "But it is an impetuous and fickle flame, undulating and variable, a fever flame, subject to fits and lulls, that holds us only by one corner" and thus unlike the friendly flame that gave off "general and universal warmth, moderate and even," of "all gentleness and smoothness, with nothing bitter and stinging about it." As Montaigne channeled Ciceronian terms of stable selfhood, he blamed the "fickle" and "fever[ish]" nature of heterosexual love on women, concluding, "The ordinary capacity of women is inadequate for that communion and fellowship which is the nurse of this sacred bond; nor does their soul seem firm enough to endure the strain of so tight and durable a knot."[16]

In contrast to these orthodox—if debated—understandings of similarity, difference, and material change, the colonial method of amalgamation fashioned sameness into a source of productive desire. As they referenced the same authorities as their peers in Europe, refiners in Latin America argued that similarity ("analogia," "amistad," "conveniencia") catalyzed metallic penetration and conversion. Writers like Barba and Cárdenas extended to chemically related matter a new explanatory potential for the logic of mixture; amid racial and ethnic mixing in colonial society, scientific writers who described New World methods of amalgamation made sameness, not difference, into a source of generation.

This new way of thinking was central to the success of the industrial-scale technology, but the redefinition of like and unlike was lost in translation. English translator Edward Montagu, for one, did not recognize the sophisticated epistemological work of the colonial language of desire; nor did Johann Lange, who worked from Montagu's translation rather than Barba's book. Throughout their translations of Barba's *Arte de los metales,* Montagu and Lange ren-

16. Marcus Tullius Cicero, *De amicitia* ([London], 1481), 85, 97; Michel de Montaigne, *The Complete Works: Essays, Travel Journal, Letters,* trans. Donald M. Frame (New York, 2003), 167.

dered the term "abrazar" (embrace)—"que el açogue abrace," "para que mejor abrace," "el açogue abraçará la plata"—into nonaffective phrases like "lay hold on," "that it may the better take hold of," and "the better lay hold of." When Barba uses "unirse" (to unite), "recoger" (to collect), and "abraça" (to embrace) in three successive lines, Montagu and Lange translate the sequence as "to unite itself," "be gotten together," and "be collected together."[17]

As we have seen, when Montagu and Lange mistranslate "conchos" as "Oyster shells" and "Auster-Schalen" (Chapter 8, above) and "Negrillos" as "black Oar" and "schwartz Erze" (Chapter 9), they fail to see the New World roots of these technical terms. In a similar way, they do not realize how the erotic expression "abrazar" indexes a new way of thinking about the nature of similarity—one that departs notably from established European traditions. The word is Spanish, but the logic is not; it reflects syncretic technologies and epistemes from the colonial Americas. In defaulting to the conceptually available, emotionally neutral verbs of alchemists like Ercker and Plattes, and disregarding the ways in which an erotic union of friendly matter rewrote those scientific conventions, Barba's translators misunderstood the theoretical underpinnings of colonial amalgamation and mistranslated the epistemological sophistication of the technology. Their language suggests that the procedures described in the treatise, the knowledge of which their readers were eager to acquire, were theoretically impossible and unprofitable to practice.

Eighteenth-Century Iterations of Like and Unlike

If it seems a curious intellectual feat for late-seventeenth-century writers to deny, based on theoretical grounds, the viability of a technology that had promoted global economic trade since the mid-sixteenth century, it is even more surprising that such writers were joined by eighteenth-century authors. But that is precisely what happened when, in 1786, Baron Ignatius von Born, director of the prestigious Natural History Museum of Vienna, published a 227-page treatise on the amalgamation of precious metals. In 1781, following the death of Austrian sovereign Maria Theresa, Holy Roman Emperor Joseph II began to reform the censorship laws that had isolated Habsburg subjects from the larger world of Enlightenment letters. In this new environment of scientific

17. Barba, *Arte de los metales,* [42v], [46v], 50, 53; Barba, *The Art of Metals, in Which Is Declared the Manner of Their Generation and the Concomitants of Them: In Two Books . . . ,* trans. [Edward] Montagu (London, 1674), II, 23, 39, 56, 68; J[ohann] L[ange], trans., *Albaro Alonso Barba, Eines Spanischen Briesers und hocherfahrnen Naturkündigers Berg-Büchlein: Darinnen Von der Metallen und Mineralien Generalia und Ursprung . . .* (Hamburg, 1676), 147, 158, 171, 181–182.

openness, Baron von Born printed a German-language edition of a book that vowed to go "beyond" its intellectual predecessors, the *Ueber das Anquicken der gold und silberhältigen Erze* (1786). Two years later, he translated it into French and dedicated his *Methode d'extraire les métaux parfaits des minérails* (1788) to Spanish monarch Carlos III. In 1791, Rudolf Erich Raspe, a German scientist who fled to England to avoid charges of theft, translated Born's work into English and published it in London as *Baron Inigo Born's New Process of Amalgamation of Gold and Silver Ores.*[18]

According to Born, Spanish practitioners had relied primarily on chance, rather than science, to produce wealth rather than knowledge. He did not deny that the methods worked. In a footnote omitted from the French translation but included in Raspe's English-language text, Born described using Barba's method to extract two-thirds of the silver-bearing ores from Zinnopel (Hungary) and process 16 percent more silver than he did with traditional techniques. However, this practical effectiveness was not the same as real scientific value or true scientific language. In contrast to colonial languages of friendship and metallurgies of desire, Born described his theories of amalgamation using terms like "Verwandtschaft" (affinité [elective affinities]), to describe a process of purification in which chemical similarity allowed for the separation of mixed metals and other mechanical applications.[19]

Born's book consisted of two parts. The first narrated the history of amalgamation in the Americas, drawn from nearly seventy pages of Spanish colonial reports on mining and metallurgy. The second presented the author's own theories and scientific explanations, concluding with twenty-one highly tech-

18. Ignaz Edlen von Born, *Ueber das Anquicken der gold und silberhältigen Erze, Rohsteine, Schwarzkupfer und Hüttenspeise* (Vienna, 1786); Ignace de Born, *Methode d'extraire les métaux parfaits des minérails et autres substances métalliques par le mercure* (Vienna, 1788); R[udolf] E[rich] Raspe, trans., *Baron Inigo Born's New Process of Amalgamation of Gold and Silver Ores, and Other Metallic Mixtures...* (London, 1791). On the Austrian Habsburgs, see R. J. W. Evans, "The Origins of Enlightenment in the Habsburg Lands," *Austria, Hungary, and the Habsburgs: Essays on Central Europe, c. 1683–1867* (Oxford, 2006), 36–55; Derek Beales, *Enlightenment and Reform in Eighteenth-Century Europe* (London, 2005), 214–223. In the Americas, Bourbon reforms led to remapping underground mines and restructuring silver production systems. See Heidi V. Scott, "Taking the Enlightenment Underground: Mining Spaces and Cartographic Representation in the Late Colonial Andes," *Journal of Latin American Geography,* XIV (2015), 7–34; and John J. TePaske, *A New World of Gold and Silver,* ed. Kendall W. Brown (Leiden, 2010), 219–233.

19. Born, *Ueber das Anquicken der gold und silberhältigen Erze,* [1], 10, 84; Born, *Methode d'extraire les métaux parfaits des minérais,* [1], 10–11, 84–85; Raspe, trans., *Baron Inigo Born's New Process of Amalgamation of Gold and Silver Ores,* 1, 8, 71.

nical drawings of mechanized wash vats, stamp mills, and sorting devices—all labeled, drawn to scale, and engraved on copper plates, allowing for greater detail and attention to perspective than any of Barba's twelve pages of woodcuts or tables of mathematical correlations.[20]

The first part of the *Ueber das Anquicken der gold und silberhältigen Erze* concludes by inviting readers to compare the unstandardized practices and inconsistent methods of Latin American refiners with Born's own procedures and protocols. In a lengthy passage that Born footnotes differently in his German- and French-language texts, he affirms:

> Wie unzureichend aber die hier angeführten Anquickungsarten seyen, wie wenig dadurch der ganze Gold- und Silbergehalt ausgebracht werden könne, was für eine übergrosse Menge Silbers in den ang quickten Schlichen jährlich zurückbleibe, wie unnütz die Zusätze von Pferdemist, Weinstein, gerulverten Hörnern, wie unsicher die ausgegebenen Hilfsmittel zur Verminderung des Quecksilberabganges, und wie unbestimmt die Kennzeichen von dem guten oder schlechten Fortgang der Anquickung seyen, davon kann sich ein jeder selbst überzeugen, der solche nachmachen, und dann die rückständigen Schliche mit der gehörigen Genauigkeit untersuchen will (*). Endlich mag der Leser das Verfahren der Spanier mit demjenigen, welches ich im folgenden Abschnitte angebe, vergleichen, und dann selbst entscheiden, ob

20. Barba, *Arte de los metales,* 57v, 62, 64, 73, 76, 78v, 80v, 82, 84, 98, 100, 108v. Tables with metallic proportions appear on 83 and 110. Born cited the following authors and editions (pagination follows the German-language text): Córdoba, manuscript evidence from 1588 and the replies of Lazarus Ercker from February-March of the same year (14–21); Joseph Acosta, *Histoire naturelle et morale des Indes . . . ,* trans. Robert Regnault Cauxois (Paris, 1598); Acosta, *Historia natural y moral de las Indias . . .* (Seville, 1590), 21–24; Barba, *Arte de los metales,* 25–50; M. Frezier, *Relation du voyage de la Mer du Sud aux Cotes du Chili, du Perou et du Bresil: Fait pendant les années 1712, 1713, et 1714* (Amsterdam, 1717), 50–54; P. Wolfgang Bayer, *Reiz naar Peru* (Nuremberg, 1776), 54–55; Francisco Xavier Gamboa, *Comentarios a las ordenanzas de Minas* (Madrid, 1761), 56–67 (including sections marked as glosses from Barba, 62–63); Lorenzo Felipe de la Torre Barrio y Lima, *Arte ó cartilla del nuevo beneficio de la plata en todo genero de metales frios, y calientes . . .* (Lima, 1738), 68–70; Juan Ordoñez Montalvo, *Arte o nuevo modo de beneficiar los metales de oro y plata, y de plata con ley de oro, por azogue . . .* (Mexico City, 1758), 71–73; Antonio de Ulloa, *Noticias americanas: Entretenimientos phisicos-historicos, sobre la América meridional, y la septentrianal oriental . . .* (Madrid, 1772), 73–78; Guillaume Bowles, *Introduction à l'histoire naturelle et à la géographie physique de l'Espagne,* trans. [Gratien Jean Baptiste Louis] de Flavigny (Paris, 1776), 79–80; Giovanni Ignazio Molina, *Saggio sulla storia civile del Chili del signor abate Giovanni Ignazio Molina* (Bologna, 1787), 81–85.

> meine Anquickungsmethode wirklich nichts weiter als der spanische Amalgamazions-Prozeß seye (**).
>
> Cependant en se donnant la peine d'essayer ces diverses méthodes et d'en examiner les residus avec les précautions nécessaires, on peut se convaincre aisément à quel point elles sont toutes insuffisantes pour opérer l'extraction complette des métaux parfaits contenus dans les minérais, que bien au contraire il en doit rester une portion très-considérable dans la farine minérale, traitée par ces méthodes (*), que rien n'est plus inutile que les doses de siente de chevaux, de créme de tartre, de cornes pulvérisées etc. qu'on y prescrit comme autant d'ingrédiens nécessaires, et que les remèdes qu'on y recommande pour diminuer les pertes en mercure sont d'un effet aussi équivoque, que les indices qu'on y donne sur le bon ou mauvais succès de l'opération sont vagues et incertains. Enfin le lecteur pourra jugar en comparant ces méthodes Espagnoles avec celle qu'il trouvera détaillée dans la seconde partie de cet ouvrage, si cette dernière n'est autre chose qu'unne simple imitation des premières.

The English-language translator, working from the original Germanic volume, follows the footnotes of Born's 1786 edition. Raspe writes,

> However, that the above methods are insufficient, and that the accounts we have of them are unsatisfactory; that the full gold and silver produce cannot be obtained by any one of them; that a great quantity of silver must every year remain in the leavings; that the addition of dung, tartar, and pulverized horn, is absolutely useless; that the methods recommended as effectual for preventing the loss of quicksilver are very unsafe; and that the pretended symptoms of the good or bad success of the amalgamation are very fallacious: all that will and must plainly appear to any person who will be at the trouble of repeating these processes, and assay the leavings *. The reader is now enabled to compare these different Spanish methods with the process of amalgamation which will be described in the following section, and to determine upon their respective merits, differences, and advantages †.[21]

This passage marks a critical transition from book 1 to book 2. It positions Born as a singular scientist who was capable of translating imprecise colonial knowledge into sound technical practices and correcting the beliefs of impor-

21. Born, *Ueber das Anquicken der gold und silberhältigen Erze,* 83–84; Born, *Methode d'extraire les métaux parfaits des minérais,* 84–85; Raspe, trans., *Baron Inigo Born's New Process of Amalgamation of Gold and Silver Ores,* 70–71.

tant thinkers in Europe. Even when presented with evidence of the effectiveness of large-scale amalgamation methods, Europe's leading lights, including Johann Andrea Cramers, Dr. Johan Gottschalk Wallerius, and Christlieb Ehregott Gellert, who published widely in Stockholm, Uppsala, and Leipzig, provided alternative explanations of the technology, suggesting that these methods worked only on native gold and silver. Such voices generally declared, in an exchange that Born did not translate into French: "'S ist ja eine alte Sache!—der leidige spanische Amalgamazios-Prozeß!" As Raspe put it, *"There is nothing new in it! It is but the old Spanish process of amalgamation!"* Throughout book 1, Born doubted colonial Latin American technologies, and his contemporaries treated his work skeptically. Book 2 promised to tell a different story, with a favorable scientific reception.[22]

Raspe, working in English, and Born, translating his own work into French, handled these intellectual exchanges in different ways, but they dealt similarly with the picture that accompanied the last page of book 1. Neither translation reproduced the image that paired Baron von Born's dismissive reading of Spanish amalgamation technologies with a square frame of two partially clothed, deeply shaded men who dug for metals in the foreground (Figure 16). Behind them, to the viewer's left, were two smaller figures who ground metals at a *trapiche,* a simple but effective mill made of two stone slabs. One stone was planted on the ground with a hole drilled through its center to allow for a post; the other stone was affixed to the post and rotated around the base slab by animal or human power. Both teams were visually enclosed by two houses on the left, one shuttered and the other thatch-roofed; on the right, ample palm trees bent in the breeze. In contrast, both the French- and English-language translations reproduced all of Born's twenty-one technical plates of refining furnaces, stamping devices, stirrers, and boilers, creating a visual register that emphasized mechanized refining technologies and novel devices rather than the embodied labor of black and brown miners in the Americas. The images of the Anglophone edition, translated by a third party, and the Francophone volume, translated by the author, thus told a different visual story about colonial Latin American mining than the one that German readers encountered. However, the dismissal of Latin American technologies in prose remained consistent across the editions.

The tropical Potosí imagined in Born's first book was a far cry from reality of the *altiplano,* but in eighteenth-century Europe, this was the image of Latin

22. Born, *Ueber das Anquicken der gold und silberhältigen Erze,* 6–7, 85; Born, *Methode d'extraire les métaux parfaits des minérais,* 7; Raspe, trans., *Baron Inigo Born's New Process of Amalgamation of Gold and Silver Ores,* 5, 71.

FIGURE 16. Representation of American mining. In Ignaz Edlen von Born, *Ueber das Anquicken der gold und silberhältigen Erze, Rohsteine, Schwarzkupfer und Hüttenspeise* (Vienna, 1786), 85. Courtesy of the John Carter Brown Library at Brown University, JCB 1-SIZE J786.B736u

American mining: rudimentary, remote, and racialized. In his English-language "Address to the Subscribers," Raspe endorsed the Spanish court's educating its South American mine inspectors in Saxony so that they could learn the new method of amalgamation and, with a team of German and Swedish experts, "introduce it in Mexico and Peru." Although Born drew largely from Barba and his contemporaries, his language, institutional position, and publication record convinced readers that large-scale amalgamation methods originated in Europe. Baron von Born made important contributions to refining technologies, but he did not invent them. Historian Tristan Platt argues that Born simply—and effectively—"reinvented American techniques within a German theoretico-practical discourse." In other words, by carefully controlling the visual representations and vocabularies in which he presented his theory of amalgamation, and framing his experiments with appeals to eighteenth-century definitions of empiricism and mechanization, Born made a convincing argument for his own scientific accomplishments and marginalized the contributions of Indigenous and colonial miners in the Americas.[23]

The irony of Born's "empiricism" is that it depended upon denying scientific evidence and sources of Amerindian metallurgical knowledge—even when such knowledges appeared in European sources that Born imitated, such as the encyclopedia of French natural philosopher Denis Diderot. Consider Born's 21 technical drawings, which use fine degrees of shading, precise scales, and comparative top views and cross-sections to show the inner workings of metallurgical devices. Some of these devices combined mechanization with traditional refining practices, such as a cart for installing a boiler and a pressing bag ("Der zur Ab- und Zufuhr der gefüllten Kessel dienende Wagen") (Figure 17). The pressing technique resembles the cheesecloth method that Biringuccio described in 1540, but the boilers were now powered by engines ("Der Sudofen im Kerutzprofil") (Figure 18). This visual language is reminiscent of Diderot's mechanized displays of technical instruments, such as his use of cross-perspective and top-down views to show an elaborate reverberatory furnace for refining copper (Figure 19) ("Métallurgie, travail du cuivre"). Over time, Diderot's *Encyclopedia* included supporting volumes that were

23. Raspe, trans., *Baron Inigo Born's New Process of Amalgamation of Gold and Silver Ores,* xi–xii; Tristan Platt, "The Alchemy of Modernity: Alonso Barba's Copper Cauldrons and the Independence of Bolivian Metallurgy (1790–1890)," *Journal of Latin American Studies,* XXXII (2000), 1–53, esp. 3. Platt compares methods of "hot" and "cold" processing in Mexico, the Andes, and Europe, documenting how Bourbon reformers like José de Gálvez, serving in Mexico, changed their beliefs about metallurgical sciences to reflect "opinions current in Central Europe" (34). In contrast, mineralogical writers in late-eighteenth- and early-nineteenth-century Bolivia eagerly cited and reprinted Barba's influential treatise. Although they were interested in some of the technical components of the *Arte de los metales,* such as the use of copper boilers to reduce mercury consumption, they were especially drawn to the political potential of enlisting "a still-buoyant American scientific tradition" that formed "part of a protectionist national project for the new Republic" (48). Like Platt, this chapter studies Enlightenment interpretations of colonial scientific ideas, although I focus on the role of Indigenous knowledges, rather than creole patriotism, in those transatlantic genealogies.

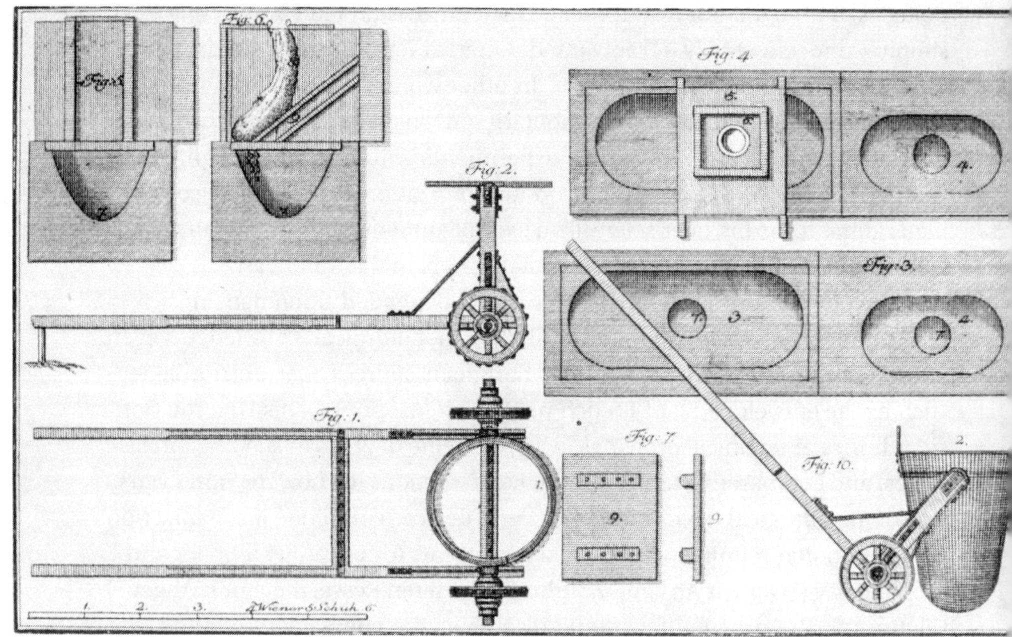

FIGURE 17. "Der zur Ab- und Zufuhr der gefüllten Kessel dienende Wagen, und der Preßkasten." In Ignaz Edlen von Born, *Ueber das Anquicken der gold und silberhältigen Erze, Rohsteine, Schwarzkupfer und Hüttenspeise* (Vienna, 1786), plate XVII. Courtesy of the John Carter Brown Library at Brown University, JCB 1-SIZE J786.B736u

filled with detailed plates of animal, botanical, and mineral life, as well as mining and refining instruments, published as *Recueil de planches, sur les sciences, les arts libéraux, et les arts méchaniques, avec leur explication.* The sixth volume of the series, which includes 294 plates, depicts ovens for different kinds of metalwork, such as copper *(cuivre)*, lead *(plomb)*, tin *(étain)*, zinc *(zinc)*, alum *(alun)*, and different varieties of iron *(fer)*, including white iron *(fer blanc)*.[24]

Unlike Born's illustrations, Diderot's artwork includes refining ovens from various world regions, including Indigenous metallurgical technologies from the Andes. Barba, in his fourth book, depicts two Indigenous Andean ovens:

24. [Denis Diderot], *Recueil de planches, sur les sciences, les arts libéraux, et les arts méchaniques, avec leur explication,* ed. Jean Le Rond d'Alembert and Pierre Mouchon, 12 vols., VI (Paris, 1762), n.p. Diderot described these printing techniques as part of his study of "mechanical arts." See "Printing from Copper Plates," in I. M. L. Donaldson, trans., *The Encyclopedia of Diderot and d'Alembert Collaborative Translation Project* (Ann Arbor, Mich., 2010), http://hdl.handle.net/2027/spo.did2222.0001.128; Diderot and Alembert, eds., *Encyclopédie; ou, Dictionnaire raisonné des sciences, des arts et des métiers, par une société de gens de lettres,* VIII (Paris, 1765), s.v. "Imprimerie en taille douce."

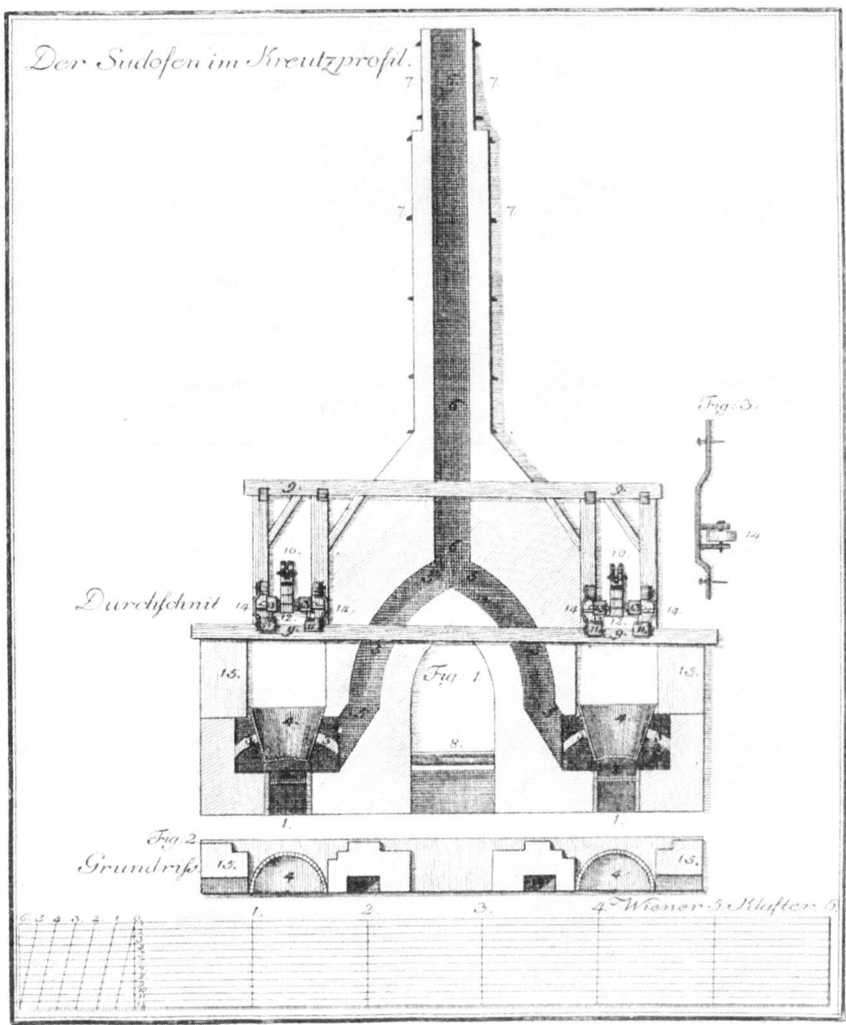

FIGURE 18. "Der Sudofen im Kreutzprofil." In Ignaz Edlen von Born, *Ueber das Anquicken der gold und silberhältigen Erze, Rohsteine, Schwarzkupfer und Hüttenspeise* (Vienna, 1786), plate XIII. Courtesy of the John Carter Brown Library at Brown University, JCB 1-SIZE J786.B736u

a *guaira* ("guaira de los Indios"), a wind oven used to separate lead (Pb) from other elements, creating a flux to process silver in later rounds of processing, and a *tocochimbo,* a refining hearth located within the homes of Andean refiners. Although Barba does not label tocochimbos as an Indigenous technology, archaeological evidence suggests Indigenous Andean origins for the oven. However, because intimate domestic spaces were not accessible to Spanish outsiders, we know less about tocochimbo technologies than we do of the

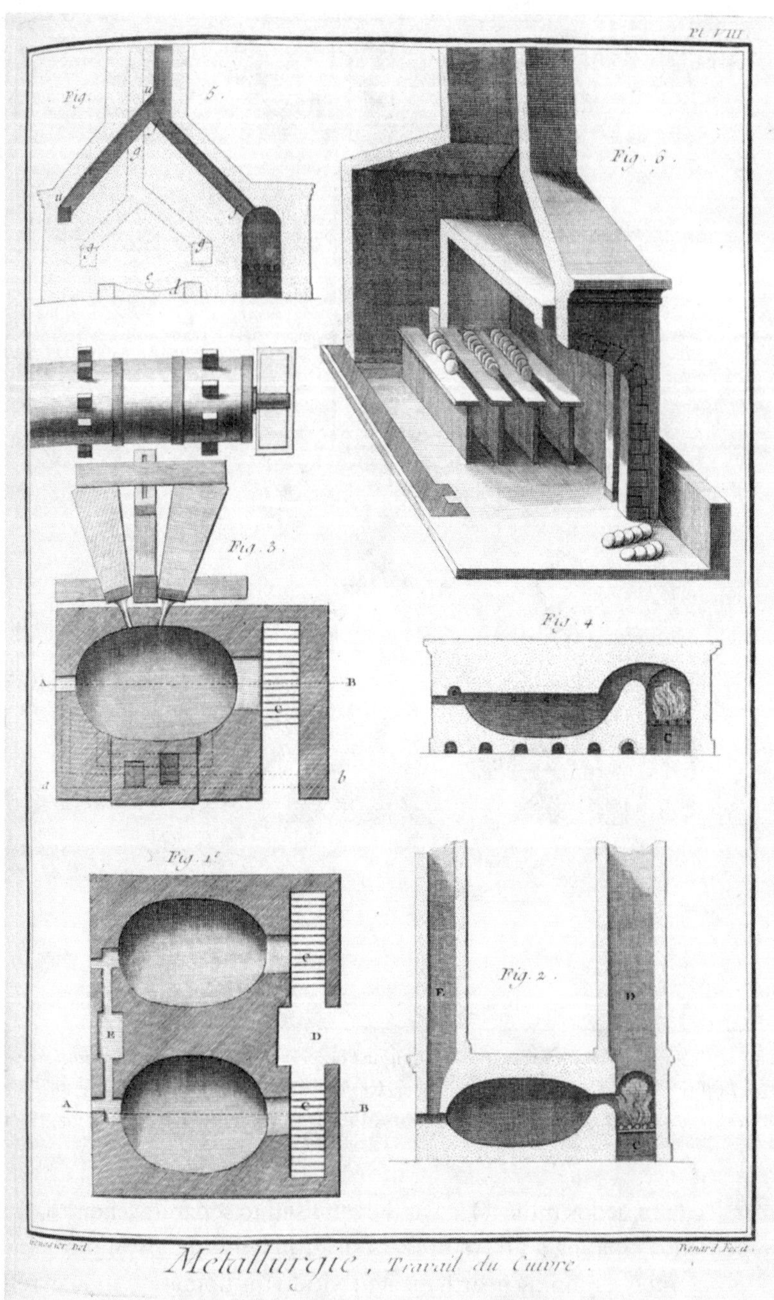

FIGURE 19. "Métallurgie, travail du cuivre." In [Denis Diderot], *Recueil de planches, sur les sciences, les arts libéraux, et les arts méchaniques, avec leur explication,* ed. Jean Le Rond d'Alembert and Pierre Mouchon, 12 vols., VI (Paris, 1762), plate VIII. RB 761772. The Huntington Library, San Marino, Calif.

methods used by Andean *guairadores* (refiners who operated guairas). Barba is one of the few firsthand sources to describe and depict Indigenous refining ovens (Figure 20).[25]

Whereas Born complained that colonial sources contradicted each other "in many material points, such as calcination, vitriol, and other respects," Diderot included Indigenous and colonial metallurgical technologies in his visual study of "Minéralogie et métallurgie; or, Calcinage et fonte" (Mineralogy and Metallurgy; or, Calcination and Melting). He reproduced the images from Barba's book with greater detail, more precise shading, and cleaner lines than the original print run in Madrid (Figure 21). Thirty years earlier, these images had already circulated in France, as they were reprinted in Charles Hautin de Villars's translation of the *Arte de los metales.* However, whereas Barba and Hautin de Villars represented the tools outside of practical contexts, Diderot reinterpreted the visual story by placing the images in a three-page sequence of minework and technical devices. The top 40 percent of each page depicts an operational mine or refinery, allowing readers to understand the scale of the devices relative to the size of a typical man or woman. (All of the workers in this series are male. However, the second plate in the "Fer Blanc" [White Iron] sequence depicts five women sorting metals, suggesting, as had Agricola's visual enactments of mining women in sixteenth-century Germany, that some aspects of metalwork were gender-inclusive.) In the bottom 60 percent of each page, Diderot zooms in on the tools used in the frame above. Hautin de Villars preserved the labeling of Barba's original images, and Diderot followed suit, such that "A" in Diderot's plate I refers to the base of a copper recipient used in gold and silver metallurgy, "H" in Diderot's plate II depicts a chimney in round and square furnaces, and "C" and "D" in Diderot's plate III replicate guairas and tocochimbos from Barba's *Arte de los metales.*[26]

25. Barba, *Arte de los metales,* 80v; Mary Van Buren and Claire R. Cohen, "Cambios tecnológicos en la producción de plata después de la conquista española en Porco, Bolivia," *Boletín del Museo Chileno de Arte Precolombino,* XV (2010), 29–46; Van Buren and Barbara H. Mills, "Huayrachinas and Tocochimbos: Traditional Smelting Technology of the Southern Andes," *Latin American Antiquity,* XVI (2005), 3–25.

26. Raspe, trans., *Baron Inigo Born's New Process of Amalgamation of Gold and Silver Ores,* 70; Born, *Ueber das Anquicken der gold und silberhältigen Erze,* 83–84; Born, *Methode d'extraire les métaux parfaits des minérais,* 84–85; Hautin de Villars, *Traité de l'art métalique,* 88–89, 120–121, 142–143, plate inserted after p. 142; Barba, *Arte de los metales,* 62, 76, 80v; [Diderot], *Recueil de planches,* ed. Alembert and Mouchon, VI, n.p. The volume is largely unpaginated, but the images are labeled "Histoire naturelle: Minéralogie et métallurgie; or, Coupe d'une mine; tirage de la mine" (plate I), "Mineralogie et étallurgie; or, Pilage et lavage de la mine" (plate II), and "Minéralogie et métallurgie; or, Calcinage

Libro quarto del

A. horno Caſtellano quadrado. B. horno Caſtellano redondo. C. guaira de los Indios. D. tocochimbo. E. ſu puerta grande por donde entra la mufla. F. mufla. G. puerta de barro con que ſe tapa la del tocochimbo. H. puerta pequeña. I. tapon con que ſe cierra el tocochimbo por arriba, por donde ſe echa el carbon.

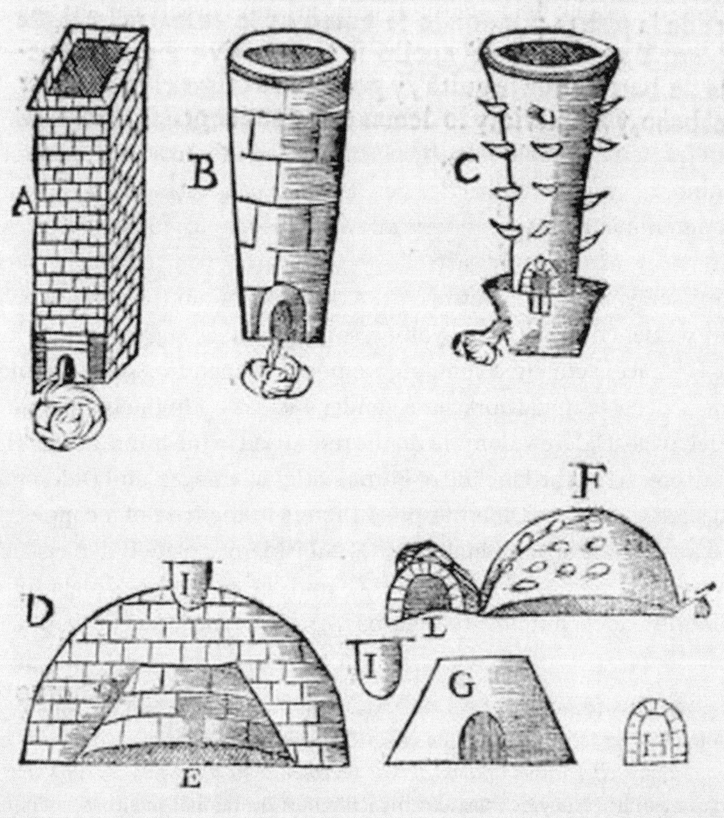

Cap.

FIGURE 20. Guaira (C) and Tocochimbo (D) refining ovens depicted in Alvaro Alonso Barba, *Arte de los metales en que se enseña el verdadero beneficio de los de oro, y plata por açogue. . . .* (Madrid, 1640), 80v. Courtesy of the John Carter Brown Library at Brown University, JCB B640.B228a

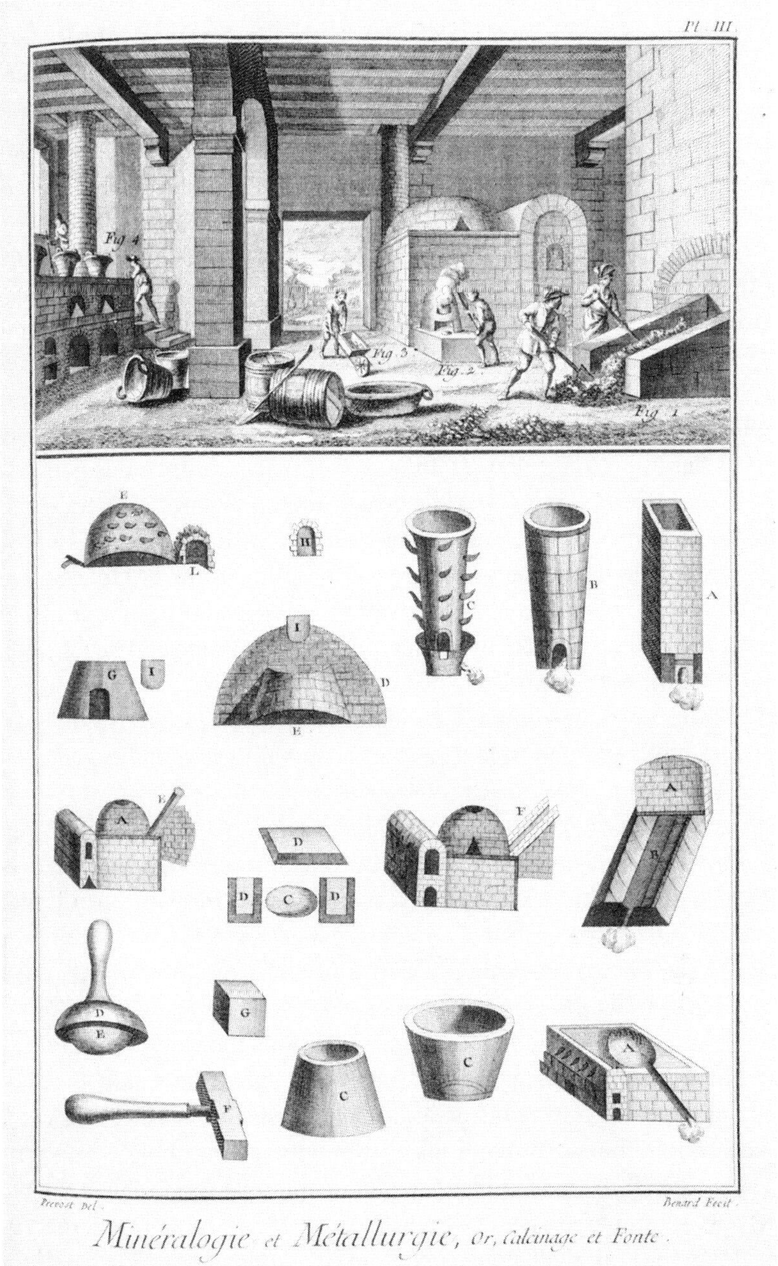

FIGURE 21. “Minéralogie et métallurgie; or, Calcinage et fonte.” Guaira (C) and Tocochimbo (D) refining ovens, depicted in [Denis Diderot], *Recueil de planches, sur les sciences, les arts libéraux, et les arts méchaniques, avec leur explication* (Paris, 1762), plate III. RB 761772. The Huntington Library, San Marino, Calif.

In the accompanying captions, Diderot explains the purpose and form of both Andean ovens. The guaira, labeled “C” in the figure, is a “fourneau de fusion pour les mines riches; il est percé de trous dans toute sa circonférence” (reduction oven for rich ores; its entire circumference is pierced with holes). Barba calls guairas an Indigenous technology (“guaira de los Indios”), but Diderot does not follow him; he is more interested in describing the technical properties of the oven than in identifying its cultural origins. Instead, he classifies tocochimbos, or muffle furnaces (“ou moufle”), labeled “D,” as a kind of “fourneau de fusion Indien” (Indian fusion oven). These ovens were notable because their main chambers held multiple points of access (“la grande portre par où entre la moufle,” “Porte dont on bouche celle du fourneau”), and their high chambers allowed refiners to regulate the amount of smoke that exited by opening and tamping shut the door (“Tampon du haut de tocochimbo”), illustrated as figures “E,” “G,” and “I.” In both cases, Diderot includes guaira and tocochimbo refining ovens for their utility, not as evidence of metalworking traditions from specific Indigenous communities with their own histories. In this way, Indigenous technologies appear in the *Encyclopédie* alongside Castilian refining furnaces, which were worked, as in plate III, by refiners who wore the tricorn hats popular in eighteenth-century Europe and Revolutionary North America, not the Andes. Whereas Born erased evidence of Indigenous contributions to amalgamation technologies, in Diderot’s hands, Indigenous Andean metallurgy—subordinated into the general class of “Indien”—here became part of the global history of metallic production.[27]

Diderot’s influential reproduction of Barba’s images of Indigenous refining ovens gave them greater circulation in Europe and placed them in different scientific and print contexts. And yet, as much as Baron von Born imitated the artistic and technical style of Diderot’s plates, he took a very different approach to the history of mining in Latin America—one that dismissed the value of Indigenous and colonial technologies.

Born’s audience eagerly supported the work. Some seventy-one readers appeared in the German-language volume’s list of subscribers, largely concentrated among merchant, political, and scientific classes in cities like Vienna, Leipzig, and Freiburg. Although the Anglophone edition boasted only fifty-nine subscribers, the work had a broader geographic reach. Subscribers included British imperial agents who were stationed in India or charged with managing trade with the colony, including Governor General Cornwallis and

---

et fonte” (plate III). Compare with images in Agricola, *De re metallica,* trans. Hoover and Hoover, 268, 306, book 8.

27. [Diderot], *Recueil de planches,* ed. Alembert and Mouchon, VI, n.p.

the "Honourable Company of Merchants Trading to India," as well as diplomats like Luis Pinto de Sousa Coutinho, "His Excellency Chevalier Pinro, late Minister of the Court of Lisbon, and now Minister of State at Lisbon," and merchants such as Samuel Vaughn, Esquire, "at Philadelphia in America." Born's language of rationality, empiricism, and objectivity was supported by a Josephist state on the rise, and it was pitted in global literary markets against a Spanish empire of decadence and decay. It is perhaps not surprising that politically prominent scientific readers in Europe, such as Dr. Carl Johann Bernhard Karsten—who edited a twenty-volume journal of metallurgical science during his tenure as royal counselor to the Prussian monarch and member of the Akademie der Künste of Berlin—declared Baron von Born to be the inventor of the amalgamation technologies that revolutionized the production of silver in the early modern world. The work's positive reception, and the celebration of its intellectual merits, had as much to do with the politics and economics of the German language in the Enlightenment as with the scientific ideas that Born presented.[28]

By the eighteenth century, refiners in Mexico and Peru also credited Enlightenment Europe with inventing large-scale amalgamation technologies. In an undated treatise from New Spain, but one whose typographic features and reference to "el Colegio" (probably the Colegio de Minería) suggest a late-eighteenth-century composition, Manuel Roces affirmed that he had related, with great fidelity, all of the metallurgical secrets that had been revealed abroad, although he retained the kitchen terminology and recipes of earlier writers. Even as he located metalworking traditions and their knowledge-making potential outside of Spanish America, Roces instructed readers to mix their materials in "un puchero de cuatro escudillas, una onza de sal, y otra de rasuras molidas, todas passadas por Cedazo, con dos libras de azogue bien mezclado con un cuchillo en agua clara" (a pipkin the size of four small bowls, add an ounce of salt and another of ground shavings, all passed through the sifter, with two pounds of mercury well-mixed with a spoon in clear water). Noticeably absent from this description are the erotic verbs that figured so formatively into Barba's and Cárdenas's work. As miners in Latin America

28. Born, *Ueber das Anquicken der gold und silberhältigen Erze,* 83–84; Born, *Methode d'extraire les métaux parfaits des minérais,* 3–4; Raspe, ed., *Baron Inigo Born's New Process of Amalgamation of Gold and Silver Ores,* a2–vi; C. J. B. Karsten, *Grundriss der Metallurgie und der metallurgischen Hüttenkunde* ([Breslau], 1818), cited in Modesto Bargalló, *La minería y la metalurgía en la América española durante la época colonial: Con un apéndice sobre la industria del hierro en México desde la iniciación de la Independencia hasta el presente* (Mexico City, 1955), 173.

came to believe that amalgamation originated in Europe rather than America, writers like Roces and Juan Ordoñez Montalvo, cited by Born, adopted a register that was free from the "love" and "appetite" of earlier writers, instead describing metallic incorporation in terms of "recogimiento" or "recoger" (collection, collecting). Following his appointment as director of the reformed Mexican lottery, Francisco Xavier de Sarría lamented in 1784 that, what Latin America enjoyed in metallic wealth, it lacked in knowledge. He used almost every available verb other than "abrazar" to explain amalgamation: "agrega," "incorporacion," "recoger la plata," "embeber," "incorporar," "limpia," "recoger," "unirse," "incorporarse" (adds, incorporates, to collect silver, drink up, incorporate, clean, collect, unite itself, incorporate itself).[29]

The shifting vocabulary of late-colonial refiners signaled larger scientific understandings of similarity and difference, as well as the intellectual origins of amalgamation and the potential of colonial scientific communities to develop, in collaboration with Indigenous miners, technologies of global value. One mine owner, writing from Lima in 1738, argued that silver and mercury had to be understood in terms of difference, for one was fluid and the other was solid. Lorenzo Felipe de la Torre Barrio y Lima, also cited by Born, denied the possibility of alchemical transmutation "por la total repugnancia, que es preciso que tenga la figura de las partes de un Metal fluido, como el del Azogue, con la de uno tan solido como el de la Plata" (for the complete repugnance that is required of the form of the parts of a fluid metal, like mercury, with that of such a solid form, like metal of silver). Although he conceded mercury's ability to form condensation on glassy surfaces, be sublimated, and mix with other metallic bodies, Torre Barrio y Lima understood silver and mercury in oppositional terms of form and matter. By the eighteenth century, scientific writers throughout Latin America explained the relationship of silver and mercury in terms of difference, not similarity. Like refiners in the early colonial period, eighteenth-century miners redefined foundational terms in the technical arts.[30]

29. Manuel Roces, *Modo de Afinar Plata con otra manera de cendrada* (n.p., n.d.), 2, 3v; Juan Ordóñez Montalvo, *Arte o nuevo modo de beneficiar los metales de oro y plata, y de plata con ley de oro, por azogue . . .* (Mexico City, 1758), 16, 17, 22; Francisco Xavier de Sarría, *Ensayo de metalurgia; ó, Descripcion por mayor de las catorce materias metálicas, del modo de ensayarlas, del laborío de las minas, y del beneficio de los frutos minerales, de la plata* (Mexico City, 1784), n.p. (preface), 124, 125, 126, 128, 129, 134, 136, 137, 145. Eugenio Maffei and Ramón Rúa Figeroa identify Roces as guild secretary; see Maffei and Figeroa, *Apuntes para una biblioteca española de libros, folletos y artículos, impresos y manuscritos, relativos al conocimiento y explotación de las riquezas minerales y á las ciencias auxiliares . . .*, 2 vols. (Madrid, 1871–1872), II, 97.

30. Torre Barrio y Lima, *Arte ó cartilla del nuevo beneficio de la plata,* 14v, 26.

As they celebrated foreign knowledge and bemoaned the backward state of colonial science, eighteenth-century refiners began to think and write about similarity and difference in ways that separated them from early colonial writers. The technical language of writers like Sarría, Ordoñez Montalvo, and Torre Barrio y Lima sounds much closer to Montagu, Lange, and Born than it does to Cárdenas or Barba, suggesting that the early modern discourse of amalgamation—including its communication through printed images—had come full circle. From seventeenth-century translations that wrote Indigenous knowledges out of metallurgical technologies to eighteenth-century treatises that marginalized the whole of Iberian science, the translated and visual languages of science and technology indexed much more than new ideas about mining and refining. They reflected, organized, and gave power to particular cultural ideas about the relationship of race to color, the nature of mixture, and perceptions of the knowledge-generating value of language itself.

Hacia una conclusión

COMPARING METALS, MATERIALS, AND IDEAS ACROSS ARCHIVES

Colonial archives are fraught spaces. They bear testimony to the asymmetries of colonial power, the legacies of white supremacy, and the brutal economic, political, narrative-making forces of early modern European empires. Their records, especially in the case of the Spanish empire, amaze us with their abilities to document so much and so little, all at once. Their physical spaces, too, testify to the weight of colonial history. For this book, I worked in large, well-funded archives and rare book libraries as well as smaller, more precarious institutions where steep budget cuts forced researchers to pay small fees to plug in their laptops. In these radically different physical and institutional environments, I was supported by teams of archivists and librarians who were deeply dedicated to their professions and to the collective work of telling the past. Their contributions, like those of colleagues working across the disciplines in the history of colonial science, are central to this book.

Histories of Iberian science and technology once focused on the marginalization of their fields from the grand narratives of scientific revolutions in early modern Europe, engaging in patriotic defenses of the Spanish and Portuguese empires rather than interrogating the logic behind concepts like scientific modernity, the dissemination of technical knowledge, or the nature of knowledge production within imperial frameworks. As Juan Pimentel and José Pardo-Tomás point out, arguments about Iberian marginalization emerged in response to Spain's transition from dictatorship to democracy in the post-Franco years, as historians of science who argued that Spain was similar to the rest of Europe created a discipline that served the needs of the state. By situating these historiographic trends within the context of twentieth-century Spanish politics rather than sixteenth- or seventeenth-century scientific thought and practice, we can address new kinds of questions about knowledge, science, and power. As this book has shown, the issue of epistemological marginalization looks quite different when viewed from the perspectives of Indigenous and African mining communities in the early Americas.[1]

1. Juan Pimentel and José Pardo-Tomás, "And Yet, We Were Modern: The Paradoxes of Iberian Science after the Grand Narratives," *History of Science,* LV (2017), 133–147.

By applying a literary approach to sixteenth- and seventeenth-century metallic works, *Mining Language* joins a scholarly community that is critically reassessing the production and transmission of scientific knowledge within Iberian imperial systems. This work represents collective efforts from art historians, literary scholars, and historians of science who draw from their disciplinary trainings and incorporate critical methods and theoretical frameworks from related fields. Daniela Bleichmar's sophisticated analysis of the visual languages of scientific communication reveals where imperial power structures and local modes of knowledge overlapped and diverged in colonial botany and natural history. Ralph Bauer's keen attention to the languages and conceptual frameworks of competing alchemical traditions from antiquity and the medieval era proves how pagan and Christian ways of knowing influenced sixteenth-century Spanish colonization schemes and seventeenth-century colonial scientific writing. An exciting group of historians of science, including Hugh Cagle, Matthew Crawford, Pablo F. Gómez, Marcy Norton, and Molly A. Warsh, has shown how the study of objects that we once considered "commodities"—such as plant-based resins, quinine bark, hammocks, and pearls—functioned as active sites of knowledge production in the colonial Americas.[2]

I am trained as a comparative literary scholar, but research for this book made it clear that colonial sources do not distinguish between fields that we now separate into discrete areas of history and literature. An analysis of sixteenth- and seventeenth-century texts that seeks to draw a hard line at the border between anthropology and history, or linguistics and religious studies, will prove unable to answer some of the most pressing issues of the colonial period and its aftermath, such as imperial power, colonial systems, and the roots of racial injustice.

The Spanish and Portuguese empires were powerful engines of the extrac-

2. Daniela Bleichmar, *El imperio visible: Expediciones botánicas y cutura visual en la ilustración hispanica* (Mexico City, 2016); Ralph Bauer, *The Alchemy of Conquest: Science, Religion, and the Secrets of the New World* (Charlottesville, Va., 2019); Hugh Cagle, *Assembling the Tropics: Science and Medicine in Portugal's Empire, 1450–1700* (Cambridge, 2018); Matthew James Crawford, *The Andean Wonder Drug: Cinchona Bark and Imperial Science in the Spanish Atlantic, 1630–1800* (Pittsburgh, 2016); Crawford and Cagle, "Enlightened Reformism in Iberian Culture and Science," in Fernando Bouza, Pedro Cardim, and Antonio Feros, eds., *The Iberian World, 1450–1820* (New York, 2020); Pablo F. Gómez, *The Experiential Caribbean: Creating Knowledge and Healing in the Early Modern Atlantic* (Chapel Hill, N.C., 2017); Marcy Norton, "Subaltern Technologies and Early Modernity in the Atlantic World," *Colonial Latin American Review*, XXVI (2017), 18–38; Molly A. Warsh, *American Baroque: Pearls and the Nature of Empire, 1492–1700* (Williamsburg, Va., and Chapel Hill, N.C., 2018).

tion, production, and transportation of wealth around the early modern world. In ecological and social terms, they were brutal, violent, devastating regimes. They also created spaces in which women and men throughout the East and West Indies developed strategies to live their lives in meaningful ways, sometimes profiting from imperial power and sometimes resisting it, covertly or overtly. In taking language and materials in equally important terms—as evidentiary sites that reveal the intellectual and epistemological workings and unworkings of empire—this book has provided texture to the story of precious and base metals in diverse colonial spaces.

By attending to the key terms of "mining" and "metallurgy," *Mining Language* has shown how the language of technical and scientific writing indexed broader cultural patterns of life, thought, meaning, and value. Chapters on precious metals detail the incorporation and rejection of Indigenous epistemes in the gold and silver industries of the Americas. My work on base metals attends to the aspirations and fictions of empire that projectors and dialogists advanced in their work on copper and iron in the East and West Indies. Taken together, these sections reveal how a renewed attention to visual and alphabetic languages enables us to study the past in ways that uncover traces of natural scientific ideas, spiritual beliefs, and technical practices that are not immediately discernible in colonial sources or imperial letters. In tracing how Indigenous and colonial miners responded in different ways to raw, refined, and imagined base and noble metals, this book has documented the lives of metals as material objects and symbolic concepts. In the early Americas, metallic matter was a site of knowledge and a conceptual node of colonial potential. The description of such objects and ideas in image and word, and their transformation by human hands, reflected larger beliefs about this world, the world to come, and humankind's place in it. Indigenous, African, and European agents in the early modern Iberian world collaborated and competed to design mining tools and technologies and to variously communicate and conceal their scientific ideas and technical practices. This book has charted how the ideas of under-studied historical scientific actors, including Indigenous miners, African metalworkers, and South Asian informants, shaped some of the critical physical and intellectual infrastructure of the colonial period. By following the sources that document these knowledges and showing how subaltern epistemologies and technical practices are erased from written and printed records, *Mining Language* tells a new story about sixteenth- and seventeenth-century mining and metallurgical sciences—a story in which incorporation and erasure represent two sides of the same imperially minted, globally traded coin. Even amid the ruptures of colonialism and the fragmented realities of colonial archives, this book has shown that diverse ways of knowing, being, and believing are accessible to us if we are willing to look for new kinds of evidence and read conventional sources in creative ways. These ways require a methodological flexibility that takes us squarely outside of our scholarly comfort zones.

While I was writing this conclusion at the Huntington Library in 2017, I returned to the words of literary scholar Robert Reid-Pharr, whose talk about archives, asymmetries, and historical legacies of inequality I had heard at William & Mary in 2012. At the time, the ink was not yet dry on my graduate degree, and I had not even unpacked what little furniture I had brought with me to Williamsburg from Chapel Hill. Reid-Pharr's *Archives of Flesh: African America, Spain, and Post-Humanist Critique* is now in print, and I have finished my book. In his supremely written and expertly researched work, Reid-Pharr argues for developing "forms of humanistic inquiry that move beyond the stale compromises and brittle ceremonies that typify so much in the current practice of the humanities and human sciences." These new kinds of research require different archival practices and methods, what he calls "Critical Archive Studies," meaning "critical in the sense of operating to end the terror of white supremacy while also naming how the split between Man and (not)man has been achieved and maintained." Methodologically, this critical archival turn requires that we approach the archive, not for coherent stories with satisfying narrative arcs, but instead to embrace "awkward pairings" that reveal "both the functioning and dis-functioning" of dominant ideological frameworks. Such a project is not about archival recovery. Rather, it acknowledges—and makes central to the work of deciphering the past—what historians Laura Helton, Justin Leroy, Max A. Mishler, Samantha Seeley, and Shauna Sweeney identify as "the impossibility of recovery when engaged with archives whose very assembly and organization occlude certain historical subjects." In other words, critical archival work means documenting these strategic silences and allowing the sources to speak for themselves, but actively interpreting their patterns of appropriation and omission.[3]

Reid-Pharr is not alone in calling for new kinds of critical archival approaches; scholars working in different historical moments, language traditions, and interconnected world regions are practicing these kinds of archival turns with methodologies that draw from diverse humanistic fields. When done poorly, comparative scholarship can make things worse, flattening crucial differences with a broad brush of similarity, obscuring key local details in the name of a bird's-eye view or global perspective, reinscribing the binaries

3. Robert F. Reid-Pharr, *Archives of Flesh: African America, Spain, and Post-Humanist Critique* (New York, 2016), 10–13; Laura Helton et al., "The Question of Recovery: An Introduction," *Social Text*, XXXIII (2015), 1–18, esp. 1.

that comparative analysis purports to escape, or framing historical questions in such a way that "there is often an implied evaluative aspect of comparison, whereby it becomes an exercise in ranking." This final aspect, analyzed by political scientist Juliet Hooker in her study of racial thinking in the nineteenth- and twentieth-century Americas, is perhaps the most serious methodological challenge that we face in comparative scholarship. Such hierarchical positioning of the past sets up a "grammar of comparison" that reifies "Man's existent hierarchies" instead of helping to "design novel assemblages of relation," as literary scholar Alexander G. Weheliye beautifully puts it. The challenge, then, is how to take the best of comparative scholarship—the ability to read across linguistic, protonational, and cultural traditions—without falling into the trap of evaluative classifications.[4]

With its "awkward pairings" of Indigenous creation narratives, colonial reports, imperial decrees, medical dialogues, technical treatises, prose-pictographic proposals, and promotional histories, *Mining Language* contributes to this necessary work of archival reimagining and (self-) critical literary and historical scholarship. This book, organized around the metallic materials that people from different language, racial, and cultural communities read in a variety of ways, from material goods and practical technologies to the abstract markers of human civilization and racial difference, has applied literary methods to texts that fall somewhere between history and literature. A literary approach to nonliterary texts reveals key moments of disjuncture in the early modern Iberian world: why the Spanish empire rearranged its gold refineries to accommodate the sprouting of a fragrant yellow plant in the Caribbean; when medical writers dialogued about iron and "indios" in ways that challenged traditional modes of imperial knowledge collection; where African copper miners were proposed to found largely autonomous communities of enslaved people; how Andean spatial concepts were mistranslated into racial vocabularies and marginalized from the history of scientific writing in western Europe.

There are many examples of innovative research in new archival studies and contrapuntal criticism, but here will suffice three works that span the colonial period and early nation-statehood in Africa, Asia, and the Americas—sites whose colonial histories persist through the nineteenth and twentieth centuries. None of these books focuses on mining, metallurgy, or mechanical arts, but all three have shaped my understanding of comparative scholarship and

4. Juliet Hooker, *Theorizing Race in the Americas: Douglass, Sarmiento, Du Bois, and Vasconcelos* (New York, 2017), 11–12; Alexander G. Weheliye, *Habeas Viscus: Racializing Assemblages, Biopolitics, and Black Feminist Theories of the Human* (Durham, N.C., 2014), 13.

archival research. By adopting some of these comparative methodologies and critical archival turns, scholars working in colonial science studies could extend the modes of analysis that I have developed here into other knowledge-making domains, such as cochineal cultivation in Mexico, furniture making and metalwork in Afro-Andean communities, or women working in technical professions that were ancillary to the mining industry, such as candle makers and ceramic artists who repurposed *ingenios* (refineries) for their own trades.[5]

First, anthropologist Ann Laura Stoler reads seventeenth-century sources "along the grain" to produce insights that cut against the aims of empire, offering a model of analysis in which "Dutch colonial archival documents serve less as stories for a colonial history than as active, generative substances with histories, as documents with itineraries of their own." In her study of Dutch efforts to govern reproduction in Indonesia and categorize multiracial children who were born into the colonial system, Stoler treats "colonial archives both as a corpus of writing and as a forcefield that animates political energies and expertise"; such archives both constitute and record the making of political authority.[6]

Second, literary scholar David Kazanjian is less concerned with the physical artifacts of colonial power than with how we read such materials. In his study of the concept of freedom in nineteenth-century Yucatán and Liberia, Kazanjian argues for "transversal" approaches to spaces that were engaged in similar intellectual and political projects at the same time—sometimes without awareness of each other. To our knowledge, Mayan-speaking communities of Yucatán and Anglophone proponents of Liberian statehood had no direct

5. On cochineal, primary sources for comparative translation analysis would include Spanish-language sources like Mexican natural historian José Antonio Alzate y Ramírez's *Memoria en que se trata del insecto grana ó cochinilla* . . . (Madrid, 1795) and the anonymous eighteenth-century treatise *Instruccion para plantar los nopales, cultivar y beneficiar la grana cochinilla fina* ([Guatemala?], n.d.) juxtaposed with French botanist Nicolas-Joseph Thiéry de Menonville's *Traité de la culture du nopal et de l'éducation de la cochenille dans les colonies françaises de l'Amérique: Précédé d'un voyage à Guaxaca* (Cap-Français, 1787), which was quickly translated into German (1789), Portuguese (Conceição Velloso, 1799), and English (Pinkerton, 1812). On Afro-Andean artisan communities (mining and furniture makers), see La Plata, Sept. 28, 1568, Archivos y Bibliotecas Nacionales de Bolivia (hereafter cited as ABNB), Escribanía Pública, XXII, 156–157v; and Lolita Guitiérrez Brockington, *Blacks, Indians, and Spaniards in the Eastern Andes: Reclaiming the Forgotten in Colonial Mizque, 1550–1782* (Lincoln, Neb., 2006). See also Potosí, Feb. 16, 1701, ABNB, Minas, 120.14 (candles); Lampa, La Plata, Dec. 12, 1772–Oct. 22, 1777, Minas, 105.11 (ceramics).

6. Ann Laura Stoler, *Along the Archival Grain: Epistemic Anxieties and Colonial Common Sense* (Princeton, N.J., 2010), 1, 22.

points of contact. As interconnected regions in an Atlantic world that was profoundly and irradicably shaped by the slave trade, they share a meaningful history. Kazanjian's interpretation of "differently global" spaces of Indigenous and black Atlantics offers a way to read around archival silences and reveal points of apposition that are otherwise obscured by documentary sources.[7]

Third, literary scholar Lisa Lowe's brilliant analysis of prose, paintings, textiles, and state papers from and about Africa, Asia, Europe, and the Americas shows how the same Enlightened thinkers who recognized universal human rights consistently defined humanity in ways that foreclosed the possibility of personhood for the majority of the world's population. To recognize the paradoxes that constituted eighteenth-century liberalism, Lowe develops a "practice of reading across archives" that are traditionally separated by language, region, and custom to reveal "the constructedness of the past" and its category-making processes. This research "unsettles the discretely bounded objects, methods, and temporal frameworks canonized by a national history invested in isolated origins and independent progressive development," allowing us to examine the history of colonialism as a "defamilarized" process rather than an inevitable outcome, "mak[ing] possible alternative forms of knowing, thinking, and being."[8]

The colonial archive, when read in the ways I have explored in this book, reveals no shortage of the kind of functional disfunctions that Reid-Pharr, Stoler, Kazanjian, Lowe, and important scholars of colonial, postcolonial, and subaltern studies have called on us to interrogate. Racial classifications in the Americas were influenced by a history of confused translations underground, in refineries, and in literary marketplaces, where they were projected into art, law, and lettered life. But they were not produced in the New World alone. Throughout medieval and early modern Europe, racist thinking underwrote "state experiments in tagging and herding people, and ruling on their bodies with the violence of law" and "exterminations of humans under repeating conditions, and disparagement of their bodies as repugnant, disabled, or monstrous." They epitomized the machinations of political power that were enlisted in the process of marking human difference.[9]

7. David Kazanjian, *The Brink of Freedom: Improvising Life in the Nineteenth-Century Atlantic World* (Durham, N.C., 2016), 5–10. On critical divergences in Atlantic studies, see James H. Sweet, "Mistaken Identities? Olaudah Equiano, Domingos Álvares, and the Methodological Challenges of Studying the African Diaspora," *American Historical Review,* CXIV (2009), 279–306, esp. 279.

8. Lisa Lowe, *The Intimacies of Four Continents* (Durham, N.C., 2015), 6, 136–137.

9. Geraldine Heng, "The Invention of Race in the European Middle Ages I: Race Studies,

As literary scholar Geraldine Heng powerfully argues, it is only the concept of Western temporality—in which modernity is "an account of self-origin" and of the West's arrival as a "unique, vigorous, self-identical and exceptional entity," whereas the medieval era remains "somehow outside real time"—that keeps early modernists and modernists from seeing how the medieval past reinscribes itself in later eras. In other words, well before 1492, the logic of racial thinking and anti-blackness was deeply rooted in Western Europe and displayed upon a range of legal codes, learned texts, and artistic works such as paintings, statues, and tapestries. In the early Americas, the ethos and aesthetics of racial and ethnic policies of discrimination were articulated through the flimsiest lexical, iconographic, and conceptual data, such that the logic and logos of whiteness were and remain ridden with inconsistencies. And yet, this intellectually incoherent doctrine exerted real power in the world from the earliest moments of colonial contact, and it lives on at the core of our most serious problems today.[10]

Our sources document the emergence of white supremacies as they were defined, debated, and constituted over the course of the colonial period and as different people responded to the ideologies that took root in their communities. It is not enough to follow these kinds of sources or to pretend that the archives they produced and continue to reflect are ideologically or intellectually neutral spaces. Historians and literary critics working in the early modern era have an opportunity—and a responsibility, as teachers and scholars—to look for the moments when sources do not make sense, when archives reveal doings and undoings, and when our own blinders prevent us from critically evaluating the making of humanity. This is especially true for historians of science, whose sources provide definitions and taxonomies of humans, non-

---

Modernity, and the Middle Ages," *Literature Compass,* VIII (2011), 315–331, esp. 318. I thank Nico Wey Gómez for pointing me toward Heng's work.

10. Heng, "The Invention of Race in the European Middle Ages I," *Literature Compass,* VIII (2011), 319, 320. See also Heng, "The Invention of Race in the European Middle Ages II: Locations of Race," ibid., 332–350; Peter Erickson and Kim F. Hall, "'A New Scholarly Song': Rereading Early Modern Race," *Shakespeare Quarterly,* LXVII (2016), 1–13, esp. 4–5; Sandra Young, "Race and the Global South in Early Modern Studies," ibid., 125–135. On debates over periodization in colonial literary studies, see Sandra M. Gustafson, "What's in a Date? Temporalities of Early American Literature," *PMLA,* CXXVIII (2013), 961–967. For historians who disagree with Heng on racism in medieval and early modern Europe, see Joan-Pau Rubiés, "Were Early Modern Europeans Racist?" in Amos Morris-Reich and Dick Rupnow, eds., *Ideas of 'Race' in the History of the Humanities* (London, 2017), 33–87; Anthony Pagden, *The Burdens of Empire: 1539 to the Present* (New York, 2015), esp. "The Peopling of the New World: Ethnos, Race, and Empire in the Early Modern World," 97–119.

humans, and less-than-humans. What it meant to be human, and how one's humanity was defined in the early modern era, cannot be disentangled from the political and economic machinations of Indigenous and African slavery in the Americas, the functioning of the imperial political economy in global markets for goods, services, and human beings, or the entrenchment of these structures in our archival sources and scholarly infrastructure.

As we think about the future of our field, it is my hope that we will continue to redefine concepts like "science" and "knowledge" in light of what our archives reveal and conceal. Following the methods and frameworks articulated by scholars across the disciplines, such as Reid-Pharr, Stoler, Kazanjian, and Lowe, would be a welcome next step in colonial science studies and the history of science more broadly. That kind of critical reflection would complement the field's productive turn from the study of canonical figures like Sir Isaac Newton and its movement away from questions of scientific patriotism into modes of analysis that are grounded in the languages, objects, and practices that characterized the many domains of early modern science and technology. Such a move would thus continue the work of bringing to the fore the substantial contributions of subaltern knowledge makers to the science and technologies of global Iberian empires in the early modern era.

APPENDIX 1

Chapters in [García d'Orta], *Colóquios dos simples e drogas e cousas medicinais da India* (1563), Carolus Clusius, trans. and ed., *Aromatum et simplicium aliquot medicamentorum apud Indos nascentium historia* (1567), Juan Fragoso, *Discurso de las cosas aromaticas, arboles y frutales y de otras muchas medicinas simples* (1572), and Annibali Briganti, *Due libri dell'historia de i semplici, aromati, et altre cose* (1576)

ARCÍA D'ORTA (1563)	C. CLUSIUS (1567–1574)	JUAN FRAGOSO (1572)	A. BRIGANTI (1576–1582)
oems to M. Afonso de ousa, L. de Camões; tters from Dimas Bosque Port. & Latin)	Privilege granted by Philip II ("Regis Hisp. & Ducis Brab."), signed by I. de Witte	Medical and legal certification; Errata; Royal privilege; alphabetic table	Dedication to don Ferrante de Alarcón e di Mendozza; alphabetic table of contents
pril 2, 1563 (Goa)	September 3, 1566 (Brussels)	March 23–27, 1572 (Madrid/El Pardo)	April 25, 1575 (Chieti)
Introducção	1. Ambaro	1. Ambar	1. Ambra
Aloes	2. Aloë	2. Anacardo	2. Aloe
Ambre	3. Altiht	3. Amomo	3. Altith
Amomo	4. Opio	4. Anime	4. Opio
Anacardo	5. Benjui	5. Azibar	5. Bengiuino
Arvote triste	6. Thure	6. Assafetida	6. Incenso
Altiht	7. Myrrha	7. Açafran Indico	7. mirra
Bangue	8. Lacca	8. Aljofar	8. Lacca
Benjuy	9. Caphura	9. Arbol triste	9. Canfora
. Ber	10. Cate, sive Lycio	10. Avacari	10. Cate, overo del Licio
. Calamo aromatico	11. Manna	11. Ambare	11. Manna
. Camfora e Carambolas	12. Tabaxir	12. Alaqueca	12. Tabaxir
. Cardamomo e Carandas	13. Tutia	13. Añir	13. Tutia
. casia fistola	14. Ebore	1. Bangue	14. Auorio
. Canela	15. Canella	2. Betre	15. Canella
. coquo	16. Agallocho	3. Benjuy	16. Agallocho, overo legno Aloe
. Costo	17. Sandalo	4. Brindones	17. Sandalo
. Crisocola	18. Betre	5. Bdelio	18. Betre
. Cubebas	19. Folio	6. Ber	19. Folio
. Datura e doriões	20. Maci	1. Canfora	20. Macis
. Ebur ou marfim	21. Garyophyllis	2. Canela	21. Garofalo
. Faufel e figos da India	22. Pipere	3. Caña olorosa	22. Pepe
. folio indio	23. Cubebis	4. Cardamomo	23. Cubebe
. Galanga	24. Cardamomo	5. Cañafistola	24. Cardamomo
. Cravo	25. Faufel	6. Clavos de especias	25. Faufel
. Gengiver	26. Nuce Indica	7. Coco Indico	26. noce d'India
. Hervas contar as ca maras	27. Myrobalanis	8. Carambolas	27. Mirabolani

GARCÍA D'ORTA (1563)	C. CLUSIUS (1567–1574)	JUAN FRAGOSO (1572)	A. BRIGANTI (1576–1582)
28. jãca e Jambolões e jambos, e Jangomas	28. Tamarindis	9. Carandas	28. Tamarindi
29. lacre	29. Cassia solutiva	10. Coru	29. Caßia solutiva
30. Linaloes	30. Anacardio	11. Caceras	30. Anacardio
31. Cate do vulugo	31. Amomo	12. Chyna	31. Amomo
32. Maça, e noz	32. Calamo aromatico	13. Costo	32. Calamo Aromatico
33. Manná purgativa	33. Nardo	14. Cubebas	33. Nardo
34. Mãgas	34. Iunco odorato	15. Cypero	34. Giunco odorato
35. margarita ou aljofar	35. Costo	1. Diamante	35. Costo
36. Muugo e melam da India	36. Turbit	2. Doriones	36. Turbit
37. Mirabolanos	37. Rhabarbaro	1. Esmeralda	37. Reubarbaro
38. Mãgostães	38. Radice Chinae	2. Encienso	38. radice China
39. Negundo ou sambali	39. Croco Indico	1. Faufel	39. Croco Indiano
40. Nimbo	40. Galanga	1. Galanga	40. Galanga
41. Amfiam ("seu nome he opio")	41. Gingibere	2. Gingibre	41. Gengevo
42. Pao da cobra	42. Zedoaria	3. Granate	42. Zedoaria
43. Pedra diamão	43. Zerumbet	1. Hoja Indica	43. Zerumbet
44. Pedras preciosas	44. ligno Colubrino	1. arbol Iaca	44. legno Colubrino
45. Pedra bezar	45. lapide Bezar	2. Iacinto	45. Pietra Bezar
46. Pimenta preta, e branca	46. lapide Malacensi	3. Iaspe	46. Pietra di Malaca
47. Raiz da China	47. Gemmis: Adamante	4. una fruta Iambos	48. *[sic]* Gemme: Diamante
48. Ruibarbo	48. Smaragdo	5. Iunco oloroso	49. Smeraldo
49. Sandalo	49. Rubino	6. arbol Iangomas	50. Rubino
50. Espiquenardo	50. Sapphiro	1. Lacca	51. Zaffiro
51. Espodio	51. Hyacintho & Granato	2. Linaloe	52. Giacinto
52. Esqueinanto	52. Iaspide	3. Lycio	53. Iaspide
52. *[sic]* Tamarinhos	53. Alaqueca	1. Marfil	54. Alequecca
53. *[sic]* Turbit	54. Oculo Catti	2. Mana	55. occhio di Gatta
54. *[sic]* Thure ("he em cenço, edemirra")	55. lapide Armeno	3. Mangas	56. Pietra Armena
56. Tutia	56. Magnete	4. Macias y nuez moscada	57. Calamita
57. Zedoaria e zerumbet	57. Margarita	5. Myrabolanos	58. Perle
58. algũas cousas que vieram		6. Musa	Il fine del primo Libro
Praestantissimo doctori Thomae Roderico		7. Myrra	
Ad Gartiam ab horto medicum apud Indios …		1. Nardo Indico	
Errata		2. Nimbo arbol	
Alphabetic table of contents	Liber secundus	3. un arbol llamado Negundo	Libro secondo
do Betre e outras cousas	1. Arbore tristi	1. Opio	1. arbore melanconico
	2. Nimbo	2. piedra Ojo de Gato	2. Nimbo
	3. Negundo	1. Palo Colubrino	3. Negundo
	4. Iaca	2. Pimienta	4. Iaca
	5. Iamgomas	3. Piedra bezaar	5. Iamgomas
	6. Carandas	4. Piedrayman	6. Carandas
	7. Coru	1. Ruybarbo	7. Coru

ARCÍA D'ORTA (1563)	C. CLUSIUS (1567–1574)	JUAN FRAGOSO (1572)	A. BRIGANTI (1576–1582)
	8. Auacari	1. Spodio	8. Auacari
	9. Mangas	Los autores de quien en este libro se haze mencion	9. Mangas
	10. Musa		10. Musa
	11. Doriones		11. Dorioni
	12. Mangostans		12. Mangostans
	13. Iambos		13. Iambos
	14. Cydoniis Bengalensibus		14. Cotogni Bengalensi
	15. Carambolas		15. Carambolas
	16. Ber		16. Ber
	17. Ambare		17. Ambare
	18. Iambolones		18. Iambalones
	19. Brindones		19. Brindones
	20. Indico Melone		20. Melone Indiano
	21. Mungo		21. Mungo
	22. Curcas		22. Curcas
	23. Caceras		23. Caceras
	24. Datura		24. Datura
	25. Bangue		25. Bangue
	26. Anil		26. Anil
	27. Anonymo		27. Anonimo
	28. quibusdam Indiae regibus		28. alcuni Re dell'Indie

urces: [García d'Orta], *Colóquios dos simples e drogas e cousas medicinais da India: Reprodução facsimilada a edição impressa em Goa em 10 de abril de 1563; comemorando o quarto centenário da edição original . . .* oa, 1563); Carolus Clusius, trans. and ed., *Aromatum, et simplicium aliquot medicamentorum apud Indos ascentium historia: Ante biennium quidem Lusitanica lingua per dialogos conscripta, D. Garcia ab Horto, oregis Indiq medico, auctore; Nunc verò primùm Latina facta, et in epitomen contracta à Carolo Clusio rebate,* 2 vols. (Antwerp, 1567); Juan Fragoso, *Discurso de las cosas aromaticas, arboles y frutales y de otras uchas medicinas simples que se traen de la India oriental, y que sirven al uso de medicina* (Madrid, 1572); and nnibali Briganti, trans., *Due libri dell'historia de i semplici, aromati, et altre cose, che vengono portate dall'Indie ientali, pertinenti alla medicina* (Venice, 1576).

APPENDIX 2

Mining terminology in Barba (1640), García de Llanos (1609), González Holguín (1608), Bertonio (1612), Montagu (1674), Lange (1676), Hautin de Villars (1730), and Lenglet du Fresnoy (1751)

SPANISH (BARBA, LLANOS)	MODERN TRANSLATION	QUECHUA (GONZÁLEZ HOLGUÍN)
paco (color), bermejo (B 39v; GL 79)	silver chloride (AgCl); in Mexico, iron oxide (Fe_2O_3)	ppaccu (cosa bermeja rubia roxa, 271)
Mulato (B 39v; GL 86); bazo (B 39v), ceniciento (GL 86)	(AgCl)-(Ag_2S)	pactascak, chaupi mitta, pactas mitta (medio entre dos extremos, 584)
negrillo (B 39v; GL 86); negro (no todos) (B 39v)	silver copper-sulfide ($Ag_6[Cu_4Fe_2]\ Sb_4S_{13}$-x)	yanallimpi (morena color, 593); yanaruna (negro, 600)
cimarrón (GL 89–90)	mineral found outside of the vein	qquita (cimarrom huydor, 310)
tacana (B 40; GL 80)	form of argentite (Ag_2S)	tacani (dar golpes, 334)
soroche (B 39v)	silver-lead alloy (Pb, Ag)S	suruchiq (Cerrón-Palomino, 113)
pella (B 48, 53; GL 69)	partial amalgam	
concho (B 53v; GL 22–23, 69)	sediment	cconcho (heces o el assiento, 544)
pallar (escoger, B 40; GL 97–98, 109–110)	to sort	pallani (coxer a mano, 274)

Sources: Alvaro Alonso Barba, *Arte de los metales en que se enseña el verdadero beneficio de los de oro, y plata por açogue. . . .* (Madrid, 1640); García de Llanos, *Diccionario y maneras de hablar que se usan en las minas y sus labores en los ingenios y beneficios de los metales* (1609), ed. Rose Mary Buchler, Gunnar Mendoza, and J. V. Murra (La Paz, 1983); Diego González Holguín, *Vocabulario de la lengua general de todo el Perú llamada lengua qquichua o del Inca* ([Lima], 1608); P. Ludovico Bertonio, *Vocabulario de la lengua aymara,* 2 vols. (1612), ed. Xavier Albó and Félix Layme (Cochabamba, 1984); [Edward Montagu], trans., *The Second Book of the Art of Mettals, Wherein Is Taught the Common Way of Refining Silver by Quicksilver: With Some New*

AIMARA (BERTONIO)	ENGLISH (MONTAGU)	GERMAN (LANGE)	FRENCH (VILLARS; LENGLET DU FRESNOY)
pako (bermejo, II, 91)	Paco, "Red colour" (II, 8)	Paco, "rothe Farbe" (134–135)	Paco, "veut dire Rouge" (HV 30; LF 137n)
taypirana (II, 340); sanni (negro medianamente, I, 329)	Mulatos, "of a Brown colour" (II, 8–9)	Mulato, "braunen Farbe" (135)	Mulato, no color (HV 31; LF 137)
cchaara yana (moreno color, I, 321); cchaara (negro, II, 72)	Negrillo (II, 8–9), "Black" (not all); "black Oar" (I, 39–41)	Negrillo (135), "schwartz" (nicht alle); "schwartz Erze" (33)	Negrillo, "la couleur noir" (HV 31, LF 137)
kita, huacora, sallca, huanaco, kuñu kuñu (cimarrón, I, 160)	—	—	—
cumpatha (quebrar con piedra, huancatha, I, 160); ttakhllitha (II, 346)	"La Tacana" (II, 9)	Tacana (136)	"La Tacana" (HV 31; LF 139)
suruxchi (Cerrón-Palomino, 115)	"The Soroches" (II, 10)	Soroches (136)	sorroche (HV 32)
	Mass (II, 25); Pellets (II, 68)	klumpen (146); Silber-Kugeln (181)	Pella (LF 151n, 188)
concho (I, 264); hama sacarara (hez escoria, I, 264)	"Oyster shells" (II, 8)	"Auster Schalen" (184)	corps (LF 191)
pallatha (recoger poco a poco, 246)	"Of the sorting of Ore" (II, 12)	"Bon allerley Arten des Erzes" (137)	"Du choix des Minerais" (LF 140)

Rules Added for the Better Performance of the Same . . ., 2 vols. (London, 1670); [Johann Lange], trans., *Albaro Alonso Barba, Eines Spanischen Briesers und hocherfahrnen Naturkündigers Berg-Büchlein: Darinnen Von der Metallen und Mineralien Generalia und Ursprung . . .* (Hamburg, 1676); Charles Hautin de Villars, *Traité de l'art métalique: Extrait des oeuvres d'Alvare-Alfonse Barba, célébre artiste dans les mines du Potozi . . .* (Paris, 1730); [Lenglet du Fresnoy], trans., *Métallurgie; ou, L'art de tirer et de purifier les métaux . . .*, I (Paris, 1751); Rodolfo Cerrón-Palomino, *Voces del Ande: Ensayos sobre onomástica andina* (Lima, 2008).

APPENDIX 3

OFFICIAL WEIGHTS AND MEASURES

Currency

1 peso = 8 reales de plata or 20 reales de vellón (copper alloy)

1 real = 34 maravedís de plata

1 escudo = 350 maravedís de plata

1 ducado = 375 maravedís de plata

1 marco = 8 ounces (silver) or 50 castellanos (gold)

1 castellano = 96 granos or 8 tomínes of gold

Mineral weight (pesos)

1 onza = 8 ochavas

1 ochava = 6 tomines

1 tomín = 12 granos

1 arroba = 11.4 kilograms or 25 pounds

4 arrobas = 45.6 kilograms or 100 pounds

Sources: Joseph García Cavallero, *Theorica, y practica de la arte de ensayar oro, plata, y vellon rico: Danse reglas para ligar, religar, alear, y reducir qualesquiera cantidades de oro, y plata a la ley del Reyno . . .* (Madrid, 1713), 17–21; Michael Thomas D'Emic, *Justice in the Marketplace in Early Modern Spain: Saravia, Villalon and the Religious Origins of Economic Analysis* (Lanham, Md., 2014), 64–65. It goes without saying that official rates were not always respected.

INDEX

Page numbers in italics refer to illustrations.